Design
for Six Sigma
Innovation for
Enhanced Competitiveness

Gregory H. Watson

Business Systems Solutions International, Inc.

GOAL/QPC
IMPROVING THE WAY ORGANIZATIONS RUN

First Edition

Janet MacCausland, *Graphic Design and Layout*
GOAL/QPC, *Publisher*

GOAL/QPC
12B Manor Parkway, Salem, NH 03079-2862
800.643.4316 or 603.890.8800
Fax: 603.870.9122
E-*mail*: service@goalqpc.com
www.goalqpc.com

Printed in the United States of America

First Edition 10 9 8 7 6 5 4 3 2 1

ISBN 1-57681-078-X

For
"maya solnushka" Crista,
who is learning much too early
that growing up
is "so very hard to do."

Contents

Preface

"There is no substitute for process knowledge."

~ W. Edwards Deming

Design for Six Sigma: A birth of necessity

Design for Six Sigma (DFSS) is truly an evolving discipline. DFSS evolved out of an operational business requirement—the need to move product quality beyond the 4.5 sigma barrier that is often created because the base design of products, processes, and services is unable to support a higher-quality performance. In order to achieve higher quality levels, it became recognized that total rethinking of the design—leading to a redesign—was essential. It became clear to the early practitioners of Six Sigma that the statistical problem-solving process (typically called DMAIC—an acronym that summarizes its five steps of define, measure, analyze, improve, and control) needed adaptation to serve the application of product development. Further, it became clear that this methodology did not fit a "one-size-fits-all" process description. Customization was required to fit business environments, corporate cultures, regulatory compliance requirements, and industry-specific norms, and DFSS needed to be integrated into the new product development or product-creation process for very different applications (e.g., design of hardware, software, and services). Perhaps the combination of a pressing business need and unclear operational definition of DFSS have kept Six Sigma both at the front-of-mind for business leaders while concurrently frustrating them that a clearer solution was not available.

Purpose of this book

The objective of this book is expansive: It seeks to establish a comprehensive overview of DFSS for an audience of business leaders. This book seeks a balance between a populist book that ends up doing no more than cheerleading and a detailed textbook that is targeted at implementers and tool users but drowns the reader in its details. It also seeks to fill a gap that is perceived in previous books on this subject[1] by purposefully focusing on its targeted customer as the business leader who needs to have the subject of DFSS demystified and by providing a coherent, comprehensive manuscript that would clarify the DFSS concept and thereby serve as a beacon to organizations interested in navigating these improvement waters.

---

[1] Previous books on this subject include: Subir Chowdhury, *The Power of Design for Six Sigma* (Dearborn, MI: Dearborn Trade, 2002); Clyde M. Creveling, Jeffrey L. Slutsky, and David Antis, Jr., *Design for Six Sigma in Technology and Product Development* (Upper Saddle River, NJ: Prentice-Hall, 2003); Kai Yang and Basem El-Haik, *Design for Six Sigma: A Roadmap for Product Development* (New York: McGraw-Hill, 2003); Greg Brue, *Design for Six Sigma* (New York: McGraw-Hill, 2003); Dana Ginn and Barbara Streibel, *The Design for Six Sigma Memory Jogger* (Salem, NH: GOAL/QPC, 2004).

The roots of this book are in articles written for *Quality Progress*, *Six Sigma Forum Magazine*, *Manufacturer's Monthly*, and speeches at numerous conferences over the past seven years and the author's experience in product development at Hewlett-Packard, Compaq, Xerox, and Nokia. The book itself has been borne out of two and a half years of thinking, writing, brooding, rewriting, and editing. This has been a tough project—perhaps for the same reasons others have had in characterizing this subject. This work is unfinished. It will remain unfinished because the real work is not in writing a book but in transitioning these ideas and tools into the business environment of a firm and making a difference in the way that it defines and introduces its new products and thereby serves its customers.

A suggestion to the reader: If you are already familiar with the literature in this field or have little interest in the theoretical concepts leading up to the concept of Design for Six Sigma, then I will suggest that you skip the foreword and go right to the first chapter. The foreword is meant to be a comprehensive survey that leads to the conclusion that business leaders must consider the implementation of DFSS in order to develop and maintain their competitive advantage. If you have already come to this conclusion, then the foreword might inhibit your appetite for getting to the main course!

Publisher's Preface

Every now and then there comes along a book that is able to consolidate diverse thoughts and disjointed concepts into a coherency that provides a systemic framework for future knowledge. Books that have accomplished this have included those like Frederick W. Taylor's *The Principles of Scientific Management*, Armand V. Feigenbaum's *Total Quality Control*, W. Edwards Deming's *Out of the Crisis*, and Philip B. Crosby's *Quality Is Free*. These books share the characteristic that they are classics in the field because they have integrated ideas in such a way as to extend the body of knowledge and define a new perspective from which to interpret the future. It should be evident from the acclamation of this book's reviewers that this volume is one of the few truly exceptional works in the field of quality management and process thinking.

This book, *Design for Six Sigma: Innovation for Enhanced Competitiveness*, by Gregory H. Watson, joins this distinguished literary circle and establishes Watson's reputation as one of our generation's leading quality thought-leaders. His previous best-selling book, *Strategic Benchmarking* (John Wiley, 1993), integrated the benchmarking process with strategic planning and competitive analysis to focus organizations on major change. This current book continues his eclectic style and focuses on the design of new products and services as well as the organizations that deliver them to the market.

Watson creates an intellectual framework that will allow the concept of Design for Six Sigma to mature by presenting the broadest possible framework for understanding the principles of quality through design and the methods and concepts that define its composition. He has done a great service to the global quality community by defining this framework as an innovative foundation upon which further work will extend his idea of design quality into a comprehensive business system, as he outlined in his previous book, *Business Systems Engineering* (John Wiley, 1994).

Enjoy this intellectual journey as Watson relates how Design for Six Sigma integrates management concepts such as program and product management, activity-based accounting, performance measurement, and innovation with technical concepts such as reliability analysis, value engineering, Quality Function Deployment (QFD), and robust design. Watson is careful to cite the intellectual roots from which he draws his eclectic model of Design for Six Sigma and to lay a firm foundation for the future by proposing a work breakdown structure as the starting point for a more comprehensive definition of the DFSS body of knowledge.

The team at GOAL is pleased to publish this book and to offer its readers the unique opportunity to journey through the foundation and development of a new body of quality knowledge that will serve as a foundation for the coming century.

Bob King,
Chairman and Publisher, GOAL/QPC

Acknowledgments

I owe a debt of gratitude to the many people who have challenged my thinking and encouraged me to pursue this project—and in advance I ask the reader's forgiveness as I practice the "Oscar" appreciation syndrome! So I say "thank you!"

Most especially to my long-suffering and loyal business partner of over ten years, Jeffrey E. Martin, and especially his most supportive and loving family.

To the many clients and professional colleagues who have challenged and stimulated my thinking and assisted me on my journey: Pekka Ala-Pietilä, Timo Hannukainen, Simo Salminen, Ahti Vaisenen, Perti Korhonen, Phil O'Neil, Raija Pollanen, and Kirsi Allonen (Nokia Group); Bob Peterson, Brian Fischer, Tony Abraham, Claude Pidgeon, Phil Valance, David Sims, David Cox, and Aldous Wong (ExxonMobil); Taizo Nishimuro and Hitoche Ootsuka (Toshiba); Mark Leidy, Ron Cooley, Deb Small, Randy White, George Brazuk, Matt Barrows, Ty Whitten, Rick Simmons, Fred Verner, Clive Deetlefs, and Neil Anderson (Monsanto); Matti Toivianen (KCI Konecranes); Larry Smith (Ford); as well as Bill Grundstrom, Joe Wexler, and Harvey Brelin (Dell Computer).

To my colleagues in the Industrial Engineering and Management Department of Oklahoma State University: Bill Kolarik, Ken Case, Paul Rossler, Camille DeYoung, Brenda Johnson, and Amanda Holley, and to the Halliburton Foundation for supporting the development of the graduate programs in engineering and technology management through their generous grants.

To my students: Thanks for making me think anew and providing a constant and provoking forum for sharpening the blunt instrument of my mind.

To my colleagues and subject-matter experts in "The Gathering"—Richard Zultner, John Terninko, Tony Rizzo, and Glenn Mazur—each in your own way, you have all made a fantastic contribution to the advancement of DFSS.

To some special friends who have encouraged me over the years: Katarina Von Firks, Bea Alanko, and Frank Toda—thanks for being there!

To my colleagues, mentors, and friends in Japan: Yoshio Kondo, Takanori Yoneyama, Yoji Akao, Noriaki Kano, Genichi Taguchi, Kenzo Sasaoka, and Katsu Yoshimoto.

To my colleagues and friends in Mexico: Gumersindo Montemayor, Moises Sandler, Humberto Canto, Xavier Lozano, Rodrigo Plancarte de la Garza, Leopoldo Pompa, Orlando Valencia, and Jose Luis Dias.

To my colleagues in Australia: Christopher F. Brendon, Michael A. Sargent, and Elizabeth M. Keim.

To my special friends in the world's quality community: Bertrand Jouslin de Noray (European Organization for Quality); Gennady Voronin, Natalia Tompson, and Yuri Samoylov (Russian Organization for Quality); Frank Steer (Institute for Quality Assurance); Paul O'Grady and Anne Marie Fallon (Excellence Ireland Quality Association); Lincoln Sim and Ken Liang (Singapore Quality Institute); Jorge Gerdau Johannpeter (Movement Quality Brazil); and, especially, Risto Lintula (Center for Excellence Finland).

To my colleagues in the International Academy for Quality (not otherwise named in other categories): Armand V. (Val) Feigenbaum, Marcos Bertin, Spencer Hutchins, John Hromi, David Luther, Lennart Sandholm, Tito Conti, Juhani Anttila, Bob Cole, Jens Dahlgaard, Miflora Gatchalian, Bland Godfrey, Jim Harrington, Jean-Claude Savard, Ken Stevens, and Shoji Shiba.

To my colleagues at the American Society for Quality: Paul Borawski, Bill Tony, Catherine Valentine, Erin Hogg, Karen Prosser, Linda Zysko, Annemmieke Hytinen, and the cast of hundreds of staff and board members who made my experience as president so memorable.

To my publisher and friend Bob King, who has been patient with me in the development of this project—along with the kindness of his wife Ellen, as well as the supportive assistance of the entire publications team at GOAL/QPC, Janet MacCausland (graphic designer), Rob King (emotional support), and Lee Alphen for just being so kind.

Special thanks for the dedication of my book reviewers, as they have definitely made this a much better book: Dr. A. H. "Jack" West, Dr. Kenneth E. Case, Dr. Paul E. Rossler, Dr. Yoji Akao, Dr. Ellen Domb, Larry Smith, Glenn Mazur, and David B. Luther.

And finally, to my wife Inessa Aleksandra and our entire family spread abroad in Helsinki, Moscow, and Richmond: Thank you for providing a meaningful and loving context to think afresh about the real world and priorities. You have taught me many things that cannot be put into my books, but can be lived in my life.

In this book, as in life, the inspiration was yours, but the mistakes have been mine!

Gregory H. Watson
Espoo, Finland
2005

"You don't have to do this...survival is not compulsory."

~ W. Edwards Deming

Introduction

Business leadership moves ahead, gains advantage over competitors, achieves forward motion, and establishes a winning position.

Most business leaders were complacent before the "wake-up" call issued in the historical 1981 NBC documentary about Dr. W. Edwards Deming titled "If Japan Can, Why Can't We?" The ability to move a business forward did not require anything more than having a basic product that the public wanted. Life was simple then, but accelerating technology growth and runaway business competition have changed everything.[2]

Bold leadership is required to win enduring competitive advantage for an organization. If an organization loses its momentum, stagnates, or becomes the victim of entropy, then it is not likely to sustain success over time. Only through conscientious effort can an organization grow and prosper over the long term. The obligation of leaders is to deliver long-term organizational strength in increments of short-term successes. In many businesses the key increment for moving a business forward is the continuous release of exciting new products to the market.

Competition drives business success

A truism in today's technologically volatile markets is that no existing market share is safe and no product life is immortal! This is as true in the high-technology sector as it is for all consumer products. Competition destabilizes

---

[2] The purpose of this foreword is to set the stage for Design for Six Sigma by identifying its significant precursor business thoughts. Developments in quality thinking of the past twenty-five or so years are used to focus this book on the emerging approach to DFSS. While much of these developments might be considered old, they establish the framework by which the current state of DFSS has evolved. A clear foundation for DFSS is seen in the work of Dr. Armand V. Feigenbaum, whose classic work *Total Quality Control* (now in its fifth edition, this book is published by McGraw-Hill) defined an engineering system approach to quality management called total quality—this systems viewpoint is reflected in the current DFSS as its fundamental architecture and the integrating principle for all of the tools and methods presented in this book. While there are many books about quality, Feigenbaum's work remains one of the most focused, engineering-based, and business-oriented definitions of what quality is and how it can be applied to management of a total business enterprise. He must be credited with establishing a systems perspective for achieving business excellence.

both protected market niches and technological advantages that have endured in established businesses. The basic force that drives market destabilization is innovation. Highly successful companies can be relegated to a mere shadow of their "glory days" and have the potential for vanishing if they do not find ways to re-create their market success through a steady stream of innovative products and customer-oriented solutions. These types of conditions represent "strategic inflection points"—a disturbance in the market forces or a discontinuity in the way customers perceive their needs.[3]

The business challenge for any company is to obtain and retain its customers, while at the same time growing into new market niches. "Competitive excellence" is achieved when a company has the ability to grow sales revenue through both increasing transactions with current customers (growing "product share" within its customer base) and by extending its offerings to additional customers (growing its "share of the market" by attracting potential customers). Profitability of a firm is ensured by a concurrent focus on decreasing the cost to deliver products and services and simultaneously growing the number of customer sales transactions.

Since share of competitive markets is captured at the expense of an adversary, the winner must be able to provide a perceivably superior product or service and subsequently be able to sustain that performance perception as its customers continue to experience the product or service throughout its life cycle. In other words, the ability to sustain "performance" over time is more valuable to a company than its ability to "inform" or advertise at a point in time. As practiced by companies such as the Dell Computer Corporation, this type of innovation requires the constant delivery of excellence in each customer's experience.

One thought leader on innovation is the German economist Joseph Schumpeter. Schumpeter had defined innovation as the planned abandonment of established, familiar, and customary or comfortable ways of working... whether in products or in services, competencies or human relationships, or the whole organization itself.[4] He called this concept of innovation "creative destruction." By planning to rapidly replace their own products or services in the market, organizations preempt the opportunity for competitors to gain advantage. Some of the high-technology companies have driven this market tactic to the level of a science. For instance, Intel executives have been known to talk about this practice using cannibal-like descriptions such as: "You've got to learn to eat your young." This practice of constant innovation places some very special requirements on an organization's ability to study, interpret, and meet the needs of consumers. In such a rapidly moving environment, consumers do not always know what they need or what benefits could be brought to them with a new generation of technology.

---

[3] See both the book by Intel CEO Andrew S. Grove, *Only the Paranoid Survive* (New York: Random House, 1996), and Grove's Stanford University teaching colleague Robert A. Burgelman and Leonard R. Sayles, *Inside Corporate Innovation: Strategy, Structure, and Managerial Skills* (New York: Free Press, 1986).

[4] Joseph A. Schumpeter, *Capitalism, Socialism, and Democracy* (New York: Harper & Row, 1950).

As the late Dr. W. Edwards Deming once quipped: "The customer never asked Mr. Edison for a light bulb." The burden for development of applications for such breakthrough technologies is on the producer, not on the consumer.

The operational meaning of competitiveness

All organizations compete: competition can be direct, indirect, latent, or virtual. With direct competition, there is a clear "head-to-head" marketplace confrontation between organizations. With indirect competition, the degree of competitiveness might not be transparent to the market (e.g., where an OEM [Original Equipment Manufacturer] supplier also sells directly to the market under its own unique brand, usually with a great deal less value [price] than the sales under its branded label). Latent competition occurs when there is another organization that has the requisite competence, technology, capability, and capital to move into your business, but has not chosen to do so (yet). Virtual competition is a type of competition that applies to not-for-profit and public-sector organizations—while they have no specific group that competes directly, it is possible to evaluate one's organization against "close substitutes" or organizations that do similar things with a for-profit motive. Whatever form competition takes, all organizations do compete for the attention of customers—as Peter Drucker observed, some "still believe in Benjamin Franklin's dictum: 'If you build a better mousetrap the world will beat a path to your door.' It does not yet occur to them to ask what makes a mousetrap 'better' or for whom?"[5]

Creating customer relationships is always a matter of customer choice, no matter what business or economic sector is considered. It is the nature of customers to choose from among alternatives. Customers will choose from among the alternative product offerings in a market the one that gives them the most value (maximizing the benefit received for the cost paid—answering the questions: "Is the product or service worth the price that is being asked? Is it worth more than other alternatives that could be chosen?).

One definition of competitiveness is: "The degree to which a nation can, under free and fair market conditions, produce goods and services that meet the test of international markets while simultaneously maintaining or expanding the real income of its citizens." This definition was established in the late 1980s by the President's Council on Competitiveness, chaired by John A. Young, then the CEO of Hewlett-Packard.[6] When this definition is transitioned in application from the macro-economic environment of nations to the micro-economic environment of the firm, it makes one clear statement: Markets rule and the customer is king—they have the buying power—when it comes to competitiveness. That is what is meant by the "test of international markets" in the council's definition. The job of the micro-economy is in

---

[5] Peter F. Drucker, *Innovation and Entrepreneurship* (New York: Harper Books, 1985), p. 12.

[6] President's Council on Competitiveness, *Report on National Competitiveness*, Washington, DC, 1987.

understanding this test and ensuring that it produces goods and services that are better able to meet these market tests than the competitive offerings. The test itself is simple—value based on the price/performance relationship as perceived by customers—does it help them "get their job done" better? However, technology by itself goes only so far in generating new value, as there is a natural limit for customer acceptance of technological change. This is represented in a diffusion process that delays the time by which innovations can be successfully launched into the marketplace.[7]

What does it take for an organization to be a winning competitor? The first step is that leaders of the organization must have the vision and foresight to know what advantage must be gained; what vulnerabilities must be eliminated; what opportunities must be seized; and also what alliances or partnerships must be garnered in order to have the proper combination of competence, capability, and capacity that will give it a sustained edge over competitors. One operating definition of a company that is a "world class" competitor is that it:

- "Knows its processes better than its competitors know their processes;

- Knows the industry competitors better than its competitors know them;

- Knows its customers better than its competitors know their customers;

- Responds more rapidly to customer behavior than do competitors;

- Engages employees more effectively than do competitors; and

- Competes for market share on a customer-by-customer basis."[8]

Business leadership (sustained success) is achieved when an organization coordinates all of its activities to deliver quality above its competitors, costs below its competitors, and technology ahead of its competitors. Each of these must be appropriate for the business enterprise model that describes how the organization competes and delivers its goods or services to its customers. When describing the competitiveness of a firm, it is the long-term capability of the firm to compete that delivers enduring success. There have been many one-product or one-concept firms that have not lasted beyond their original idea. True competitiveness is based on establishing continuing relationships with customers so that the firm captures its customers' experiences and is able to use this knowledge to stimulate innovation and develop products and services that are even more useful for these customers. This process is inherently a learning or discovery process.

What is the quality job of a business leader?[9] Well, unlike many jobs, true leadership does not come with a pre-issued position description. The fundamental outcome of leadership is effective management of business resources

---

[7] Everett M. Rodgers, *The Diffusion of Innovation*, 3rd edition (New York: The Free Press, 1983).

[8] Gregory H. Watson, *Strategic Benchmarking* (New York: John Wiley & Sons, 1993), p. 34.

[9] For a more comprehensive view of the quality job of a CEO, see: Gregory H. Watson, "Selling Six Sigma to Upper Management," *Six Sigma Forum Magazine*, August 2002.

(finances, assets, and people) in a way that creates shareholder value (growth in stock price plus dividends) while at the same time creating lasting brand value (sustained value through enduring customer relationships). Sustainable competitive advantage means that a company is delivering profit in the short term (thereby satisfying investors) and strength in the long run (thereby providing a secure working environment for employees) while simultaneously delivering excellence in its products (thereby satisfying customers). The job of a business leader is to create value in the dimensions of shareholder value and brand value through the effective, efficient, and economic use of its resources—capital, equipment, and people.[10]

Leaders create profitable growth to generate shareholder value

Shareholder value is increased by the profitable growth of a business. Shareholder Value-Add (SVA) is an indicator of the incremental improvement achieved for the investment capital that has been entrusted to a company. SVA reflects the quality of the financial performance of an organization and takes into account cash, return, and growth. Cash-flow analysis helps determine if the organization has enough cash to fund its operations and also looks at the way cash is being managed (terms for payment and receipt of cash as well as categories of cash distribution). The return generated on the investment indicates the profit an organization makes on its operations. Return has two major ingredients: margin of revenue over costs and velocity of cash, or turnover rate—the so-called order-to-cash cycle in a business. The third component is growth: profitable growth is necessary, because sales purchased at great discounts do not make an organization strong. The typical economic rule that organizations follow is that profits generated by business actions must exceed the "cost of capital" or the long-term rate over which an organization can obtain loans.

Shareholder value is created by several specific business practices:

- Growing revenue through new product sales, business acquisitions, building market share, or increasing the scope of the product line;

- Improving profit margins through improved pricing power due to market dominance, increasing the product differentiation advantage over the direct competitors, and operational excellence defined by defect elimination, cycle time improvement, and cost reduction;

- Reducing the cost of capital by reducing capital intensity (fixed asset-to-sales ratio, days of inventory, and days of receivables), reducing the percentage cost of capital, and also by decreasing the debt/equity ratio.

---

[10] Here, the term "value" is restricted to financial calculations—business leaders must also create employee value and community value (as well as for other stakeholders in the organization), but these are expressed in terms of levels of satisfaction rather than in financial terms.

Of course, the best type of growth comes organically—growing revenue from new product sales. This is why a continuous stream of new products that meet customer needs is so important to a business. However, business leaders must be mindful of the inherent choices that they make in considering alternative product investments. Product plans must meet dual objectives of adding to the shareholder value while adding to brand value by increasing the organization's market reputation.

Leaders create brand value to generate customer loyalty

Brand value is really an expression of customer value that is sustained over time. Brand value is created by giving customers what they need to be successful in their business and by responding quickly to changing market conditions that generate new product opportunities (an enhancing strategy) and taking rapid action to counter any problems observed with the current product line (a maintaining strategy).[11]

The net effect of a strong focus on quality should not just be the increase of customer satisfaction, but it must also increase the brand value. Brand value is achieved through the sustained delivery of "moments of customer satisfaction." Customer satisfaction focuses on individual events in the relationship with customers, while brand value maintains an enduring relationship with customers despite temporary setbacks. A customer is most strongly influenced by the quality of the latest engagement that they have with a company in their relationship with it. Customer satisfaction is a perception of performance by an individual that is then combined to provide a collective view to determine the average performance an organization has in a market. Brands are different. A brand represents the effect of a company's sustained performance over time. Brand is the image that is imposed by the actions of a company on its market. Brand has a unique point of origin that might be different from or aligned with the individual product concept perspectives. A brand represents the enduring value of the customer's experiences with an organization. When senior management pays attention to building strength in its customer dimensions, this strength must deliver two moments of success: the immediate moment of quality at the initial experience and the enduring moment of reliability as their experiences are savored over time. So, brand value is created one loyal customer at a time, and customer loyalty is achieved by delivering differentiable value that customers appreciate.

Understanding the customer value proposition

Ultimately quality is whatever the consumer determines it to be as judged by a product's enduring or sustained commercial success in the competitive market. A critical starting point for thinking about quality is value. The final

---

[11] The distinction between disruptive technology and sustaining technology is a key in the work of Clayton M. Christensen and Michael E. Raynor; see their book *The Innovator's Solution* (Boston: Harvard Business School Press, 2003).

customer is the ultimate determinant of value. It is true that customers want those things that they value. The issue for customers is to determine: What is the best value proposition among the alternative choices? Competitive excellence demands that the processes that support creation, production, and distribution of products be centered on customer-perceived value. This is very different from building a customer-centered company that only asks its current customers what they want and does not seek to generate creative quality attributes that attract new customers.

Christensen and Raynor, in *The Innovator's Solution*, define the purpose of a product as to get the customer's job done by targeting circumstances in which certain customers require the product and then determining how to add value to these circumstances.[12]

In *The Dynamics of Market Leaders*, Michael Treacy and Fred Wiersema observe that there are "three important truths that characterize the new world of competition:

- "Different customers buy different kinds of value. You can't hope to be the best in all dimensions, so you choose your customers and narrow your value focus.

- As value standards rise so do customer expectations, so you can stay ahead only by moving ahead.

- Producing an unmatched level of a particular value requires a superior operating model—a 'machine'—dedicated to just that kind of value." [13]

However, there is a point of diminishing returns in delivering additional functions and features. This relationship is identified by Christensen: "When the performance of two or more competing products has improved beyond what the market demands, customers can no longer base their choice on which is the higher-performing product. The basis of product choice often evolves from functionality to reliability, then to convenience, and, ultimately, to price."[14] In order to stay in tune with customers, it is essential that business leaders create what Treacy and Wiersema call a "customer intimate" company. This type of company is characterized by:

- "An obsession with the core processes of solution development (such as helping the customer understand exactly what's needed), results management (or ensuring the solution gets implemented properly), and relationship management.

- A business structure that delegates decision-making to employees who are close to the customer.

- Management systems that are geared toward creating results for carefully selected and nurtured clients.

[12] *Ibid.*, p. 75.

[13] Michael Treacy and Frederick Wiersema, *The Discipline of Market Leaders* (Perseus Books: Reading, Massachusetts, 1995), p. 19.

[14] Clayton M. Christensen, *The Innovator's Dilemma* (New York: Harper Collins, 2000), p. xxviii.

- A culture that embraces specific rather than general solutions and thrives on deep and lasting client relationships."[15]

Companies that are driven to create this degree of intimacy have a cult-like fascination with the customer that is continuously expressed in people's attitudes and behaviors. In companies with this focus there are two strong motivating beliefs:

- Customer value is the ultimate measure of their work performance.

- Accelerating value development for customers is the driver of business success.

Building this strong customer focus into the culture and values of an organization is the job of the business leader. Leaders confirm their personal commitment to the value proposition by communicating its implications for their organization in a crisp, easily comprehended manner. Leaders must get employees not just to understand this commitment but to personally embrace it in their daily work routines. To achieve emotional acceptance by all members of the team, leaders must identify the right operational levers that permit managers to take definitive actions that deliver customer value. Managers must recognize these opportunities to deliver value and seek conscientiously to accelerate actions that build and sustain the value proposition. This means removing obstacles that inhibit effective action by the front-line workers and giving people the tools and resources needed to work effectively and efficiently.

Quality: A competitive business advantage

How is high performance guaranteed in the long term? To produce enduring success, companies must learn to thrive on change and uncertainty, not merely to cope with them. Senior managers must reinvent the company repeatedly to focus better on delivering core competence for meeting the changing needs of its most critical customers. Routinely, the company must be repositioned in its competitive market, adjusting its organizational structure, product, or service lines; business processes; managerial practices; personnel and technology policies; and marketing strategies to deliver excellence consistently in the face of changing customer opportunities, concerns, and requirements.

To achieve this degree of long-term performance excellence that delivers sustained competitive business advantage, managers must embrace a proactive quality policy. Such a policy must focus the resources of the entire organization on delivering the value propositions required by the key stakeholders—by its customers and investors as well as its employees and suppliers. By optimizing this portfolio of value propositions, business leaders can design and deliver sustained performance that is able to dominate their market.

---

[15] Treacy and Wiersema, *op. cit.*

In the 1970s and 1980s, a study was conducted by General Electric's strategic planning office of the various market factors that influenced profitability of the firm. This study was extended by the Wharton School of Business and became known as the Profit Impact of Market Strategy (PIMS) Study (afterward, this methodology was commercialized by the Strategic Planning Institute). The most important finding of the PIMS study was the establishment of a definitive relationship among perceived quality, market share, and profitability. The study found that the driving force for product profitability was the customer's perception of its quality. It observed that when the relative perceived quality and relative market share are both high, then a company's profitability is virtually ensured. The PIMS study also observed that customers make their quality judgments using a criterion of value (the relationship between price and quality), not just based on the quality characteristics alone.[16]

This perceived relative value of the total offering (both products and services) influences the purchasing behavior of customers. Relative perceived quality is not the same as product quality or conformance to a design specification—it is quality from the customer's perspective, relative to alternative choices in a competitive market and the price of the offering. Customer desires drive market performance and establish the minimum standard for value—performance that is delivered for a given price. The PIMS study discovered that the customer's value proposition is the most significant factor in the competitive business equation. PIMS was a cornerstone in the research into customer perception and quality.

Subsequent to the PIMS results, a number of further studies pushed the boundaries of knowledge about the customer's perception of quality and its impact on business management. These research efforts attempted to clarify the meaning of customer satisfaction, commitment, and trust in the purchasing relationship and to quantify in financial terms the value of business investment in quality-enhancement efforts. Two of the leading investigators in this field have been Roland T. Rust, the David Bruce Smith Chair in Marketing at the University of Maryland at the Smith Graduate School of Business, and Michael D. Johnson, the D. Maynard Phelps Professor of Business Administration and Professor of Marketing at the University of Michigan at the Ross School of Business.[17, 18]

Some of the interesting observations and definitions that were generated by related research on this subject include:

---

[16] The results of the PIMS studies were published as: Robert D. Buzzell and Bradley T. Gale, *The PIMS Principles: Linking Strategy to Performance* (New York: The Free Press, 1987).

[17] Their key works are: Roland T. Rust, Anthony J. Zahorik, and Timothy L. Keiningham, *Return on Quality: Measuring the Financial Impact of Your Company's Quest for Quality* (Chicago: Irwin, 1994), and Michael D. Johnson and Anders Gustafsson, *Improving Customer Satisfaction, Loyalty, and Profit: An Integrated Measurement and Management System* (San Francisco: Jossey-Bass, 2000).

[18] Findings of Rust's research were also reported in the following publications: Roland T. Rust, Anthony J. Zahorik, and Timothy L. Keiningham, "Return on Quality (ROQ): Making Service Quality Financially Accountable," *Journal of Marketing,* vol. 59 (April 1995), pp. 58–70.

- The definition of customer satisfaction as the long-term customer attitude that allows profitable customer retention where customer satisfaction is a proxy performance measure for future economic returns.[19]

- Commitment is an enduring value to maintain a valued relationship[20], and commitment is an implicit or external pledge of relationship continuity.[21]

- Trust is the willingness to rely on a party in whom one has confidence[22] and the belief that a party's word or promise is reliable and a party will fulfill their relationship objectives.[23]

- Trust and commitment are the determinants of successful long-term commercial relationships that generate enduring value for customers and lead to sustainable market advantage.

Thus, delivering value that is appreciated by customers is the most important consideration for a business and requires the total attention of the management team as well as the coordinated efforts of all employees. It requires a total commitment to the delivery of quality. Quality focuses on achieving desired results through excellence in process performance targeted at objectives aligned with customer expectations. Management by fact is the approach used to coordinate organizational components to work together as a team—integrating their professional competence, technical capabilities, and human skills to achieve the shared plan for obtaining sustained success. So, given all these ideas: How should we define quality?[24]

What is quality?

Quality is used more broadly as distinguished from reliability.[25] Reliability is quality in the dimension of time and is typically more technically defined—using failure rates, customer consumption models, statistical sampling plans, accelerated testing methods, and statistical analysis methods

---

[19] Duncan I. Simester, John R. Hauser, Birger Wernerfelt, and Roland T. Rust, "Implementing Quality Improvement Programs Designed to Enhance Customer Satisfaction," *Journal of Marketing*, vol. 37 (February 2000), pp. 100–112.

[20] Christine Moorman, Gerald Zaltman, and Rohit Deshpandé, "Relationships between Providers and Users of Marketing Research," *Journal of Marketing Research*, vol. 20 (August 1992), pp. 314–329.

[21] Robert F. Dwyer, Paul H. Schurr, and Sejo Oh, "Developing the Buyer-Seller Relationships," *Journal of Marketing*, vol. 51 (April 1987), pp. 11–27.

[22] Christine Moorman, Gerald Zaltman, and Rohit Deshpandé, *op. cit.*, p. 316.

[23] Paul H. Schurr and Julie L. Ozanne, "Influences on Exchange Processes: Buyer's Preconceptions of a Seller's Trustworthiness and Bargaining Toughness," *Journal of Consumer Research*, vol. 11 (March 1985), pp. 939–953.

[24] Asking this question is like asking: What is beauty, or what is value? While the answer might be "it is in the eye of the beholder," we are not satisfied with the answer, and so debates have raged for ages over the meaning of these terms. This discussion might not be a final answer to this debate about the meaning of quality, but it is intended to give a different perspective and be helpful in making better decisions about how to design business processes and use customer information in the creation of new products.

[25] Design for Reliability (DFR) is the subject of chapter 7 in this book.

to create a probabilistic model of failure as a function of time over the life cycle of a product.[26] Quality can be defined using a three-phase model in a way that explains the role of quality in product development.[27] In this model, quality is embedded into the transformation process (innovation excellence) where technology is converted into an innovative product (as defined by the market promise) while operational excellence is the quality characteristic that is delivered through the disciplined daily management process that supervises routine work in the production of the product or service (the delivery of promises made to customers). Sustained performance, or performance that is consistently delivered over an enduring period of time, requires that the dimensions of both innovation excellence and operational excellence are able to meet their commercial, competitive performance requirements.

Customers can experience quality gaps that originate from two distinct causes: one related to the misunderstanding of the true design requirement, while the second is a function of the execution of the identified design requirement as it is delivered to the market. The design gap exists between what the customer requires and what the customer is promised. The conformity gap exists between what the customer is promised and what is delivered. These two gaps are illustrated in the figure below, which depicts a simple process for defining products and delivering products. The first gap comes from design shortfalls and is a gap in "expectations" because the promise that is offered to the customer does not deliver the functionality necessary to meet the opportunity that satisfies the customer's key requirements. The second gap is an "entitlement" gap, as the customer is not receiving a level of performance that they are entitled to receive based on their reliance on the value proposition embedded within the product offering (the promise from the advertising, guarantees, or specification). This gap represents a shortfall in the stated functionality of the product—it doesn't meet its performance objectives in a dimension that is critical to satisfaction of the customer.

How is quality consistently delivered?

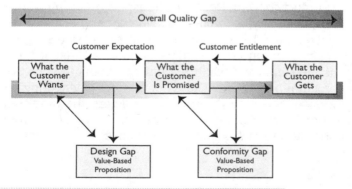

---

[26] A preferred definition of reliability is: "consistent delivery of product or service performance features over time" where "consistent" is described using probability models of performance.

[27] This model was introduced in: Tito Conti, Yoshio Kondo, and Gregory H. Watson, *Quality into the 21st Century: Perspectives on Quality and Competitiveness for Sustained Performance* (Milwaukee, WI: ASQ Quality Press, 2003).

The design gap represents a problem in the value proposition delivered to the market by a company's business model. There are two aspects to the value proposition of an organization—one is this market dimension of delivering value to customers, while the second aspect is the concept of values as a way of working within an organization. The design gap indicates that there is a lack of appreciation for the outcome desired by customers—the delivery of value. The conformity gap identifies a problem in the values-based proposition—the way an organization works to achieve a stated goal for quality of delivery. Value entitlement is the expectation that customers have for performance excellence in both of these dimensions of the quality-delivery equation.

The PIMS study identified that customer-perceived quality is a much more significant factor in profitability than originally thought.[28] It is important to emphasize that customer perception is reality. If your customers believe there is a problem or flaw in your product or service offering, then that is the reality, whether or not it conforms to an internal engineering specification. The root cause of the problem might be that the specification does not reflect your customers' desires. Remember the golden rule: Those who have the gold make the rules—and in business it is the customer's gold that carries the weight!

What is design?

The presence of this design gap creates the question: What is design? Design is the task that is faced when developing a new product—its objective is to create a product that will meet the needs of others in a manner that is commercially viable.[29] This task has three components that must be successfully executed: understanding and addressing the commercial need, designing the product, and engineering the design. Understanding the commercial need is the part of the innovation process where research into customer needs or consumer purchasing trends exposes a unique product development opportunity—the job that a customer needs to accomplish that can be uniquely provided by a product concept. Design is the aspect of the innovation process where the concept of a product is created to match this perceived commercial need of the marketplace. The engineering process translates a design into a product that can be produced in sufficient volumes to meet the projected demand of the marketplace. Concurrent engineering is the practice of overlapping the program management tasks of product engineering and manufacturing process engineering in order to accelerate the time-to-market of the product. Concurrent engineering removes the waiting time from product conceptualization to product launch and sequences management's decision

---

[28] Buzzell and Gale, *op. cit.*

[29] While the language describing DFSS is focused on products, most organizations also apply this same logic to the design of their business processes and services that are offered to customers. In order to more clearly describe what is meant by DFSS, product development will be the focal point of the discussion, and the extension of these methods to business processes and services will be left to another book. This simplification does not belittle the value of the application of DFSS to these areas, but it helps to focus this book in a way that is meaningful.

milestones so that the product is not only delivered as fast as possible to the market but it also meets the market's window of opportunity where customer demand naturally builds from prior products, yet the new product is launched into this sea of market opportunities prior to competing products—the timing to the market. Business leaders in new product development must be responsive to customers' needs and answer the question: What is the role of quality in this design process? This answer must be experienced by customers as they use the product that the engineers designed.

What is design for quality?

Simply put, design for quality is a process for ensuring the delivery of both innovation excellence and operational excellence to customers. When this delivery process is achieved, then financial success can be obtained and the opportunity for business performance excellence exists. The approach to deliver quality in design occurs in DFSS through the five-step process called DMADV (Define-Measure-Analyze-Design-Verify), which defines a Six Sigma innovation process. DFSS places quality as the objective of the design process and defines quality in the broadest sense as the value proposition that is offered and delivered to customers. In the DFSS process, the quality objective is to achieve a Six Sigma level of performance for selected critical-to-satisfaction product-performance parameters that have been validated against real customer requirements.

In addition to having quality as a design objective, DFSS also makes quality considerations part of the planning and execution of the product design by embedding quality-performance criteria into the design reviews conducted to support program milestones and ensure consistent progress toward the program goals. Overall program measures are tracked to ensure that consistent improvement is achieved across the milestones of the product development project. Program-design review milestones are selected based on the need for management intervention at pre-determined decision points. These decision points typically require a financial or resource decision to be made relative to the progress on the program and the potential risks and benefits that are associated with further investment.

Typical design-quality reviews occur to support the adequacy of the business case (usually called a concept review) as well as progress in the transition of the concept into a product at a series of reviews that evaluate prototype testing and demonstrate progress toward production readiness, and then a final post-mortem that is conducted about six months after release to the market (also called product launch). Each of these decision milestones represents a measurement control point (tollgate) where specific design or engineering tasks must be accomplished, resources assigned, and choices must be made as to the degree of adequacy of progress as well as management's commitment for the continued allocation of future resources required to complete the next incremental project phase.

Design quality is ensured through this design-review process by a continuous-improvement process where test data is analyzed to determine if design or engineering problems exist, as well as to discover the degree of improvement in product reliability and production capability over prior prototypes. Corrective actions are taken in the next prototype development, along with engineering extensions of functionality and packaging for mass production and market consumption.

Aligning work to customer priorities

One of the key problems in business is the lack of alignment between the way people work to design and produce products and the concerns and interests of customers in those products. This lack of alignment is caused by a fundamental discontinuity in the language of consumers and producers. Producers tend to focus on organizational performance, while customers are most concerned about product performance. Their priorities are greatly different. The customer is most concerned about issues like ease of use, timeliness, certainty of performance, cost to own, and variety or choice in the product's features. Most producers tend to be more inwardly focused on such concerns as productivity, schedule, standards, cost to produce, and volume of output. It is no wonder that customers are not well satisfied by the market offerings—the American Customer Satisfaction Index shows a chronic 20% dissatisfaction rating across all industries. How can a company improve its performance? One thing that designers can do is to be sure that the product's functional specification describes all the features that must be implemented to ensure customer acceptance of the product. This means understanding the job that the customer needs to accomplish as well as how the technology in this new product will do this job better than alternatives available to the customer.[30] What is the underlying relationship among product innovation, market dynamics, and customer satisfaction? The quality concepts embedded in DFSS can be better understood by overlaying the Theory of Attractive Quality on the application of the preceding definition of quality to help design and define products that convey market-share-winning customer value.

---

[30] The functional specification should be the single source document that defines functions that the product will deliver to its users. Functions describe the outputs of the product based on its inputs and past performance—the set of transformations that the product will make of material, energy, or information to accomplish the task that it was intended to perform for the end user. If a feature or function is not described in the functional specification, then it shouldn't be a design feature of the product; in fact, any unspecified feature or function that is required to support the primary functions should be the result of the lowest-cost design option, regardless of the enhancement that it might provide to the user—these enhancements are spurious, as they are not required by the specification and can therefore result in additional cost to the product without delivering valued capability—not worth what the customer is willing to pay for it. While the functional specification describes the "what" that gets done and the product development specification defines "how" it is accomplished, QFD illustrates the translation of the "what's" into "how's" and the further translation into the detailed engineering design for production.

Over the past two decades, the Theory of Attractive Quality, developed by Dr. Noriaki Kano of Tokyo Science University, has gained increasing exposure and acceptance. This theory can be applied to strategic thinking, business planning, and product development to demonstrate lessons learned in innovation, competitiveness, and product compliance.[31] A graphical presentation of Kano's theory is constructed using two axes that define three relationships in the ability of customers to identify their requirements for a product's features (see the figure on the following page).

One axis describes the range of customer satisfaction/dissatisfaction, and the other describes the physical fulfillment/non-fulfillment of the requirement (or, as I interpret it, the excellence level in execution of the design features or functions as measured from complete fulfillment to non-fulfillment of the requirements). A useful definition of customer satisfaction is the degree to which customers appreciate the product or service offering, are willing to recommend it to others, and follow up with a purchase at the next point where they require a similar product. A definition of physical fulfillment (execution excellence) is the degree to which the design of the product or service is able to perform its function relative to the capabilities of the competing products or industry standards. The better the design, the more enhanced the relative position of the product or service as a choice option for customers. Execution excellence provides a head-to-head comparison of product differentiation as compared to competing market choices of customers.

The process of defining the features, functions, and product capabilities that customers require can be characterized using three different curves. The center curve represents an openly stated or explicit purchase requirement, or what Dr. Kano calls a "spoken" requirement, for product features or quality characteristics—such as might be found in a request for a quotation or proposal. In addition to this explicit description of the needs by customers, Dr. Kano identified two other curves that represent different categories of "unspoken" customer quality requirements. The first relationship defines quality characteristics as "unspoken" because these requirements are so well known that they are assumed to be obvious by a knowledgeable consumer. In this case a product might be so well known and understood that people do not think explicitly about specific features, functions, or characteristics when defining their needs. In the second relationship, the quality requirements remain unspoken because consumers have not discovered them and they have no idea how this type of application can be delivered to increase the value and quality of their work or enhance their personal productivity or experience in using the product or service. This curve represents unspoken quality because customers might not even be aware of the potential for the

---

[31] Dr. Noriaki Kano of Tokyo Science University created and developed the Theory of Attractive Quality. In 1997, the Japanese Union of Scientists and Engineers (JUSE) awarded Dr. Kano the Deming Prize in recognition of the significant contribution of this theory to the body of quality knowledge. The original article on this theory is: Noriaki Kano, Nobuhiko Seraku, Fumio Takahashi, and Shinichi Tsuji, "Attractive Quality and Must-Be Quality" (translated by Glenn Mazur), *Quality Journal* (Tokyo: Japan Society for Quality Control, 1984, vol. 14, no. 2, pp. 147–156).

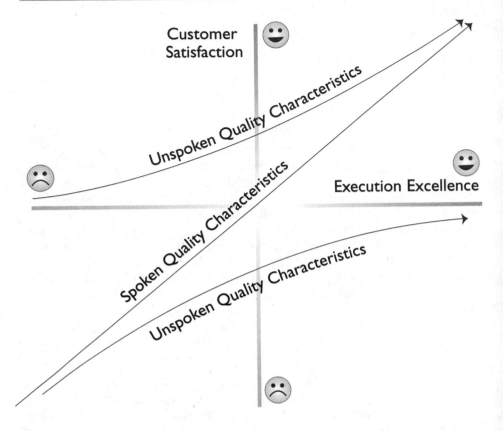

existence of this feature, function, or capability, or how it could improve the circumstances of their working environment.

The Kano Theory of Attractive Quality integrates these ideas to explain the fundamental relationships between consumer behaviors and product design. In the next sections, each of these three relationships is described in more detail.

Spoken quality and competitive performance

The better a product is designed, the more likely it is to achieve higher satisfaction of its intended customers. In addition, the more poorly executed product (or service) designs are most likely to dissatisfy customers. This relationship holds true for each of the features included in the criteria used for decision-making by customers.

The basic competitive idea is that the best performance for value wins the consumer's choice. Product features located on the middle curve of the Kano Model have one common characteristic: the customer is able to define their purchase criteria for evaluating the differences that exist among the competitive offerings. Thus, winning for these cases means that the relative score on the customer's stated preferences is the highest for that set of procurement criteria. A "spoken need" typically is a set of procurement-decision criteria (as in the technical statement of work in a request for proposals) that, when most fully delivered (e.g., the "best" degree of execution excellence for a particular design feature), results in highest customer satisfaction, and therefore also wins the sale.

This middle curve also represents the traditional definition of a competitive market as described by Michael Porter.[32] In Porter's view, a company must differentiate itself through either cost leadership or product differentiation. When focused on a particular marketplace, the relative merits of competing products can be judged—much as *Consumer Reports* evaluates alternatives among competing commodities to recommend its buyer's choice or "best of breed" in the Darwinian sense of survival, where only the "fittest" survive the tests of time.

An example of spoken quality characteristics that everyone should be able to relate to is the choice of an automobile. When shopping for a vehicle everyone has their own particular "wants" or "musts" that need to be satisfied. We might make a list of the things that are required in the car for our family or personal use. When we examine this list we might observe such characteristics as fuel economy, number of passengers seated, color, music system, and type of transmission.

However, this middle curve does not provide a complete description of competitive conditions. There are two other curves that need to be considered in order to understand the complete relationship between customer satisfaction and product design.

Unspoken quality: Surpassing standards

Those features that are so closely related to the basic product concept that they are not perceived to be in any way distinct from the operation of the product as a whole are core product features. These features define a product but do not differentiate its performance against competitors.

Products that are on the second curve have "assumed quality characteristics." In other words, customers do not speak about these most basic requirements for product performance because they "assume" that each of these product design fundamentals is understood by all of the most serious bidders for their business. Kano calls this behavior "unspoken quality" because the customers do not state these requirements explicitly, nor are they considered in the set of purchase criteria used to evaluate alternative offerings. The customer actually considers these factors only in their absence.

---

[32] Michael E. Porter, *Competitive Advantage* (New York: The Free Press, 1985) and Michael E. Porter, *Competitive Strategy* (New York: The Free Press, 1980).

The most interesting observation about this "standard" level of product performance is that no matter how well these product features are designed, they will never provide a "competitive" level of satisfaction for customers. These features deliver only a threshold of satisfaction. The performance on these factors must be above a certain minimal level, but incremental performance beyond that level does not enhance customer perception. Since these sets of product features are not satisfaction drivers, this implies that competition for products whose features are dominated by this category of feature are able to compete only on "price," as all other differentiators no longer matter. In this market condition, the company with the lowest cost of operations can win the dominant market position.[33]

To illustrate the concept of this lower level of unspoken quality, let us reconsider the purchase of a car. In making the list of characteristics that are desirable, we failed to consider the following: the car starts, goes, turns, and stops! But, you say, every car does this! Precisely! We have so defined a car that we no longer speak of these fundamental characteristics explicitly—they are tacitly understood, unspoken characteristics. They don't contribute to our satisfaction with the product precisely because we don't think about them. But, consider what happens when they do not perform with excellence? We become absolutely livid in dissatisfaction! Products that have a significant standard feature that "can go wrong" are in jeopardy from neglect in their design. It is essential to safeguard standard features from poor performance, lest their poor performance overwhelm the competitive advantage gained by those design characteristics that lead to an initial purchase decision. Since these standard product characteristics are not usually included in an initial purchasing decision, the only result they can have is to alienate consumers when they fail.

Unspoken quality: Attractive quality

This type of unspoken quality offers performance-excellence results by delivering "innovation" in the product design in ways that unexpectedly delight its consumers. Here, the job of a design engineer (or "imagineer," as they are called by Disney) is to find "unknown future requirements" of their customers and imaginatively apply the magic of advanced technology to create a satisfaction advantage that distinguishes the product (or service) as truly unique in its competitive market. This product development strategy can establish a new product as "prime-mover" or "first-in-class" with all of the advantages that being first in time-to-market entails, and might launch a disruptive discontinuity that fundamentally changes the industry's total value proposition.

---

[33] A counter-point to this discussion can also be offered where companies are observed to be competing on features or functions based on over-design that is delivered at a value-point that the market perceives as excellent. Two of the examples that could follow this definition are Lexus automobiles and Starbucks coffee. What differentiates the way these organizations have performed is that they have value-engineered their products to serve different markets and have changed the value proposition as perceived by customers (see chapter 5 for a discussion of value engineering).

Distinctive products capture the imagination of customers. If a product's features are so unique that it virtually has no competition, then its creator has a dominating competitive niche. Note that this will occur whenever the unique features are highly desirable for customer-valued product (or service) applications. When customers both "perceive" and "believe" in the value of a feature, then a distinction is created that drives buying behavior.

It is important to note that features in this category do not have competition. They represent the product leaders who have established a new frontier in a particular product arena. This means that there is a desire to possess the uniqueness for many early adapters of technology, who will cope with any design problems in order to have the opportunity to find a new way to gain new knowledge using this unique feature.

There is a downside to this type of unspoken quality. Due to attractive nature, it "attracts" the creative imitation of competitors. Perhaps an example will help to illustrate this downside. In purchasing a car, many buyers consider the product and its features to be a commodity at worst, and at best requiring only a cursory competitive product analysis to determine what purchase to make. When these types of market conditions prevail, then products have lost any distinction in characteristics. Customers then tend to rely more on brand perception than product analysis to make their purchase decision. Brand perception is driven by the history of the customer with a particular make of product rather than by the creation of perceptions about a specific product model. If a competitor does not have a strong brand image and products are not particularly differentiated, then the company must build an extended product (bundling service features with the product) to create a differentiated market offering. This is why companies are offering 0% financing charge for new car loans. The customer expects to pay interest on their loan. Eliminating interest fees produces an "unexpected customer delight" by meeting an unspoken request not to "waste money" on interest paid to banks.

The natural force of entropy introduces a dynamic shift

There is a natural progression in the distribution of innovative product features. While a feature is innovative it will lead to product "leadership" in the market; however, it will fall to the "competitive" performance level as competitors see its value and imitate its capability. Over the long term, such a feature might eventually become a "basic" feature of the product as customers start to expect that all viable products have this capability.

This natural transition of innovative product features leads customers to anticipate certain trends in the path of "feature migration," which each competitor must learn to observe as a marketplace expectation. It is also true that customers expect that each new product will be equal to or surpass the prior generation's capability. This is particularly true for product quality.

Perhaps a little perspective on automotive history will help to illustrate how entropy influences the viability of a product design. In the mid-1950s—this was an era of cheap gasoline, rising customer expectations, and expanding automotive engineering know-how—the first inkling of the concept of a "muscle car" was born, and Americans fell head-over-heels in love with this raw form of "controllable" power. The muscle car provided a high-horsepower, high-torque, V-8 engine that showed great distain for such mundane economic considerations as the price of its gasoline or the interval between required service appointments to keep the engine purring. The key feature became the ability of the car to "excite" the customer on acceleration. Non-exciting acceleration was for the older generation. Engineers pushed the limits of physics to deliver the thrill of raw power to consumers—until they ran out of engineering options and this sense of raw power became an expected feature in all vehicles, including the economy class—they accelerate much faster than the family cars of the 1950s. The ability to go fast was transitioned into an expectation of society by the innovation of engineering.

Innovation eventually decays into mediocrity

If products are unable to be truly differentiated based on innovative and competitive feature design, then those features that were once innovative or competitive become incorporated into the product's standard features. This transition relegates these once "differentiating qualities" to the realm of a commodity. The time that it takes for features to make this transition (from the "leadership" level to "basic" performance) is a function of the product's viable market life and the endurance of the innovative "technology," which changes with the commercial attractiveness of the technology.

It is important to note that these three relationships in the Kano Model are not independent, but over time "exciting" features will migrate into "competitive" features as competitors and the purchasers understand their value. Likewise, "competitive" features will become "standard" as the market accepts their routine benefits and associates these features with the basic product concept (e.g., the ability to steer a car is not a competitive benefit, but its absence is much more notable). The law of entropy applies, and all features degrade in "competitive significance" over time.

The net impact of this "gravity effect" is to lose competitive product positioning (and market advantage); therefore, it is important for a company to continuously refresh its products in order to keep them from becoming commodities and to ensure that they are perceived as "innovative." This product re-creation cycle is the driver for introduction of a product line's continuous flow of new product concepts, each in its own way extending the customer capability in a way that directly improves perceived performance in the customer's application environment. The customer must perceive "value" in order for the company to maintain an edge.

In a practical application of this theory of attractive quality, design engineers can assign the set of product features under consideration a descriptive characteristic using the Kano Model to help identify what to focus on for integration into the product concept. Individual product features can be characterized using this set of curves (e.g., each feature is ranked "exciting" or "standard" or "competitive") and thereby assist the design team to set design parameters for the feature in order to align the customer's requirement with their design objectives.

What product development strategy should a company take in order to overcome this application of the law of entropy? In the late 1980s Hewlett-Packard made the choice to pursue IU^{2}N (John Doyle, then a Hewlett-Packard corporate senior vice president, defined IU^{2}N as "an Imaginative Understanding of User Needs"). Following this strategy, engineers should apply their talents to the creative application of technology in the interpretation and realization of the unstated needs of their targeted customers. How does this work? A case study of the Ford Taurus will illustrate how product-design engineering can apply Kano's theory.

Interpreting the theory of attractive quality: Ford Taurus example

Much has been written about the customer value proposition that was embedded into the Ford Taurus during its design process (Watson, 1993). Ford benchmarked the entire spectrum of its competitors and identified "best practices" in design features in order to establish competitive targets for the design of its new product. The result: *Motor Trend Magazine* voted the Ford Taurus as "Car of the Year" for 1986—and its headlines noted the attention paid to its details: "It even has a coffee cup holder!"

Taking the example of the coffee cup holder as an innovative feature with attractive quality, let's consider how the Kano theory has worked out in the real world. The design of the coffee cup holder for the 1986 Taurus was accomplished in the Dearborn engineering facilities of Ford. As a working model of a coffee cup, the engineers used a "standard" 8-ounce Styrofoam cup that is used by many commercial food institutions. The problem with the design is that people do not drink out of these cups at home, and half of most daily automobile trips begin at home, where the driver is most likely to want a cup of coffee on the way to work. Given this usage model, the first coffee cup design can be seen as faulted, even though it was innovative and worthy of honorable mention as an automotive feature. Upon seeing this design weakness, competitors quickly sought to create more "humanized" designs: increasing the size of the cup, adapting the holder for juice boxes in addition to cups, designing the cup holder for mugs as well as glasses, etc.

This "war of the coffee cup holder" was eventually won by Lexus in its "relentless pursuit of excellence" in the design of the coffee cup holder: walnut paneling, hydraulic activation, and positive mechanical locking, combined with a soft rubber holder that would adapt to any cup that was placed in it! All this design excellence was delivered at a manufacturing cost of over $100, compared to the initial Ford Taurus $20 cost and the cost of an after-market coffee cup holder of around $2! This illustrates the competitive battle for differentiation that is found in the price/performance trade-off of the spoken quality curve—now that the automobile manufacturers have come to understand that one of the key purposes of an automobile is to safely transport coffee! However, the battle also raised consumer expectations.

A friend of mine once told me that he had not realized how dependent he was on the coffee cup holder until his first child was born. He decided to get a new car and have his wife drive his safe Volvo! As he started looking at new cars, his only requirement was economy—until he discovered that an economic car did not necessarily include a coffee cup holder. This discovery increased his purchase price by almost $2,000—this is the cost of an emotional decision! His choice was made based on an emotional response to the failure to receive an expected product feature and is typical of consumer behavioral response when a "standard" feature is not adequately delivered.

Consumers tend to react to products in a predictable manner that can be related to the Kano Model. Most of us react whenever our "spoken and unspoken" quality requirements are not fully met by a product or service! We move from the creative mind-set that is engaged by the "attractive" quality curve to the rational mind-set of the "competitive" quality curve to the emotional mind-set that takes over our behavior when confronted with dissatisfiers on the "standard" quality curve.

The concept of technology half-life

Intellectual property is inherently perishable. This is the implicit nature of product design. Just as a radioactive isotope has a half-life function—the period of time over which half of its level of radioactivity decays—so technological innovation also has a decay function that results in the loss of competitiveness for specific design features. It is essential for companies to anticipate the transition of technology and its impact on both product and production technologies. Technology half-life is a measure of the time it takes for the turnover in an organization's fundamental area of technology application (e.g., it indicates the half-life of change for turnover in technology—for instance, in the electronics industry, Moore's Law indicates the rate of turnover of technology for computer memory devices. Half the duration of the current cycle for the transition in one cycle of Moore's Law as applied to the semiconductor industry would equate to the technology half-life for these innovations).

This technology half-life determines the minimum frequency for strategic business scanning of an organization's technology environment to look for changes in the critical technology assumptions of their business model. This frequency ensures that an organization will not miss detection of a strategic change in technology direction, but it also allows product development reaction time to counter the moves of competitors. This observation provides a fundamental reason for using the idea of a stretch goal for an organization. Why set a stretch goal for an organization? It is not because anyone believes that the goal is "correct" or even "achievable"—one reason for a stretch goal is to establish the frequency with which an organization evaluates its design performance to determine what technology focus areas require management attention for strategic change. This analysis will also help to establish priorities for investment in research compared with alternative investments in marketing or capital equipment.

Technology transition and the speed of competition

The key question for any company is: What is the speed of transition for innovative concepts to become competitive concepts and then to move on down to the basic product concept level? It is the time that it takes an industry to accept a technology and for that technology to become "ubiquitous" within that industry. This is an observable and measurable time. Once this factor, or capacity to change, is known, then an innovative company must adjust its planning horizon to ensure that its strategic thinking stays ahead of industry trends. The industry's planning horizon—the period used to encourage the "creative destruction" of its product line—should be set so that the "half-life" of its technology base (half of the industry's transition time from one generation of technology to the next) approximates the strategic planning horizon. This implies that in some industries, strategic product planning should become a continuous event!

Since innovation represents the "creative destruction" of the familiar or "current" in order to make way for distinctive product advances or differences in applications, understanding the rate of technological change for the fundamental technologies that drive an industry's product and production capabilities is a most significant component in designing the proper strategy for continuing competitiveness and sustained profitability. What is the relationship between the degree of product innovation and customer perception of quality performance in a product? Do the more highly innovative products get away with higher failure rates?

Innovation dilutes quality concerns

Customers really do care about innovation, but while they purchase "features" they also buy the quality of the total market offering (a bundled product and its related services). However, in the final analysis it is the quality of the products and services that determines the level of customer loyalty and commitment to a particular brand or company. In essence, customers buy quality.

Customers do not desire failure. While a customer never excuses catastrophic product failure, products at the "bleeding edge" of technology will typically enjoy a high degree of customer forgiveness for relatively minor quality issues or bugs. This occurs because "early technology adopters" have become conditioned to accept that they must "pay a price" for being the first to apply a new technology. Generally they believe that they will obtain a competitive advantage by learning how to use a newly emerging technology and that this advantage will far outweigh any disadvantage that is suffered from lack of product maturity.

However, there are two related concerns that these customers share. First, they do not want to feel that they are being systematically taken advantage of by serving as a beta test site for all new product releases. Second, they expect that problems reported with the product will be rapidly corrected and their operations or application of the product will not be interrupted as a result of any product-related problems. In this competitive environment there are two basic quality rules for new product introduction:

1. Companies must be exceptionally responsive to all reported customer issues reported in the early months after an initial product release. Companies must investigate each voiced concern and, recognizing that many customers remain silent, must have a proactive way to reach out and discover any latent consumer issues that are not reported.

2. As a design rule, product performance should be subject to continuous improvement of its quality—each product generation must not repeat any previously discovered problems and must perform at a higher level of reliability.

The conclusion is clear: While there is a relatively high degree of tolerance for quality problems with "innovative" products, there is no tolerance for quality problems in commodity products. As a corollary to this conclusion, consumer confidence is undermined whenever a company has a prolonged trend of releasing new products that have problems into the market. They are treating their customers as if they were part of the product development and testing process and waiting for the customer to detect the problem. Customers want value in the products and services that they purchase, and consistently delivering a promise that is perceived to be valuable is a critical aspect of competitiveness. How should a company create its customer value proposition?

Value propositions and competitiveness

A company's value proposition contains two elements. The first is the explicit promise of value that is given to customers. The second element of a value proposition is a combination of actions that are taken internally to deliver a "consistent way of working" that delivers this proposition of value in a way that reflects constancy of purpose in the organization's fulfillment of its promises.

Both of these elements of a value proposition—its goal (the promise) and its delivery process (internal way of working)—have been investigated over the past decade. Looking at these studies, it is clear that a consistent theme emerges as a synthesis supporting these two elements.

In the book *Built to Last*, authors Jim Collins and Jerry Porras identified companies that were able to sustain performance over time, which they called "visionary companies"—recognized as the "crown jewels" in their industry for their ability to sustain leading performance. Collins and Porras observed that these companies followed a dualistic path to achieve success—they preserved their core values while at the same time acting innovatively to stimulate progress. Core ideology is the focal point—a blending of guiding principles, the belief structure of the firm, and business purpose, the vision or direction that determines why the firm exists. The type of value proposition that is put forward by Collins and Porras is the values around the way of working as a group that create the sustainable corporate engine allowing the company to clearly focus on delivering its customer proposition over the long haul.[34]

A second aspect of the value proposition describes what the firm actually does and extends on the belief system by choosing a specific value proposition as a market discipline and a way to deliver enduring customer value. *The Discipline of Market Leaders* describes three aspects of delivering value to customers. The first aspect is a company's value proposition: the promise that it makes to customers to deliver a certain combination of service, convenience, price, quality, selection, etc. The second aspect of value is the operating model that defines precisely how value is transferred to customers: the set of business processes, cultural norms, operating systems, and functional competence that creates the ability to deliver on the value proposition. The third aspect is the value discipline of an organization. A value discipline describes the way in which companies combine the features of their operating model for the delivery of their value proposition in order to be the best in their chosen market. Treacy and Wiersema identify three different value disciplines that create different types of customer value.[35] They further state that, in order to achieve "lasting excellence" (described by Collins and Porras) and achieve business leadership through sustained growth, a company must make an explicit choice to demonstrate consistent excellence in one of the following competence areas: innovative products, marketing leadership, and operational excellence.What are the three market disciplines they describe?

Product leadership—concentrate on offering innovative products that continually push the known performance boundaries. The value proposition for customers is that these products will be the best in the market from the aspect of innovative features and capabilities. The second value proposition is customer intimacy—focus not on delivering what a generic market wants, but what a specifically targeted customer wants. Customer-intimate companies do not pursue every market opportunity or individual business transactions; they cultivate long-term relationships that deliver value through a continuing relationship that becomes more and more seamless between a customer's need and the company's product and service support. The third market dis-

---

[34] James C. Collins and Jerry I. Porras, *Built to Last* (New York: HarperCollins, 1995).

[35] Treacy and Wiersema, *op. cit.*

cipline that delivers value to customers is operational excellence—focus on delivering capable, but "middle-of-the-market" products and services at the best possible market price and with the least possible inconvenience. The value proposition of companies pursuing this market discipline is delivering both low price and hassle-free service.

A company's choice of value discipline resulting in market leadership represents a distinct and strategic choice by its leadership team. According to Treacy and Wiersema, these three choices are exclusive—a company can excel only in one market discipline, and this discipline defines what a company does at its core, framing its subsequent strategic plans and operating methods.

In *Lean Thinking*, Womack and Jones focus companies on the methods by which they create value for their customers.[36] When companies focus on existing organizational structure and outdated value propositions, then managers create waste and the economic strength of the firm falters. Lean thinking focuses on value-creating activities for the product or service—the value stream that flows smoothly based on a pull of customer demand through the company's processes for delivering that demand and providing the highest satisfaction of customer requirements.

How does a company make such a strategic choice as to what discipline it should pursue and how it translates that choice into internal activities that drive market results? John Kay defines an approach for adding value and identifies four ingredients as value drivers: product innovation, reputation (brand), strategic assets (factors that create a market barrier to entry for other potential competitors), and architecture (relationships with employees, suppliers, and customers).[37] The focus on value comes from a strictly financial perspective. Kay defines value as a comprehensive financial difference between the value of goods and services produced and the cost of their production. This value definition can serve as both a motivator and an appropriate measure of achievement. Creation of value permits a company to determine how to share the value produced among the organization's stakeholders (customers, shareholders, and employees). Kay describes the outcome of success as a product of these four value ingredients. Success comes when managers act on their company's specific capabilities and advantages and make appropriate changes that move it in the direction of becoming a consistent value producer. What is the best way to effect such designed change?

Harvard Professor Rosabeth Moss Kanter describes value production process as "crystallization" of new action possibilities (new policies, new behaviors, new patterns, new methodologies, new products, or new market ideas) based on "reconceptualized" patterns in the organization. The architecture of change involves the construction of new patterns, or the reformulation of old ones, to make new, and hopefully more productive, actions possible.[38] Kanter be-

[36] James P. Womack and Daniel T. Jones, *Lean Thinking* (New York: Simon & Schuster, 1996).

[37] John Kay, *Why Firms Succeed* (London: Oxford University Press, 1995).

[38] Rosabeth Moss Kanter, *The Change Masters* (New York: Simon & Schuster, 1983).

lieves that in order to make change happen, it is important to be aware of the foundations of the organization. The innovative building blocks of change must be laid on chosen departures from the foundation of tradition in order for change to reach the point of institutionalization (full integration across the organization into the approach taken for its routine ways of working). Productive change is able to take an organization to a new level of performance in its delivery of value to customers and thereby more fully secure its place in a competitive market. Kanter's approach provides an operational definition for implementing Schumpeter's innovation through "creative destruction" in the operating processes of an organization.

Linking value disciplines to the theory of attractive quality

How does this digression into value disciplines of a company relate to the Kano Theory of Attractive Quality? Consider the Kano Model as a two-by-two matrix describing individual competence over the axes of the Kano Model. This structure (see the figure below) creates four distinct quadrants that can be envisioned as strategic approaches to value delivery. In each of these four quadrants a different competitive focus is required of an organization. In the upper left quadrant a company focuses on the value discipline of product leadership—consistently giving value to customers through technology exploitation and innovation. In the upper right quadrant, a company delivers the value discipline of customer intimacy—consistently beating competitors by its knowledge of customer desires and its ability to deliver them at a higher

Value Propositions and Competitive Positioning

quality (measured by a price/performance indicator) than can its competitors (in a Darwinian "only the strong survive" approach to business). In the bottom right quadrant, a company delivers the value discipline of operations excellence by being the cost leader so it can compete on price and reliability of its products. The bottom left quadrant is simply not a competitive place to remain. A business in this quadrant is on its way to bankruptcy!

Many people have treated the Kano Model as a static model of the customer dynamic, just as the Treacy-Wiersema value-disciplines model has been treated as static. However, in the real world environment of business, both of these models are dynamic and change as a function of the transformation in a product's life cycle within a specific product category. The technology half-life of a product allows an organization to calculate an anticipated "duration" for specific product features. This calculation also establishes a market transformation cycle time. In other words, it establishes the "beat" of the market in terms of the willingness of its customers to accept all the new technology—an estimate of the technology diffusion susceptibility of a market. The speed of change becomes a distinguishing characteristic in leading companies. Companies must not only welcome change—they should actively seek change to stimulate progress in all dimensions of performance.

Companies that enjoy sustained success must discover within themselves the ability to reinvent their greatness. The new approach to quality described in this foreword underlies the philosophy of DFSS and provides an important insight into the set of actions that such a company must consider when it decides how to reinvent itself through its product line. If a company makes a mistake in the bottom two curves of the Kano Model, then no matter how much innovation is in a product or how extensive the capability to design exciting products and features, it simply does *not* matter. Mistakes on these bottom curves invoke a response that is very similar to the Hierarchy of Needs identified by Abraham Maslow—survival needs, such as security or safety, will always overwhelm the need for personal development or self-actualization.

In today's dynamic markets, with their rapid innovations in technology, companies are finding that a highly capable product-creation strategy must be matched with marketing agility to continuously position it as a superior offering based on an in-depth and intimate knowledge of customer needs, issues, and concerns. Not only must the positioning be superior to competitors', but it must be clear from the viewpoint of the customer's own value system that superior value is also being delivered. Following the creation of the value proposition and the promotion of this value proposition (selling it to customers), then a company must be able to consistently produce reliable results and demonstrate their operational excellence to deliver the value proposition in a flawless manner to customers. How can this example be seen in a competitive world? Let's reconsider what happened to the Ford Taurus.

What is the rest of the story about the Ford Taurus? While the Ford Taurus was one of the most creative new product concepts in automotive history, it had reliability problems in its drive train, which causes history to judge this product that made an initial splash as the "Car of the Year" as a Blue Book "lemon" rather than a market "leader." Reliability is defined as quality performance over a long period of time—or sustained performance excellence. Whenever a basic quality level is not delivered, this experience will wipe out the reputation gained from innovative features or better competitive positioning.

Product life cycles describe product dynamic dimensions

Since a company consists of several product lines with many different products, it is difficult to extrapolate from the Kano Model to corporate strategy. The reason for this difficulty is that the company actually has an entire portfolio of products, each of which is at a different moment in its product life cycle. When products are first released, they might fall into the innovative domain of product leadership. As competition recognizes the value acceptance by customers, they will seek to replicate the same capability. As competition increases and the customers begin to rely on this capability, then the product will transition into the expected or "must be" quality characteristic that is found in a commodity view of the product's capability.

The speed of this transformation from innovation to commodity feature is characteristic of each particular industry. In the cellular phone or laptop computer businesses, this cycle time is now measured in months (using single digits!). The implication of this observation is that a company must be able to simultaneously produce all three value disciplines if it wants to remain a market leader over the long haul. This means that companies must continuously "look over their shoulder" to understand competitive moves, regulatory changes, technology developments, and other factors that affect their business environment.[39] Competitive excellence is achieved when a company is able to constantly re-create high levels of "exciting quality" while paying attention to the foundations of both product reliability and the design of product functions or features that correctly anticipate the true needs of its customers.

Quality in the value proposition

While Treacy and Wiersema believe that a company must choose only one market discipline in which to excel, their proposition must be challenged in the circumstance where the speed of the product life cycle turnover is so rapid that the business model never rests in equilibrium. Such high-technology telecommunications firms as Nokia, which must learn to thrive in a business

---

[39] For more on integration of strategic planning and environmental analysis, see Watson, *Strategic Benchmarking.*

environment where quarterly innovations are introduced into their business, cannot maintain a single, stagnant value discipline. Under the pressure for a constant stream of new products, it is essential that these companies manage their entire product portfolio to balance out innovation with customer intimacy, which leads to significant understanding of the buying behaviors of the leading adaptors of new technology, and at the same time deliver products fault-free (Six Sigma level of quality) because there will be no time to correct deficiencies in a product once it has been introduced.

DFSS is the operational discipline of product leadership! The input to DFSS is the voice of the customer, which comes from customer intimacy, while its output is delivery of the highest total value—not lowest total cost, which is derived from operational excellence. Thus, true leadership requires integration of all three disciplines to drive the fullest competitive benefits! DFSS is the means by which to integrate these three disciplines!

How does design deliver quality?

The saying that "quality begins and ends with the customer" is especially evident in the design process. Strategic understanding of market requirements, competitive analysis, and customer applications are key elements for development of a business case to initiate a product program. The first step in a program development is identification of a market need that can be addressed by available technology. What will the customer buy, how will they use it, and how many people have this need? The final step in the program development process is the delivery of the product to customers, where a crucial determination is made whether the design is right or not. In order to prevent surprises when the product is delivered to the market, a series of DFSS management interventions are made to ensure that progress is made toward the project's goals and that the customers are engaged in appropriate ways throughout the entire process.

Understanding how quality is implemented in design requires understanding of two fundamental new product development processes: the product conceptualization process, which results in a decision to transition a specific product concept into a product, and the design realization process, which transforms the product concept into a design that is ready for detailed engineering. Design quality is focused on product conceptualization, while transfer of the design to product realization is the task of manufacturing and production engineering (see the figure below).

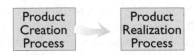

The product creation process creates business success by sustaining the value proposition of product leadership over time as technology changes—or, as Christensen and Raynor describe in *The Innovator's Solution*—a persistent leader in developing both sustaining technology and disruptive technology. Managing the transition of a product to production is the job of the product realization process—with the oversight of manufacturing management and production engineering. The result that occurs when these processes operate together in the context of quality as described in this foreword is the persistent exercise of the product leadership discipline, which is capable of sustaining business success.

Product design imperative: Win customers!

For a company to consistently win its "daily" battle for customers, it must compete in both gaining and keeping its customers. Sustained growth is not just a market or revenue-centered goal; it is the essential ingredient in a recipe for overcoming entropy and the economic effect of inflation. If a company does not continue to grow it is not standing still; it is actually losing economic ground. "Business change initiatives should be balanced between continuous improvement and breakthrough activities, with the decision for selection based on both resource requirements and business performance needs."[40] Thus, the balance business leaders must find is between their improvement efforts for winning new customers (through DFSS) and keeping their customers (through flawless execution as delivered by DMAIC projects).

Success will always require customers and particular knowledge of them that will deliver focus in everything the organization does. To obtain sustained success in business results, excellence must be expressly embedded in our customers' experience. Such activity must be directed at delivering the best value—flawless execution—to customers. Flawless execution requires organizations to deliver Six Sigma levels of performance through both design and execution of the organization's products and services. Organizations don't compete for markets as a whole; they compete one customer at a time, based on their ability to consistently fulfill their value proposition for quality performance.

While the DMAIC process of Six Sigma will return an organization to a state of effective and efficient operation, business leaders must implement the DMADV process of Design for Six Sigma to win new customers and ensure the long-term competitiveness of their organization.

---

[40] Gregory H. Watson, *Business Systems Engineering,* pp. 94–95.

Chapter 1

Introducing Design for Six Sigma

*"The whole of science is nothing more than
the refinement of everyday thinking."*

~ Albert Einstein

Introduction

Six Sigma was initially defined in 1983 by the late Motorola engineer Bill Smith, who used it as a practical means to quantify the business improvement strategy of CEO Bob Galvin: to improve the performance of Motorola by a factor of a hundredfold over a five-year period. Motorola worked with a number of companies in the semiconductor industry through its participation in the Six Sigma Research Institute, headed by Dr. Mikel J. Harry, to define the methodology that would deliver this stretch performance objective.[1] CEO

---

[1] In 1981, Bob Galvin, Chairman of Motorola, followed the example of Hewlett-Packard's CEO John Young and established a "10X" improvement program. He outdid Young in that he asked Motorola to achieve 100X in five years, instead of the decade that HP chose to achieve its 10X goal. Motorola went looking for ways to make these improvements by cutting waste and also improving process efficiency. Bill Smith, a Motorola engineer, was studying the relationship between a product's field life and how often the product was repaired during the manufacturing process. In 1985, he presented a paper concluding that if a product were found defective in the production process and repaired, then it was likely that other errors would escape the test process and be found later by customers during their early experience with the product. However, if the product was assembled free of errors, then the likelihood of failure during initial customer usage was significantly lower. At this same time, Motorola discovered that the best-in-class manufacturers (such as Hewlett-Packard) were making products that required no repair or rework during the manufacturing process. The challenge of producing defect-free products is the fundamental challenge of Six Sigma. Motorola joined forces with Texas Instruments, IBM, Digital Electronics, Intel, and Harris Semiconductor to establish and fund a Six Sigma Research Institute in Schaumburg, Illinois. Dr. Mikel J. Harry headed up this effort to clarify the statistical meaning of Six Sigma and develop the specific tools and tactics to deliver the promise of improvement.

Larry Bossidy successfully applied the resulting methodology as a turnaround strategy for the AlliedSignal organization. After Jack Welch adapted the Six Sigma methods for General Electric, Six Sigma rapidly became a mainstream management methodology that has been applied at hundreds of organizations around the world. Why has Six Sigma taken such a successful journey? In the words of Jack Welch: "Six Sigma gives us a route to the business control function, the hardest thing to do in management."[2] While Welch's statement focuses on one aspect of Six Sigma, there is much more to the initiative. Six Sigma provides discipline for executing a Total Quality Management strategy in the areas of change management, project management, problem solving, and innovation (or the design of products and processes)—it supports fundamental business processes that define an organization's mission with a methodology that links its individual change projects to the overall change management strategy that management designs to deliver its vision.

What is Six Sigma?

The phrase "Six Sigma" has taken on several different meanings. It is more of a business strategy than it is a quality program. Six Sigma improvements should be tied to an organization's corporate strategy and goals for business performance in order to achieve the maximum benefit from its analytical power. But, just what is Six Sigma? Consider the following four meanings of Six Sigma[3]:

As a metric, Six Sigma (6σ) is a statistical measure of process performance. Sigma is an indicator of variation. Statisticians use the Greek letter sigma (σ) to express standard deviation, which refers to the average difference between a given point in a set of data and the average of all other points. The higher the sigma value, the better a process is performing. If sigma is used as a common metric across processes, then it is possible to compare relative quality levels across similar and dissimilar products, services, and processes. The current competitive level of performance in business is in the range of three to four sigma, with many companies operating below this level. The sigma scale is exponential when translated into defects per million opportunities. Performing at a one-sigma level means that a process is producing more defects than it is good results according to a customer-defined standard of goodness. So, Six Sigma means near-perfect quality performance for a particular process characteristic. The sigma performance scale can also be translated into measures of process capability—for both indices of Cp (capability for design performance relative to customer requirements) and Cpk (capability for real-world performance in the presence of variation)—as well as a corresponding estimate of the cost of poor quality that an organization bears at each level of sigma performance (see the following table).

---

[2] As quoted in: Gregory H. Watson, "Cycles of Learning: Observations of Jack Welch," *Six Sigma Forum Magazine*, vol. 1, no. 1, November 2001, p. 13.

[3] Six Sigma is a federally registered sales mark and trademark of Motorola.

Sigma performance level[4]	Defects per million opportunities to make a defect	Process capability (Cp)	Process capability (Cpk)	Cost of poor quality (% revenue)
1.0σ	670,000	Not capable	Not capable	
1.5σ	500,000	Not capable	Not capable	
2.0σ	308,300	Not capable	Not capable	30–40%
2.5σ	158,650	Not capable	Not capable	
3.0σ	66,807	1.0	0.5	20–30%
3.5σ	22,700	1.17	0.67	
4.0σ	6,210	1.33	0.83	15–20%
4.5σ	1,350	1.5	1.0	
5.0σ	233	1.67	1.17	10–15%
5.5σ	32	1.83	1.33	
6.0σ	3.4	2.0	1.5	<10%

Cp describes intended or design performance, while Cpk describes what happens when the real-world implementation occurs and the discipline of maintaining design performance is not possible due to inherent shifts and drifts in the design parameter's average. Note that there is a higher defect level in the real-world distribution (indicated in the Cpk) than in the ideal-world distribution (indicated in the Cp). As today's leading statistical guru, Dr. George E. P. Box observes: "The authors of the Six Sigma concept wisely assume that the process does not have a fixed mean value but undergoes drift—specifically, that the local mean might drift on either side of the target by about 1.5 standard deviations."[5]

Second, Six Sigma is also a data-driven, statistical analysis process-improvement methodology for achieving these levels of near-perfect performance. This methodology combines a rigorous, step-by-step analytical approach to statistical problem-solving with a library of statistical tools that address multi-variable problems and are used in a specific sequence in order to expose the sources of variation and demonstrate how they can be put under control in a way that optimizes and controls process output. This sequence of application for the statistical tools has been demonstrated to provide profound knowledge of both engineering and business processes and represents a significant breakthrough as a learning sequence for discovering how these

[4] Note that this table is built using the Six Sigma convention of applying a 1.5σ shift to the short-term value that is found in statistical tables. This means that the numerical value for Six Sigma taken directly from the normal distribution statistical Z-table would be 0.002 parts per million (ppm), but subtracting the 1.5σ shift would move this value to 4.5σ or 3.4 ppm in recognition of the extra effect of long-term variation. This is a much-debated heuristic, and it is always advisable to calculate the shift as the performance difference between observed short-term (variation within a short-term sample) and shifts that occur in the mean performance between short-term samples (variation between short-term samples collected over a longer time period).

[5] George E. P. Box, "Six Sigma, Process Drift, Capability Indices, and Feedback Adjustment," *Quality Engineering,* vol. 12, no. 3, March 2000, p. 298.

processes operate and for building an understanding of the interrelation-ships among the various process factors that influence its performance.

Third, Six Sigma is a philosophy of management. As a philosophy for busi-ness operations, Six Sigma recognizes the direct linkage among the number of product defects, wasted operating costs, and the level of customer satis-faction with a company's goods and services. As an operating philosophy, Six Sigma provides a framework that ties together business improvement and quality initiatives and aligns the organization to a common set of goals that are evaluated using measures of productivity, cost-effectiveness, and quality. Six Sigma improvement targets should be linked to both an organization's strategy and its business results by using customer expectations and market requirements as the defining point for all improvement projects.

Finally, the Six Sigma analysis process becomes a culture in and of itself, motivating teams to work on a common problem to achieve higher lev-els of performance effectiveness and productivity at lower cost. In mature organizations (after about three years of operating the Six Sigma way), man-agement by fact, root cause analysis, and definition of problems according to the source of variance become part of the business language and form a common bond among all levels of employees. Each different level of deci-sion making (enterprise-wide, business area, and front-line operations) has a unique contribution to Six Sigma, and, through their joint efforts, a long-term process for problem prevention and corrective action can be put into place built around Six Sigma thinking and its action-oriented philosophy.

Six Sigma methods can be summarized as a business improvement approach that seeks to find and eliminate causes of mistakes or defects in business processes by focusing on outputs that are of significance to customers. The concepts underlying Six Sigma deal with the fact that process and product variation are known to be strong factors affecting product production lead times, product and process costs, process yields, and ultimately customer satisfaction. One of the most important aspects of the work of a Six Sigma "Black Belt" is to define and measure variation with the intent of discover-ing its causes and to develop efficient operational means to control and re-duce variation. The heart of the fresh approach that is implicit in Six Sigma lies within packaging of the toolkit relative to its rigorous problem-solving approach, the dedicated application of trained business analysts to well-structured process or product improvement projects, and the attention to bottom-line results and sustaining those results over time.

A Six Sigma improvement initiative contains both management and technical components. On the management side, it concentrates on getting the right process metrics and goals, the right projects and people to work on them, and the use of management systems to complete the projects successfully and sustain the gains over time. On the technical side, it focuses on enhancing process performance (e.g., improving the average level of performance and reducing variation) by using process data, statistical thinking and methods, and a disciplined approach to process improvement methodology, which has five principal steps: define, measure, analyze, improve, and control. The statistical and quality improvement tools are linked and sequenced in a unique way that is both easy to use and effective in analysis. This Six Sigma approach focuses on the identification of the key process drivers (primary sources of variation) and relies on statistical software to simplify the calculations.

The essence of Six Sigma

Six Sigma thinking begins with the customers of a business—understanding what is critical to quality in the business outcome that leads to customer satisfaction as well as financial return for shareholders and competitive advantage in the market. By understanding customer requirements as the starting point in a Six Sigma analysis, the definition of an opportunity for defects is anchored directly to a facet of performance that is significant to customers and their experience with a product or service.

There are three aspects of Six Sigma that can be considered either "new" or not properly emphasized in past approaches to quality improvement: integration of the human and process aspects of business improvement; clear concentration on obtaining bottom-line results and a structured method that links the analytical tools into an overall framework; and a fixed analytical "recipe" for resolving chronic work problems and attacking emerging issues.

Six Sigma integrates both process and human improvement aspects. Some of the human issues that are involved include: leadership by all levels of management, operating with a sense of urgency to both evaluate and correct issues, focus on customer concerns, working in project teams, driving for bottom-line results, and deploying the program to ensure a culture change toward management by fact and the emphasis of continuous improvement of business as a natural aspect of everyone's work experience. Some of the process issues that are included in Six Sigma include: a disciplined approach to the issues at hand; dedication to process improvement; use of quantitative measures, methods for understanding the sources of variation, and statistical methods; and emphasis on process management to sustain the gains. Six Sigma creates "constancy of purpose" in an organization by adding a new dimension to business process measurement: variation as an indicator of process performance. Sigma now stands alongside financial indicators as a business metric indicating systemic excellence in execution of the management improvement agenda.

Management in Six Sigma companies has come to understand that their chief responsibility is to foster and encourage such improvement efforts. They do this by making it absolutely clear that improvement of business processes and product (both goods and services elements) is part of the everyday job of all employees; by providing appropriate training at all levels of the organization; and by making improvement of quality into a "competitive sport" through the application of the roles of "Champions" and "Black Belts" to drive these improvements.

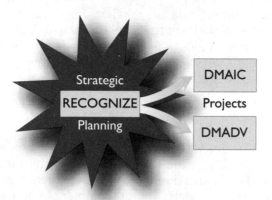

The customer expectation for flawless execution of the value proposition that they "buy into" has its own internal problems. What is the distinction between flawless execution and perfection in the way work is done? Consider the question that we are continually confronted with: Is perfection too much to hope for in human activities?

Flawless execution vs. perfection as a Six Sigma performance target

Perhaps an example is best to introduce the distinction between these two concepts. Consider the Motorola "Bandit" pocket pager. This product was designed to deliver Six Sigma as an absolute performance target—essentially no defect in any of the product-design features. The outcome of the effort of the Motorola engineers was a product that had a Mean Time to Failure (or MTTF—a statistic that describes the average point of expected failure—half of the failures will occur before this time and half afterward) of over 150 years! Motorola cites this performance as a phenomenal indicator of customer satisfaction, when in reality it indicates a lack of knowledge of the customer's perspective. How long does a customer want to use a "disposable" pocket pager? What is the useful product life? Is this level of perfection really the desired goal? Most people would be quite pleased if the performance of their pager provided complete reception and also reliable messages during a two-year useful life. What was the problem in the Motorola approach to defining this critical performance characteristic? Lack of customer perspective! And this lack cost Motorola dearly as Nokia beat it to the market on digital cellular technology, causing Motorola to lose business. Performance fell because Motorola defined flawless design execution as perfection in an engineering sense, rather than a customer-oriented sense. The difference is a loss of time to market. Notice how this distinction impacts competitiveness in the figure below. While Motorola's engineers slaved to minimize the risk for every potential defect that could occur out to a 150-year MTTF, it left itself vulnerable to a swift-moving competitor that delivered exactly to the market's expectation for useful life. In this case, too much quality cost too dearly in total business terms.

Flawless Execution versus Perfection

Consider the Motorolla "Bandit" pocket pager. This product was designed to deliver Six Sigma as an absolute performance target. The outcome is a product with a Mean Time to Failure (MTTF) of over 150 years! What is the useful product life? Is perfection really the desired goal?

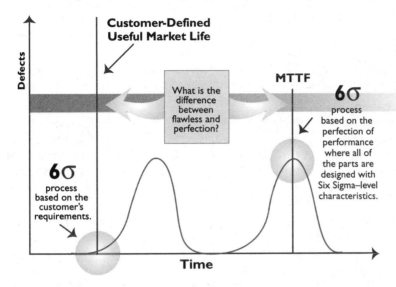

Which process costs more? Which process delivers more customer value?

On the other hand, the approach identified for flawless execution delivers Six Sigma performance relative to the customer's expectation. This means that companies must understand the requirement of their customer for the useful life of their product, as well as the features that they desire it to have sustained during this performance period—for both the spoken (essential) features and the unspoken (differentiating) features. These observations lead to the next discovery in the extension of the Kano Model: In this dynamic environment, there is a different concept for delivering quality to customers.

In order to determine how much impact closing these gaps can have on an organization, it is essential to measure the performance gap. One measure of this type of performance is the process capability (Cp) index—this ratio measures the width in a customer requirement specification (their tolerance for variation around a nominal performance level) to a measure of process variation using six standard deviations of the process variation. This statistic indicates how well a process has been designed and is a reasonable indicator of the performance that is anticipated in an initial capital investment in a process. Of course, Cp represents the best that a process can achieve in terms of its performance. A process does not operate at this level—variation happens, and the process operates at a lower level that, as measured using the related performance index Cpk, accounts for variation from the designed performance level.

For the purpose of this discussion, it is sufficient to recognize that the Cp index estimates the highest return on capital investment a process could obtain. The process is purchased based on a requirement, and the requirement establishes the "expected value" of process performance. If the process is operating at its designed target level of performance and under its design conditions for variation, then Cp will be achieved. When the process is operating at less than its Cp level, then the performance metric return on capital employed will demonstrate the loss due to this "off-centered" condition. If Cpk is improved to the design Cp, then return on capital employed is maximized.

It is a significant observation that the process capability index links together the voice of the customer (customer requirement) and the voice of the process (variation inherent in the process design). The difference between the "idealized" or process potential of Cp and the "real-world" or process performance of Cpk provides an estimate of the gap in performance that must be closed to optimize the value proposition for a product or process. The difference between the levels of Cp and Cpk is the cost of keeping the process centered on its nominal performance level. However, many times the problem lies not in this gap, which measures the potential to improve a process to achieve "flawless execution" as indicated by the chosen nominal or desired performance level based on a fixed level of capital investment. Often the problem is that process performance does not have an adequate level of Cp—which is a function of the design capability established during the product-creation process.[6]

Influencing performance results

Flawless execution can be measured using sigma (standard deviation or its probabilistic expression using the bell-shaped normal distribution, which statisticians refer to as a Z-distribution) as an indicator of performance. There is always some performance shift from the ideal condition for which a process has been designed (Cp) as it is executed over time. (Note the equivalence between Cp and sigma: When Cp is multiplied by 3, then the result is the design sigma level of the process.) Also, short-term observations of process performance have less opportunity for performance variation to occur than do long-term observations. In the mathematics of Six Sigma, this effect is noted heuristically as a 1.5-sigma shift between the short-term and long-term distributions. The same type of difference can be observed when evaluating components of variation estimated using samples (sometimes noted as Zst for the short-term normal probability calculation used to obtain a sigma value). In the terms of ANOVA (Analysis of Variance), this is the same component of variation as "within" sample variation—an average of the variation within the samples. However, there is a second component of variation that must be considered—the shift between means that occurs across the samples. This component of variation is the "between" samples variation

---

[6] Note that in a competitive business environment the product-creation process designs both products and processes that deliver these products. True competitiveness is achieved when products are unique, processes are not readily duplicated, and the design cycle time is so fast that competitors can't keep up with a company's innovations in both the product and process domains.

that represents long-term process drift (and this is calculated using Zlt for the long-term component of variation). The difference between short-term and long-term variation indicates the combined or total effect of variation on a process. While "1.5 sigma" is used as a rule of thumb, the exact gap can be calculated based on the actual, observed differences of "within" and "between" ANOVA components of variation.

The impact of this distinction between short-term and long-term effects of variation is lost as a business improves its performance beyond the 3–4 sigma levels (today's most common performance targets). As one evaluates the sigma offset as a function of the short-term process performance when short-term process approaches Six Sigma, then the absolute level of the sigma shift has less of an impact on process performance, and the correction between short-term and long-term performance becomes diminished in value. Using the chart below, the absolute impact of a process shift can be observed to decrease significantly as its process performance level improves.

Higher Quality Decreases Significance of the Sigma Shift

Note how the impact of the shift (as measured in parts per million) decreases—as the process improves, the short-term sigma (Zst) and long-term sigma (Zlt) converge:

Sigma Offset	Sigma Short-Term (Zst)						
	3	3.5	4	4.5	5	5.5	6
0	1,350	233	32	3.4	0.39	0.017	0.001
0.25	3,000	665	88	11	1	0.1	0.0063
0.5	6,200	1,350	233	32	3.4	0.7	0.017
0.75	12,200	3,000	665	88	11	1	0.1
1.0	22,800	6,200	1,350	233	32	3.4	0.39
1.25	40,100	12,200	3,000	665	88	11	1
1.5	66,800	22,800	6,200	1,350	233	32	3.4
1.75	105,600	40,100	12,200	3,000	665	88	11
2.0	158,700	66,800	22,800	6,200	1,350	233	32

This discovery is critical when it comes to understanding the significance of the pursuit of flawless execution. It is only processes that are performing at industry "average" (3 to 4 sigma) that are impacted most heavily by process shift and drift. High-performing processes are much more robust across an entire range of shift and drift as the absolute effect of these conditions decreases with increasing process quality. Thus, higher process quality has an effect that is observed as a "predictable outcome" by customers. Such predictable outcomes lead to exceptional customer experiences as a result of robust process performance and sustainable business performance.

There are many definitions of Design for Six Sigma (DFSS)—here are a few:

▶ "While Six Sigma helps fix what is broken...Design for Six Sigma helps to design things that don't break in the first place, things that do more and cost less." [7]

▶ "The ultimate goal of DFSS is to: (1) Do the right things; and (2) Do things right all the time."[8] "The term 'Six Sigma' in the context of DFSS can be defined as the level at which design vulnerabilities are *not effective* or minimal. Generally two major design vulnerabilities can affect the quality of a design: (1) Conceptual vulnerabilities that are established because of the violation of design axioms and principles. (2) Operational vulnerabilities due to the lack of robustness in the use environment. Elimination or reduction of operational vulnerabilities is the objective of...Six Sigma."[9]

▶ "DFSS adds another dimension to product development, called Critical Parameter Management (CPM). CPM is the disciplined and focused attention to the design's functions, parameters, and responses that are critical to fulfilling the customer's needs.... DFSS is about preventing problems and doing the right things at the right time during product development. From a management perspective, it is about designing the right cycle time for product development of new products. It helps in the process of inventing, developing, optimizing, and transferring new technology into product design programs. It also enables the subsequent conceptual development, design, optimization, and verification of new products prior to their launch into their respective markets."[10]

DFSS has three major components: product line management, design and new product development project management, and the Six Sigma toolkit (DMADV) that is applied in the product-creation process. The definition of DFSS that we will use is:

Design for Six Sigma is a process to define, design, and deliver innovative products, processes, and services that provide competitively attractive value to customers in a manner that achieves the critical-to-quality characteristics for all the significant functions.

Some of the activities conducted during a DFSS project include:

▶ Choose product development projects by weighing risks and benefits.

▶ Focus the allocation of design resources to maximize return on investment.

[7] Subir Chowdhury, *Design for Six Sigma: The Revolutionary Process for Achieving Extraordinary Profits* (Dearborn, MI: Dearborn Trade Publishing, 2002), p. 13.

[8] Yang and E-Haik, *op. cit.,* p. xi.

[9] *Ibid.,* pp. 50–51.

[10] Creveling, Slutsky, and Antis, *op. cit.,* p. xvii. Parameter design, originally developed at MIT (the Massachusetts Institute of Technology), is the fundamental concept underlying this methodology.

- Identify and address the critical-to-quality customer functional requirements.
- Assess alternative designs to innovatively resolve design conflicts.
- Define high-value, low-cost product functions.
- Eliminate potential failure modes in the functions that affect customers.
- Ensure customer tolerances for design parameters are met.
- Reduce variation for critical functional parameters.
- Designs that are robust to the inherent material and process variation.
- Products and services that are robust to the environment in which they are used.
- Complete commercial transition within the window of market opportunity.
- Minimize the total life-cycle cost of the product.

Components of Design for Six Sigma

Innovative design drives business competitiveness

The best starting point for understanding DFSS is by focusing on its influence on business competitiveness. In DFSS, business competitiveness is ensured through the design function—which is responsible for delivering continuous growth in shareholder value through development of new products and services that generate future revenue flows and fulfill the promises for both increased growth and continued profitability.

Designs can be classified as either conceptually static or dynamic. A conceptually static design has reached a plateau in terms of its innovative development. Such a design has been developed in an iterative fashion, and it has converged on a relatively fixed or static concept that is susceptible only to minor developments that will enhance capability for production, decrease production cost, or correct minor defects in design or production. At this point, major investments in the continued refinement of the design result in diminishingly marginal returns. Conceptually static design changes are often engineered by the production operations group as part of their efforts at continuous improvement in the production process by reducing its cost and cycle time while improving the quality of results.

On the other hand, conceptually dynamic designs are characterized by inherently unstable technology that has not yet converged into an industry standard based on stable design architecture. Examples of such convergence include transitions to: IBM PC/Windows, VHS tape format, the internal combustion engine, etc. In each of these cases, prior to market acceptance of the standard, there was a turbulent period of dynamic design development in which alternative designs fought for customer and market acceptance to become a dominant standard. Ideas that generate these standards come from the whirlwind of dynamic conceptualization and are driven by a continuous stream of technological innovation so that stability in design of product, service, and production process cannot lie in a dormant condition for long—they must adapt to changing conditions of the new reality or become extinct in the competitive marketplace.

An organization's design strategy should use "controlled dissatisfaction" as a means to challenge itself to continuously improve today's design to meet the customer needs of tomorrow. This strategy can work well with either conceptually static or dynamic designs. In the case of dynamic designs, this strategy challenges the organization to actively search for the next innovative breakthrough in technology. In the case of a static design, this strategy forces the need for incremental improvements that generate market repositioning opportunities and refresh the image of the product among loyal customers to encourage their continued commercial relationship.[11]

Competitive rhythm: Both time to market and timing the opportunity

A major issue in design is the selection of the design concept that is commercially viable, not commercially vulnerable. This issue arises due to the extended time that it takes for "diffusion of innovation" from ideation or its technical conceptualization to acceptance by the mass market. Rogers hypothesized that about 2.5% of a market are pioneers who will try any new form of technology. Such people are eager to discover better ways to do things, but their purchases do not drive market penetration into the mass market. In a second category are the early-adopter segment (about 12.5% of the total market), which is between the pioneer segment and the early-matu-

---

[11] This description extends the thinking of the late Professor Stuart Pugh of the University of Strathclyde, whose concept of "total design" was foundational for DFSS. Of course, dynamic designs can be tested using Monte Carlo simulation to evaluate the "corner cases" of their performance envelope. This is most helpful when simulation is used in the framework of an experimental design (see chapter 8).

rity segment (35% of the market), which represents the mass market. Once a product has sales among consumers in the early-maturity segment, it can be considered a commercial success. Based on this trend, management might well decide that the key group for focusing design and marketing attention on is the early-adopter segment.[12]

The design environment places significant emotional pressure on a development team through the emphasis on "speed-to-market" and the need to meet the perceived market window of opportunity to commercialize the product. However, when observing how well new development projects perform relative to their initially projected shipment date, there is a one-word summary available—slippage!

Design integrates business strategy and technological innovation

Why is design so important to business success? Design is a process that requires the integration of the marketing, engineering, manufacturing, and purchasing disciplines to provide the best solution. While these disciplines combine their operational efforts to produce current shareholder value, only design focuses on development of future shareholder value—the ability to deliver future cash flows as a result of the innovative products and services that are developed investing current resources to find and fulfill anticipated market demands. Thus, DFSS focuses on future value-adding while Six Sigma problem-solving focuses on improving performance of the value proposition for current products and services by developing more effective, efficient, and economical processes. How can we specify this distinction more clearly?

The framework of DFSS

While the steps of the Six Sigma Innovation process (also called Design for Six Sigma [DFSS]) are named in a similar way to those of the Six Sigma Problem Solving process (DMADV for DFSS [Define, Measure, Analyze, Design, Verify] versus DMADV for problem solving [Define, Measure, Analyze, Improve, Control]), their objectives are very different. DFSS is a comprehensive set of strategies, tactics, and tools that enable an organization to characterize, quantify, and mitigate the risk in all phases of development of its products, processes, and services. It is implemented as a part of an overall Six Sigma strategy and relies on an infrastructure of Black Belts to support the design projects. DFSS does not replace an organization's design process—it is a customized application of the organization's product development process integrating Six Sigma methodologies into the basic engineering and business requirements of product design.

---

[12] The lifetime work of the late Everett M. Rogers focused on studies of the diffusion of innovation. Rogers developed the model of diffusion that identified different categories of product users according to their willingness to accept innovative products: pioneers, early adopters, early maturity, late maturity, and laggards (see chapter 2 for more information about the Rogers model).

The overall objective of the Six Sigma innovation process is to design products, processes, or services to consistently meet customer expectations. This objective requires knowledge of both the customer requirement and the organization's inherent capability to produce results (such as process output) that meet that requirement. In order to meet the customer's requirement (which, once known, becomes a fixed variable), the process must be designed so that the variation in its output is consistently better than that performance level. When the design goal for this process capability is specified to be six standard deviations beyond this requirement, then the product can be declared a "Six Sigma design"—once statistical data has been presented to validate that the product meets this design goal, then the product can be described as a "Six Sigma product." The process for creating such a product, process, or service follows the following five-step sequence that is typically called DMADV based on the first letters of the five steps as described for a new product development process of a hardware product (DFSS applications for software, process, and service are different). Once a product completes the design process, any subsequent problems, issues, or concerns about its performance or its business management are managed using Six Sigma problem solving using the DMAIC process.

The elements of DFSS

While there are a number of different processes that have been offered as "standards" for doing Design for Six Sigma[13], in this book we will discuss the "DMADV" definition of Design for Six Sigma, following the convention of the GOAL/QPC Memory Jogger™.[14] According to the use by GOAL/QPC, the DMADV steps stand for: Define the project; Measure customer requirements; Analyze the alternative concepts; Design the product and its delivery process; and Verify that the design performance has been achieved and is sustainable.

Much of the thinking that is incorporated into DFSS owes a debt of intellectual gratitude to the late Professor Stuart Pugh of the University of Strathclyde. Pugh differentiated between production engineering–led design and design engineering–led design. The emphasis on corrective action inherent in the DFSS DMAIC process is strongly related to the production engineering–led design process, which results in the developments of variants on the core conceptual design. Here, the emphasis is on the incremental change that is required to make small improvements that increase quality or enhance production capability, reduce cost, or improve performance at the margin of the core product. The emphasis on preventive action and clean-sheet product development is inherent in the R&D engineering-led design process that is

---

[13] For example, Chowdury suggests IDDOV (Identify the project; Define the opportunity; Develop concepts; Optimize the design; and Verify the design). However, according to the author's research, the DMADV form appears to have the broadest corporate acceptance, and all the other definitions of the DFSS process appear to fit its phases well.

[14] Dana Ginn and Barbara Streibel, *The Design for Six Sigma Memory Jogger: Tools and Methods for Robust Processes and Products* (Salem, NH: GOAL/QPC, 2004), pp. 8–9.

identified in DFSS as DMADV.

Pugh observed that new products can fail in three ways—each produces a different type of business risk:

1. Failure due to specification: vulnerability due to need interpretation—this type of failure creates market risk.

2. Failure due to design: vulnerability due to conceptual misalignment—this type of failure creates consumer risk.

3. Failure due to production: vulnerability due to implementation discipline—this type of failure creates producer risk.

DMADV incorporates many of the tools and methods that Pugh emphasized: Kano Model for feature analysis, enhanced QFD (Quality Function Deployment), Theory of Inventive Problem Solving (TRIZ), Pugh concept selection matrix, Taguchi experimental design, and statistical tolerance analysis. Even the controversy about how to engage the computer-aided design tools that was a core of Pugh's design concept is embedded into DMADV, where the use of CAD/CAM tools is focused in the last two steps of the process, following the conceptual design and elimination of design vulnerability to error at the level of the initial product-design specification.

Cultural artifacts of Six Sigma

While the name of this quality initiative has received much publicity in the past five years, Six Sigma, along with its associated martial arts "artifacts"—Black Belts, Green Belts—has become part of the language used within many global businesses, and it is important to understand what this language means. However, in many organizations and national cultures this language is a foreign language and is associated with negative connotations. Therefore, not all organizations that have implemented Six Sigma have accepted these artifacts as they have implemented the core elements of Six Sigma. For instance, Bombardier calls its Black Belts "Agents," while Toshiba refers to them as "Quality Experts," and other organizations call them "Improvement Specialists" and "Process Advisors." But whatever terms are used within a local culture, it is very important to understand the following individual roles found in successful Six Sigma implementations:

Executive Sponsor

The organization's business leaders serve as Executive Sponsors and provide strategic alignment for Six Sigma projects and ensure that the initiative is focused on improving critical business area problems, while the organization's routine continuous improvement efforts are addressed by its embedded, team-based quality processes. The senior management team sponsors Six Sigma, but it typically designates one individual to serve as the focal point for Six Sigma implementation activities and communication focal point. Typically the organization's CEO is the spokesman for Six Sigma, while the

Deployment Champion manages the logistics of implementation.

Deployment Champion

Deployment Champions serve as "implementation coordinators" in a Six Sigma initiative. This person is responsible for the logistics of implementation for the Six Sigma effort across the organization—that means scheduling training, ensuring management has selected Black Belt candidates and defined their training projects prior to training, tracking improvement project progress, and communicating about the Six Sigma initiative and its results through a wide variety of internal communication channels (this also includes intranet or internal web sites as well as more traditional means, such as success stories that are published in organizational newsletters). Many times the Deployment Champion will also serve as the contract administrator for consulting services related to Six Sigma.

Project Champion

The Project Champion is a process owner who provides "business focus" for Six Sigma projects. They have the primary responsibility for identifying, selecting, and defining projects for the Black Belts. In cooperation with the Master Black Belts, Project Champions perform the "Define" phase in both the DMADV (see Six Sigma Innovation section below) and DMAIC (see Six Sigma Problem Solving section below) processes. Project Champions also conduct regular project progress reviews at each of the milestones to ensure that the project meets its intended business objectives. When a process owner is also the Project Champion, then they are charged with implementation of the recommendations of the Six Sigma project.

Black Belt

Black Belts are the "analytical engines" of Six Sigma: Black Belts lead the improvement project teams and conduct the detailed analysis required in both the DMADV and DMAIC methodologies. Black Belts can also serve as instructors for their project team members and Green Belts, educating them in the tools and methods of Six Sigma. It is important to know that successful Six Sigma implementations occur more frequently when the Black Belt is not charged with responsibility for implementation of the project's recommendations—this role remains for a line manager or process owner. This is the reason that most organizations choose the Project Champion as one of these two individuals to ensure that they understand the analysis and build familiarity with the insights provided through the Six Sigma analysis.

Master Black Belt

Master Black Belts are the internal technical consultants to Black Belts and provide coaching in the use of tools as well as assistance in getting through "stuck points" in their project analyses. In addition, Master Black Belts can help coordinate "mega-projects" that breach functional and process areas, assist business leaders and process owners in definition of projects, as well as provide routine technical milestone reviews for Black Belt projects. Master Black Belts can also serve as the organization's measurement owner for implementation of their Six Sigma Customer Dashboard or Business Scorecard as well as training future generations of Black Belts.

Green Belt

Green Belts provide the "multiplier effect" in Six Sigma. Green Belts are not trained to the same depth as Black Belts, but are focused on learning some of the basic tools that permit an acceleration of projects. Two different strategies are taken to implement this approach. In one, Green Belts receive two weeks of training and are asked to conduct their own Six Sigma projects, while in the other they receive an even more abbreviated training in basic quality and statistics, process mapping, failure analysis, data collection, and report preparation. In this role they serve as a journeyman to a Black Belt, who mentors them in their development and provides them with on-the-job training to improve their proficiency and ability to operate independently facilitating the more routine continuous improvement projects.

The core elements of Six Sigma

There are four major processes in conducting a Six Sigma implementation: change management, project management, problem solving (referred to by its process steps as DMAIC), and innovation (typically referred to by its process steps as DMADV).

Change management

Implementing Six Sigma requires cultural change—and this change emphasizes accountability for results, measurement, and management by fact. When doing Six Sigma, business processes shift from "Theory O"—opinion-based decision-making—to fact-based, statistically supported analyses. As Six Sigma becomes part of an organization's process of management, there are some tools and processes that help management manage the transition to a Six Sigma company:

▶ *Six Sigma readiness assessment*—This management-level assessment is conducted to evaluate the readiness of an organization for implementing Six Sigma. It assesses the organization's history of deploying quality systems and the lessons learned from these experiences, the human resources system and the organizational culture, the Six Sigma–related skills and competence available inside the organization, and the ability of the organization to assimilate change.

▶ *Six Sigma deployment plan*—This plan is an outcome of the readiness assessment. It identifies the proposed deployment sequence with performance milestones, and it also describes the requirements for assigning Black Belts to training classes as a function of coverage of the key business areas. In addition, a Deployment Plan also addresses the education of senior business leaders, process owners, Master Black Belts, and Green Belts, plus generic training for the organization. Deployment Plans can also include the communication plan for the initiative (see below).

- *Six Sigma cultural alignment and program customization*—Once the readiness assessment has been conducted, the management team must evaluate how their own organizational culture aligns with the expectations for a successful implementation of Six Sigma (e.g., customer-focused, learning organization with knowledge base, value achievement and results orientation, respect for individuals, etc.). The culture of the organization and historical linkages to previous improvement initiatives should be integrated with the Six Sigma training program so that employees perceive that Six Sigma is a natural extension of previous improvement efforts and that the current effort amounts to "sharpening the blunt tools" deployed in the previous efforts.

- *Customer requirements analysis*—Research must be conducted by the organization to determine where it fails to understand customer requirements or satisfy performance levels desired by customers. Organizations can use Quality Function Deployment (QFD) as a methodology to describe customer requirements and to translate them into business actions. This analysis is needed to ensure that critical-to-satisfaction characteristics[15] are identified and that Six Sigma projects can be aligned to the customer's experience with the organization's products and services.

- *Enterprise map*—This value stream analysis of the business describes the high-level operation of a business and how core business processes are decomposed into work-level processes. Completion of an enterprise model makes "hidden factories" more evident, as unnecessary feedback loops and long decision-authorization pathways are two key indicators of work that customers would not pay for if they were aware of its existence. Together with the business measurement system, the enterprise map helps to identify projects for Black Belts by illustrating where performance gaps are first noticed in the work process flow.

- *Business measurement system*—Business performance indicators (Business Y's in the language of Six Sigma) that indicate excellence has been achieved from the point of view of the overall organization (sometimes called a Balanced Scorecard or Customer Dashboard) are identified and translated into measures of the work process (e.g., quality, cost, and cycle time). This system identifies problems.

- *Strategic benchmarking of key performance indicators*—Benchmarking key business processes to understand the performance of the Business Y's should be done using external validation of observed problems noted in the business measurement system. External comparisons help to validate current

---

[15] Critical-to-satisfaction (CTS) characteristics are those aspects of a product's performance that allow the customer to do their job better and provide them with satisfaction. These product characteristics are actually critical-to-quality (CTQ) in the performance of the customer's job. One early objective of a DFSS project is to identify customer CTQ factors and to define them. CTQ characteristics define what is being delivered to the customer, should be aligned to the customer need (through QFD and VOC), and possess four traits: (1) Identification of the function to be achieved or performed, (2) Quantitative measure of performance desired for the function, (3) Target value for achievement of this desired performance, and (4) Specification limits to define how much variation from this performance target customers will tolerate without complaint or degradation.

performance capabilities and establish where excellence really exists while also serving as a valuable source for discovering new improvement ideas.

▶ *Business governance self-assessment*—A self-assessment using the criteria of the Malcolm Baldrige National Quality Award or the European Quality Award is a good way to identify opportunities for improvement. Gaps in performance among the best practices outlined in these business models are a potential source for defining Six Sigma improvement projects.

▶ *Policy deployment planning system*—Policy deployment, also called *hoshin kanri*, provides a system for defining the strategic direction of an organization and then organizing the organization's resources to achieve this direction, one project at a time. This management system presents opportunities for defining Six Sigma projects that are fully aligned with the business change management strategy.

▶ *Reward and recognition system*—It is important that the work of Black Belts and Six Sigma project teams be recognized for its valuable contribution to improving organizational performance. Human resource specialists and staff compensation managers should develop an appropriate reward and recognition system that is aligned with the culture of the organization and its policies for payment of salaries and compensation.

▶ *Quality management system*—The organization's quality management system is part of its framework for business control and represents a natural means to deploy the improvements from Six Sigma projects and to ensure that they become part of the routine operations of the organization.

▶ *Six Sigma communication plan*—The communication plan describes the messages that must be presented to the organization along with the channels that can be used to best communicate these messages. This plan includes such support mechanisms as an intranet web site for news, project information, and training materials. Other aspects of this plan include networking sessions among Black Belts and Project Champions, as well as annual internal meetings where Black Belts can compete for the "project of the year" or other recognitions.

▶ *Employee environment*—Teamwork and employee involvement are essential aspects of Six Sigma projects. In order to reduce resistance to change and to encourage a more positive working environment, the participation of those employees who will be implementing the change is essential. All Six Sigma projects are team projects where the Black Belt facilitates the team using the statistical and management tools of Six Sigma to stimulate improvement ideas of the team. This collaborative work environment is essential for successful project work.

Six Sigma cultural changes require the satisfaction of the following definition of strategic work: Strategic work is effort that is valued by the organization and its customers while personally satisfying to the workers. If strategic work receives the support of management by provision of adequate resources and applies the skills of the organization's human resources effectively, then this work will make a difference and provide the climate for successful Six Sigma projects. In order to meet this definition, Six Sigma projects must be officially sponsored by management and receive support in terms of a written charter and regular management reviews (see the following Six Sigma project management section):

This human environment exists in both Six Sigma innovation projects and in Six Sigma problem-solving projects.

Project management

When organizations turn the steps of DMADV and DMAIC into tollgates or milestones in order to manage project reviews, they have taken a step toward Six Sigma project management. These milestones are aligned with the steps of the Six Sigma project (either DMADV or DMAIC) for technical reviews by the assigned Master Black Belt and business progress reviews by the Project Champion. In addition, senior management might initiate projects during the strategic planning cycle at the end of the Recognize step (which precedes Define) and approve experiments to be conducted that might interrupt production operations. Executive sponsors conduct a final review to ensure that benefits are obtained and that budgets reflect the financial improvements (this is called a "Realization Review").

Problem solving

The Six Sigma problem-solving process is normally called DMAIC, following the acronym formed by its five sequential steps: Define, Measure, Analyze, Improve, and Control. The specific activities of these steps are highlighted below:

▶ **Define**: Translate a current business problem into a Six Sigma improvement project. Charter a team to conduct the analysis and implement the recommendations. Establish a schedule for the project reviews and determine resources required to perform the analysis. Gain the active participation of process owners and other significant stakeholders in the project outcomes. Develop a high-level definition of the business problem from the perspective of its customer, determine what is critical-to-satisfaction for customers, and provide input to the team to align the project to the original business problem. The project charter is a Black Belt's formal "variation hunting license," and it formally demonstrates that this project has the power of the organization, and its management team, supporting it.

▶ **Measure**: Identify those characteristics of the product or process that are critical to the customer's requirement for quality performance and that contribute to customer satisfaction with their use of the product or process output. These are the response variables that will be improved during the Six Sigma DMAIC phases ("Y's" or output variables). Clarify how the process operates by developing a map of the activities and determine how the process can fail using a Failure Mode and Effects Analysis (FMEA). Evaluate which process factors are controllable—and therefore desirable—aspects of a final solution. Define a performance standard for the delivery process of products or services to the customer and measure the current performance against this standard as well as available external benchmarks. Determine the cost of poor quality and establish a target for improvement. Validate the inherent capability of the measurement system to detect significant changes in the process performance. At the completion of the Measure phase of the analysis, a Black Belt should know the nature of the statistical problem (needing to shift the mean for the "Y," reduce its variation, or do both) and have a performance baseline that defines how the current process operates in terms of its design capability (Cp), benchmark against comparative process performance, achieved average performance, as well as variation in performance over time (Cpk and trend analysis).

▶ **Analyze:** Evaluate the current operation of the process to determine the potential sources of variation for critical performance parameters ("X's" or independent variables). Link the sources of variation to the control points in the process to provide physical "levers for improvement" once the analysis indicates how the process must be set for optimal performance results. Characterization consists of sequential "data mining" with statistical tools to identify factors that impact variation. Begin with hypothesis testing to evaluate differences between factors, move on to analysis of variance to determine if samples come from the same population, and apply regression analysis to determine how much of the total variation is explained by the factors that have been identified. The Analyze phase of a Six Sigma project identifies the "vital few" or significant X's from the collection of all X's or the "trivial many" performance parameters based on their statistical and practical significance. This phase ends when business leaders agree on improvement objectives based on findings from this process characterization.

▶ **Improve:** Screen potential sources of variation to determine their effects on shifting the process mean and reducing the total process variation. Discover inter-relationships and dependencies between the process variables (solve the equation "Y = f (X)") and determine which factors ("X's") drive process performance ("Y"). For the critical parameters of the process, determine the best operating characteristics (set points and tolerances) and the range over which optimal process performance can be maintained. The principal tools of the Improve phase include: design of experiments, simulation analysis, and the tools of lean management for setup-time reduction, cycle-time reduction, and value enhancement. The Improve phase applies experimentation or conducts pilot demonstrations of the performance capability of the recommended solution to discover optimal process settings for the critical-to-quality parameters.

▶ **Control:** Based on the recommended process changes, validate the measurement system to ensure that it is capable of detecting and accurately reporting significant changes in process performance for the critical parameters.

Calculate the process capability achieved by making the recommended changes. Develop a control plan to maintain the improved level of process performance. Implement the process controls on the revised process and train the operators to ensure their personal capability to interpret instructions and execute the process improvements. The Control phase "locks in the gains" from the process-improvement project by transitioning the improvement to the daily management system and ensuring that changes are managed using appropriate business controls.

Following the Control phase, there is an additional project activity that might involve the Black Belt. This activity is conducting the "Realization Review" following a protracted implementation phase where the process owner makes the recommended changes. The objective of this review is to conduct an assessment of benefit capture by the process owner—Were all the projected benefits of the project realized? Did these benefits transfer to the bottom line? In many organizations, this is a review that is conducted by the finance organization or by internal audit.

What is the DMADV innovation process?

When an organization begins working problems using the Six Sigma DMAIC process, it has the ability to achieve a local maximum performance (the inherent process capability [Cp] that has been designed into the process). However, if this performance is not sufficient to meet the organization's competitive requirement, then it must begin the DMADV process to design the process to be more competitive—designing to a goal of flawless execution against both the market (targeted customer) requirement and the organization's desired competitive position. In this case, the organization designs its business processes to become a "predictable factory"—one that is able to flawlessly perform at a higher level of process capability. This design process is called Design for Six Sigma and is represented by the process steps DMADV.

What is the Six Sigma innovation process called DMADV, and how does it work? While the steps of the Six Sigma innovation process (also called Design for Six Sigma [DFSS]) are named in a way similar to those of the Six Sigma problem-solving process, their set of objectives are very different. DFSS is a comprehensive set of strategies, tactics, and tools that enable an organization to characterize, quantify, and mitigate the risk in all phases of development of its products, processes, and services. It is implemented as a part of an overall Six Sigma strategy and relies on an infrastructure of Black Belts to support the design projects. DFSS supplements an organization's

---

[16] While the purpose of this book is to focus on DMADV applications to design products for Six Sigma levels of performance, DMADV can be applied to DFSS business processes and services as well. The front-end business analysis of all three applications does not differ, and many of the tools that are described in this book are transferable to these applications of DMADV. Indeed, the application of these concepts to business processes was the subject of a prior book by the author: *Business Systems Engineering* (New York: John Wiley & Sons, 1994).

design process—it is typically developed as a customized application of the organization's product development process, integrating Six Sigma methodologies into the engineering and business requirements of product design.[16]

One way to stay ahead of your market competitors is to Design for Six Sigma using the DMADV innovation process. The DMADV objective is to ensure that products are designed to meet current customer needs and requirements and also anticipate the changing needs and requirements of the future market.

The overall objective of the Six Sigma innovation process is to design products, processes, or services to consistently meet customer expectations. This objective requires knowledge of both the customer requirement and the organization's inherent capability to produce results (such as process output) that meet that requirement. In order to meet the customer's requirement (which, once known, becomes a fixed variable), the process must be designed so that the variation in its output is consistently better than this required performance level. If the design goal for this process capability is specified to produce failures with a probability of less than six standard deviations at this requirement, then the product can be declared to have a "Six Sigma design"—and once statistical data has been presented to validate that the product meets this design goal, then the product can be described as a "Six Sigma product." The process for creating such a product, process, or service is the following five-step sequence called DMADV, which is described for a new product development process of a hardware product (DFSS applications for software, process, and service are different).

How does the Define step of DMADV work?

▶ **Define.** The Define step engages the program-planning process to establish the product concept. The design management team begins a project by developing a business case for capitalizing on an opportunity that is presented from its technology portfolio or its product line plan. They must determine, through customer and market research, how this opportunity can address the commercial needs of the marketplace. The initial assessment of the

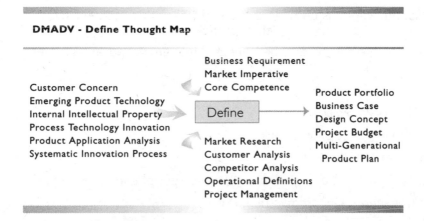

DMADV - Define Thought Map

	Business Requirement	
	Market Imperative	
Customer Concern	Core Competence	Product Portfolio
Emerging Product Technology		Business Case
Internal Intellectual Property	Define	Design Concept
Process Technology Innovation		Project Budget
Product Application Analysis	Market Research	Multi-Generational
Systematic Innovation Process	Customer Analysis	Product Plan
	Competitor Analysis	
	Operational Definitions	
	Project Management	

product concept and its commercial viability is presented in the business case along with the projected budget and a multi-generational product line plan that identifies how features and concepts will be sequenced for introduction into the market (as new product variants). Upon completion of the initial conceptual design review, the product budget and project plan are approved, and a development team is assigned to staff the project.

▶ *Define step objectives*: Specify a business case and design concept for development of a new product, define how the product structure and its subsequent releases of variant designs will change across your multi-generational product development plan, and then establish a target competitive position for the new product in your product portfolio.

▶ *Define step definition*: The Define Step evaluates market feasibility and risk that is associated with alternative concepts for new product development and establishes the scope and the charter for selected projects.

▶ *Define step fundamental questions*:

? What customer experience with our products and services needs to be improved from their perspective?

? Where is the market going—what developments are happening that can threaten our current position?

? What competitive moves are taking place that can shift the market-share balance?

? What business priorities of my customers can our products and services fill better than our competitors—Where is our advantage and how can we extend it?

? What "unspoken" needs of my customers have not been recognized yet and will yield competitive advantage if we deliver them first in the market?

? How can our technology portfolio of intellectual property and licensable emerging technology be applied in an innovative way to our products and services?

? Are there technology areas that we require in the future where we have no access?

? What innovation is possible that could make our customers' lives easier, smarter, quicker, and less defect-prone?

? Can our core competence be leveraged into greater advantage over competitors?

▶ *Define step deliverables*:

- Technology acquisition plan.

- Product portfolio.

- Product business case (including design concept and product budget).

- Multi-generational product plan (MGP).

▶ *Measure*. The Measure step evaluates the market requirements for both the product concept and the potential market demand for the product. During this step, research is planned to determine customer needs and competitive performance, as well as to identify those features and options that are differentiators of the product. The team seeks to identify those design elements that are critical-to-quality for the product in that they deliver satisfaction for identified customer requirements. This step in the design process is documented using Quality Function Deployment (QFD) matrices as well as design scorecards, which are used to record the progress of the project. Design control is managed through tollgate reviews of checklists for critical activities to ensure that adequate progress is made toward the planned product launch date.

▶ *Measure step objectives*: Translate a design concept into a product definition that is aligned with customer needs in the targeted market segments for the product.

▶ *Measure step definition*: The Measure step identifies expectations of targeted customers through in-depth customer analysis and determines which functions are aligned to these customer needs while providing the most product competitiveness when compared to alternative designs.

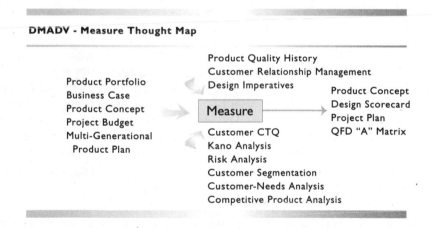

DMADV - Measure Thought Map

Product Portfolio
Business Case
Product Concept
Project Budget
Multi-Generational
Product Plan

Product Quality History
Customer Relationship Management
Design Imperatives

Measure

Customer CTQ
Kano Analysis
Risk Analysis
Customer Segmentation
Customer-Needs Analysis
Competitive Product Analysis

Product Concept
Design Scorecard
Project Plan
QFD "A" Matrix

▶ *Measure step fundamental questions*:

? What are the specific product (or service) features that are required by specific customer segments?

? How do requirements, needs, and expectations differ according to the different types of customer (market segment, application persona, decision level, etc.)?

? Which functions have the highest priority as customer requirements?

? Which functions provide competitive advantage according to a Kano analysis?

? How do the top-priority customer needs translate into CTQ product features?

? Where are there opportunities to develop performance advantages over competing product features?

? How do high-level functions relate to the CTQ priorities of customers?

? What types of risk are anticipated in product development, and where are these risks most intensive?

? Which customer segments define the "target audience" for the product or service, and how do these segments relate to the historical market acceptance for these types of products?

▶ *Measure step deliverables*:

- Product conceptual definition.

- Design scorecard for Define step.

- Research and development (R&D) project management plan.

- Quality function deployment (QFD) "A" level matrix.

How does the Analyze step of DMADV work?

▶ *Analyze*. The Analyze step completes characterization of the product and includes the following key activities: functional analysis of the features and their capability to address the identified customer requirements, benchmarking of performance for these features, conceptual design of the product, process maps of both the production and service delivery processes, and a design requirement specification. The milestone or tollgate review that completes the Analyze step evaluates the design scorecard along with a comparison of the design requirements against the business plan to authorize the detailed product design.

▶ *Analyze step objectives*: Translate a product concept into a high-level product design and characterize technological and business risks associated with full-scale product development.

▶ *Analyze step definition*: The Analyze step completes the high-level design of the product, demonstrates market suitability of the design concept, determines the degree of technological risk associated with further development, and develops initial plans for marketing the product.

DMADV - Analyze Thought Map

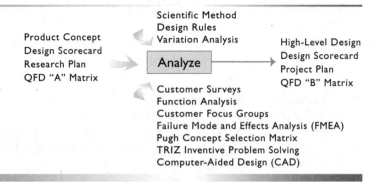

Product Concept
Design Scorecard
Research Plan
QFD "A" Matrix

Scientific Method
Design Rules
Variation Analysis

Analyze

High-Level Design
Design Scorecard
Project Plan
QFD "B" Matrix

Customer Surveys
Function Analysis
Customer Focus Groups
Failure Mode and Effects Analysis (FMEA)
Pugh Concept Selection Matrix
TRIZ Inventive Problem Solving
Computer-Aided Design (CAD)

▶ *Analyze step fundamental questions*:

❓ What functions are necessary to support the design requirements?

❓ How do these functions translate into acceptable product features for targeted customers?

❓ What can go wrong (system-level) with the operation of these product functions?

❓ What are innovative ways to implement these features into a high-level design?

❓ How to choose the best design from among alternatives?

❓ How to reduce the time to market of the product through the use of CAD tools?

▶ *Analyze step deliverables*:

- Product high-level design.

- Design scorecard for the Analyze step.

- Market development plan and project management plan.

- QFD "B" matrix.

How does the Design step of DMADV work?

▶ **Design.** In the Design step, detailed process maps are created for the production facility layout, along with the engineering detail of the product specification. All the critical process parameters are identified, failure analysis is conducted to determine the potential risks, capability analysis is conducted to determine design robustness, and statistical analysis is used to establish tolerances for critical parameters. Value analysis is conducted to ensure that the product value proposition is optimized. Detailed designs are documented in functional performance specifications that are demonstrated as ready for release to manufacturing. In this step, reliability testing of prototypes is conducted to demonstrate growth in the stability of the design as well as its readiness for the commercial marketplace.

▶ *Design step objectives*: Translates a high-level design into an engineering detailed design that is ready for hard tooling and preparation for full-scale production.

▶ *Design step definition*: The Design step of DMADV develops the detailed product design and control plans that ensure robust performance in the eventual production environment and also prepares the project for management's final design decision to implement the product in full-scale operation.

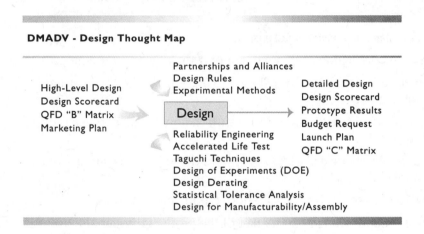

DMADV - Design Thought Map

High-Level Design
Design Scorecard
QFD "B" Matrix
Marketing Plan

Partnerships and Alliances
Design Rules
Experimental Methods

Design

Reliability Engineering
Accelerated Life Test
Taguchi Techniques
Design of Experiments (DOE)
Design Derating
Statistical Tolerance Analysis
Design for Manufacturability/Assembly

Detailed Design
Design Scorecard
Prototype Results
Budget Request
Launch Plan
QFD "C" Matrix

▶ *Design step fundamental questions*:

? How should the parts be designed to deliver the required functionality?

? How can the parts be designed for high reliability?

? What is the expected useful market life of this product?

? What is the best operating envelope for the critical design parameters?

? What tolerance limits will produce the most reliable product design?

? How can the parts fit together in a way that reduces production cycle time?

? Is the product ready to be considered for full-scale production?

? What is the plan for launching the product into the marketplace?

? What is the plan for tooling the product for full-scale production?

? Are the production facilities ready to accept the product?

? Have the production procedures been written so that all jobs are specified?

? Is the design robust to material, process, customer, and environmental variation?

▶ **Design step deliverables:**

- Detailed engineering design.

- Design scorecard for Design step.

- Prototype test results ("beta" testing with customers).

- New product launch plan from marketing.

- Budget request for full-scale implementation and product launch.

- QFD "C" matrix.

How does the Verify step of DMADV work?

▶ **Verify.** The Verify step engages the customer in product testing through pilot tests that demonstrate the marketability of the product as well as its production readiness. Pilot tests are used to verify the details for transition to full production, as well as the implementation of the control procedures for routine production after ramp-up to the full forecast volume is achieved. There are two components of testing that are combined in this step: verification and validation. Verification testing refers to testing conducted to ensure that appropriate progress is being made in the development process. Validation testing refers to testing that is done at the end of the product development cycle to ensure that the product meets all of its functional specifications. A third type of testing might be done, called customer acceptance testing, which evaluates the acceptability of the product as delivered in the production-ready prototype and as documented in the final product development specification to satisfy the user's needs. The product control plan that ensures consistent production once the product is released for manufacturing is embedded into the assembly procedures, test procedures, and acceptance criteria. The product completes development and transitions to full production upon completion of the Verify step as marked by an official commercial product launch.

▶ **Verify step objectives:** Translates a detailed engineering design into a product that is offered to customers in the market.

▶ **Verify step definition:** The Verify step of DMADV validates design plans and provides formal documentation for full-scale production in order to transition the product design from a development project to an operational owner for daily management oversight.

DMADV - Verify Thought Map

Detailed Design
Design Scorecard
Prototype Results
Budget Request
Launch Plan
QFD "C" Matrix

Quality Management System
Work Content Analysis
Principles of Standardization

Verify

FMEA - Process
Mistake Proofing
Work Standardization
Design for Service
Design for Logistics
Capability Analysis
Measurement Systems Analysis
Preventive Maintenance
Statistical Process Control (SPC)
Computer-Automated Test Equipment

Full-Scale Design
Design Scorecard
Production Plan
Procurement Plan
Distribution Plan
Service Plan
QFD "D" Matrix

▶ **Verify step fundamental questions:**

? What are the opportunities for defects in the production process?

? What countermeasures are possible to mistake-proof the production process?

? What detailed procedures must be followed to produce the product?

? What is the strategy to service the product?

? What is the plan for distributing the product and ensuring market availability?

? How capable is the production process (what is its full-scale entitlement)?

? Is the measurement system sensitive enough to detect significant changes in the critical process-control parameters?

? Are the maintenance requirements for production equipment established, and has a cycle been prepared to anticipate problems and prevent failures?

? Has automated test equipment been implemented to decrease the non-value-added time required for in-process testing?

? Is statistical process control implemented in conjunction with engineering process control to ensure that the production process consistently delivers the quality level that it was designed to produce?

? Is there a plan to review all early product returns to ensure that problems are fixed as soon as they are detected?

? Are there any "showstoppers" that would delay the product's release to the market?

▶ **Verify step deliverables:**

- Full-scale product design.

- Design scorecard for Verify step.
- Production plan.
- Procurement plan.
- Distribution plan.
- Service plan.
- QFD "D" matrix.

The imperative to lead change management

Effective change doesn't just happen to an organization; it must be led. Otherwise, change will just happen to the organization, and variation in the business factors that drive the organization will be the determinants of its success—serendipity will direct the outcomes of the business. But because Six Sigma manages variation, it can provide a solution to long-term change management. However, even Six Sigma implementation must be managed effectively as a change initiative! A clear distinction exists between the two Six Sigma project methods: DMAIC and DMADV. This leads to the questions: Should management choose one or the other, or both to pursue? What is the right order for doing Six Sigma? What should be the driving factors in making this decision?

To address these questions, consider the following comparison between DMAIC and DMADV, which clearly shows that these two approaches provide different types of business value:[17]

Characteristic	DMAIC Process	DMADV Process
Profit Delivery Method	Cost Reduction	Revenue Enhancement
Primary Focus	Internal Processes	External Market
Dominant Metric	Defects per Million Opportunities	Customer Satisfaction
Competitive Emphasis	Standardization	Customization

DMAIC is focused on defect elimination and cost reduction; DMAIC is focused on product creation and revenue building. Both approaches can add value to an organization. But what is the strategy that business leaders should pursue to implement an effective approach to Six Sigma? Research by Roland T. Rust, Christine Moorman, and Peter R. Dickson suggests a sound rationale for addressing this decision.[18] Rust, Moorman, and Dickson raised doubts about the efficacy of a concentrated, simultaneous, dual focus by management on both cost reduction and revenue expansion. Their research showed

---

[17] The distinction between these types of value is not clearly recognized in all communities. For instance, the Software Engineering Institute's (SEI) Capability Maturity Model (CMM) for product development defines business value that focuses on "savings as a ratio of the cost to produce these savings" and totally ignores the positive revenue component of business value. See further the SEI Report: "Benefits of CMM-Based Software Process Improvement—Initial Results," Technical Report CMU/SEI-94-TR-013 (Pittsburgh: The Carnegie Mellon University, 1994).

[18] Roland T. Rust, Christine Moorman, and Peter R. Dickson, "Getting Return on Quality: Revenue Expansion, Cost Reduction, or Both?" Journal of Marketing, vol. 66 (October 2002), pp. 7–24.

that not both of these emphases had equal effects on the value produced by the firm, although they didn't clearly specify the time frame over which value could be produced. However, their research clearly showed that an emphasis on revenue expansion resulted in better financial outcomes for the organization over the long term. This observation is reinforced by research by Michael T. Johnson and Lars Nilsson[19], where they demonstrated that there is a much stronger effect of product customization (the DMADV approach) over reliability development (the DMAIC approach) for both products and services as defined by the measure of customer perception. Together these findings align with the broadly accepted recommendation for implementing Six Sigma as a two-phase effort[20]—implementing a DMAIC program first, followed by a DMADV initiative. In this way, the cost savings generated by the DMAIC program can fund the revenue expansion efforts of DMADV. Additionally, it should be observed that today's DMADV/DFSS projects gone wrong or poorly done will become tomorrow's DMAIC projects for corrective action and cost control. Thus, having a solid DMAIC program foundation is essential to the long-term success of DFSS!

How to use this book

This chapter has introduced the following eight chapters, which focus on key decisions and analysis methods used in DFSS. Emphasis in these chapters is not on technical methodologies but on managerial applications and integration of these methods into a system of decision making and project management that leads to successful products. A summary of the content of the rest of this book follows:

▶ *Chapter 2: Managing Design Programs.* This chapter establishes a more detailed business context for Design for Six Sigma and builds on information presented in the foreword and this first chapter. The chapter introduces product-line management (PLM) for managing the organization's technology portfolio, analyzing and managing business, conducting market and customer research, and Quality Function Deployment[21] for organizing design information that is generated during the product-creation process.

▶ *Chapter 3: Managing a Product Design Project.* This chapter applies DFSS project management principles to DFSS projects with particular emphasis on lean methodologies and on multi-generational and multi-project planning, ap-

---

[19] Michael T. Johnson and Lars Nilsson, "The Importance of Reliability and Customization," *Quality Management Journal*, vol. 10, no. 1 (January 2003), pp. 8–19.

[20] For example, see: Gregory H. Watson, *Six Sigma for Business Leaders* (Salem, NH: GOAL/QPC, 2004).

[21] The terms used to define the QFD methodology have interesting meanings—*function* refers to the features or functions of a product or service—*quality* describes the degree or level of implementation—*deployment* signifies that there is a combination of translation from one language to another (e.g., from the voice of the customer to the voice of the process, from system-level specifications to part-level specifications, from the voice of the marketing discipline to the voice of the engineer, to the voice of the production operator, etc.) and team-based, integrative decision making that reaches consensus on the features delivered as well as their quality levels.

plying critical chain management ideas developed by Eli Goldratt to project management, project measurement, and product pricing.

▶ *Chapter 4: Measuring Program and Project Progress*. This chapter describes some issues in the application of accounting methods and defines a design scorecard and tollgates for measuring DFSS project progress.

▶ *Chapter 5: Engineering Value into Designs*. This chapter describes how value analysis methods are used to engineer low-cost design alternatives and how the Pugh Concept Selection matrix can be used to choose between competing design concepts.

▶ *Chapter 6: Planning Innovative Design Developments*. This chapter introduces the set of tools used while applying the theory of inventive problem solving (TRIZ) to define innovative concepts and resolve design feature conflicts to deliver good commercial value for customers. Also, an introduction to Axiomatic Design is presented in the context of TRIZ.

▶ *Chapter 7: Building Reliability into Products*. This chapter focuses on the use of DFX tools—especially Design for Reliability (DFR) and how product testing is used to develop robust products with predictable failure modes and performance.

▶ *Chapter 8: Experimenting to Create Robust Performance*. This chapter describes how experimental design and Taguchi analysis are applied for defining the critical operating characteristics, design parameters, and their tolerances.

▶ *Chapter 9: Controlling Product Realization*. This chapter describes the transition of a product from the design environment to the production environment as the design becomes realized as a commercial product. Emphasis is on the integrated use of control plans, statistical process control, and mistake proofing to establish a disciplined production process.

▶ *Appendix A: Evaluating Your Readiness for* DFSS. This appendix provides a complete self-assessment process to determine how well your organization can adapt to a DFSS business-improvement initiative.

▶ *Appendix B: Design for Six Sigma Body of Knowledge*. This appendix is the inaugural attempt at codifying a formal body of knowledge for DFSS. The author hopes that a body like the American Society for Quality will take up the challenge and extend this work to completion.

▶ *Appendix C: Data Analysis and Experimentation*. This appendix provides a technical view of experimental design that has been prepared to demystify the subject for business leaders.

▶ *Appendix D: References*. This appendix is a comprehensive reference list for those who seek deeper study of topics related to quality in design and new product development.

Each of these book sections is relatively stand-alone, and if the reader has a particular interest in a specific tool or methodology, they are invited to jump into the midst of the text and pursue their interest!

Chapter 2
Managing Design Programs

"All models are wrong, but some models are useful."

~ George E. P. Box

The strength of DFSS is not in its stand-alone performance, but it comes from integration of methods and concepts that have been independently developed into a system of thinking and working that result in product designs that serve customers better while generating attractive profit. DFSS is not strategic planning, but it builds on the "recognize" component in strategic planning where business improvement needs are unveiled. DFSS is not program management, but it provides a philosophy and methodology for more effectively coordinating multiple project programs. DFSS is not project management, but it supports project managers with an analytical process that facilitates a "right-the-first-time" approach to product creation. Finally, DFSS is much more than the DMADV process, but DMADV is a way to summarize how it fits into the overall business system. While DFSS is somewhat amorphous in this format, it becomes specific within the context of a particular business system. Thus, there is no one-size-fits-all definition of DFSS; rather, DFSS concepts and methods must be adapted and customized to support a particular business purpose, cultural style, and design technology in order for it to have real substance. DFSS supports management of design programs in the product-creation process.

The purpose of Design for Six Sigma (DFSS) is to help develop innovative products that meet customer needs while providing an attractive return to your company! In pursuing this objective, DFSS grows business by obtaining new customers, extending sales into the current customer base, and attracting lost customers who have deserted to the competition. DFSS focuses on creating new or better products that meet market needs and anticipate emerging market needs. DFSS develops innovative approaches for applying new technology. DFSS begins with the identification of concepts for the application of technology to customer problems that should be included in a portfolio of new projects for the product-creation process through participation in the recognize phase of strategic planning, which generates business improvement projects for the total Six Sigma effort. DFSS has three other components that are related:

▶ Program management of the portfolio of DFSS projects, which manages issues such as identifying and defining product concepts, selecting new product development projects, defining product features, and assigning staff with appropriate skills and competence to the new product development programs.

▶ Project management issues, such as managing the new product development life cycle through quality reviews conducted at each of the design milestones.

▶ Analytical tools of the DMADV process supplement the concurrent engineering process of the organization.

DFSS integrates project management with application of the DMADV tools across the development of the product life cycle to define the project's daily management system or the standard design process for the product-creation process. This chapter will describe how the Recognize and program management elements of DFSS operate, while the next chapter will focus on project management, and the rest of this book will describe elements of the DMADV toolkit. This chapter establishes a more detailed business context for Design for Six Sigma and builds on information presented in the foreword and chapter 1. The chapter introduces product-line management (PLM) for managing the organization's technology portfolio, analyzing and managing business, conducting market and customer research, and Quality Function Deployment (QFD) for organizing design information that is generated during the product-creation process.

Competitive innovation: Stimulus of Design for Six Sigma

Competitive innovation is the ability of an organization to innovate faster, better, and smarter than its competitors. Harvard professor Shoshana Zuboff observed that "the status quo eats up innovation." This observation is particularly profound as it describes the energy drain that comes by sustaining the status quo, which takes away energy and resources from creating the opportunities that invent the future through new product developments. Managing the distinction between sustaining technology and disruptive technology is indeed a lingering challenge for most product-design groups.[1]

---

[1] Shoshana Zuboff, "Groupware at Work: It's Here, But What Is It? *CSCW Conference Proceedings*, ACM Conference on Computer Supported Cooperative Work, November 1996, Cambridge, MA, and *In the Age of the Smart Machine* (New York: Basic Books, 1988).

Harvard Professor Clayton M. Christensen noted that there are two different types of innovation—sustaining and disruptive innovation—that are differentiated based on the circumstances of the innovation. Sustaining innovation might be either continuous improvement or a technology breakthrough that serves a current customer base and brings them better-performing functions than were available previously. However, a disruptive innovation disrupts an industry by redefining the S-curve in such a way that it offers a different appeal to a market and thereby changes the market environment and decision criteria by which customers make choices. A great example of this was the personal copier that Canon introduced in the mid-1980s—it was disruptive to the central copying equipment sold by Xerox as it distributed copying throughout an organization and sold "slower" copying by offering the convenience of not walking to the central location. Thus, for a few copies, the total time invested was actually less. "In *sustaining circumstances*—when the race entails making better products that can be sold for more money to attractive customers—we found that incumbents almost always prevail. In *disruptive circumstances*—where the challenge is to commercialize a simpler, more convenient product that sells for less money and appeals to a new or unattractive customer set—the entrants are likely to beat the incumbents."[2]

However, organizations that are delivering sustaining technology fall victim to their status quo and often forgo the opportunity to develop a disruptive technology that can threaten their bottom-line performance. In the case of Xerox, they allowed four years of "free market reign" to Canon before they realized that attacking their soft market in this way was actually destroying their main market also! This leads to the dilemma that Christensen describes: catering to the needs of your best customers can lead to an ultimate failure in the market. Science fiction author of 2001: A *Space Odyssey*, Arthur C. Clarke's third law states that "Any sufficiently advanced technology is indistinguishable from magic." Continuing innovation delivers a continuous stream of new products and relies on progressive revelation of technology applications that serve customer needs—this is the traditional approach to innovation that leads to the dilemma. So how does an organization integrate both types of innovation in order to "keep the magic going?" Magic must be "de-magicized" in order to make it useful in the real world—it must be transitioned into the language of the customer and translated into an approach to help them get their job done better so they understand how it operates. To the magician, magic is a process, BUT to the uninitiated, it is still magic![3]

So how does innovation relate to managing new product design?

---

[2] Clayton M. Christensen and Michael E. Raynor, *The Innovator's Solution* (Boston: Harvard Business School Press, 2003), p. 32.

[3] This book will build upon the excellent work of Christensen and focus on how to develop exceptional products once the proper focus has been met. Rather than repeating any of what Christensen says in his book, I most strongly recommend a detailed study of his work as a pragmatic preliminary to designing a DFSS system that is appropriate for your business, as his work sets the strategic context for DFSS.

Economist Joseph A. Schumpeter described innovation as a process of creative destruction: innovation requires the planned abandonment of established, familiar, and customary or comfortable ways of working...whether in products or in services, competencies or human relationships, or the whole organization itself.[4] Innovation finds applications of technology in the things that customers need to get done and finds a solution to what the customer needs to accomplish. Marketing defines transitions for promotion of products to unique customer needs and positions the product as the best tool to accomplish the customer's job. Sustaining innovation continues on the development trajectory of the previous products through either variant products or by breakthroughs in the underlying technologies. Disruptive innovation changes the fundamental structure of the market by attacking at vulnerable points, or in markets that don't currently consume the sustaining innovation products. Truly disruptive innovation will "creatively destroy" mature markets.

As described in the first chapter, the objective of a commercial venture is to achieve consistently profitable growth (which will be further described in chapter 4). Achieving this objective requires an astute understanding of how work is accomplished and learning from the past about what lessons should be preserved to build a new future that the workers will find compelling. This is a job of leadership. It has been said that historians look at the past—managers look to the future—but leaders destroy the past to create a new future! Innovation creates a compelling future that engages customers, employees, and shareholders alike!

Lessons learned from the past include important relationships that can generate increased competitiveness for an organization. There are three relationships the author has observed that are fundamental to the sustainable competitiveness of an organization and that are summarized in the figure on the next page:

▶ Competitiveness is achieved by improving product technology, while at the same time improving the process technology that delivers the product to the market.

▶ When time to market is reduced, scheduling risk is reduced in a product because the impact of schedule uncertainty operates on a shorter period of time.

▶ As time to market increases, product development cost increases. This might not be a bad thing, as a 1980s generation McKinsey study indicated that the cost of new product development has a relatively minor impact on lifetime profitability as compared to getting the product launched properly into its window of market opportunity.

---

[4] See Joseph A. Schumpeter, *Capitalism, Socialism, and Democracy* (New York: Harper Torch Books, 1951; republished 1962, 1984); *The Theory of Economic Development* (New York: Transaction Publishers, 1983); *History of Economic Analysis* (London: Oxford University Press, 1996), and *Essays on Entrepreneurs, Innovations, Business Cycles, and Capitalism* (New York: Transaction Publishers, 1989).

Important Relationships

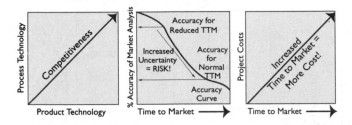

Shorter development time leads to:
- Increased product life-cycle revenue and market penetration
- Success in time-sensitive markets due to improved predictability of release
- More successful products at lower engineering costs
- Less development waste and better resource use

Thus, innovations must be focused on both the delivered product and the process by which it is delivered. Reliable innovation—innovation that can be counted on to succeed in the market—is delivered by quality processes. Stanford University professor Robert A. Burgelman describes the emphasis that needs to be placed in the development of new product thinking as a combination of technology push and market pull—or, in his words, "need linked" and "technology linked"—but he says that even when this "double linking" occurs, there is no guarantee of success, and he encourages the building of a stronger interface between the business people and the technology people in an organization.[5]

In *The Innovator's Solution*, Christensen and Raynor define the purpose of a product as to get the customer's job done by targeting circumstances in which certain customers require the product and then determining how to add value to these circumstances.[6]

Burgelman suggests the use of a new venture organization, as does Christensen, as a means to focus the organization on a unique development opportunity (disruptive technology) and to avoid the "status quo," which could devour the innovation. When products are aligned in both the dimensions of marketing and technology, then they are a "star"—however, they might be a sustaining technology star that is vulnerable to a disrupting technology!

How is such an alignment obtained? The answer is through the quality methods used in DFSS! Technology is an enabler of sustained success, but it is innovation that transitions technology into successful products when it focuses on delivering "the job of the customer." Quality is delivered in the long term through keeping all product promises that are made about the job it will do, including performance, reliability, delivery, usability, and flexibility. This model for quality delivery was described in the foreword to this book; quality

[5] Robert A. Burgelman and Leonard R. Sales, *Inside Corporate Innovation* (New York: Free Press, 1986), p. 46.

[6] Christensen and Raynor, *The Innovator's Solution*, p. 75.

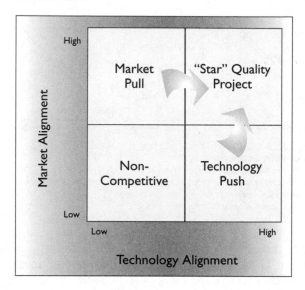

is an imperative of business—a "must have" that cannot be compromised without sacrificing current levels of customer satisfaction. This means that the expectation of customers for future products or services will be moving in the direction of "flawless execution," so Six Sigma levels of performance will become requirements of future product performance for those functions that help customers get their job done. However, innovation is also an imperative of business in order to ensure delivery of both long-term strength and profitable growth—both to be able to sustain the current cash flow and to provide insurance against disruptions that are unanticipated—and thereby safeguard future cash flows. Thus, quality and innovation are inseparable parameters of continuing business success!

How does a quality program begin to make a business impact? The first thing that it needs to accomplish is to analyze the customers in order to discover what they need to have next.

Analyzing customers and the diffusion of innovation

Christensen's third book in his innovation series, *Seeing What's Next*, provides a fresh way of looking at customers that offers insights into their needs. He describes three types of consumers as differentiated by how product design addresses their buying rationale:

▶ **Overshot customers**: customers whose needs have been already served by the product features and will no longer pay a premium for further developments (the product design is too good for the customers' needs).

▶ **Non-consumers**: people who lack the ability, wealth, or access to conveniently do a job for themselves and cannot afford the solution offered, so they settle for a less-than-adequate capability.

▶ *Undershot customers*: customers who purchase a product but are frustrated by its lack of capability and desire to purchase further improvements (the product design is not good enough for the customers' needs).[7]

Another way of viewing the way that technology is mainstreamed into society is by diffusion research, and the key study in this field is by Everett M. Rogers, as reported in his book *The Diffusion of Innovation*. In this book, Rogers presents a basic model for change that is based on the willingness of people to accept new technology. This model has been widely applied, and Rogers has validated it in a variety of industries:[8]

▶ *Pioneers*: tend to be technologically oriented people who seek new capabilities to help them get their jobs done. They are always ready to try new technology and to accept new ideas. There are not many pioneers in a market, but gaining sales to them helps to assure the early adopters that the product technology is viable.

▶ *Early adopters*: tend to be intuitive and visionary—able to readily understand the value proposition that is offered by the new technology in terms of its contribution to improving the way they work. They make investment decisions based on their insight rather than on reference sales to other parties.

▶ *Early maturity*: tend to be more practical than the early adopters. While sharing the same drive for improvement, they need more evidence and persuasion that the technology will accomplish the job they need to get done. The early majority will wait until they see reference sales that indicate the technology is not a fad and that it will deliver its promise. This group is particularly important, as it represents the mass market (about a third of the total market), and when it has accepted a product, then the product has achieved a critical success point in its life cycle.

▶ *Late maturity*: tends to be less comfortable with technology than early maturity, and they want to purchase "standard" products that they are assured will integrate seamlessly with the job that they need to get done. This group represents the class of individuals who are generally skeptical of new concepts and technologies and will adopt them only when it is proven that they won't "hurt" them or their process. The preponderance of the evidence and the endorsement of their most respected peers will convince them to make an experiment to try it for themselves.

▶ *Laggards*: tend to be the resisters to change—the last group to take on a new idea or technology, and typically they do so only because there is no other choice, since the product support for their current technology is be-

---

[7] Clayton M. Christenson, Scott D. Anthony, and Erik A. Roth, *Seeing What's Next* (Boston: Harvard Business School Press, 2004), p. 5.

[8] Everett M. Rogers, *The Diffusion of Innovation*, 5th edition (New York: Free Press, 2003).

ing eliminated. This group is traditional in its way of doing things. A word of caution must be offered about this class of your customers—they might be what Christensen calls "over-served" customers—they don't need any more technology than they already have, so any move to force them to a new technology can only disrupt their work and cause them to seek a more simple solution that better fits their working environment.

These groups can be plotted as a normal probability distribution:

Rogers Model of Change Acceptance

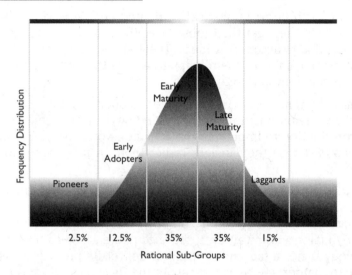

When Rogers' model is presented as a frequency distribution detailing the number of individuals by category, then the result is a bell-shaped or normal curve in which the technology adopters appear to be evenly distributed around the early to late maturity market segments. When the market penetration of a product is presented differently as a cumulative probability distribution, then the resultant graphic is the S-curve, or rate of market growth curve. The S-curve was first proposed by Bryce Ryan and Neal Gross in 1943 as an explanation for the adoption function for improved products. But it was the application by Purdue University Professor Frank M. Bass that converted the S-curve function into a plausible explanation for market behavior for introduction of new products. The Bass Forecasting Model assumes two types of communication will influence the rate of adoption of technology according to this function. Early adopters are more influenced by mass media, while late adopters are more influenced by personal recommendations. Bass made his market forecasts based on three driving influences: mass media influence, interpersonal influence, and market potential.[9]

Rogers points out that innovations present individuals or organizations with new ways to solve their problems, but they don't know if the probability of

---

[9] Frank M. Bass, "A New Product Growth Model for Consumer Durables," *Management Science*, vol. 15, no. 5, 1969, pp. 215–227.

solving their problem is higher with the innovation or with their current way of doing their job. Thus, they are "motivated to seek more information about the innovation in order to cope with the uncertainty that it creates."[10] The less information available to them that is targeted to the job they need to get done, the greater their delay in accepting the innovation. If this delay occurs across many segments of the market, then the market penetration of the new product is effectively stalled, creating a gap or "chasm" in the market-growth function. Thus, the key to a smooth introduction of a new product is understanding customers and their needs.

Of course, markets do not exist in a vacuum; there are always past customers, current customers, and potential future customers. When looking at a customer base, it is most important to understand how they are being served today. As Christensen points out, customers might be underserved or overserved—and each of these alternatives has a unique implication for developing market strategy for new technologies. How does a company learn "What job needs to get done by which customer?" and determine how it will address these jobs in its product design and marketing strategy? Albert Einstein once observed, "technological change is like an ax in the hands of a pathological criminal!"[11] How can technological changes generated in a new product development project be managed more sanely?

Insight into this problem is provided by consultant Geoffrey Moore as he points out that Rogers' distribution is not really continuous, but has a discontinuity following the early adopters, which he calls the "chasm" between the preliminary market and the mass market—indeed, Rogers himself recognized this as he called this the "take-off" period before the transition to the mass market is achieved.

What is the best strategy to cross this chasm from those customers who are willing to accept more risk in order to appropriate the new technology to "get their job done" (these are the pioneers and the early adopters) and those customers in the mass market who demand more proven technology performance (early maturity customers)?

Rogers points out that there are really two different functions operating here—one measures the rate in growth in awareness of the innovation, while the second measures the decision period for adoption of the technology by the customers. Early adopters are more influenced by mass media and technological breakthroughs, while the early maturity market is more influenced by "proven" technology as cited by reference sales or case-study materials. These insights provide the foundation for a strategy to approach the market, when coupled with other tools and insights that are grouped into the DFSS program management function.

Some conclusions can be drawn about how to market the introduction of a new technology based on the five categories of technology adopter that

[10] Rogers, op. cit., p. xvii.

[11] As quoted in: Richard S. Rosenberg, The Social Impact of Computers, 2nd edition (San Diego: Academic Press, 1997), p. 56.

Rogers defined. The basic strategy should be to focus on the early adopter segment, as it provides a transition to the mass market in the early maturity segment, which represents the growth in product sales where the natural market forces take over when critical mass is achieved. After this initial inflection point, the diffusion of innovation "takes off" and enough "individuals have adopted an innovation so that the innovation's further rate of adoption is self-sustaining." Thus, the early adopter segment must be very carefully managed to ensure that appropriate reference sales are obtained in order to convince the early maturity market of the readiness of the technology for their use. The early adopters need to be identified and segmented to determine how to appeal to their needs. The conclusion from Rogers' studies is that organizations should focus on the early adopter segment, segmenting them based on the job that they want to get done! Segmentation of division of the market into logical sub-groups should focus on attacking those market niches that move rapidly toward getting "critical mass" so that the natural market forces take over. This strategy is illustrated below:

Focus Your Design Effort!

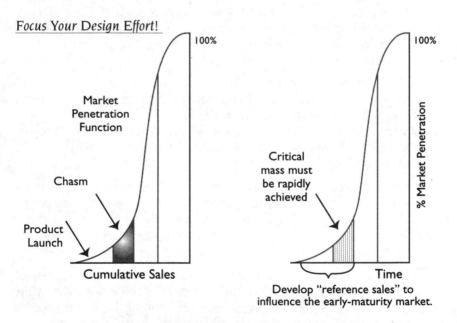

Develop "reference sales" to
influence the early-maturity market.

A generic set of decision criteria to consider how to focus a business to transition this chasm should include the following parameters:

▶ Financial condition of the targeted customers in the early adopter segment.

▶ Accessibility of the targeted customer to your sales team.

▶ Job the customer needs to get done—compelling reason to buy?

▶ Availability of a "whole product solution" that fulfills this reason to buy.

▶ Status and strength of entrenched competition.

▶ Ability to leverage this sale to other targeted market segments.[12]

Rogers points out that the diffusion of innovation across these categories is actually a chain of five events: building awareness of what the innovation is, how it works, and how it applies to your situation; forming an opinion about the innovation and its utility; deciding to adopt or reject the innovation; putting the innovation to use; and reviewing feedback from the pilot application to reinforce and confirm the decision.[13]

The consequences (or, as consultant Joel A. Barker refers to them, implications) of innovation refer to the impact or effect of change on the social system, whether it be a business or a community. Rogers believes that up to three generations of direct and indirect effects (the intended or unintended consequences of a change) must be defined and tracked in order to determine their impact on the system.[14]

These statements are actually extensions of the Law of Unintended Consequences, which describes the unanticipated consequences of purposeful social action and was developed by sociologist Robert K. Merton in 1936. Consequences of actions can be either intended or unintended and might be unforeseen by either proponents or critics of the action. Nobel Prize–winning economist Milton Friedman has called this same concept "the law of unintended consequences."[15] No matter how well-intended an undertaking, there might be unforeseen repercussions that can overshadow the original action. Technological innovations that are intended to eliminate physical stress can create emotional stress due to lack of job security. In fact, unintended consequences might be positive (serendipity or windfall gains), sources of problems—according to Murphy's Law (usually stated that "if something can go wrong, then it will"), or definitely negative (the perverse effect or opposite of the desired outcome).

How do unintended consequences come about? Merton has described six different sources of unintended consequences: ignorance, error, self-interest, basic values, self-defeating prediction, and self-fulfilling prophecy. While the first two of these sources are self-explanatory, the others require a brief description. Self-interest occurs whenever willful ignorance occurs—a policy or outcome is so strongly desired that the consequences are ignored, even though they could be foreseen. Basic values refer to the value structure that is inherent to a society, corporation, group, or individual (such as religious values or national pride). These values are so strongly held that they create "blindness" to their effects and thus the inability to understand what might

---

[12] Adapted from a set of criteria offered in a case study on Moore's work in Robert A. Burgelman, Modesto A. Maidique, and Steven C. Wheelwright, *Strategic Management of Technology and Innovation*, 3rd edition (New York: McGraw-Hill, 2001), p. 270.

[13] Rogers, *op. cit.*, p. 20.

[14] Barker's approach is described in his best-selling book, *Discovering the Future* (St. Paul, MN: ILI Press, 1985), and he cites his descriptions as a continuation of the work of Thomas Kuhn on paradigms, as described in his book *The Structure of Scientific Revolutions* (Chicago: University of Chicago Press, 1962).

15 Robert K. Merton, "The Unanticipated Consequences of Purposive Social Action," *Sociological Ambivalence and Other Essays* (New York: Free Press, 1979), pp. 145–155.

be potential outcomes of value-based decisions. Self-defeating prediction refers to the effect of making a prediction, which by itself changes the outcome (acting as a warning against undesired behavior). Finally, self-fulfilling prophecy is the opposite of self-defeating prediction—the fact of predicting an outcome causes people to want to work to achieve the forecast result.

However, studying customers and market needs is not always a sure-fire way to ensure success in new product development, particularly when new technologies emerge that lead to the potential for disruptive market technologies. As observed by John Seeley Brown, Chief Scientist of Xerox and Director of the Palo Alto Research Center (PARC):

> "Too often, it seems that an obsessive focus on customers eliminates judgment from the game of innovation. Innovation requires judgment, informed by a wide range of analytic tools, and it requires discipline. But, in many companies, it doesn't matter whether something is a good idea or if it makes strategic sense. All anyone cares about is what the current customers say that they want. The problem is that customers can't always articulate what they want, and what they want is not what they need."[16]

He goes on to provide his definition of innovation, pointing out the need for intuitive judgment in order to see differently:

> "Innovation means finding new markets for existing technologies, new technologies for existing markets, and new technologies for new markets. It means finding new ways of doing business: reaching customers, listening to the market, distributing products, managing people, managing uncertainty, and connecting to the ecologies surrounding *something* differently. Moreover, we need to have the courage to follow our intuitions."[17]

Brown's thesis on innovation spotlights the need for diversity—diversity in terms of the culture of people, the age of people, and the disciplines of people. Organizations that tend to have a dominant discipline (e.g., mechanical engineering, electrical engineering, finance, marketing, etc.) have a difficult time because they tend to use a language for internal communication that is discipline-specific, and all their colleagues must then learn this language. However, the language of the customer comes from a different perspective, and it is essential that organizations develop a means to translate between these languages. Brown comments: "Much of what we think of as innovation is the product of creative tension between different perspectives."[18] Also, international QFD expert Glenn Mazur has noted that customers tend to mumble as they report on what it is that they need, want, or desire in a new product—they are not reliable reporters of their own interests:

> "The eminent linguist S. I. Hayakawa, in *Language in Thought and Action* (1990), defines three major types of language data. When customers

---

[16] John Seeley Brown, Seeing Differently: *Insights on Innovation* (Boston: Harvard Business School Press, 1997), pp. xx–xxi.

[17] *Ibid.,* p. xxvi.

[18] *Ibid.,* p. xxvii.

speak they mumble all three together, which makes understanding their *true* needs difficult. Reports are verifiable, inferences are a statement about the unknown based on the known, and a judgment expresses approval or disapproval. To the QFD team, verbatim customer language data will contain a mixture of requirements (reports), wishes (inferences), and complaints (judgments)."[19]

Customer focus must be combined with insight from technology to gain an intuitive viewpoint of what can be achieved. Value must be measured from the customer's viewpoint using a standard that judges how well they can get their job done using the product. The degree to which product functionality achieves this level of performance is a measure of its marginal economic utility. When value diminishes, then the market price is no longer warranted; as the products transition to a commodity, then the company's profit margin is destroyed. The job of management is to deliver a continuous stream of value, as perceived by customers, based on timing of the market and competitive forces. Therefore, technology alone is not the answer! Both market and customer insights must be "double-linked" in order to deliver the right value proposition to customers.

However, if technology and customers cannot provide the right answer by themselves, how can an organization gain the right insight? Harvard Professor Philip Kotler has observed that "marketing is not the art of finding clever ways to dispose of what you make. It is the art of creating genuine customer value."[20] Customer value creation is the desired outcome of the product creation process, but how do you harness intuition to deliver the right technology for the right customer job?

In his book on software development titled *The Inmates Are Running the Asylum*, Alan Cooper, inventor of the Visual Basic programming language and designated a Microsoft Fellow by Bill Gates, presents the thesis that software products fail because of a lack of knowledge of the users' requirements.[21] Cooper recommends creating personas—psychometric profiles that define conditions of purchase for "customer types"—in each of the market segments to put flesh and blood into their understanding of the customer knowledge gained in research. Cooper emphasizes what the person does with the product, not what will cause them to buy the product. These personas are "developmental archetypes" that can be used to test creative applications of emerging marketing concepts or new product features for their ability to "get the job done" for customers.

Taking this idea one step further, a company should focus on those personas that produce clarifying knowledge about early adopters—segmenting by early adopter archetype until the market transition path across this market segment (based on the generic model from Rogers, this means that only about

[19] As quoted by Gregory H. Watson, "Kano Analysis for QFD," *Proceedings of 13th QFD Symposium*, QFD Institute, November 5, 2001, slide 35.

[20] Philip Kotler, *Marketing Management*, 11th edition (Englewood Cliffs, NJ: Prentice Hall, 2002).

[21] Alan Cooper, *The Inmates Are Running the Asylum* (Indianapolis, IN: Sams Publishing, 1999).

13% of the market must be targeted and investigated in depth) is clearly defined. This implies that the market penetration strategy can be modeled as a Bayesian-based Markov chain—a sequence of events or marketing activities that lead to success or failure that are linked as conditional probabilities for the transition across their states of achievement. Sequential events in the marketing communication strategy and transition probabilities of success between these events define how a market moves, and the definitions of personas bring it to life in a human form.

So, critical to the success of a product is gaining a "proper" understanding of user needs, or, as senior vice president of HP John Doyle called it, "an imaginative understanding." Some of the tools used for investigating and describing customer needs include: customer focus groups, customer surveys, and customer data analysis. These methods are analyzed using descriptive statistics, comparative statistics (e.g., conjoint analysis and pairwise comparisons), and Kano Feature Analysis, and summarized in customer tables and QFD analyses. The key methodology that is applied in DFSS is QFD, which is a mechanism for developing the voice of the customer (VOC) or the statement of what is "critical to satisfaction" (CTS) in their "job to be done" (work application). QFD then translates the VOC into the voice of the process (VOP), or the way that the product is designed and constructed in order to deliver the desired CTS functions. QFD applies throughout the product life cycle, and it can be used to preserve the knowledge gained in a new product's development, so it is preserved for a future product generation.

Yoji Akao is the co-inventor of Quality Function Deployment (QFD) with Shigeru Mizuno.[22] The origins of QFD were influenced by value analysis and the need to determine how the functions were deployed (delivered) through the design and production processes to the customers to ensure that the quality characteristics as envisioned by listening to the VOC were achieved through the VOP. QFD converts the consumers' demands into "quality characteristics" and develops the design of the finished product by systematically deploying relationships between the customer requirements/demands and the design characteristics, starting with the quality of each product function and extending this relationship to the quality of each part and process. The terms used to define the QFD methodology have interesting meanings. "Function" refers to the features or functions of a product or service. "Quality" describes the degree or level of implementation for the functional design. "Deployment" signifies that there is a combination of translation from one language to another (e.g., from the voice of the customer to the voice of the process, from system-level specifications to part-level specifications, from the voice of the marketing discipline to the voice of the engineer to the voice of the production operator, etc.) and a broadened, team-based, integrated decision-making approach that reaches consensus across different organiza-

[22] Yoji Akao and Shigeru Mizuno, *QFD: The Customer-Driven Approach to Quality Planning and Deployment* (Tokyo: Asian Productivity Organization, Japanese 1978, English 1994); Yoji Akao, *Quality Function Deployment: Integrating Customer Requirements into Product Design* (Portland, OR: Productivity Press, 1990); and Jack B. ReVelle, John W. Moran, and Charles A. Cox, *The QFD Handbook* (New York: John Wiley & Sons, 1998).

tional groups on both the functions that are incorporated into the design as well as their quality levels.

QFD is an immense subject; however, it is best known for its four organizing matrices, the first of which is typically called "the house of quality," as it translates external quality characteristics into internal quality characteristics, while the remainder of these matrices act as "transaction processors" to convert this quality VOC to the VOP. This sequence of matrices is illustrated below:

Translation of Requirements as Qualities Are Deployed

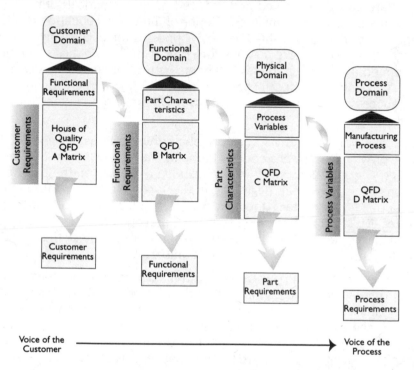

The process for applying QFD is experience-based, and the America-based QFD Institute offers a phased development program for QFD practitioners modeled after the Six Sigma methodology with QFD Green Belt®, QFD Black Belt®, and QFD Master Black Belt® levels of achievement.[23] QFD is an excellent methodology for preserving sensitivity to the customer's job throughout the design process, and it also helps in clarifying the organization's competitive position at the function level through its forced head-to-head pairwise comparison of capability versus the leading competitors.

How to do combat for market share? Christensen suggests that a divide-and-conquer strategy can work—focus one division on disruptive technol-

---

[23] These are all registered trademarks of The QFD Institute. The QFD Institute was founded by Glenn Mazur, John Terninko, and Richard Zultner under the guidance of Yoji Akao: http://www.qfdi.org. A good overview of QFD is provided in an article by Don Clausing and John R. Hauser, "The House of Quality," *Harvard Business Review*, May–June 1988.

ogy while the mainstream focuses on sustaining technology. This strategy is based on the laws of combat that were developed by Frederick W. Lanchester (1868–1946).

Combat for market share

Lanchester was a British engineer and mathematician who built the first British gasoline-powered automobile, invented power steering and disc brakes, contributed to the aerodynamic design of British aircraft, and was one of the founders of the field of operations research. Lanchester believed that warfare could be studied and reduced to mathematical form. During World War I, Lanchester formulated a series of differential equations to demonstrate the power relationships between opposing forces and subsequently published his theory and equations for combat in 1916.[24] These equations were applied by American military planners with great success in designing the Pacific island-hopping campaign during World War II. Interestingly, it was the Japanese who exploited the Lanchester Theory and equations for commercial gain.

Lanchester's work was introduced to Japan by W. Edwards Deming in 1951 when he provided a copy of a book by Philip M. Morse and George M. Kimball (*Methods of Operations Research*)[25], which included a chapter on the Lanchester equations for land combat. Beginning in the 1960s, Dr. Nobuo Taoka (1927–1984) applied Lanchester's theories for developing marketing and sales strategies. Dr. Taoka restructured the military and operations research strategies Lanchester developed into a marketing and sales strategy that could be called the "Lanchester Theory of Market Combat."[26]

The Lanchester theory applies to sales and marketing and describes a broad strategy that includes tactics for new product introduction, attacks on existing companies, and equivalent tactics for the market leader for defending its market share. Lanchester's principle of concentration shows the importance of focusing on a narrow segment of the market (or customer group, geographic area, etc.) in the drive for dominance. This theory can be defined by two laws and one principle as follows:[27]

▶ **Lanchester's Linear Law.** This law applies to traditional one-on-one combat, where the outcome of a battle is a function of the relative size of the opposing armies. Thus, the larger force has an increasingly superior position based on the gap in the difference between the force levels. Stated more

---

[24] Frederick W. Lanchester, *Aircraft in Warfare: The Dawn of the Fourth Arm* (Sunnyvale, CA: Lanchester Press; 1916 edition republished in 1995).

[25] Philip M. Morse and George E. Kimball, *Methods of Operations Research* (New York: John Wiley & Sons and Massachusetts Institute of Technology, 1951).

[26] Nobuo Taoka, *Lanchester Strategy: An Introduction* (Sunnyvale, CA: Lanchester Press, published in English, 1997).

[27] Lanchester's laws and their application are described in a three-volume series by Shinichi Yano: *New Lanchester Strategy: An Introduction* (Sunnyvale, CA: Lanchester Press, Inc., 1996); *New Lanchester Strategy: Sales and Marketing for the Strong* (Sunnyvale, CA: Lanchester Press, Inc., 1997); and *New Lanchester Strategy: Sales and Marketing for the Weak* (Sunnyvale, CA: Lanchester Press, Inc., 1998).

simply, this law says that "there is a direct relationship to the probability of winning a battle and the relative size difference between the opposite forces."

▶ **Lanchester's N-Squared Law.** Lancaster's second law applies to modern combat, where each soldier can engage multiple targets and is also subject to attack from multiple directions. In this case, the attrition rate is also proportional to the number of troops squared, and the law is called Lanchester's N-Squared Law. This law applies whenever operating with multiple participants in a battle (e.g., multiple participants in a market sector).

▶ **Lanchester's Principle of Concentration.** The basic concept in designing strategy is that of concentration—concentrating the main strength of force at one point in the field of operations to focus strength and exploit an opponent's weakness. This leads to a marketing imperative for targeting the point of attack—or, as marketing consultant Geoffrey Moore so eloquently put it: "Trying to cross the chasm without taking a niche market approach is like trying to light a fire without kindling."[28]

Thus, according to the Lanchester Theory, any force that can define the competitive engagement in such a way as to concentrate its force capability in a superior way can win the battle. Based on this knowledge, the Japanese developed two theories based on Lanchester's work. One theory applied Lanchester's equations and the principle of concentration to develop a set of strategies to gain insight into competition design for selecting appropriate marketing tactics. As applied to small companies or new product introduction, the choice of strategy should be to use one-on-one combat to secure a market beachhead. On the other hand, for the existing markets and established firms, the need to protect market share requires battle under the N-Squared Law where the survival rate is greater. The second theory that the Japanese developed involved the analysis of market structure and understanding what is the significance of break points in relative market-share rations among competitors. For example, conventional wisdom (as expressed by Geoffrey A. Moore)[29] states that it takes a 50% share to gain control of a targeted market; however, when the Lanchester equations are applied, the need to dominate is not nearly so great, as a 41.7% share will yield market control.

According to this theory, a superior force should always choose to fight under the N-Squared Law conditions, because the end result will leave the victor with a greater number of survivors than when fighting under the Linear Law. Second, there is an opportunity for an inferior force to win by tactically splitting the larger force and engaging in smaller increments to sequentially annihilate each segment of the enemy force (e.g., when into weaker sales regions or territories or product categories, as was observed by Christensen for low-end market disruptions).[30]

---

[28] Geoffrey A. Moore, *Crossing the Chasm* (Boston: Harvard Business School Press, 1997), p. 67.

[29] Geoffrey A. Moore, *op. cit.,* p. 70.

[30] Christensen and Raynor, *op. cit.,* p. 46.

How does innovation relate to Lanchester's theory? If the quality of a force (product) is increased through application of innovative technology, then the superior advantage of an established force that does not have this innovative technology (a competitor) is reduced according to Lanchester's equation such that an N-squared-fold increase in quality makes up for an N-fold increase in quantity and maintains the parity between forces. However, when force size is constant, then this quality enhancement results in a gain in market share. Thus, there is a consequence of quality improvement such that quality can indeed offset quantity in a competitive business environment.[31]

Applying Lanchester's principle of concentration to marketing, organizations should define the competitive battle and target their point of attack to an area where they can concentrate their resources in the most effective manner. To achieve victory, an organization should attack the market with speed and expand distribution as fast as possible in an attempt to gain a dominant market share before their competitors can understand what is happening. Speed is of the essence, and the first to reach the destination always has the opportunity to obtain a battlefield advantage. The benefit of an opportunity always depends on what you do with it.

What is the role of design in this competitive process?

In his book *Competitive Strategy*, Harvard Professor Michael Porter discusses how, why, when, and what one does to analyze and assess an organization's competitors. Interestingly, little mention is made of the product as a key business concern, and design is mentioned only perfunctorily. In his wheel of competitive strategy, Porter does not include design or engineering as a driver of competition—it appears to exist only at a sub-level under the product line.[32]

Design is a process that occurs across the four QFD matrices. Its job is to create a concrete product that will meet the needs of customers in a commercially viable way. The design process has three major phases: understanding and addressing commercial needs, inventing the product, and engineering the product design to fulfill commercial needs. We have been discussing the first component of this process to this point in the chapter; now we need to focus on how the market analysis transitions into the design, and the key job to be done is to match the product functional design to the perceived commercial need in the market.

---

[31] However, the Lanchester Theory is not without its weakness. For instance, Lanchester's Laws only apply to battles of attrition, where the objective is annihilation of the enemy. If "winning" is defined in a more humanitarian way, then the Lanchester Laws do not help understand which side can win. Also, other tactical considerations, such as terrain, morale, weapon range, movement and maneuver, surprise, weather, and many other issues, have decided battles over the centuries. Additionally, technology advantages from long-range weapons and remote sensors and their ability to coordinate the command-and-control problem in order to concentrate firepower yield immediate battlefield superiority that an inferior force is not able to replicate. Lanchester's Laws help planners develop a "grand strategy," but planning only helps a force to conceptualize a battle, not to fight it according to every potential detail.

[32] Michael E. Porter, *Competitive Strategy: Techniques for Analyzing Industries and Competitors* (New York: The Free Press, 1980, republished in 1998).

The transition across the QFD matrices defines a unique product concept and project development opportunity—the job that a customer needs to accomplish—and translates this product design concept into a product that is capable of meeting its functional requirements with "flawless excellence." The methods of DFSS focus the organization on achieving excellence in the design of those critical-to-satisfaction functions while balancing cost, functional performance, and risk as criteria for design excellence. The standard of performance to be achieved in design of a product is excellence in value delivery (perceived benefits compared to market price) as defined by your customer (value delivery in the design process is the subject of chapter 5).

The design process consists of several steps: setting design performance targets that satisfy a specific set of customer requirements; generating design alternative concepts that are plausible solutions to the customer's problems; analyzing these alternative solutions to determine which one best satisfies the design objectives; and then doing the detailed work required to implement the selected design.[33] Decisions that are made during each step of this design process will profoundly affect product cost, quality, and manufacturing productivity. As described previously in the QFD view of the product life cycle, there are four perspectives of design that must be taken into account: customer, functional, physical, and process viewpoints. The design process involves the continuous processing of information across these four distinct views and requires a concurrent satisfaction of all their requirements.

This connectivity among these perspectives is the core reason why QFD is such a powerful methodology in the DFSS toolkit. QFD maps "what is required" in terms of the functional requirements to "how it is delivered" in terms of design parameters for the functions and those process variables that translate the design parameters into the production process. The design process is iterative and has cycles of prototype engineering, testing, analysis, review, and corrective actions that seem to revolve around each other—the process is not linear in any real sense, although it is often depicted as a linear process. Often testing will expose a different way to understand the design, which results in an iteration of the design to evaluate the new discovery. DFSS helps to make this process ordered and less haphazard by providing a means to organize these product experiments and make the design learning process more efficient (see chapter 8 on planning designed experiments).

How does management engage this "design engine" by assigning it projects to be done and allocating resources to accomplish these tasks? This is the job that is done by the Six Sigma Recognize process, which is embedded in the strategic-planning process of the organization.

---

[33] A very instructional article on the linkage of methods in DFSS was written by Larry R. Smith: "Six Sigma and the Evolution of Quality in Product Development," *Six Sigma Forum Magazine*, no. 1, vol. 1, November 2001.

In an August 2001 interview with Peter F. Drucker, I asked a question that has been a concern for many professionals: How can we convince our CEOs to "do" process improvements such as DFSS? His answer was intriguing and educational. He said, "It is not your job to train your CEOs. They are bright people and can understand quickly what needs to be accomplished. However, it is the job of staff to clearly report necessary information that CEOs can easily assimilate and understand, so they can draw their own conclusions."[34]

The philosophy of former General Electric CEO Jack Welch is that the job of a CEO is to deliver profit in the short term and strength in the long term.[35] It is interesting to observe that John A. Young, former CEO of Hewlett-Packard, made a similar observation about twelve years ago: "There is no long term without the short term—the long term is a series of short terms."[36] Clearly, it is important for a CEO to create a business environment that generates profitable growth so the organization can sustain its success. But what is sustainable profitability, and how does an executive balance the short term with the long term?

Sustained profitable growth delivers a consistent profit to shareholders and generates it using means within tolerance limits investors have for risk that also will satisfy their desire for return on their investment. If these twin conditions of return and risk are not met, investors will seek alternative investments. If no one else wants to invest in the business, there will be a shortfall in capital, creating a crisis that could lead to downsizing, restructuring, and redeployment of capital to maintain the value of the business.

What product-related strategic decisions are made that address this basic need for competitive products over the long term? The enterprise organizational level must invest in technologies and products that have commercial potential to deliver financial performance that satisfies shareholders. The business organization must focus on effectively delivering a continuous stream of products over the long term (a job for product-line managers) that build a competitive difference for the organization. And at the operation's organization level, the job is to consistently deliver the promises made by the organization relative to its products and services. The objective of these integrated design activities is to enable a business system that is capable of generating and sustaining profitable growth.[37] How does the strategy process "recognize" that it has an opportunity?

The imperative is to achieve breakthrough and evolutionary improvement—doing both change management and routine management—addressing both sustaining and disruptive technologies at the same time. This is what Collins

---

[34] Gregory H. Watson, "Peter F. Drucker: Delivering Value to Customers," *Quality Progress*, May 2002, pp. 55–61.

[35] Gregory H. Watson, "Cycles of Learning: Observations of Jack Welch," *Six Sigma Forum Magazine*, November 2001, p. 13.

[36] John A. Young, then-CEO of Hewlett-Packard, in an address to the managers of Chevron in 1989.

[37] Gregory H. Watson, *Business Systems Engineering* (New York: John Wiley & Sons, 1994).

and Porras call "the genius of AND"—an inclusive approach to planning and executing change that requires organizations to embrace both aspects of change simultaneously: "If you can think of new methods to preserve the core, then by all means put them in place. If you can invent powerful new methods to stimulate progress, then give them a try. Use the proven methods and create new methods. Do both."[38] How to accomplish this task? We will return to this subject when we discuss product-line management.

Business strategic planning must identify the critical assumptions that underlie the organization's commitment to products, technologies, markets, and customers. The design process must deliver the "ideal" product to generate future growth. It must focus on the question "What?" first before it can focus on the question "How?" Thus, organizations must continuously examine their market intelligence to determine how to look for early warnings that one of their critical business assumptions is approaching an inflection point that could signal a market or technology discontinuity and assess what it "could do" (or options) if this "what if" (business scenario) were to unfold.[39]

The other side of risk management is managing opportunities. How are opportunities recognized? How to decide where to invest? How to deploy an opportunity into the business so it is captured? Is this market environment as represented by a cumulative sales curve (S-curve) really a limitation to growth, or is it just a signal of the need to transition to a new product that has a different relationship to sales (e.g., instead of "$Y = f(X)$" it is the function "$Y = g(X)$")? Is there a new function that must be designed?

Learning to See Functions Differently

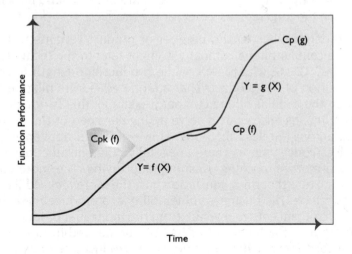

[38] Collins and Porras, op. cit., p. 216.

[39] For information on scenario-based strategic plans, see: Peter Schwartz, The Art of the Long View (New York: Doubleday Currency, 1996); Kees van der Heijden, The Art of Strategic Conversation (New York: John Wiley & Sons, 1997); Arie de Geus, The Living Company (London: Nicholas Brealey, 1997); Pierre Wack, "Scenarios: Uncharted Waters Ahead," Harvard Business Review, September–October 1985; Pierre Wack, "Scenarios: Shooting the Rapids," Harvard Business Review, November–December 1985; and Ged Davis, "Foreseeing a Refracted Future," Scenario Strategy and Planning, April–May 1999.

Note that in this graphical view of the transition from one function to another, the transition point is defined as the achieved process capability (Cpk) approaches the designed process capability (Cp) for the function of interest to the customer (CTS). This can be achieved through either a technology shift (shifting the average value of the functional performance or reducing its variation so its performance is more consistent) or through a market shift (changing the specified performance based on a new insight into customer requirements). This illustrates the two forces that drive DFSS: technology push and market pull, which were described by Burgelman. How is this S-curve managed in the practical world? The answer is through effective product-line management.

Product-line management

Product-line management (PLM) integrates marketing, engineering, and production into a coherent process for understanding customer needs and specifying requirements for products; designing products and production processes; pricing the product for the competitive market; delivering products to the market; and promoting products to customers. A product line is the set of product variations that are commercially available to meet a particular customer need through the offer of differing functions or forms to fulfill variations of the same general class of need. A product line might offer a range of prices to address the same functionality with differences in the product's value proposition—a function of options or enhancements offered to a basic product (as in a mobile phone product line for GSM cellular phones, where the basic telephony is the same but the software offerings and packaging will differ based on the targeted customer for the product).

Product-line depth refers to the number of product variants in a product line (e.g., in a cellular phone company it might refer to the technologies addressed: TDMA, CDMA, GSM, etc.), while product-line length refers to the total composition of the products that are offered—or its mixture (referred to as mix). In the cellular phone company example, this is a highly consistent product line, as all products serve a singular need of the customer by communicating via wireless methods. However, in an appliance company the mix is less consistent, as there are totally different functions served in terms of food storage, cooking, washing, and drying. The more consistent the product mixture that an organization has, the more focused its development efforts can be. The business vulnerability of a product line is based on the breakdown of percentage revenue from the individual products. A highly vulnerable product line has most of its revenue derived from relatively few of the products offered. When revenue of the product line is evenly distributed across the products, then the product line is less vulnerable to attack by competitors, as the competition would have to address all of the variants in order to gain advantage. When a new product is added to a product line that is already in existence, this is called a product-line extension. When a new product replaces a product that is in the product line, then this is called a product rollover. When the new product is of higher quality (perceived value to the customer), then this is trading up, which leverages the brand by increasing its value. When a new product is of lower quality than the prior ones (or the one it replaces), then this action is referred to as trading down, which has the effect of reducing the brand equity.

Determining the long-term customer orientation of a company's offerings is part of product-line management—should products be pushed from available technology or pulled by market demand to help customers get their job done better?[40] Decisions made in managing a product line include the following:

? Which technologies should be pursued?

? Which markets should be developed?

? What products should we produce?

? What new products should be added to the current portfolio of products?

? What existing products should you discontinue offering to the market?

? How should your products be differentiated from your competitors' products?

? How should your products be positioned in the marketplace?

? How should products be branded and offered to customers?

These questions might seem naïve, but they can lead to a profound understanding of the way to focus an organization's design process.

These decisions are developed in a process for product-line management that is integrated into the organization's strategic planning process. These questions are tied to methods and tools that support the product-line management process. For instance, the question "What do we have?" is addressed by taking a technology inventory of the current capability of an organization's intellectual property and knowledge capital. The question "What will probably happen?" is addressed by a technology forecast that evaluates the relative maturity of emerging new technologies and evaluates their potential for commercialization. The question "How does this technology fit customer needs?" leads to conducting a technical assessment of the road map of technologies that will be required to develop future products for customers. The question "What do we do about it?" leads to the development of and commitment to a technology strategy for investing in future product capabilities that the organization can offer to the market through technology development, acquisition, or licensing. This set of questions and their related activities combine to create a portfolio of new technologies that must be developed or acquired to address future customer needs. This process of management planning is illustrated on the next page:

---

[40] This approach follows Theodore Leavitt's recommendation from his classic 1960 *Harvard Business Review* article "Marketing Myopia," where he remarked that customers don't buy drills, they buy holes!

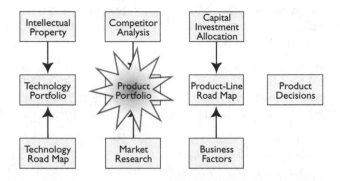

The question "How do we compare?" leads an organization to benchmark itself against its competitors to discover where it has advantages and where it has vulnerabilities that need to be addressed. The question "What is needed?" leads to market research to discover what jobs customers need to get done and how competitors have chosen to address these jobs. The question "What do we do first?" leads to prioritization of the organization's effort as reflected in its product development strategy. Along with the decisions made regarding the portfolio of new technologies to be pursued, the answers to the questions supported by both competitor analysis and market research lead to the decision about what products need to be developed and included in the product portfolio (the sum of all products across all the product lines offered by a company). When combined with the capital investment available and other important business factors, an organization can then create its product-line road map (decisions about what product-line extensions to develop) and make product-specific decisions regarding functionality and form to be offered in variants to current products or in totally new products.

When these decisions are made, several outcomes might occur:

▶ First, the current product line might be found to have significant weaknesses that create business vulnerabilities that must be addressed immediately as a product upgrade (corrective action to product-related issues).

▶ Second, critical improvements or functional upgrades to the current product line might be identified that must be achieved in the near term to ensure competitiveness of the product line (sustainable product features and functions).

▶ Third, new technologies have been identified that will totally change the business and require focused development and management to ensure that the product line is able to transition to the next level of the S-curve by taking advantage of the discontinuity and using it to generate its own new future.

▶ Fourth, there are no problems! This is rarely the outcome of such an analysis!

Business Assessment   **Technical Assessment**

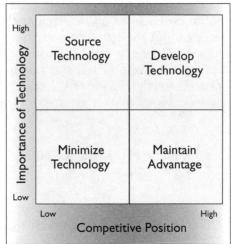

Such an analysis focuses the organization on both its business and technical ability to compete. The business assessment is built on a method that was developed in the 1970s by the Boston Consulting Group, where they cross-plot the profit potential of products against their relative competitive position. When these factors are scaled, then a two-by-two decision matrix is created where a low-low combination results in a decision to exit this particular product line; a low-high factor combination results in the decision to "milk the cash cow" and not further invest in the technology; a high-low combination results in the need to create strategic technology alliances so that other organizations will develop the future technology required to achieve the profitability so that the organization doesn't squander its limited new-technology resources on projects that don't lead to competitive advantage; and a high-high combination results in the decision to commit the organization's resources to developing or acquiring the intellectual property for these technologies. The choice of what to do about the technology is governed by the technical assessment. It takes both of these perspectives to clearly understand the strategic decision. Considering the importance of the technology against competitive position leads to a second two-by-two decision matrix where a low-low combination results in the decision to minimize this technology; a low-high combination results in the decision to maintain the advantage; a high-low combination results in the decision to outsource the technology (through joint ventures or licensing); and a high-high combination results in the commitment for internal development (as long as funding and technology resources—mostly the right-skilled people—are available). These decisions are summarized in the figure above.

There are two key decisions in the process outlined above: selection of the technology portfolio and choice of product concepts to be developed. Each of these decisions can be interpreted as a risk-based decision regarding potential payback for an investment that is financially constrained—there is never enough money to do everything! The organization has alternatives that it might choose to address customer needs. Thus, the choice is not purely financial—it must include the "goodness of fit" with requirements of customers and also the degree of risk that is inherent in each of the choices due to the technology, market, competitors, and ability to produce it.

Decision-Making Hierarchy in AHP

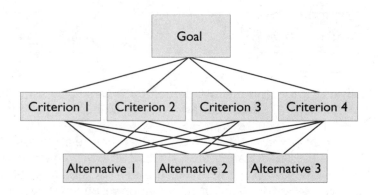

One methodology for assisting in making a more rational decision regarding these competing alternatives is the Analytic Hierarchy Process (AHP). AHP was created at the Wharton Graduate School of Business by Professor Thomas Saaty in the 1980s to improve marketing decision making (currently, Professor Saaty is University Chair of the Quantitative Group at the Katz Graduate School of the Business in the University of Pittsburgh).[41]

The AHP methodology compares decision alternatives against a standard set of criteria using pairwise analysis and ranking the choices and converts individual preferences into a ratio scale and combines these into a linear additive weight for each alternative. (Note that in one variant of AHP the ratio is the product of benefits times opportunities divided by costs times risks.) The resultant weighted alternative can then be used to compare the relative rank-

---

[41] Thomas L. Saaty has published a number of books and hundreds of articles on this subject. Among the most notable books are: *The Analytic Hierarchy Process* (New York: McGraw-Hill, 1980); *Multi-Criteria Decision Making: The Analytic Hierarchy Process* (Pittsburgh: RWS Publications, 1990); and *Decision Making for Leaders* (Pittsburgh: RWS Publications, 2000).

ings of the alternatives to determine the priorities of the alternatives based on the decision criteria considered.[42,43] How does this work specifically? AHP begins by specifying the goal of the decision, the alternatives that will be considered, and the decision criteria that will be used to decide which alternative has the highest priority. This can be shown in a hierarchy as shown on the previous page.

First, the decision-makers grade the criteria using pairwise evaluations to determine the relative importance of the decision criteria (the number of criteria should not exceed nine as a practical rule). This pairwise evaluation of criteria answers the question: "Which one is more important?" and then makes a relative judgment regarding "How much more important is it?" Then the alternatives are evaluated using pairwise comparisons for each of the decision criteria to determine which is superior for each of the decision factors. The relative ranking of the alternatives by each criterion can be summarized by normalizing the columns (so they all add to 1.00) and then summing all of the rows and dividing each by the number of alternatives to get the average per row. At this point, the relative magnitude of these weighted averages indicates the alternative that has the highest performance for this criterion. Recording this information for all of the criteria comparisons provides a local solution to the decision. When these values are multiplied by the relative importance of the criteria as assessed in the initial pairwise comparison, then a global ranking can be made following this same process. The process is complete when a sensitivity analysis (using "what if" scenarios) is done and an assessment is made of any inconsistent judgments.

The AHP methodology has been documented in thousands of projects and over one hundred doctoral dissertations, and software is available to conduct the analysis and calculate a more precise ranking than available from this methodology (this more advanced calculation method uses matrix mathematics and eigenvector analysis to calculate the relative comparisons).[44]

The result of this AHP analysis is a rank-ordered listing of the relative importance of the alternative decisions based on the chosen decision criteria. When the decision that is being considered is which project to fund in the portfolio of potential new product developments, then the result is an initial sorting of the options. Projects also need to be evaluated for technology sequence (e.g., Does one technology or product need to precede another in order to appropriately develop a family of products?) and for their strategic importance to the business as a whole. Once a product line is selected for

---

[42] ANP is a further development of AHP. See Thomas L. Saaty, *The Analytic Network Process (ANP) for Decision Making and Forecasting with Dependence and Feedback* (Pittsburgh: RWS Publications, 2001).

[43] Thomas L. Saaty, "The Seven Pillars of the Analytic Hierarchy Process," available for downloading from the web at http://www.creativedecisions.net/papers/show_sub.php3?Submission_Id=2 (accessed on January 6, 2005), along with a PowerPoint presentation by Saaty. This article describes the technical issues involved in the AHP method, and it is most strongly recommended for anyone considering the use of AHP for multiple-criteria decision making.

[44] ExpertChoice™ software for AHP is available from www.expertchoice.com.

funding, then management decisions focus on how to manage its development using the PLM process shown below:

Third-Generation Product-Line Management

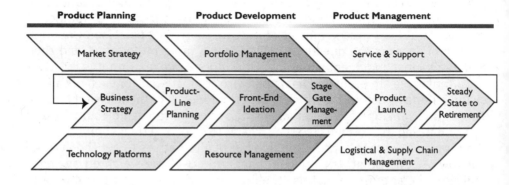

Product Planning	**Product Development**	**Product Management**
Market Strategy	Portfolio Management	Service & Support
Business Strategy / Product-Line Planning	Front-End Ideation / Stage Gate Management	Product Launch / Steady State to Retirement
Technology Platforms	Resource Management	Logistical & Supply Chain Management

How is product-line management conducted?

PLM broadly consists of three processes: product planning, product development, and product management.

The front end of PLM is the process of selecting projects for development as we have been describing. It develops a market strategy based on the organization's business strategy and the technology platforms that it is committed to develop. The decision to fund a project transitions it into the product-line planning process, which formally launches the project into product development. In the product development process, the product proceeds from functional ideation (idea + creation) through the phase-gate or stage-gate process by which the product is prepared for the commercial market. This transition is aided by portfolio management and resource management processes that coordinate activities and allocate resources across the portfolio of products that are under development. A product transitions from development to management when it has been launched into the market. Product launch marks the end of product development and the building of market acceptance for the product such that it is able to engage the market such that self-sustaining forces take over (or it has transitioned through the chasm, in the language of Geoffrey Moore). From that point on, a product is in a steady state of production until the decision is made to obsolete the product and manage it to the end of life (EOL). This final phase of the product life cycle delivers service and support to the customers as well as logistic and supply-chain support to production.

PLM is not a new concept—it has probably existed in one form or another since the first dawn of the industrial revolution. There are three generations of PLM that can be observed. The first generation of PLM existed until the mid-1990s—it was a manual system of work management that engaged one project at a time and was characterized by high variability in application of management methods with resultant poor performance in business measures. This generation organized work according to the tasks required.

The second generation of PLM was born in the mid-1990s and exists today. It features a collaborative work environment facilitated by information systems connectivity, globally accessible knowledge bases, and standardized software solutions. This generation of PLM uses standard processes, allows work to flow across the processes, and focuses management on the effective use of its resources.

Third-generation PLM is in development and exists in marketing promises (but it will be coming soon to a computer near you!). Third-generation PLM features a set of tools that track requirements from their point of initiation with specific customers who have definite jobs that need to get done to the point where these jobs are accomplished. Third-generation PLM will rely on the use of the statistical tools and methods of Design for Six Sigma to improve the business management, project management, and design processes of PLM.[45] How will DFSS be integrated into the basic PLM model? A series of graphics will help explain the tasks that are included.

In product planning, the following emphasis areas are added to the second-generation PLM to incorporate DFSS:

▶ *Business strategy*: Objectives are set for the design project to maximize return-on-capital employed based on the process capability that is designed into the product. The shareholder value proposition is ensured through tracking the reduction in risk associated with the project as it progresses through its life-cycle development.

▶ *Market strategy*: Customer needs are developed based on market segments that are developed by analyzing the behavioral environment in which the customer uses or applies the product in order to determine "What is the job that the customer needs to get done?" Customer needs are tracked from concept development to the point of realization in their working environment. All engineering design analysis and functional trade-offs (conflicts among design parameters) are resolved based on how they serve the customer-need priorities (chapter 6).

▶ *Technology platforms*: Technology growth mapping and discontinuity analysis are used to define critical assumptions, and design conflicts are resolved in favor of delivering the most "ideal" product functionality to market (chapter 6).

▶ *Product-line planning*: The choice of products in the development portfolio is based on a corporate risk profile that details how much risk, and what

---

[45] I owe a debt of gratitude to CEO Brian Semkiw of Rand Worldwide, the largest independent value-added retailer of CAD/CAM systems in the world, for the use of his model and the opportunity to work with Peter Zitis, CEO of Rand Australia, in integrating their PLM approach with DFSS for executive briefings on Design for Six Sigma that Rand sponsored in Melbourne, Australia.

type of risk, management is comfortable with managing as compared to the potential financial return that the project generates from its market opportunity. Multi-generational product-line plans are road-mapped for design and development in order to deliver a continuous stream of innovations to the market. Product performance measures will change over the total life cycle of the project to reflect changing management priorities and the shift in focus on what is important to the customer (chapter 4).

Third-Generation PLM: Integrating Design for Six Simga

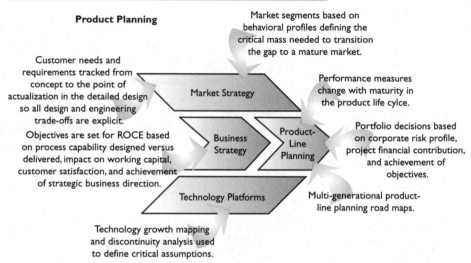

Product Planning

Market segments based on behavioral profiles defining the critical mass needed to transition the gap to a mature market.

Customer needs and requirements tracked from concept to the point of actualization in the detailed design so all design and engineering trade-offs are explicit.

Performance measures change with maturity in the product life cylce.

Objectives are set for ROCE based on process capability designed versus delivered, impact on working capital, customer satisfaction, and achievement of strategic business direction.

Portfolio decisions based on corporate risk profile, project financial contribution, and achievement of objectives.

Market Strategy

Business Strategy

Product-Line Planning

Technology Platforms

Multi-generational product-line planning road maps.

Technology growth mapping and discontinuity analysis used to define critical assumptions.

In product development, the following modifications to the second-generation PLM are made to incorporate DFSS:

▶ *Front-end ideation*: Functional idea generation and concept selection are used to focus design development on the job that the customer needs to get done and ways to ensure that a customer-aligned design is provided that has an effective approach for "double-linking" the technology push with the market pull (chapter 5).

▶ *Portfolio management*: Performance management is applied and scorecards are used to link financial performance with growth in technical and quality maturity of the product as it proceeds through the stage-gate detailed design management process. Customer value is maximized during the design, while business risk is minimized in order to ensure that this new product opportunity meets both market and shareholder criteria for success (chapter 4).

▶ *Resource management*: Resources are allocated to projects based on probability models that determine skills requirements and project need. Project management methods identify critical resources that must be managed across projects and map the availability of these resources to minimize cross-project waiting time while at the same time maximizing the utiliza-

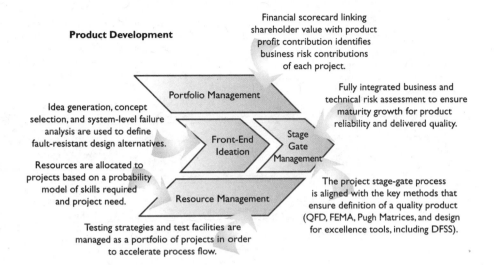

Product Development

Financial scorecard linking shareholder value with product profit contribution identifies business risk contributions of each project.

Portfolio Management

Idea generation, concept selection, and system-level failure analysis are used to define fault-resistant design alternatives.

Fully integrated business and technical risk assessment to ensure maturity growth for product reliability and delivered quality.

Front-End Ideation

Stage Gate Management

Resources are allocated to projects based on a probability model of skills required and project need.

Resource Management

The project stage-gate process is aligned with the key methods that ensure definition of a quality product (QFD, FEMA, Pugh Matrices, and design for excellence tools, including DFSS).

Testing strategies and test facilities are managed as a portfolio of projects in order to accelerate process flow.

tion of these resources. In particular, testing strategies and test facilities are managed across the portfolio of projects that are in development to ensure that the overall business strategy is met (chapter 7).

▶ **Stage-gate management**: The stage-gate process is aligned with the application of key DFSS methods (e.g., QFD, TRIZ, Value Analysis, Pugh Concept Selection Matrix, FMEA, Taguchi Analysis and experimental design, etc.) (see chapter 8) to ensure that the most learning can be achieved during within-stage activities where preproduction prototype designs are constructed. Business and technology risk assessments are embedded into the design reviews conducted at each decision gate to ensure that an ongoing growth in reliability, maturity, and customer satisfaction is achieved with progress through the product development stages (chapter 9).

In product management, the following improvements to the second-generation PLM are made to incorporate DFSS (chapter 9):

▶ **Product launch**: The commercial launch of the product is a formal process, not a marketing event. The process of product launch management analyzes the method of communication with customers to ensure effectiveness in response by targeted markets and good payback on the advertising investment. The process also will monitor customer feedback and sales trend data to ensure highly responsive action is taken to correct any customer-perceived problems and to enhance perception of the product in the market.

▶ **Service and support**: The product is launched into a production environment that is managed by an effective business and quality-control system that

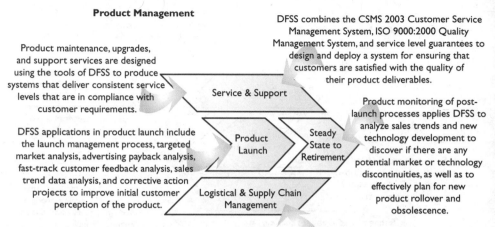

Product Management

Product maintenance, upgrades, and support services are designed using the tools of DFSS to produce systems that deliver consistent service levels that are in compliance with customer requirements.

DFSS combines the CSMS 2003 Customer Service Management System, ISO 9000:2000 Quality Management System, and service level guarantees to design and deploy a system for ensuring that customers are satisfied with the quality of their product deliverables.

DFSS applications in product launch include the launch management process, targeted market analysis, advertising payback analysis, fast-track customer feedback analysis, sales trend data analysis, and corrective action projects to improve initial customer perception of the product.

Product monitoring of post-launch processes applies DFSS to analyze sales trends and new technology development to discover if there are any potential market or technology discontinuities, as well as to effectively plan for new product rollover and obsolescence.

Service & Support

Product Launch

Steady State to Retirement

Logistical & Supply Chain Management

DFSS is applied to the entire supply chain to ensure timely delivery of high-quality parts as well as services. Suppliers and distributors are involved in the planning process before launch in order to develop an effective end-to-end logistics system that has the flexibility to meet an uncertain market demand for the product without sacrificing quality of the product or jeopardizing delivery time.

ensures that the customer's experience with ongoing service and support is exceptional. Product upgrade, maintenance, and support services are all executed using the same DFSS methods and design rules as the original product development process.

▶ *Logistical and supply chain management*: Six Sigma methods are incorporated in the work processes of suppliers to ensure a continuous stream of high-quality parts to support the production process. Suppliers and distributors become involved in the planning process prior to launch to develop an end-to-end logistics system that has flexibility to meet the ramp-up in product demand without sacrificing either its on-time delivery or product quality.

▶ *Steady state to retirement*: Product performance in the field is monitored after its launch to assess potential customer issues and to detect any potential upsets or discontinuities that could signal a change in the way your customers are using the product to get their job done.

How is PLM conducted in DFSS?

PLM is managed through a series of DFSS design management reviews that are conducted throughout the life cycle.

The sequence of DFSS activities follows four major phases: Recognize, Characterize (the DMA phases of DMADV), Optimize (the DV phases of DMADV combined with the Document activity that is required for product standardization prior to launch), and Implement (which is made up of three steps: Execute, Monitor, and Control). In this total DFSS project scope, the

Critical DFSS Management Reviews

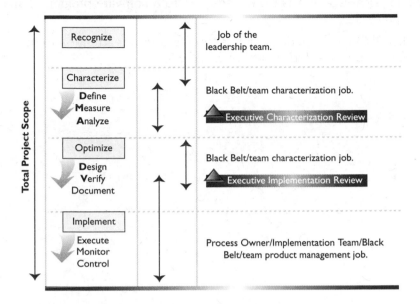

job of the leadership team is in the Recognize phase to the Define step, where they identify the projects that should be funded to meet both customer needs and business requirements. The DFSS Black Belt is involved with the initial project team in the Characterize phase in order to define the product functions from the customer's perspective.

Once executives have reviewed and approved the design characterization, then the full product team launches the Optimize phase, which designs and verifies the product as producible and meeting the design requirements of the Characterization review. When the product has been successfully designed, then a final review of documents to determine their suitability for production is conducted as a formal transition from design to production. (It almost goes without saying that these design documents have been in preparation throughout the Characterize and Optimize phases!) The implementation phase represents the full-scale production, which is the job of the operations, sales, and field-service organizations.

Quality function deployment for PLM knowledge management

A critical role of QFD in the design process is that of the "gate-keeper," where QFD is the management tool that enforces compliance with the design rules and development stage-gate process. Combined with this role of QFD is its role as the manager of the product knowledge base. Because QFD stimulates and tracks technical progress of the product development from concept through realization, it can be linked to the key design documents (e.g., functional requirements, design drawings, test results, final product design specification, etc.) and serve as a means to record the knowledge that is generated during the design process. While this concept is conceptually difficult in the physical world, it is readily adapted to a software program management approach.

Now that PLM has been defined, it is time to turn our attention to the management of projects—the subject of chapter 3.

Chapter 3
Managing a Product Design Project

"All change happens one project at a time and in no other way."

~ Joseph M. Juran

The natural laws of productivity

Bossidy says that "the people process is more important than either the strategy or operations processes." In fact, the people process allows the strategy process to be executed in the operations process. Bossidy continues: "After all, it's the people of an organization who make judgments about how markets are changing, create strategies based on those judgments, and translate the strategies into operational realities." He concludes by observing that "if you don't get the people process right, you will never fulfill the potential of your business."[1] While the people process is critical to the success of a business, a warning must also be considered based on the principle coined by the late Laurence J. Peter (1919–1990), who observed: "In a hierarchy, every employee tends to rise to his level of incompetence." The warning embedded in this so-called Peter Principle is actually a challenge for management: If operations are to succeed in a business, then people must have their competence developed beyond the capability that is required just to "get the job done"—they must become masters of the work that they do, not just be barely competent functionaries in their rigidly defined job. One way to extend the capability of people is to have them operate together in a team and following a shared process for accomplishing their work, rather than working alone in an isolated environment that is loosely coordinated, as in the work done by a guild of craftsmen in the Middle Ages.

[1] Bossidy and Charan, *op. cit.,* p. 141.

One of the basic principles of Total Quality Management is that all work is done in a process and that all processes can be improved. Processes have inputs and outputs and consume resources in the transformation between the two. Performance measures for processes can look at the outputs (results measures) and the transformation that occurs inside the process (process measures). When an output measure represents a critical success factor to the organization, it can be considered a key process output variable (KPOV) or a Y-factor in the Six Sigma equation $Y = f(X)$. When an input or process variable is a critical design parameter that defines how well the process operates, then it can be considered a key process input variable (KPIV) or the X-factor in the process transfer function $Y = f(X)$. The fundamental units of measurement for these process factors are cycle time, or the time to complete the process transformation or the transaction; quality, or the goodness by which the work is accomplished according to an established standard of performance; and cost, or the expense that is incurred in order to facilitate the transformation. There are two basic laws that govern the way processes operate: Little's Law, from queuing theory in operations research, and Coase's Law, from the theory of the firm in economics, which must be interpreted in the light of Ockham's Razor as a basic principle of scientific investigation.

The first natural law of productivity that governs the relationships among process factors has been named Little's Law for its originator, Dr. John D. C. Little, Institute Professor at the Massachusetts Institute of Technology and Chair of the Management Science Department at the Sloan Graduate School of Business. Little's Law is often expressed by the formula $L = \lambda W$, and it relates production rate and work-in-process to cycle time. In plain English, this law states that the average number of customers in a stable system (L) (over some time interval) (this is an equivalent of work-in-process [WIP]) is equal to their average rate of arrival (λ) (the production rate or throughput), multiplied by their average time in the system (W) (cycle time). A corollary has been added: "The average time in the system is equal to the average time in queue plus the average time it takes to receive service." This law is a key to understanding process inefficiency, and it can be restated as:[2]

> Cycle time = work-in-process / production rate
>
> where:
>
> cycle time = waiting time + service time

The measure of cycle time used in lean thinking (*takt* time) is actually the inverse of the arrival rate or throughput (TH) in Little's Law. What is the practical meaning of this law? Imagine a small factory with a single operation and an area for shipping, and a receiving location where only one item can be in the process at a given time, so the system could be represented as:

---

[2] John D. C. Little, "A Proof for the Queuing Formula: $L = \lambda W$," *Operations Research*, vol. 9, no. 3, 1961, pp. 383–387.

The three important measures are the average time product takes to go through the work process, the utilization of the work process, and the rate at which products move through the system. The rate of throughput is what the factory wants to maximize. To understand how to make this system work effectively, we can apply Little's result to the process. This shows that the number of products on average at the process is the rate at which the items move through the system, multiplied by the time it takes to transform them in the process. Since the number of products in the process is its utilization, it can therefore be shown that the throughput rate is given by utilization, divided by the time per customer. Therefore, to make a really productive process, you should strive to take as little time as possible shipping, and you should try to keep your process as busy as possible. However, the Theory of Constraints (TOC) says that the process that paces the entire factory flow (the bottleneck) constrains the output of the entire factory based on its achieved capability, and it is the one place where the process flow should be continuous, and its production pace should set the beat for the flow of the entire factory. Eli Goldratt, inventor of TOC, defines a "constraint" as anything that keeps an organization from making money and satisfying its customers. In the TOC, Goldratt considers each constraint an opportunity to be exploited. Constraints can be physical (as in material or equipment), logical (as in response time), managerial (as in policies and rules), or behavioral (as in activities of specific employees).[3]

The second natural law of productivity is named Coase's Law, after University of Chicago Clifton R. Musser Professor Emeritus (retired) of Economics and Nobel Laureate, Ronald H. Coase. Coase's Law on transaction costs and productivity states that "cost per transaction decreases as number of transactions increases," and for this statement he received the Nobel Prize in Economics (1991). Why does this law represent profound knowledge of a process? Coase first proposed this law in 1937.[4] In this article, he argued that firms (companies or organizations) are grown within an economic system and their existence is justified by transaction costs of production. Firms (and other economic organizations) exist because an entrepreneur finds that they are a useful way to minimize costs of marketing transactions. Coase developed a basic insight about why firms exist. Firms are like centrally planned economies, he wrote, but unlike the latter, they are formed because of people's voluntary choices. But why do people make these choices? The answer, according to Coase, is "transaction costs." Because markets are costly to use, the most efficient production process often takes place in a firm. As transaction costs decrease, the complexity of a firm also decreases. Firms will continue to grow as long as the internal cost of doing work is less than the external cost—at the point where these costs are the same, the firm will cease to grow and people would make

---

[3] Eliyahu M. Goldratt and Jeff Cox, The Goal, second edition (Boston: North River Press, 1992).

[4] Ronald H. Coase, "The Nature of the Firm," The Firm, the Market, and the Law (Chicago: University of Chicago Press, 1990 [originally published in Economica in 1937]), pp. 33–56.

arm's-length transactions with other organizations. If markets were costless to use, then firms would not exist.

Both Little's Law and Coase's Law help to explain productivity in organizations and the benefits of lean thinking—especially when they are mitigated by what is called Ockham's Razor—the scientific principle that whenever two explanations are offered for the same phenomenon, then the most simple, full explanation is preferable. This principle argues for simplicity in process design—that the complexity of a process should not be increased without necessity, perhaps based on the value it adds to the customer-required output.[5]

The final element of theoretical background to lean thinking comes from TOC, which observes that every production process has a bottleneck, or a constraint on the process such that the flow through the process is restricted. When the throughput of a process is managed at this bottleneck, then the process operates at its most efficient level of performance. In order to maximize the output of a process, it is essential that the flow through the bottleneck be unconstrained. The TOC rules applied to the production process include:[6]

▶ Balance flow, not capacity.

▶ The utilization of a non-bottleneck should be determined by its own requirements for operation, not by some other constraint on the system.

▶ Utilization of a piece of equipment is not synonymous with the period of time that it is actively used. Activation is efficient only when equipment is operated at the rate required to balance flow for the bottleneck operation.

▶ An hour lost at the bottleneck is an hour lost for the entire production system.

▶ An hour saved at a non-bottleneck is worthless because it doesn't affect the total factory throughput.

▶ Bottlenecks govern both factory throughput and inventory and should be used to control the rate of production for the factory.

▶ The amount of inventory moved between workstations should not be equal to the total production quantity, but should change to balance the flow of equipment and work in the process—it is a variable, not a constant.

▶ Lead times are the result of operating schedules, and they cannot be pre-specified as a fixed period of time as in standard production systems.

▶ Schedules should be developed based on all the constraints: production, marketing, distribution, and administration.[7]

Coase's Law can be used to explain productivity benefits because transaction costs decrease as transaction volume increases. However, this must be mitigated using Little's Law and applying Ockham's Razor—arguing for simplicity in work design of transaction processes and managing at the bottleneck for maximum effectiveness.

---

[5] This principle is named after William of Ockham (1285–1349).

[6] Goldratt and Cox, op. cit. Additionally, the impact of TOC on accounting is described in chapter 5.

[7] As paraphrased from Goldratt's works.

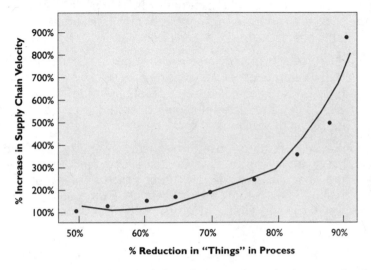

One theoretical study observed that the speed at which a supply chain operates or performs its work (the velocity of a supply chain in its production environment) increases as the number of transactions (works in process) in the supply chain is reduced, as illustrated above (thus, improvement in processes results when work is eliminated—see the function above for an illustration of how the speed of process throughput changes as a function of complexity):[8] This illustration raises a further question: How should the productivity of work be measured?

Measures of productivity

Standard financial measures of performance are net profit (an indicator of the quality of the organization's throughput), working capital (measures the way that operating expenses are managed), and return on assets (describes the effective use of resources by the organization). In the operational perspective, dollars are not counted; rather, the number of items that flow through the business are counted. Thus, inventory level is not described in financial terms as a revenue or turnover rate, but in the number of units that are held at various levels of completion (e.g., raw parts, works in process [WIP], and finished goods inventory [FGI]). In order to manage a production process in the most effective way, management must control work flow through the bottlenecks, eliminate all process-quality or part problems, develop flexible lead times for both the material and production time dimensions, and deliver the output on time, every time, to the paying customers. This process is controlled in the physical domain rather than in the financial domain. What priorities should be set for managing performance and controlling the business?

---

[8] John D. Sterman, *Business Dynamics: Systems Thinking and Modeling for a Complex World* (New York: Irwin McGraw-Hill, 2001).

There appear to be three "levers to move" that help to manage the business better: One is to reduce operating expenses, the second is to reduce inventory, and the third is to improve throughput. Which one should be the priority? The answer is one of the basic lessons from Goldratt's book *The Goal*.

▶ If an organization sets its priority on reducing operating expenses, then the issue is that all operating expenses are equal in priority, and reduction of any operating expense becomes an acceptable solution for business improvement, even when a reduction in some operating expenses might have a negative impact on the business.

▶ If the organization sets its priority on reducing inventory, then the issue it faces is that some inventory is needed to ensure smooth shipments to customers and also manage work flow through the use of inventory buffers to smooth the flow of tasks that take different cycle times in the production process. However, by controlling and reducing inventory, operating expenses are improved (through the cost of carrying inventory), and the production process becomes more flexible because there is a need to improve the responsiveness of the linkage between production and sales when there is no buffer of inventory between the two.

▶ However, when an organization works on increasing throughput, then in order to produce a sale to the final customer, the entire operation must work together in a consistent way for a sustained period of time. By linking the production plans to sales to external customers and managing this throughput, then both inventory level and operating expense are reduced. Thus, the answer is to emphasize increase of throughput as the operating priority for a business.

An organization should begin measuring its performance by measuring output productivity. It does this by measuring the outputs of the design process, as these outputs are the inputs to the operating process (because the product-creation process feeds the product-realization process, as described below). Operational measurement should begin by looking at the effective-

How to Start Measuring?

Process Measures

Measure Requirements of Both Customer and Process Owner

Results Measures

- Effectiveness
  - Defects
- Efficiency
  - Productivity
- Economy
  - Expense

Suppliers ──Inputs──▶ Process ──Outputs──▶ Customers

Measurement Questions:
- How good is our measurement system?
- How should we measure our current performance?
- What is our current performance level?
- How good could our performance be?

ness, efficiency, and economics of the results of the work processes, working backward through the process sequence to the suppliers by evaluating the chain of measurements that produced the results (e.g., for cycle time, look at the timing of the processes and the types of activities that are accomplished during these times—this is the essence of value stream mapping). Chapter 4 will describe more fully how to create a measurement process that addresses the set of measurement questions listed in the previous figure.

Performance management is facilitated by measurement

Performance management is the practice of managing for results by applying best practices to develop an exceptional experience for your customer with your products and services. Performance management is measured by the results that it generates in terms of both short-term profit and long-term strength. Sustainable performance by an organization at the level of excellence requires continuous growth, or else entropy will cause degradation and the business will decline. The two key measures of results for a business are shareholder value-added and brand value-added. These metrics are indicators of the growth in value of the organization as perceived by its owners and its customers.

A business can be considered successful if its growth is stimulated by innovation (an indicator of its natural ability to out-think and excel above its competition) and when its gross revenue increases faster than the cost of its operations (an indicator that the firm is efficient and economical in the effective delivery of its products and services).

The measurement system for performance management will service all three tiers of the organization's structure, as indicated in the following breakdown of performance management:

Performance Management

Organizational Level	Primary Customer	Chief Objective	Main Metrics
Enterprise	Shareholder	Maximize the value propositions of both shareholders and target customers	• Shareholder Value • Brand Value
Business	External Customer	Establish a demand-driven pull for products & services	• Profitable Growth • Customer Loyalty • Delivery to Promise
Operational	Internal Customer or Next Process	Deliver to promise and establish a truly reliable organization	• Productivity • Cycle Time • Quality Level • Cost of Operations • Job Satisfaction

Organizations tend to focus their work into three levels of performance, which are arranged in a hierarchical structure:

▶ At the top of the hierarchy is the enterprise level. This level serves shareholders as its primary customers and has a goal of maximizing the value proposition of business owners and targeted customers, as measured by shareholder value and brand value.

▶ The middle tier of the hierarchy is the business level, which serves external customers and has the objective of matching the customer demand (market pull as opposed to technology push) for new products and services, as measured by profitable growth, customer loyalty (repurchase performance), and delivery to its promise (on-time delivery).

▶ The third tier of the hierarchy is the operational level, where work is conducted at the process level. The objective of this level is to achieve the status of a reliable organization—one that delivers according to its promises (this is the concept of a predictable factory, which is the outcome of Six Sigma); its performance can be measured by factors such as productivity, cycle time, quality level, cost of operations, and job satisfaction of employees.

In order to fully understand the concept of shareholder value (as introduced in the foreword to this book), two prerequisite concepts must be described: product pricing and return on investment (ROI).

The first component to understand is the structural breakdown of product pricing. Product pricing is based on standard cost (the sum of labor, overhead, and direct material that goes into the product) plus periodic costs (the sum of indirect and overhead costs that are required to prepare the product for market, including the sum of the costs of product design, sales and marketing, general administrative expenses, etc.). Product pricing must fully absorb the costs that have been incurred in producing the product in order to return a profit. If there is no profit, then shareholder value cannot increase.

Product Pricing Structure Breakdown

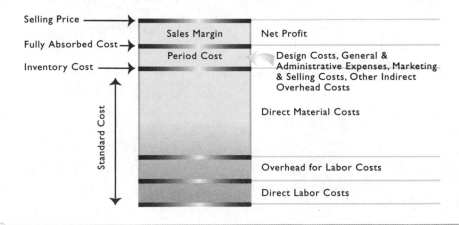

Furthermore, pricing is itself a subjective business exercise. As illustrated below, there is an elasticity of pricing that is related to the customer's value perception. Christensen observes that when the price requested exceeds the value that customers believe is reasonable, then the customer has become "overshot"—given more in the product than they need to satisfy their needs—and they are no longer willing to pay extra for this "lack of value" at the "margin" of the product design. However, "underserved" customers have demands that are not met by the current products, and they are still willing to purchase their needs at a higher price point. Marketing managers must differentiate customers to determine which are at their limit of sustaining additional price increases and which would welcome price when it is accompanied by the value that they are seeking. The balance that exists between these two categories of customers determines the marketability of any further product developments or functional extensions.[9]

Customer Price Sensitivity

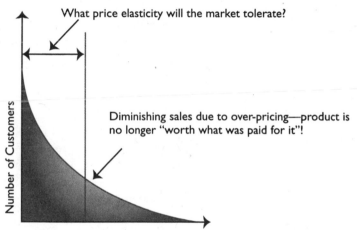

The pricing question creates a zone of intellectual competition among the three business disciplines of marketing, engineering, and accounting. Typically, market pricing studies are made to assess overlap in the criteria that each of these groups uses for recommending the price point of new products and establishing "discount structures" for volume-based pricing. A pricing study attempts to answer questions about the price that customers are willing to tolerate and the limits of pricing elasticity that are available to the management team for setting the price point in their initial market-launch decision process. Within the confines of the pricing framework, a market analysis establishes the upper limit of market pricing tolerance as well as the lower limit of customer functional performance required, while the engineering analysis establishes the upper limit of technical design capability, and the accounting discipline determines the production-cost impact.

---

[9] Clayton M. Christensen and Michael E. Raynor, op. cit.

The second concept is return on investment (ROI) (one of the financial performance indicators described more fully in chapter 4). Decisions that are made about funding individual projects are typically based on their ROI analysis, which assesses the profit potential from alternative applications or uses of the organization's assets. The analysis done to create this financial ratio is summarized in a tree diagram called a DuPont analysis because it originated in the DuPont chemical company in the 1930s. This analysis forms the basis of most investment decisions made by organizations. ROI is calculated using the breakdown analysis as presented in the figure below—multiplying the net profit generated by sales (this is the total revenue minus the total expenses as a percentage of revenue generated) by the ratio of the sales produced by the total assets of the organization required to produce the product and generate the sales.

Return on Investment Calculation

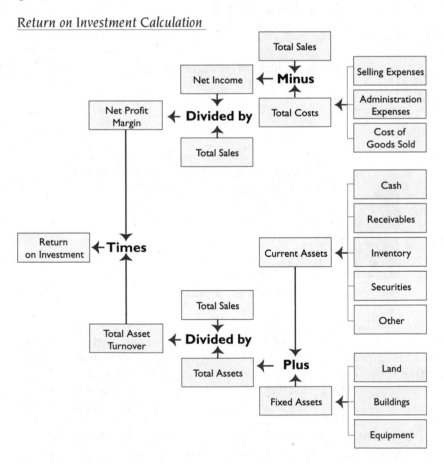

The relationship of product pricing to return on revenue is very straightforward—the higher the unit price, the higher the revenue and the greater the return on investment. The relationship between return on investment and shareholder value is also very straightforward—the higher the return on investment, the higher the shareholder value. Thus, the objective of an organization should be to maximize the price of its products as is indicated by the tolerance for payment by customers based on their value perception for the product.

However, cost is an outcome of design—it is a symptom generated by management and engineering choices made during the process of product development. The root cause of all product cost is found in the design process, where both the product and the process by which it is produced are designed. Competitive products occur when both products and their production processes are designed in a cost-effective way to meet the value proposition required to help targeted customers get their jobs done in ways that are more effective and efficient than alternative choices that are available. Since cost is an outcome of the product-creation process, it is most important for management to measure its performance. How should design performance and the effectiveness, efficiency, and economics of the product-creation process be measured?

Measuring the contribution of design engineering

How can the contributions of design and the product-creation process be evaluated to determine their effectiveness in increasing long-term organizational strength? It is important to be sure that the concept of "balance" is maintained in an assessment of the performance of product creation. This means that the measures used should reflect the perspectives of the various stakeholders so that the picture described gives a comprehensive view of organization-wide performance and indicates actionable areas that focus management effort to improve the quality of its work (more on this subject in chapter 4). There at least five areas of contribution to measure: financial, market, customer, productivity, and employee perspectives. Assessing these different perspectives of the product-creation process requires evaluating several dimensions of performance. What performance indicators could make up a balanced scorecard for the product-creation process? Here is a preliminary set to consider:

▶ **Client satisfaction**: Satisfaction of customers provides an important predictor of the contribution of design to the overall business. There are three customers that must be assessed for satisfaction: the commercial customer (including both those who are economic buyers and end users of the product); the product-line manager, who is concerned with the contribution of the product development project to the overall product-line position; and third parties that have an interest in the new product (e.g., regulatory agencies, consumer protection or "watchdog" groups, professional product reviewers, registrar of patents and trademarks, etc.). For all of these dimensions of customer satisfaction, comparisons should be made against both competitive products and prior-generation products to ensure that a trend in increasing the level of satisfaction is achieved.

▶ **Revenue contribution**: The ultimate indicator of performance is the contribution to the bottom line of new products. Development projects that are funded for the product-creation process are typically required to have a return on investment that surpasses a minimum profit "hurdle rate" or achieves a required "payback period" and can be tracked in terms of achievement of this performance using the Breakeven Time (BET) metric (see chapter 4 for explanations of these financial indicators). However, this is an indicator of the contribution of a single project to the profitability of a business. How do you measure the financial contribution of the entire product-creation process? There are a number of indicators that can be used to do this:

▶ *Revenue growth contribution from new product projects*: This measure is sometimes called a vintage chart because it tracks revenue over a period of years and divides the annual income into a stacked bar chart that is grouped by the year in which the products were launched and attributes the revenue gained from those products launched in that year to the same category. This chart helps to illustrate how important time to market is for a company: How much of its revenue comes from products that were launched within the past two years?

▶ *Return on research*: This measure indicates total profit generated by products introduced in the past year (typically, it is gross margin) as a function of the prior year's annual research budget, and it provides a gross indicator of the profit contribution of new product development.

▶ *R&D program payback period*: This measure indicates the average time to pay back the investment for all new products launched in the prior year (see the payback period measure in chapter 4).

▶ *R&D investment efficiency*: This measure indicates the ability to manage the product-line portfolio efficiently. It sums the investment made in new product development over the past three years and divides this into the difference between revenues from products introduced in this period minus revenue lost from products purposefully made obsolete in this period.

▶ *Growth in royalty income from licensing*: This measure indicates the year-to-year growth in revenue from licensing technology to other organizations.

▶ *Growth in knowledge capital*: This measure is an indicator of the intangible value of knowledge capital generated through the product-creation process.[10]

▶ *Knowledge share*: The contribution of design could be measured in terms of the file size of databases produced, lines of computer code, or pounds of paper, as the outcome is a record of knowledge about how to produce a product and a definition of what the product is (specification). However, these types of measures are indicators of only activities of design and do not indicate anything about the quality of the work produced. A better measure would

---

[10] Jonathan Low and Pam Cohen *Kalafut, Intangible Advantage: How Intangibles Are Driving Business Performance* (Cambridge, MA: Perseus Publishing, 2002).

be to evaluate new knowledge that is produced during the design process according to an independent standard (e.g., a measure such as percentage of patent applications in core technology areas, the rate of conversion of applications to patents, the percentage of product knowledge that exists in "protected intellectual property" via patents, cross-licensing or copyright, or the ratio of royalties paid to royalties received for intellectual property).

▶ *Technology productivity*: This is the cycle time it takes to transition a technology application concept from theory to reality in a product that has been launched into the market. Some of the ways that cycle-time measures can be applied to indicate technology productivity include:

> ▶ *Protected property cycle time*

> ▶ *Generation-to-generation time-to-market cycle time difference*

> ▶ **Supporting measures**: The percentage share of technology-breakthrough patents awarded as compared to the competition; growth in "knowledge share" for specific enabling technologies to measure access to technology from all sources; and time to converge on Six Sigma levels of quality on new product developments.

▶ *Capacity to create*: The environment where people's work can provide a strong contribution to their ability to create. In the final two decades of the twentieth century, several studies on the subject of innovation and creativity in the workplace have highlighted factors that enhance the inventive process and are appropriate for a design environment. In technology management, people are the most valuable resource; developing their competence and establishing a challenging work environment are two factors that management must continually encourage. The capacity to create is a measure of the designer's perspective or feeling about their environment and the degree of management support that they feel to express their ideas and contribute by developing new ideas on behalf of their customer. These measures of employee perception must be correlated with business performance measures that indicate that a creativity-inducing environment has been obtained (e.g., patents awarded, products introduced, gain in time to market over prior new-product generations, professional papers produced, etc.). What questions should be asked to probe employee perception regarding their capacity to create? Begin your survey by considering that innovation thrives in a climate that encourages experimentation and tolerates mistakes! Think about how your employees feel about the following set of factors:

▶ A work atmosphere where probing questions, testing answers, free dialogue, and honest disagreement are normal, stimulating, and not intimidating.

▶ Employees are provided with the right tools and training to get their job done.

▶ The workplace has a stimulating atmosphere, and people are organized in ways to encourage innovation and creativity.

▶ Innovation and out-of-the-box thinking are cultivated and rewarded.

- Failure is acknowledged and allowed, but used as a learning experience.
- Employees have personal and professional development plans that are used for career management.
- Personnel decisions are thoughtful, decisive, and quick.
- Interim as well as major achievements are both acknowledged and rewarded, and social activities include family events.
- Performance that is greater than expected is acknowledged both privately and publicly; however, criticism is done in private but in a timely and constructive manner.
- Communication channels are open in *all directions* with respect to *all issues*.

Commitments to product cost are distributed across the design process through decisions made regarding materials, suppliers, and tolerances assigned to the product. Understanding how the project is managed is important to ensuring that the lowest-cost product that is capable of meeting the customer needs (this defines a high-value product) is delivered to the market.

Making decisions based on measurements

There are some critical up-front decisions that management must make based on the observation of their measurement system. The first concern that they should have is: How do they know if they are growing their business properly? The second should be the follow-up question: How do they know that they need to do Six Sigma?

Regarding the first concern, there are a number of artifacts indicating that a business is growing properly:

- Transaction volume increases as transaction cost decreases.
- New products have better quality than the ones they replace.
- Capital payback periods are consistently reduced.
- Product warranty claims, product returns, customer complaints, shipment and labor variances, scrap, and rework all decrease simultaneously.

There are also a number of hints that an organization can observe indicating that it is in desperate need for doing DFSS:

- The process is documented and measured.
- The process is lean, and cycle time is approaching *takt* time.
- The customer requirement is firm, and CTS requirements equal the product-design specifications.
- Operating-process performance is approaching design-process capability.

- Competition is raising the performance standard.
- You have under-served customers.
- You have under-performing processes (cost/transaction is stable or increasing).

The ultimate success of a business must be measured both financially (e.g., return on net assets, earnings per share, return on investment, return on capital employed, operating profit, and cash flow) and commercially (sustainable reputation of a business in its principal market—brand value or the sustained confidence of the market in enduring customer satisfaction).

Achievement of sustainable performance requires that an organization not only deliver on both of these dimensions but manage to deliver this performance through planned actions that are intended to achieve this performance outcome—but not from serendipitous activity that delivers the results without any relationship to the plans or actions of the organization. It is only when conscious management action delivers performance that the organization can hope for sustainable progress toward its vision. When management does not take specific action in the daily management system that it uses for directing its operations in order to generate the performance that it achieves, then the organization creates a risk that it will not be able to continue successfully into its future. Sustained success requires sound execution of the daily work processes of organizations (chapter 4 will discuss how to develop the system for measurement, while chapter 9 will discuss how to operate a system of business controls).

How is this measurement system related to the concepts of lean thinking?

Concepts of lean thinking

Lean thinking should also be applied to project management in the product-creation process! The lean concepts developed in Japanese industry (perhaps most notably at Toyota) are based on experiential learning, and generally they are summarized as sets of lessons learned. Two *Harvard Business Review* articles provide different insights into the meaning of "lean thinking." Spear and Bowen cite four rules that operate in the Toyota Production System (TPS), and Womack and Jones prescribe five elements for becoming "lean" in an organization. The four TPS rules that guide the design, operation, and improvement of every activity for every product and service are:

1. All work shall be highly specified as to content, sequence, timing, and outcome.

2. Every customer/supplier connection must be direct, and there can be no unambiguous yes-or-no way to send requests and receive responses.

3. The pathway for every product and service must be simple and direct.

4. Any improvement must be made in accordance with the scientific method, under the guidance of a teacher, at the lowest possible level of the organization.

Additionally, the five elements cited in the article by Womack and Jones are:

1. Define value from the product's end-customer perspective in very specific terms.

2. Describe how value is produced (the value stream) and eliminate waste.

3. Make the remaining value-creating steps flow continuously with no waiting.

4. Design and provide what the customer wants only when they have the need.

5. Pursue perfection.[11]

Frequently in the literature on "lean thinking," there are six principles that are offered to define what it means: determine customer value, identify the value stream, make the value visible, make value flow, pull production to the customer demand, and pursue perfection—or, in summary: produce what is needed, when it is needed, at the level of quality characteristics required, then continuously improve. How do these three sets of rules and principles that define lean systems apply in the product-creation process? Consider the following integration of these concepts:

▶ *Determine customer value*: Define value from the product's end-customer perspective in very specific terms. Design and provide what the customer wants only when they have the need.

▶ *Identify the value stream*: All work shall be highly specified as to content, sequence, timing, and outcome. The pathway for every product and service must be simple and direct.

▶ *Make the value visible*: Describe how customer value is produced (the value stream) and eliminate waste.

▶ *Make value flow*: Make the remaining value-creating steps flow continuously with no waiting or time lost so that the bottleneck in the process remains as fully productive as possible.

▶ *Pull production to the customer demand*: Initiate production with priority given to the revenue-producing orders and tightly couple the process to real customer demand. All of the customer/supplier connections must be direct, and there can be no unambiguous yes-or-no way to send requests and receive responses.

▶ *Pursue perfection*: Design products to Six Sigma levels of functional and process performance as measured against the performance requirement for parameters that are critical to customer satisfaction (related to measures of time, quality, and cost). Any improvement must be made in accordance with the scientific method, under the guidance of a teacher, at the lowest possible level of the organization.

[11] The basic resource for lean is the book by James P. Womack and Daniel T. Jones, *Lean Thinking* (New York: Simon & Schuster, 1996). Also, three excellent articles published by *Harvard Business Review* are worth studying: Steven J. Spear and H. Kent Bowen, "Decoding the DNA of the Toyota Production System," *Harvard Business Review*, September–October 1999; James P. Womack and Daniel T. Jones, "Beyond Toyota: How to Root Out Waste and Pursue Perfection," *Harvard Business Review*, September–October 1996; and Steven J. Spear, "Learning to Lead at Toyota," *Harvard Business Review*, May 2004.

The implications of this interpretation of lean thinking on DFSS project management are addressed in the following section, but first a summary of the historical approach to project management will provide a perspective for a different approach using lean methods and the Theory of Constraints to increase project management performance.

Tools of project management

There are a number of tools that are traditionally used to manage projects effectively at the individual project level. These tools fall into these categories: initiating projects, tracking projects, analyzing performance, documenting projects, and ensuring quality results.

▶ **Initiating projects:**

    ▶ **Project charter**: The formal document that initiates a project into the product-creation process under the DMADV process. This charter is similar to the one used to initiate a Six Sigma DMAIC problem-solving project.

    ▶ **Pugh product-concept statement**: Professor Stuart Pugh initiated the idea that the concept document for a new product should be a less-than-one-thousand-word statement of how the proposed product will address the job that customers need to get done. This initial description can focus the market research for developing insights into the voice of the customer from this perspective.

▶ **Tracking projects:**

    ▶ **Gantt chart**: Henry L. Gantt (1861–1919) developed the Gantt chart, which is considered the basic project management scheduling tool (it is included in the Microsoft Project software). The Gantt chart is a work-breakdown structure that sequences the tasks required for a particular job into their time sequence and identifies both the start and termination times of the tasks, as well as any dependencies that might exist between the tasks.[12]

    ▶ **Critical Path Method (CPM)**: Critical Path Method (CPM) was developed by DuPont and the Remington Rand Corporation in 1957 for managing complex projects with many interrelated tasks (such as those that occur in the shutdown of a chemical plant for facility-wide maintenance). A CPM model is a network diagram where each node represents a task and these nodes are connected by arrows that indicate the sequence of dependencies among the tasks. Each task is annotated with the time to complete the task so that the cumulative effect of each work pathway among the nodes can be added to determine which path takes the longest time to complete to get to the end state—this is the critical path.

---

[12] Henry L. Gantt, "Work, Wages, and Profit," *The Engineering Magazine*, 1910.

- **Project Evaluation Review Technique (PERT):** PERT was developed by the United States Navy and its contractors for use on the Polaris missile submarine program. PERT extends the CPM method to include the effects of uncertainty on scheduling and a method to "crash" the schedule or adjust it to conform to time and resource constraints. The existence of constraints in the schedule led to development of an application for scheduling based on Goldratt's Theory of Constraints called the critical chain.

- **Duane growth curve:** This chart is used to track the growth in product-level reliability as a design progresses through the product-creation process from the initial prototype level to production readiness (chapter 7 has more details).

- **Project slip rate:** Slip rate can be used to chart the relative schedule progress of the components of a product design (see figure below), and it measures the ability of the team to maintain its forecast project schedule at the part level. The "reality" line on the chart is the reference forecast of product delivery that is used for the calculation. The remaining lines are the calculated delivery schedules by part or sub-assembly. Using the slip rate metric allows project managers to reallocate resources among the different design functions in order to balance engineering efforts and achieve the overall design delivery schedule.

Project Assessment Using Slip Rate

$$\text{Slip Rate} = \frac{\text{Planned Duration (months)}}{\text{Actual Duration (months)}} \times 100\%$$

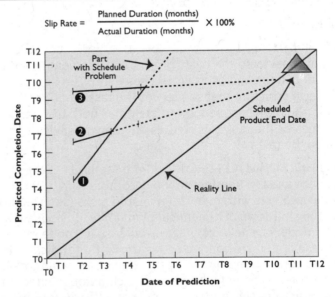

- **Analyzing performance:**
  - **Critical parameter management (CPM):** Parametric analysis is based on a combination of Taguchi methods of analysis (see chapter 8) and a process capability index (Cp) (a ratio of the specification width divided by six standard deviations of the parameter's average performance).

Monitoring the ability of a design to approach the target Cp value indicates the relative maturity of the product design. Parametric analysis is also used to investigate or characterize relationships between different factors in two-factor analyses, as recommended by Stuart Pugh for technical performance data mining. When the parametric analysis is done, the input factors for signals, noise, and control are compared to the measured functional output to determine the relationship or the "transfer function" that describes the strength of the correlation between the two. This can be described as a regression equation, with the statistic R^2 indicating the amount of variation in the functional output that is explained by one of the input factors (see the diagram below).

Parameter Diagram

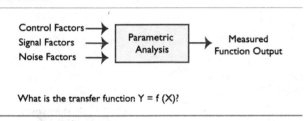

What is the transfer function $Y = f(X)$?

▶ **Target costing**: Target costing is an application of value engineering at the front end of product creation, where it is used to allocate cost targets for each of the functions based on their relative value contributions. Target costing is performed according to the logic of the following flow diagram:[13]

Target Costing

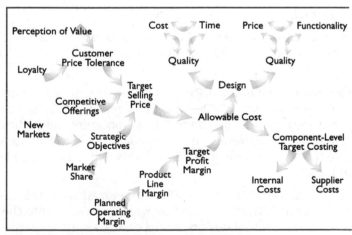

Target Selling Price – Target Profit Margin = Allowable Cost

[13] Robin Cooper and Regine Slagmulder, *Target Costing and Value Engineering* (Portland, OR: Productivity Press/Institute of Management Accountants, 1997); Robert Kaplan and Robin Cooper, *Cost and Effect* (Boston: Harvard Business School Press, 1998); and Shahid Ansari et al., *Target Costing* (New York: Irwin/ McGraw-Hill, 1997).

▶ **Price tolerance analysis:** This marketing research study determines the zone of customer indifference to price changes with a specified envelope for combinations of cost/performance based on four design limits: the production cost impact establishes the lower cost limit, while the market pricing tolerance establishes the upper pricing limit; and the equivalent functional performance from value engineering analysis (chapter 5) sets the lower performance limit as technical-design capability sets the upper performance limit. These factors create a price/performance tolerance trade-off zone, where the team can concentrate its efforts for setting the product's initial market price (see below):

Pricing Tolerance Analysis

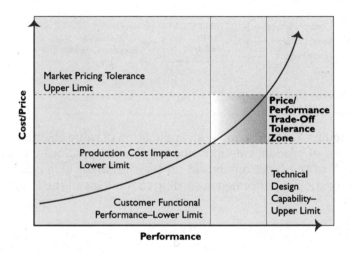

▶ *Documenting projects:*

> ▶ **Quality Function Deployment (QFD):** QFD is a method for tracking the voice of the customer (VOC) to the voice of the process (VOP). (See chapter 2.)
>
> ▶ **Customer requirement matrix (CR):** This matrix describes the detail of the voice of the customer (VOC)—who they are, what they say they want, how what they want is interpreted, how important the request is, and the degree of attractiveness of the request using the Kano Model to indicate the level of benefit perceived (this matrix is also called a customer table).
>
> ▶ **Functional requirement (FR):** The FR is developed after the conceptual design to describe the functions that will be designed into the product to meet the conceptual design. Based on the FR, the design team will design functions and integrate them into the system that will become the eventual product.

- ▶ **Product design specification (PDS)**: The PDS is the final document of the design process; it documents the technical performance that has been designed into the system for all critical design parameters. PDS supplements include detailed design drawings, test plans, and test results that demonstrate conformance to the customer requirements. A PDC is often called a "spec."

▶ **Ensuring quality results:**

- ▶ **Design Review (DR)**: A Design Review is the formal management review that is conducted at the end of a design stage in the engineering development cycle. This review acts as a "gate" through which each project must pass to move on to the next phase. Each Design Review milestone has a specific set of requirements (sometimes called "wickets"—the gates that a croquet ball must pass through) that must be successfully navigated in order for management to approve funding of the next stage.

- ▶ **Control plan**: A control plan, along with engineering drawings, test plans, the bill of materials, and the product-design specification, represents the final product of the design process. The control plan identifies critical parameters that must be managed, how they are tested, the statistical approach for data collection and analysis, and countermeasures that can be taken when a particular failure mode is observed (see chapter 9).

The constraints on project management

Project management is the act of applying resources to achieve a scoped task within a scheduled time period. This can be seen in the graphic on the next page.[14] A manager's recipe for successful completion of a project is a combination of three ingredients:

▶ **Timing and sequential dependencies**: Tasks take a certain amount of time to be performed, and they are done in a sequential order based on the requirements of the outcome.

▶ **Resource availability**: Tasks consume resources. The more resources available to get a task accomplished, the faster the task can get done (e.g., to a limit, this is true of adding more engineers to a project; however, at a certain point in time, the job of coordinating and managing the number of people becomes too large, and the value of adding additional resources is negligible).

▶ **Project scope**: The amount of work that the project team will accomplish. This can be defined as the number of functions to be engineered, the technical level of performance to be achieved on specification of the design parameters, or the level of quality in the components of the design.

---

[14] Adapted from an article by David Higgins, "Critical Chain Project Management's Visibility Problem," *Cutter Information Technology Journal*, vol. 16, no. 3, March 2003, pp. 5–9.

While the most frequent complaint from business leaders is that projects are late, it can often be observed that projects are delivered with reduced scope (functions that are desired by customers are removed from the specification in order to satisfy the schedule by reducing the level of effort or scope of work required), or they have a decreased quality level (performance is barely adequate but does not differentiate the product from the competition). Thus, the project management trade-offs made to stay on schedule might sacrifice the business success of the project. So, what causes projects to slip in schedule seems to be the major cause of the problem!

Project Constraints = Management Trade-Offs

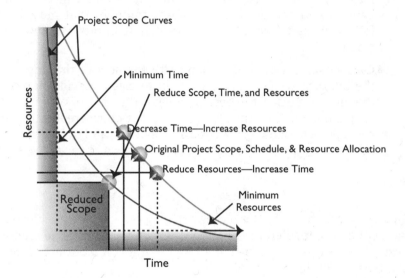

Four factors combine to cause project schedules to slip, and together they conspire to create late projects: personal safety buffers, the effect of Parkinson's Law, contention for project resources, and natural variation in process performance. Here's how they work:

▶ *Personal safety buffers*: People have a natural proclivity for self-preservation and reducing their chance for failure by adding contingency time in their estimate of the level of effort it will take for completing a task. This is what Goldratt calls the Student Syndrome—when a student is given a month to complete a task that takes a week, they invariably wait until the latest possible time to begin the work and barely get it done on time (or only after "pulling an all-nighter" to complete the work!). Thus, the planning process itself plans to waste time!

▶ *Parkinson's Law*: This law is named after former Raffles Professor of History at the University of Singapore, C. Northcote Parkinson (1909–1993), who defined what is known as Parkinson's Law: "Work expands so as to fill the time available for its completion."[15] Thus, the psychological self-satisfying act of adding buffer time to a task for which one is responsible in order to reduce perceived personal risk actually becomes a self-fulfilling prophecy!

▶ *Contention for resources*: Where there are limits on available resources that are required to support a project, then the engineers compete for the same resources (e.g., for testing fixture availability or draftsmen support time). Limited capacity at a resource converts it into a bottleneck—this is particularly troublesome when the resource is multitasking or attempting to share its services for many users (see comments below on multitasking). Whenever the constraint on resources comes from demands for the resource that are external to the project, then this drain on resource availability will magnify the effective time lost.

▶ *Natural variation in process performance*: All processes have variation. There is a tendency for process performance to drift in time around a central tendency for its performance (the average or mean value). The measure of distribution around this central value illustrates the range of performance, or its variation (the standard distance of a data point from the central tendency). Processes that are natural (e.g., the height of boys of a certain age, the background sound of the ocean, etc.) tend to have a normal distribution (represented by the "classical" bell-shaped curve), while other activities are characterized by different statistical distributions. Processes that are represented in queuing theory (waiting in lines, as in the service of a material flow by a bottleneck resource) tend to operate using a Poisson distribution for service times in the queue. The Poisson distribution is fat toward the zero service time, has a mean representing the average service time, and is a long tail composed of events that create major problems at the bottleneck.

How does the Theory of Constraints (TOC) improve this situation?

Theory of Constraints and impact at the bottleneck

Whenever there is a constraint at a bottleneck, the productivity or throughput of the system is reduced.[16] As mentioned previously, bottlenecks should be used to control the flow through a process—but how? The answer was developed by Goldratt in his book *The Goal*, and he called it "Drum-Buffer-Rope." This process is used to manage the capacity of the production system. Goldratt identifies three different types of capacity: (1) productive capacity—that part of a resource's capacity that is used to process materials, (2) protective capacity—that part of a resource's capacity that is used to regenerate buffer inventory, and (3) excess capacity—that part of capacity that is above the combined productive and protective capacity that is not required for meeting throughput requirements. A bottleneck has only productive capacity, while all other activities should have a combination of productive and protective capacity.

---

[15] As presented first in a November 1955 article in *The Economist* followed by a book: C. Northcote Parkinson, *Parkinson's Law: The Pursuit of Progress* (London: John Murray Press, 1958).

[16] Note that this also signals an opportunity to apply TRIZ to eliminate the conflict in the system!

Goldratt begins his discussion of productivity by asking the question: What determines the strength of a chain? The answer, of course, is its weakest link. The weakest link in a production system is the bottleneck—it restricts the response of the entire system so it cannot keep pace with rapidly flowing customer orders. How to eliminate this problem? Focus on the constrained bottleneck and make the rest of the process service this constraint. The "Drum" establishes the beat of the flow and represents the schedule for operating the bottleneck. The "Buffer" provides protection that ensures the bottleneck is able to operate at full capacity and indicates the time allowed for parts or materials to reach the bottleneck in the flow. The buffer also serves to protect the bottleneck from any statistical fluctuations in the flow through the process. At the bottleneck, parts with schedule constraints can be merged with unconstrained parts, and it is important that the flow of unconstrained parts should not hold back the processing of constrained parts. Finally, the "Rope" is the schedule for releasing parts and material to production for non-constrained items in order to ensure that they don't impact the bottleneck.

Decisions about capacity and flow through other production steps are subordinated to decisions made for operating the bottleneck operation—utilization of the bottleneck is the priority for maximizing the throughput of the entire operation. Productivity of the entire system is controlled through buffer management to ensure that throughput is not decreased and inventory is not increased due to fluctuations in the flow. Monitoring the buffer level at the bottleneck provides an indication of the effectiveness and efficiency of the production flow at the bottleneck and ensures that order throughput is optimized while operating expense and inventory are managed.

Three different types of buffers can be used in a system: (1) *constraint buffer*—used to protect the bottleneck and keep it operating at maximum rate to match throughput; (2) *assembly buffer*—for merging parts that must be processed at the bottleneck with parts that are coming from non-constrained operations (the buffer ensures productivity at the bottleneck by keeping non-bottleneck-produced parts from starving assembly operations at the bottleneck; and (3) *shipping buffer*—the inventory required in order to protect the shipping schedule to paying customers. If the only constraint that exists is from the market demand, then there is just a shipping buffer. If there is also a physical constraint in production, then a constraint buffer is added to the shipping buffer. If the bottleneck activity also relies on resources that come from any non-constrained operations, then an assembly buffer is added to the shipping and constraint buffers.

Critical chain for single projects

How do these TOC concepts apply to project management scheduling? Remember that the Critical Path Method (CPM) uses sequential dependencies and calculates the time-constrained pathway through the resources (process steps), where the maximum time pathway is called the critical path. CPM schedules tasks "as early as possible" from the project start date, which leads to a prioritization of all tasks based on when the work commences. The PERT methodology adds statistical variation to calculation of these pathways to account for a degree of fluctuation in the process steps. The application of TOC to the project management process adds the concept of resource dependencies and scheduling backward from completion (scheduling tasks "as late as possible" focuses the project-activity sequence more strongly on resource requirements) to the system of project-related planning (this is a key development that has created a third generation of planning tools called "critical-chain" project management—Gantt charts were the artifacts of the first generation of planning, while CPM/PERT methods characterized the second generation of tools used in project management).

However, it must be noted that the most important factors that cause schedule slips are behavioral (e.g., Student Syndrome) and not programmatic. Another behavior to be avoided is playing the game "PERT Chicken." This game is created when people in the design process are not properly prepared at a decision-review milestone. The game is relatively easy to play and requires only slight finesse and a straight face—if you can bluff in poker, then this game's for you! The design review represents that time when management seeks to understand the progress status of work on a project. However, if your team is not fully prepared to move ahead, and you don't wish to be the team that holds back overall progress, then you have a conflict to resolve. The approach taken is collusion-based in the PERT Chicken game. (This game is named after the 1950s game where two people would get in cars and accelerate toward each other head-on. The one that turned away first was the "chicken"—they lost the game. Whenever there were two winners in this game, then both lost by dying.) In the PERT Chicken game, one risks only one's career! The way to play PERT Chicken is simple: (1) Get on the review agenda at the end of the time by pleading other pressing activities not related directly to the review; (2) Have a colleague monitor the total of the schedule slips confessed up to the point in time that you are required to report and have them "summon" you to the review—using this time to inform you of the total slippage that has occurred; (3) Decide how to report your project—if the other team leaders have already confessed to more schedule slips than your team requires, then all is on track and you can use this extra time to "enhance" the current design. Of course, the other side of the coin also can occur—not enough slippage has occurred yet in the review, so you have to confess to the problem at hand. In the words of the old rock-and-roll song: "The winner of the game would holler 'Chicken!'"

While this tongue-in-cheek, humorous version of project management is not without its element of truth, it does point out the need for some essential values in effective project management, such as the need for honesty, trust, open communication, and appropriate rewards for performance so that people act in accordance with their system of performance measures. Bill Hewlett (1913–2001), co-founder of Hewlett-Packard, made a profound observation in the 1950s: "Tell me how a person is measured and I'll tell you how they will behave!" Behavior is so important in project management that it must be emphasized that the resultant market behavior of project delivery also provides a clue to your competitors about how your projects are managed. This brief observation introduces a most profound approach to project scheduling based on optimization of the Boyd Cycle.

▶ **The Boyd Cycle**: The next extension to the project management body of knowledge comes from the military in the form of the Boyd Cycle, which dictates flexibility and speed to be effective in maneuver warfare. This cycle was named after Colonel John R. Boyd, USAF (1927–1997). Boyd was a fighter pilot who was nicknamed "40-second Boyd" because he bet he could shoot down any opponent within 40 seconds—and in some 3,000 hours of aerial fighter combat training, he did! How did he accomplish this? By applying what is now called the Boyd Cycle. Boyd taught tactical engagement to USAF pilots and developed his cycle into a general theory of war that can be applied to competition. He applied his ideas in the design of the USAF F-16 fighter.[17]

Two key ideas expounded by Boyd were his definition of cycle time and the idea of "getting inside the adversary's decision cycle." Boyd believed that "he who handles the quickest rate of change survives." In other words, the competitor who acts fastest wins! What is the Boyd Cycle, and how does it operate? Business competition takes place in time, and success in business, as in any real-time competitive rivalry, depends on the ability to perform a series of steps or a cycle faster than your opponent. The Boyd Cycle is a looped decision system that accepts and processes feedback from the environment and the cumulative effect of your prior actions. It allows a competitor to better understand cause-and-effect relationships by reducing the time between observations of caused events and their outcome. This performance feedback is processed and used to recalibrate activities for the next cycle. The Boyd Cycle is often called the OODA Cycle, for its four steps of observation, orientation, decision, and action. What happens in these steps?

▶ *Observation*: Sensing yourself and the operational environment—actionable intelligence that identifies differences between your original understanding of the situation and the changed reality in the current state. Observation seeks to discover the mismatches that define opportunities that give the potential for gaining competitive advantage. Rivals should begin the competitive process by observing their positions, the environment, and their opponents.

---

[17] The original writings of Col. John R. Boyd, USAF, such as his brief essay "Destruction and Creation" and his briefing slides on "Patterns of Conflict," are included for free downloading from the web site www.d-n-i.net/second_level/boyd_military.htm. OODA is cited without reference to its originator in: Joseph L. Bauer and Thomas M. Hout, "Fast-Cycle Capability for Competitive Power," *Harvard Business Review*, November 1988. Other books and articles that reference Boyd's work include: William S. Lind, *Maneuver Warfare Handbook* (New York: Perseus Books, Westview Press, 1985); Grant T. Hamond, *The Mind of War: John Boyd and American Security* (Washington, DC: The Smithsonian Institution Press, 2001); Keith H. Hammonds, "The Strategy of the Fighter Pilot," *Fast Company*, June 2002, issue 59, page 98; Chester W. Richards, *A Swift and Elusive Sword* (Washington, DC: Center for Defense Information, 2003); Robert Coram, *Boyd: The Fighter Pilot Who Changed the Art of War* (New York: Little, Brown, 2004); and Chester W. Richards, *Certain to Win: The Strategy of John R. Boyd Applied to Business* (Philadelphia: Random House, Xlibris, 2004).

- **Orientation**: Interpreting the situation based on experience, culture, education, and data—this is the core process as it guides decisions and also shapes action as well as establishing a perspective from which observations are made. This mental snapshot of the current situation orients the implications of the tactical intelligence to their specific situations.

- **Decision**: Processes the learning from the observation and orientation steps, formulates hypotheses about the way that this information could affect the outcome of the current situation, and then makes rapid decisions about courses of action based on this understanding of the competitive environment.

- **Action**: All decisions are tested by taking action: "Decisions without actions are pointless, and actions without decisions are reckless!" Action allocates the resources to execute tactical plans and checks to see if an action has changed the situation, causing the Boyd Cycle to start anew with the next observation round. Note that Larry Bossidy would approve highly of this process, as it is parallel to his idea of "execution" as the Achilles' heel of business!

The Boyd Cycle encourages competitors to accelerate competitive activities and impact through systematic, repeatable processes. If one of the rivals in a head-to-head competition can consistently operate this cycle faster than the other, then it will gain the competitive advantage. Boyd called this "operating inside your opponent's OODA loop," which means to act quickly to out-think and out-maneuver your opponent. By the time the slower adversary reacts, the faster one is doing something different, and their adversary's action becomes ineffective. With each cycle of progress, the slower party's action becomes more ineffective by a larger margin. This rapid action appears ambiguous to your opponent and generates confusion and disorder in their thinking. The aggregate effect of this rapid, incremental improvement disorients the planning capability of your opponents. The Boyd Cycle can be illustrated across a series of new product launches, as shown at right:

The Boyd Cycle in Product Development

Boyd Cycle = OODA = Observe > Orient > Decide > Act

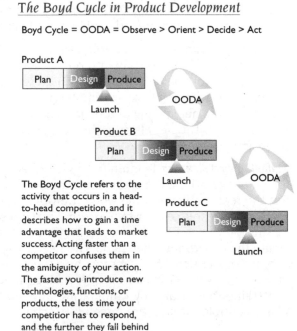

The Boyd Cycle refers to the activity that occurs in a head-to-head competition, and it describes how to gain a time advantage that leads to market success. Acting faster than a competitor confuses them in the ambiguity of your action. The faster you introduce new technologies, functions, or products, the less time your competitior has to respond, and the further they fall behind in product offerings.

What is the purpose of strategy? According to Boyd, it is to "improve our ability to shape and adapt to unfolding circumstances so that we (as individuals or groups, or as a culture or nation-state) can survive on our own terms." The secret of moving faster than your opponent lies in the continuous reduction of friction (things that hold back an organization) through simple, reliable administrative structures and the use of flexible tools that can be adapted rapidly in response to changing tactics. When this idea is applied to project management, it means reducing the "visible" cycle time to your opponent—the time between launches of new products—so the opponent does not understand what you are doing because they are always working on a technology generation or product concept that is lagging. This incremental time advantage should be called the "Boyd Cycle Time" in honor of the breakthrough thinking of Colonel Boyd.

Critical-chain project management

Boyd Cycle Time is the inter-project release time between products launched into the market. However, if projects are not released to the market in ever-shortening cycles, then there is no ambiguity to the situation, and your market rivals have time to adjust their activities to counter your moves. What holds back the release of projects or causes your schedule to slip? The biggest cause of project slippage in many companies is the fact that they rely on multitasking to manage their constrained resources. What is multitasking? It is the assignment of more than one project to a resource so that it must time-share its available processing time to accomplish both tasks simultaneously. What does this mean for projects? Consider the following points that show how the critical-chain TOC approach to project management helps to alleviate problems that are induced by multitasking:

▶ **Multitasking resources and project schedules**: Multitasking a resource will induce three different kinds of delay into projects: (1) project tasks wait while the individual is working on other tasks; (2) there is a loss in work efficiency that comes from switching tasks (estimated to be as high as 40%); and (3) there is a loss in the networking of functions based on resource misalignment to their demand. The net effect is that all tasks are delayed in a multitasking project environment!

▶ **Multiple project planning**: Planning a single project is a relatively direct problem for a manager. There is a single pathway that must be found and navigated. But the real problems come when multiple projects are competing for the same set of resources or when external activities have the ability to impose tasking on the same resources as required by a project. These situations create the constraints that signal the need for TOC thinking and the development of a critical-chain approach to the project. The critical chain takes up where CPM/PERT leaves off by focusing on how to manage the resource constraints better and by eliminating any multitasking from the project. When multiple projects are forced into the same timeline and compete for the same resources, an easy decision for managers is to tell the engineers to multitask and work on all the projects at once. However, no project can be completed until its last task is done, so, as indicated above, all of the projects in a multitasking environment get extended, and an organization that uses this approach risks delaying all of its new products. A simple approach to resolve this issue is to sequence the projects by business priority and technical readiness and to focus work on them one at a time. This results in a significant reduction to the overall timeline and the completion of more projects by the same set of resources.[18] In addition to the elimination of multitasking, the intelligent use of buffers also aids in managing the critical chain across many projects.

▶ *Managing project buffers*: When estimating project completion time, there are two different answers that can be given—one is the "expected" time of completion, which "on average" will be right. This estimate is based on the mean or averages of the time to complete the critical-chain tasks. However, one would expect that such an estimate is wrong all the time, as 50% of the estimate is longer than this mathematical average and 50% is shorter than this average. Six Sigma experts often observe that "the mean rarely happens in the real world!" The second type of estimate that might be given is the "committed time of completion," which is the time that marketing will plan on releasing the new product to the market (in a Six Sigma approach, one would want a 95% confidence level that this time is the best estimate of completion). Clearly, it is not appropriate to use a 50% maximum likelihood estimate, or MLE, for such a commitment.

It is this second estimate that the critical-chain method helps to improve; it does so by managing buffers in the project schedule. Instead of allowing each of the individual engineers to add their own personal padding to the project schedule, the critical-chain method pools the safety buffer and manages it at a higher level by the project manager. This means that each of the project engineers is asked to provide their MLE for their tasks, and the overall performance of the project will allocate safety time across the components of the critical-chain tasks as required. Critical-chain project management applies three different buffer types to improve management of the flow of project tasks, which are special cases of the basic TOC buffers: (1) project buffer—synchronizes the project across all constraints and orchestrates the individual "drumbeats" (one constraint acts like a kettle drum, while another might be bongos—each with their own tempo) into a syncopated rhythm that presents a pleasing, melodious harmony (here the parallel TOC concept is called the shipping buffer); (2) feeding buffer—ensures that non-constraining pathways will not restrict the project bottlenecks (the parallel TOC concept is the assembly buffer); and (3) capacity buffer—synchronizes performance at the project bottleneck to ensure the right overall delivery commitment (here the parallel TOC concept is the constraint buffer).

---

[18] A great explanation of the benefits from eliminating multitasking from projects is presented by QFD, software quality, and critical-chain expert Richard E. Zultner in "Getting Projects out of Your System: A Critical Chain Primer," *Cutter Information Technology Journal*, March 2003, vol. 16, no. 3, pp. 10–18.

While critical-chain project management aids in the macro-level planning for project development, the specific tasks to be navigated across the product-creation process are determined by the engineering process used to develop a mature design that is able to deliver the CTS customer requirements and be ready for commercial launch.

Engineering designs for Six Sigma performance

The design process is often referred to as concurrent engineering, and more recently it has been extended to include collaborative engineering to include external parties in a form of collaboration that is mainly via distance as facilitated by design systems over the internet. However, these are just two of the "best engineering practices" that are incorporated into the process of DFSS. DFSS activity is embedded within this project management system as a set of tools whose use is coordinated according to the DMADV logic. Perhaps the most significant contribution of DFSS is to quantify and mitigate risk during design and development of new products. The logical rationale that DFSS employs to manage risk is as follows:

▶ If our customer is not satisfied, then we did not meet their original expectations.

▶ If we did not meet their expectations, then either we did not understand them or we failed to design the product to meet their expectations.

▶ If we did not understand their expectations, then we did not properly address the "voice of the customer" during design.

▶ If we failed to design the product to meet customer expectations, then we did not establish the right priorities in the product or service development process.

▶ The risk associated with addressing the customer's problem existed before this project started, and making it explicit in the design and management of the product-creation process should have been part of the management process for this project.

▶ DFSS contributes to the management of risk through the combined use of its managerial and statistical tools throughout the DMADV process (as described in chapters 5 through 8).

Clearly, the front end of the product-creation process is most critical to its eventual success, but this has been well documented in numerous studies and is not a new observation. How does the embedding of the DMADV process of DFSS into the design-engineering process improve the situation? To understand this, we must first answer the question: What makes a really great product? The following standard design rules are the basis for beginning a DFSS program:

▶ Design to deliver the *most important* customer requirements.

▶ *Minimize the risks of failure* at the part, process, and product levels.

- Design products for robust performance in *user* environments.
- Use *proven* designs and *standard* approaches wherever practical.
- *Involve suppliers* early in the process to simplify tooling and production.
- *Stabilize designs early* to eliminate shifting requirements.
- *Design for reliability* to ensure the new design is better than the old design.
- *Test products to the point of failure* to prevent the likely failure modes.
- *Fool-proof processes* to prevent mistakes and stabilize factory output.
- *Minimize engineering changes* to reduce the risk of introducing new failures.

Embedding DMADV into the design-engineering process provides three advantages over design engineering without DMADV:

- The coordinated use of QFD helps manage the knowledge-creation process and deliver a documented design that has traceability to the roots of its customers' requirements.
- The design of the functions tracked by QFD is supported by value engineering, TRIZ, DFR, and DOE methods, which are sequentially and iteratively applied across the design process and whose sustained results are ensured by the DFSS control function (chapter 9).
- The target for critical design parameter performance is set according to statistical performance criteria (e.g., achieving a Six Sigma level of performance in design capability when compared to the customer requirement), and the growth in design maturity toward this goal is tracked throughout the product-creation process.

DFSS balances design for consistent delivery of customer expectations with design for flawless performance of internal business operations—these are just two sides of the same coin! DFSS methodologies permit the creation of designs that deliver Six Sigma levels of performance relative to both customer requirements and the capability inherent in production investment. Four engineering best practices are embedded into DFSS to improve an organization's ability to "design it right the first time—every time:"

- *Leveraged technology*: Incrementally engineering new products by adding features and functions to an already-proven design.
- *Concurrent engineering*: Uses a parallel approach to design product, process, and all market deliverables simultaneously.
- *Collaborative engineering*: The simultaneous design of different parts for the same product by different groups of design engineers (who might be distributed globally).
- *Value engineering*: A discipline for maximizing the value contained in the unique product cost elements.

Leveraged technology is a strategy based on leveraging modular components in the product design across product lines or generations of products. The remaining three best practices need to be integrated with the DMADV toolkit based on the specific organizational culture, product technology, and business management and control processes. Customizing and integrating these methodologies with DMADV is the job of Master Black Belts and business leaders in a Six Sigma company. The first three of these best practices will be discussed below, while the challenge of Six Sigma for value engineering is the topic of chapter 5.

Design leveraging

Design leveraging is used to reduce the technology risk in product development. It recognizes that less than 25% of the content in a product design is truly new. The remainder has been done before. Successful designs borrow from old products and innovate to create new products. After all, innovation is often the restatement or restructuring of what has been done before in a different way. Much of what is *thought* to be new has already been done and proven. Much of what is *believed* to be a better way has already been tried, and it has failed. Facts must triumph over opinion in order to ensure that novelty is not just a fad but a truly valued extension to the job that customers need to get done. Successful product developments are usually based on proven designs with added important innovations—what Christensen calls a sustainable technology, rather than a disruptive technology (Christensen estimates that over 90% of new products are sustainable technologies rather than disruptive ones).

However, there are some caveats that must be considered to design leveraging. First, rediscovering the wheel will, at best, delay the design of the wagon and can often result in a bumpy ride for the business. It is essential that product extensions are not repeated blindly as an organization is approaching an inflection point in its product life cycle S-curve or in times of disruptive technology in their industry. Also, it is important to choose carefully what technology is being "reinvented" for the future. Repeating failed products and features wastes time and effort and provides no added value to your customers (it also makes an organization look really dumb). In order to successfully leverage design, the product development team should search out what has been tried and determine what does and does not work—and then they should adapt the best capabilities for their design. The team should concentrate time and effort on the really "new" functions that offer an opportunity to differentiate their product in the market. If there is time left over in the development schedule, then they should seek to improve the functions that are inherited from the past. In order to have a truly leveraged design leveraging, technology managers must incorporate some proven best practices into their design process:

▶ Design the product architecture for planned reuse and expansion.

▶ Define modular blocks of features that can be reused.

- Partition the design so that it is easy to transfer to other products.
- Make the product knowledge and documentation easily accessible.
- Employ a disciplined design process with management reviews that inquire about modular design and functional reuse.
- Communicate efficiently between the design team and the customers.
- Use compatible design tools throughout the development process.
- Maintain a "book of sins" where project leaders confess both what they did right as well as the lessons learned when things went wrong.
- Develop a design environment that makes it easier to leverage on the proven designs than it is to create new ones.

Concurrent engineering

Concurrent design gets products to market faster through its parallel approach to the cost-effective design of the product, process design for producibility, part and process tooling, and a concurrent focus on the "ileitis" of Design for Excellence (DFX): quality, reliability, testability, serviceability, and maintainability.

There are a number of management artifacts that offer evidence of a comprehensive approach to the use of concurrent engineering:

- Multifunctional team (*all* functions involved in the project are represented).
- Dedicated members (people are fully assigned with no other responsibilities).
- Full team start—everyone on board at the beginning.
- Everyone located in the same place so the communication can improve.
- All day-to-day decisions are made at the team level.
- A strong team leader is appointed to manage the project.
- A technology coach is available for guidance to the project manager.
- Management oversight and support occur through scheduled design reviews.

In concurrent design there are specific roles of the senior technical manager and the functional manager, who exercise "matrix" responsibility over the project team. It is the job of the senior technology manager to ensure that the project plans, market and customer requirements, and product specification agree and are approved *early in the development life cycle and that the product architecture is approved at the conceptual stage of the product-creation process.* The senior technology manager also ensures that resources (people, facilities, equipment, budget, and capital) that are required in the project plan are assigned and available *when required* throughout the project. In addition, the senior technology manager monitors progress, provides assistance to the project manager as necessary, responds quickly to unplanned events (requiring quick business decisions), insulates the team from actions that dilute or defocus their progress, and removes obstructions that inhibit their progress. On the other hand, the job of the functional manager is to manage a staff "support" center of excellence that operates like a community of practice for the function rather than a line "decision" center. Thus, the functional manager coordinates the pooled functional resources to meet the schedule requirements of the team. These managers develop, provide, and maintain the various functional systems, resources, facilities, services, and administrative processes that are required to assist the team. However, the functional managers *do not* manage the day-to-day resources of the team members assigned from their function.

This authority structure operates in a matrix between these two managers so that the project manager and team have two bosses, creating ambiguity in management and presenting several challenges for concurrent design:

▶ Senior managers and functional managers have hard transitions.

▶ Senior managers must delegate both responsibility and the *authority to make decisions* and refrain from meddling (no micro-managing or second-guessing!).

▶ Functional managers must change their roles from in-line decision makers to a support role. (Some managers never make this transition to this style of leading.)

▶ Team leadership is critical to success. The leaderless team is an oxymoron. Concurrent design requires *more* leadership—leaders at all levels—and dealing with suppliers, technology partners, sub-contractors, etc., also requires leadership.

▶ Measurements and rewards should be based on the achievement of team targets rather than just individual efforts. People-process decisions also must be made in a systematic manner: Who does the performance appraisal? What about raises and promotions? What about career planning and transitioning the team members to the next job on their career path?

Traditional Stage-Gate Design Process

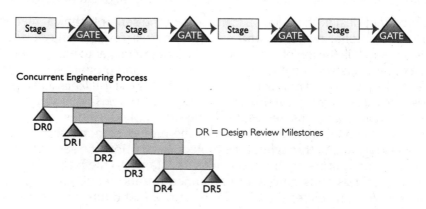

DR = Design Review Milestones

The benefits of concurrent design outweigh these problems, and this is the reason that concurrent engineering has become a de facto standard of design:

- The product is designed once—including the concurrent input and requirements of all perspectives.
- It takes less time to get the product to market.
- Because it takes less time, it also costs less to produce the design.
- Product and process development are integrated, so they work more smoothly at the time of the product launch.
- Co-development results in both higher quality and reliability.
- Inclusion of maintenance and service functions results in a better-fielded product.
- Working with customers during prototype testing helps anticipate and correct the problems found at launch and results in less customer problems at the time of introduction to the market.

Collaborative engineering

Collaborative design is a process that makes coordinated use of resources and expertise found in other organizations and exercises the simultaneous design of product parts by different engineering teams or organizations in a networked system of development across different locations. Collaborative design is organized using a stage-gate process to ensure concurrency in design efforts and to coordinate progress across the different participating organizations. Networked groupware tools, such as Lotus Notes, help to coordinate the design efforts of distributed team members and to ensure that everyone has visibility to the latest revisions of all design documents.

There are many challenges that are presented during a collaborative engineering effort. Some of the major concerns include:

- Management decision coordination is needed—who does what and how?
- Organizational structures might differ across the involved groups.
- Site teamwork, collaboration, and interdependence are required—compared to the more normal autonomy and self-reliance of knowledge workers.
- Multi-site communication, coordination, and scheduling are critical to success.
- Drawing and documentation databases, as well as information management systems, must be compatible.
- Design changes must be controlled and synchronized.
- Design/measuring/testing/diagnostic tools must be standardized, and their output must correlate.
- Remote problem solving must not sub-optimize overall performance.

▶ Manufacturing processes must be standardized so that any product can be made at any location.

In order to overcome these challenges, a collaborative engineering effort requires centralization and standardization of many functions, plus capital investment in those design systems that support electronic sharing of information. The basic rules for the process are that the same design rules, tools, processes, and systems should be used at all locations that contribute to the design (including suppliers or subcontractors that have an integral role in the product-creation process).

The program and project management systems of DFSS are grounded in the use of a sound measurement system. The development of such a measurement system is the topic of the next chapter.

Chapter 4
Measuring Program and Project Progress

*"Until a business returns a profit that is greater than its
cost of capital, it operates at a loss. Never mind that it pays
taxes as if it had genuine profit. The enterprise still returns less to the
economy than it devours in resources...until then, it does not
create wealth, it destroys it."*

~ Peter F. Drucker

Performance management relies on measurement

In the first chapter I quoted former GE CEO Jack Welch: "Six Sigma gives us a route to the business control function, the hardest thing to do in management."[1] Business control is the function of an organization that manages the current state of the business and delivers today's performance, ensuring execution of plans and rapid response with corrective action that is required to sustain the promised service levels to customers.

Effective business control is the essential element of any management process, and it requires that managers lead by example. No management system can endure leaders who do not apply the same principles to themselves that they apply to their people. Effective business control also requires that an organization manage by process in order to produce value for its customers and shareholders. Organizations that do not use process management become introspective and self-seeking and lose their competitive edge. Effective business control also requires that its people monitor measurements. It is

---

[1] As quoted in: Gregory H. Watson, "Cycles of Learning: Observations of Jack Welch," *Six Sigma Forum Magazine*, vol. 1, no. 1, November 2001, p. 13.

not just the act of measuring that is essential, it is the use of good measures to learn about the business and choose direction more carefully. Effective business control also requires that managers evaluate progress. Performance management without effective decision making results in frustration for the entire organization. It is only when measurement systems are used to identify and effect change in routine operations that people actually believe that such methods can make a difference. Finally, effective business control also requires that managers adapt to their environment. Excellence comes only by execution.

Excellence is not merely the product of a good process map, measurement system, or self-assessment scheme—excellence comes when leaders lead by example and also hold others accountable for following that example. However, in designing a daily management system for business control, one must begin somewhere, and the process map and measurement system set the context for business leadership by example.

Dr. Peter F. Drucker, in his timeless book *Managing for Results*, observed: "The neglect of the future is only a symptom; the executive slights tomorrow because he cannot get ahead of today. That too is a symptom. The real disease is the absence of any foundation of knowledge and system for tackling the economic tasks in business....There are three different dimensions to the economic task: (1) The present business must be made effective; (2) its potential must be identified and realized; and (3) it must be made into a different business for a different future."[2]

What is the goal of business?

Before any discussion of measurement can go beyond a purely superficial level, it is necessary to identify the goals or objectives that are being measured. Without this perspective, all measurement systems are subjective and subject to the operation of "Theory O"—an opinion-based judgment about what is important in business that is not grounded in a "management by facts" perspective. Dr. W. Edwards Deming is often quoted as saying that "In God we trust; all others must bring data."[3]

Peter Drucker commented: "For full effectiveness, all the work needs to be integrated into a unified *program for performance*."[4]

So, what is the goal of business? Combining Eli Goldratt's views with the analytical outcomes from the studies of successful organizations by Jim Collins and Jerry Porras, we postulate the following generic business goals:[5]

---

[2] Peter F. Drucker, *Managing for Results* (New York: Harper & Row, 1964), pp. 3–4.

[3] Gregory H. Watson, "Comments on Quality: Oh No! It's Theory O!" *Quality Progress Magazine*, October 2000.

[4] Peter F. Drucker, *Managing for Results* (New York: Harper & Row, 1964), p. 193.

[5] These ideas are drawn from the combined thinking of Eliyahu M. Goldratt and Jeff Cox, *The Goal*, second edition (Boston: North River Press, 1992), and Jim Collins and Jerry I. Porras, *Built to Last* (New York: Harper Business, 2002).

Make money for shareholders

AND

Deliver perceived value to customers

AND

Ensure meaningful work for employees

AND

Contribute to improved quality of community life

But just stating such goals is only the beginning: How do you know you've done it? By what means will you know (for sure) that you've achieved the results? To delve deeper into these issues requires a foundation on the principles of sound measurement.

Principles of sound measurement

What are the design requirements of a sound measurement system?

1. Measures must be realistic—indicating the work done and realistic progress.

2. Measures must be actionable—provide a definitive basis for taking action.

3. Measures must be quantitative—statistical descriptions of performance.

4. Measures must be auditable—capable of undergoing third-party objective scrutiny.

5. Measures must be standardized across operating units.

6. Measures must be reliable and indicate desired results.

7. Measures must be timely indicators of performance.

8. Measures must be capable of validation externally.

9. Measures must be described in terms of defects, cost, and time.

10. Measures must be owned by managers who can act on them.

11. Measures must be predictive of final, intended business results.

12. Measures must reflect the expectations of all stakeholders.

13. Measures must be an integral element of managerial accountability.

However, not all business measurement systems have been constructed applying these principles, and they have embedded problems in their approach to business measurement. What are the problems that are most often encountered in measurement systems?

While measurement systems, performance standards, and targets are important aspects for achieving accountability, if these are not grounded in the organization's value proposition relative to its customers, then holding people accountable to these standards and this system might not create the intended result. One of the shortcomings of many TQM implementations was a basic misunderstanding regarding the meaning of the phrase "the customer is always right." What this really meant to many people was that their most important customer was their boss, so whatever the boss wanted was right—although it might or might not have been connected in any way to what the end customer really wanted! Connectivity to the final customer's expectations is the best way to establish a relationship built on trust and to demonstrate to customers an organization's continuing commitment to providing excellence in their customer experience.

In addition to this basic alignment issue, some of the more common problems observed when conducting management reviews of business measurement systems include:

1. Sub-optimization of functional performance instead of optimizing processes.
2. Barriers created by organizational reporting relationships and authority or power structures in the context of personal accountability.
3. Failure to specify decision rights: who gets to decide what, and how much spending authority is delegated to them, along with the appropriate supporting measures, performance criteria, and targets.
4. Management resistance to delegate decision authority and accountability.
5. Lack of real-time feedback mechanisms to facilitate timely improvement actions.
6. Functional interpretation of work versus process orientation.
7. Minimal use of statistical methods to gain improved insights.
8. Misinterpretation of graphs and thereby hiding performance-trend data.
9. Inappropriate selection of graphics for presenting information.
10. Systemic confusion in relationships among measures and work performed.
11. Structural conflicts among organizational results, personal evaluation, and reward systems.
12. Inappropriate use of measurement scalar data.

The last item on this list is so fundamental that an expanded explanation of this issue follows.

The use of measurement scales is possible because there are patterns be-tween the characteristics of physical objects and the properties of numerical series. The following table is adapted from an article by Stevens and com-pares the characteristics of four scales of measurement: nominal, ordinal, interval, and ratio.[6] The last column of the table lists applicable statistics for these scales. Note that the application of appropriate statistics is cumulative as the applicable scale changes from nominal to ratio—with all statistics being usable on a ratio scale.

Comparison of Measurement Scales

Scale	Empirical Operations	Mathematical Group Structure	Applicable Statistics
Nominal	Determination of equality	Permutation group[*] $f(X)$ = one-for-one substitution	Frequency count Mode Contingency correlation
Ordinal	Determination of greater than or less than	Isotonic group[**] $f(X)$ = any monotonic increasing function	Median Percentiles
Interval	Determination of equality of intervals or differences	General linear group $f(X) = mx + b$	Mean Standard deviation Rank order correlation Product moment correlation
Ratio	Determination of equality of ratios	Similarity group[***] $f(X) = ax^1$	Coefficient of variation

[*] Permutation group: a rearrangement of an ordered list so there is one-to-one correspondence with itself (e.g., the different combinations possible for enumerating the order of a deck of cards). The number of permu-tatins is calculated by: $_nP_k = \frac{n!}{(n-k)!}$

[**] Isotonic group: a function $f(X)$ that always increases as X increases (e.g., the derivative domain is a strict inequality) and thus has an observable order (e.g., as a car's speed increases, gas consumption increases).

[***] Similarity group: a relationship between two groups where X^1 is similar to X in a constant way (a) (e.g., automobile gas consumption performance that depends on the size of the engine).

▶ **Nominal scale:** Of the four scales, the nominal scale is the most limited or statistically challenged, as its numerical structure could be replaced with letters or words without changing any meaning. The nominal scale dis-plays a form of attribute data (categorical information) where groups or classes are assigned numbers for identification purposes (e.g., numbering of athletes on a sports team to readily identify them during play). Since the numbering system is so arbitrary, the only statistical calculations that are meaningful are frequency count (How many individuals wear player number 99 in a professional sports league?), the mode (What is the most frequently

---

[6] In a 1946 article, Stevens provided a classification scheme for scales of measurement that indicates the appropriate mathematical applications of different types of factors. Based on the author's observations regarding many current uses of measurement, his concerns about poorly applied mathematics in this area are still well grounded. Engineers must be concerned with the type of data used and understand what statistical methods use it properly (see S. S. Stevens, "On the Theory of Scales of Measurement," Science, vol. 103, no. 2684, June 7, 1946).

occurring player number in professional sports?), and contingency correlation (How many players with the number 99 play a particular position?). There is really only one rule that is applicable to this "measurement" scale—the rule of clarity: Do not assign the same number to different physical classes or different numbers to the same physical class. After that, arbitrariness takes over, and numerical assignments are at the whim of the creator.

▶ *Ordinal scale*: An ordinal scale is created when individual data elements are structured according to their relative rank to the other members of the set of information based on a logically ordered sequence. Rank order implies an unvarying but vague relationship among the factors, and the strictness of the underlying relationship will depend on how well the relationship between the physical information and the scale's anchor points in the categorical data describe the relationship. Typically, the ordinal scale is interpreted as describing linear relationships among the data elements, as in customer responses to the degree of satisfaction that they experience from a product. Many times, the way ordinal scales are used implies that something more than relative order is known about the information (e.g., interpreting between the "anchor points" of the scale, taking average and standard deviation of ordinal scale data, etc.). Since the scale is anchored at very specific points, interpolating between these points is not a rigorous approach to data analysis, as these points are not calibrated according to the responding customer's experience (e.g., consider the following seven-point scale with its anchor points: 1 = extremely satisfied; 2 = very satisfied; 3 = satisfied; 4 = neutral; 5 = dissatisfied; 6 = very dissatisfied; and 7 = extremely dissatisfied. What is the meaning of 4.5?). Interpolation between the original points on the scale is not a rigorous approach to data analysis. An ordered scale is appropriate for such statistics only when the successive interval between the responses is equal and the scalar function is known (e.g., linear). While mean and standard deviation are not strictly "legitimate" for this type of scalar information, they can often help to provide meaningful insight into the relationships (with caveats about how to interpret these statistics). In any case, judgments or conclusions that are drawn from such data are preliminary, and business decisions should be made with caution when relying on ordinal scalar information. But, having made this observation, there are two statistical methods that can be used "without fear" (in addition to the methods that are appropriate for the nominal scale): the median or center-point of the data as observed in the rank ordering, and the division of information in the response into percentile groups (e.g., a distribution statistic such as quartiles that uses the scale to divide information into four groups, each with 25% of the membership of the data response).

▶ *Interval scale*: The interval scale follows the general linear equation $Y = mx + b$, adding to the information contained in the ordinal data the knowledge of a fixed scale that determines the interval between observations. True zero on the scale is the point at which $b = 0$ and represents a point on the scale from which the intervals are measured. As in the temperature scale

(Centigrade and Fahrenheit), the location of the zero point might be an arbitrary designation (the point at which water freezes), but the intervals above and below the point remain constant. All basic descriptive statistics can be performed on interval data: calculation of mean, standard deviation, rank order correlation, and product moment correlation. The interval scale is the one that most measurement systems aspire to create.

▶ *Ratio scale*: The ratio scale is used when all four measurement dimensions are required: equality, rank order, equality of intervals, and equality of ratios. The ratio scale is based on a similarity group, so it is appropriate to judge that one element is "X" times greater or less than another element (e.g., twice as big or half as small). All statistics of the three previous scales also apply to the ratio scale (including also the coefficient of variation, which is ratio-based analysis of variation contribution for an element).

How can an organization prevent such problems from being embedded into the basic architecture of its measurement system? The first step toward an effective measurement system is to perform a self-assessment of the current measurement system.

Measurement system self-assessment questions

Begin the measurement system self-assessment by evaluating how effective the current state is. As a guideline for this self-assessment, consider the following questions as a starting point:

1. What do we need to know? By what means will we learn?

2. What measure provides this knowledge?

3. What action does this measure enable us to take?

4. What type of data is required to support this measurement?

5. Where is this type of data available?

6. How should the measurement data be collected?

7. How much data is required?

8. What is the appropriate way to analyze this data to gain deeper insights?

9. How can this information be presented for a clear decision?

10. What graphical analysis tool will deliver the right message from this information?

After this assessment has been made, then a map of the business enterprise must be developed to relate the measurements to the business process in order to demonstrate how these measures can be used to influence business behavior. This influence will occur at control points where the measurements are taken, and there is a managerial capability to regulate the flow of the business based on the measurement system.

Measurement control points

Measurement control points offer the opportunity to create an adaptive system—one that reads its own performance and applies a statistical algorithm (based on the use of statistical process control) to adjust its behavior and maintain the desired performance result for customers. What are the characteristics of a measurement control point?

1. A measurement control point is either a physical location or a point in time in a work process where control of the quality or quantity of the throughput can be exercised.

2. A measurement control point is used to monitor the progress of a work process, including an in-process assessment of the quality of output in a prior process as a "check" step in the process.

3. A measurement control point might also be used to regulate the flow of the work through a process and balance the workloads to ensure predictable work output.

4. A measurement control point that is also a process bottleneck can be used to evaluate the capability of the entire production process to produce the desired level of output.

5. A measurement control point can be used to evaluate proposals for resource allocation to determine if the process needs more support in order to perform at the desired level.

6. A measurement control point represents an exceptional point for the management team to exercise its oversight responsibility in order to determine progress during work operating processes.

Effective corrective action to be taken at a measurement control point must be learned through process study. A measurement system must be studied in order to establish a process capability for effective performance. What elements must be considered in a measurement systems analysis?

Elements of a measurement system

There are ten ingredients that can be contained in a measurement system:

1. *Process owner*—The manager who accepts responsibility and accountability for the design, development, deployment, and determination of performance for either a business process or a measurement system.

2. *Measurement map*—The tree diagram that illustrates how data is used to manage a business, going from the highest level of abstraction (business Y measure) to the lowest level of work process measurement (a process X measure). This diagram is developed in MECE logic—each branch is mutually exclusive and completely exhaustive so that all opportunities for understanding the process have been fully investigated and are comprehensively described.

3. *Process flow diagram*—A block diagram that depicts the high-level functional flow of either a business or work process.

4. *Business Y scorecard*—A summary breakdown of a business metric into component parts (work process X's) for daily management and monitoring.

5. *Customer dashboard*—A set of inferential measures that, taken together, present the current condition of performance from the viewpoint of a customer and show its implication for the top-tier performance measures of the organization.

6. *Deployment diagram*—A graphical description of a process flow from the perspective of work contributed by different areas—illustrating hand-offs, time line, and measurement control points (including key decision points), as well as identifying participants in each activity.

7. *Thought process map*—A detailed definition of each activity in a deployment map to illustrate key process input and output results measures, as well as the in-process measures.

8. *Decision rights matrix*—A matrix that defines the accountability for stewardship and execution of a measurement system.

9. $Y = f(X)$ *analysis tree*—A breakdown of the top-level metric into its component measures to demonstrate the linkage and operational definition.

10. *Measurement specification*—A summary of all factors involved in the definition of a performance indicator.

What constitutes a complete measurement specification?

Measurement specification

The basic information items contained in a measurement specification include:

1. Name of the performance indicator.

2. Linkage to stakeholder or customer.

3. Causal relationship between indicator and customer satisfaction.

4. Actionable relationship to the work-process activities.

5. Operational definition of the measure and its defect categories.

6. Counting rules, computations, and measurement tree.

7. Indication of measurement control points.

8. Expectation for measurement sampling and reporting frequency.

9. Display requirements for the metric.

10. Guidelines on how to interpret the metric.

11. Assignment of "ownership" of the metric for definition and execution.

Given that all this knowledge can be compiled, how should you go about creating a measurement system for your business? What steps should be taken to design, develop, and deploy an effective measurement system?

The steps that should be taken to construct a measurement system include:

1. Document the business enterprise model.

2. Document the current business measurement system.

3. Determine measurement control points and controllable options.

4. Ensure that the top-tier measures balance the requirements of all key stakeholders.

5. Validate the measurement system for critical sources of variation.

6. Identify gaps where new performance measures are required.

7. Analyze the system to link the business scorecard to work measures.

How does one use such a measurement system to manage the business better?

Business focus and organizational structure

How do organizations relate the work they do to the accomplishments required to deliver the financial returns necessary to deliver long-term success?

A chief executive officer (CEO) is the process owner for the management process of the enterprise. In the most simple, generic business model, a business consists of three core processes, as illustrated in the figure below, that define the work an organization does to accomplish its commercial objectives.

To accomplish work, an organization must have processes that create (define) the product or services (product creation process) and a means to deliver this product or service to the target market (product realization process). These two processes create and deliver the organization's value to its consumers.

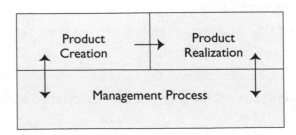

All the oversight, coordination, and direction required for management of these two processes come from the management process. At the enterprise level of business performance, the primary customer is the shareholder—the principal focus of the CEO as process owner of the management process. The CEO is the one individual who is both responsible and accountable for delivering the requirements of this customer.

At the enterprise level of a business, two factors determine long-term organizational strength:

1. Value as delivered to shareholders.

2. Value as perceived in its market.

A primary purpose of business is to build long-term value for all stakeholders: investors, customers, partners, and employees. This implies that metrics of shareholder value and brand value are critically important to sustained performance. Management must establish a win-win relationship for balancing these two factors, or there will be no sustainable short-term or long-term success.

CEOs use the management process as their dominant vehicle to ensure sustained success. A traditional management process would include actions such as planning activities, allocating budgets, executing work, collecting data, analyzing information, and reporting performance results. The actions a CEO can take to improve organizational performance, however, are limited in a way that makes the CEO's role seem more like that of the architect who establishes a design and works with craftsmen and builders to drive the design into reality.

Choices for CEOs

CEOs can focus their organizations by making only a few choices, which are the primary sources of common-cause variation in the management process. These choices include:

▶ Where should the business be focused based on the shareholder's criteria for potential profit, growth, and diversification of their investment?

▶ What is the strategic direction that will maintain persistence in the vision for sustained success and work with constancy of purpose to achieve that vision?

▶ What is the right system to develop that will provide working processes to take commercial concepts and deliver them to customers, including the support services that deliver materials and capture information that is available to improve performance and manage the processes?

▶ What is the right structure for organizing people for effective and efficient work to support business processes and centers of excellence that maintain knowledge and sustain functional expertise?

▶ How should people be recruited and developed to ensure the combination of motivation and skill necessary for delivering core competence that sustains competitive performance?

Creation of profitable growth

Fundamentally, profit is the excess of revenue beyond expenses. Profit is therefore not realized until a sale has been made to customers—or, as Drucker once commented, "The only profit center is a customer whose check does not bounce."[7] An organization achieves profitable growth when it delivers exceptional value to both its shareholders and the market.

To understand the current state of business performance (how much money an organization is making) requires an integrated view of the business—both financial and operational.

The financial viewpoint tends to provide a lagging perspective that evaluates work accomplished, while the operational viewpoint examines work that is currently being done and consuming the cost of operations in the real-time response to market forces.

A balanced and integrated understanding of both financial and operational measures is needed to gain profound knowledge of business process performance. The organization's measurement system must enlighten the top management team to both of these perspectives. To achieve profitable growth, it is essential that the actions of the organization respond to market forces in an efficient, effective, and economical manner. This requires linkage of current actions to predicted financial outcomes.

All formulas for determining profit have a similar interpretation: Shareholder value is built if the return is greater than the return of alternative investments. Shareholder value is destroyed whenever the return is less than that achieved from an alternative (usually safer or less risky) investment (for example, loaning money to a bank). In most business analyses, this threshold for return is called "cost of capital" and is used to establish a minimum return expected from internal investments to ensure management actions are focused on creating shareholder value.

Note that the measure of net assets is equivalent to shareholder's equity (total assets minus total liabilities) because net assets are calculated by subtracting total liabilities (short-term and long-term) from the sum of current assets plus working capital. When a company returns more than the cost of capital, it adds economic value to the shareholder. Value-based indicators include such performance indexes as economic value added (EVA)[8], shareholder value increase, economic value creation, and market value added (MVA). These terms are used in many companies to focus the attention of

---

[7] Jack Beatty, *The World According to Peter Drucker* (New York: Free Press, 1998), p. 23.

[8] The acronym EVA is a registered trademark of Stern Stewart.

management on the bottom line, thus delivering shareholder return that represents value on the original investment and provides a return greater than a safe investment—usually benchmarked against a government security.

The twist applied in MVA is that growth is observed between the capitalized market value of the stock and the book value of the firm's capital.[9]

Boards of directors, stock market analysts, and institutional investors evaluate corporate performance based on the ability to deliver this value. In most respects, these individuals declare themselves as surrogate customers of a CEO who is acting on behalf of the shareholder customer.

A CEO satisfies these surrogate customers through bottom-line management—delivering the profit numbers (this is sometimes called "make-the-numbers" [MTN] management). Performance of a CEO is typically judged on short-term information releases—the quarterly financial statement, which is the shareholders' report card on the profitability of the organization. This causes many CEOs to be myopic and focus only on their organization's short-term performance and to de-emphasize their responsibility for delivering results that develop long-term strength.

So, profitable growth is management's objective regarding profit. It is an imperative because it is required to offset the downward pressure on prices in the market (caused by customers wanting more value at a cheaper price) and simultaneously to offset the upward pressure on cost of goods sold from inflationary pressures (labor prices rise, and material costs tend to maintain parity with monetary buying power). Growth is required to overcome the effects of the value decrease that occurs naturally over time due to these forces. While growth in sales is necessary, it must not be achieved in a manner that eliminates profitability (for example, the cost of sales should not eliminate the marginal contribution to profit from these sales).

Six Sigma uses the language of top management to facilitate good communication with business leaders and thereby encourages more active involvement of Six Sigma Black Belts in key business decisions. Using the standard financial language of business also avoids the problem of educating business leaders in quality language—a "foreign language" that might generate misinterpretation or resistance to change.

What is customer satisfaction?

In order to understand how brand value applies to the business decisions of management, one must first understand the concept of customer satisfaction. Peter Drucker writes: "What is our business is not determined by the producer but by the consumer. It is not defined by the company's name, statutes, or articles of incorporation, but by the want the consumer satisfies

---

[9] Jonathan K. Kramer and George Pushner, "An Empirical Analysis of Economic Value Added as a Proxy for Market Value Added (MVA)," *Financial Practice and Education*, Spring/Summer 1997, pp. 41–49.

when he buys a product or service."[10] While Drucker focuses on the customer in this statement, he also appears to dismiss the value of "the company's name" or its brand. While Drucker focuses on the external criteria for value, he doesn't distinguish between the two different aspects of a purchasing decision. The economic buyer is easily satisfied with low cost at minimal functionality—this is what traditional product development delivers. However, the consuming customer has different criteria for choice. Price is only a surrogate for value as judged by economic buyers who use it to assess the relative worth of alternative decisions—however, it is not the total criteria by which consuming customers judge value. Consuming customer judgments (a user of the product, rather than just the economic buyer) are based on the job that they want to get done—how to use the product to their advantage—and they judge value by the degree of satisfaction that they have with the product for meeting their expectations to fulfill this task.

Three types of value make up this consuming customer's value perception. First is *use value*, which is a function of fitness-for-use and is typically the purchaser's highest priority—how well does it help them to get their job done? *Possession value* is the value that the consuming customer associates with the increase in self-esteem, personal pride, or gratification that occurs from the possession or exhibition of the product. *Experience value* is a value that comes from the unique and personal experience the purchaser will derive from using the product. The total perception of value will blend these types of value into an overall judgment about the worth of a product. These considerations make it difficult to engineer a single product for multiple customers with different perceptions! The more "mass customization" that must be done to meet varying customer requirements, the stronger the need for the value discipline of customer intimacy and development of in-depth knowledge of the "jobs customers need to get done!"[11]

> First, in every market there is a rate of improvement that customers can utilize or absorb...Second, in every market there is a distinctly different trajectory of improvement that innovating companies provide as they introduce new and improved products. This pace of technological progress almost always outstrips the ability of customers in any given tier of the market to use it...Thus, a company whose products are squarely positioned on mainstream customers' current needs today will probably overshoot what those same customers are able to utilize in the future. This happens because companies keep striving to make better products that they can sell for higher profit margins to not-yet-satisfied customers in more demanding tiers of the market.[12]

The point is made by Christensen and Raynor, in their book *The Innovator's Solution*, that there are two types of products or services—those that are in-

[10] Peter F. Drucker, *The Practice of Management* (New York: Harper Business, 1986), p. 50.

[11] Michael Treacy and Fred Wiersema, in *The Discipline of Market Leaders* (New York: Perseus Publishing, 1997), describe the concept of value disciplines.

[12] Clayton M. Christensen and Michael E. Raynor, *The Innovator's Solution* (Boston: Harvard Business School Publishing Corporation, 2003), pp. 32–34.

vented by sustaining innovation, and those that are invented by disruptive innovation. Sustaining innovation continues current trends for development of products or services and seeks higher returns for expanded capability to "get the customer's job done." Disruptive innovation seeks to apply new concepts in new markets—and thereby to build the capability to attack the mass market through channels that disrupt traditional sales and totally restructure the profit margins of the industry. In the case of a new-market disruption, the unserved customer either did without the function or used ad hoc alternatives. The entrepreneur's difficulty lies in identifying these unserved customers and quantifying the value of the disruptive innovation to them. Christensen and Raynor advocate the total integration of the consumer with organizational processes. It is essential to know what the customer really wants—what job are they trying to perform, and how will your product or services support them in achieving it in the most economical way? They also describe how value is created from functionality, reliability, and convenience.

Christensen and Raynor also point out that, in the typical accounting-driven analyses of the profit potential of new product developments, there is a drive to push innovation at a rate that exceeds the risk that investors are willing to bear. Decisions to grow a business are typically based on financial analysis of expected earnings that increase the rate of change in shareholder value. Thus, many organizations set "decision hurdles" that must be surpassed by forecasts of new product sales—some use a fixed percentage of return on investment (ROI), while others use a similar hurdle rate for gross profit margin. However, when these decisions are based on the uncertainties of marketing forecasts of sales and the rate is set to achieve the same (or better) financial performance as prior products, then the organization has created a bureaucratic infrastructure for killing promising ideas that do not fit into the traditional product mold—they have developed decision rules that will cause them to stay on the same trajectory of business development and sustain innovation in this pathway. In order to move to a different trajectory, fixed rules for payback (or the financial return of new projects based on analysis of the base of current customer needs) must give way to open consideration of choices based on consumers as well as the non-consumers of your products. This externally focused perspective will provide a clearer understanding of the value gap that can be filled by new products.

This is a crucial lesson: *In the process of assessing value, the customer's perspective of value must be the focus, and the way that value is interpreted must be from the customer's viewpoint, not restricted to an internal organizational viewpoint based on just accounting practice or engineering analysis.*

Philip B. Crosby stated that "the customer deserves to receive exactly what we have promised to produce."[13] That is their quality entitlement! Two issues define quality: (1) Do we really know how to make a promise that fits the circumstances of use that customers require, thereby properly setting their expectation for performance? and (2) Do we really deliver on promises that

---

[13] Philip B. Crosby, *Quality Is Free* (New York: McGraw-Hill, 1979), p. 69.

we make to customers? These two elements define a value delivery process that transfers value from conceptual design to the point where the customer is satisfied.[14]

It is important to document the customer requirements—the initial form of documentation for customer requirement is usually a table that records basic information gathered during market research. This information is then used to compile the functional specification that describes *what* it is the product will do (defined as experienced by its users). The functional specification is a contract that can be used to set customer expectation about the performance of product functions.[15] An example of an initial customer table follows:

Documenting Customer Requirements

Output	Priority	CTQ	Unit of Measure	Target	Specification
What your customer wants	How important this is to the target customer	What you can do to improve it	How you measure your performance for this factor	Desired value or level	How far it can go from its target

Specifies the operational definition of your customer requirements

Customers make comparative judgments that are limited by their personal knowledge and ability to draw conclusions from the data and knowledge at hand. However, value is based on how they rank importance of comparative attributes. Value changes and is different for every person and every situation based on many different factors. How does this work at the individual customer level? For each of the expected values, a perceived value judgment is made. This is the perception of how well the product ranks against competitors for the attribute under consideration. The customer performs a weighted average for each function (typically this is an implicit analysis) of the ratio of value perceived to value expected, using the personal importance of the function as their weighting function. From mentally assessing this ratio, the customer determines whether the product meets their needs or whether it does not. The final aspect of the consumer's choice is comparing this value assessment with the product price to make a "value for money" judgment. If the product compares favorably to competing choices for getting the job done, then a purchase is considered. An expression of this formula is given by:

[14] Gregory H. Watson, "Customers, Competitors, and Consistent Quality," *Quality into the 21st Century* (Milwaukee: ASQ Quality Press, 2003), pp. 41–42.

[15] The functional specification (FS) is the product of the DMA phases of DMADV and could be contrasted with the product development specification (PDS), which describes how the product works for the users; this "spec" is an outcome of the design phase as a deliverable for verification testing. This reminds us that the product of the design is not the prototype, but the paper that allows the product to be built consistently to its specifications.

$$\text{Customer Satisfaction Attribute Ratio} = \sum_{i=1}^{n} W_i \frac{VP_i}{Ve_i}$$

Adrian Slywotzky states that "the common lesson of diverse industry examples is the necessity to have a wide customer field of vision." Slywotzky also says that identification of emerging customers and evaluating their wealth, power, and basic needs can be critical as a first step in creating the next wave of value growth for an industry or company.[16] This is a parallel observation to that of Christensen, who advises to keep your eye on the requirements of the non-consumers of your products and services (and is supported by the QFD work of Yoji Akao). QFD also permits the tracking of emergent product concepts and the voice of non-consumers as well as design engineers across the development process.[17]

Brand value vs. customer satisfaction

So, why should the second focus of a CEO be placed on building brand value rather than on increasing customer satisfaction? Building brand value is different from increasing customer satisfaction. In reality, customer satisfaction is a relatively poor measure for CEOs because it typically uses data analysis that inherently restricts its utility as a business performance indicator. Customer satisfaction measures a feeling of the customer—a perception—based on a short-term experience, whereas brand value represents the effect of sustained customer satisfaction. The two measures should be considered together, with brand value—the long-term strength—having priority as a top-tier metric for executives.

Additionally, there are at least four major problems with the way customer satisfaction is measured. These must be corrected to ensure the best quality of information for management use in interpreting the customer dimension of business performance.

1. **How it is calculated.** Customer satisfaction is typically calculated as an average response from selected customer categories (for instance, by market segment or product application) in an attempt to indicate how well a company is doing in a market.

The problem with such an application is that the average information is relatively stable compared to the variance in responses from individual customers. But CEOs often receive complaints directly from customers and indirectly via bad press or poor product reviews.

Presenting average information results in stability that yields a false sense of security if the CEO does not listen to all available channels of communica-

---

[16] Adrien J. Slywotzky, *Value Migration: How to Think Several Moves ahead of the Competition* (Boston: Harvard Business School Press, 1996), p. 263.

[17] Yoji Akao, *Quality Function Deployment: Integrating Customer Requirements into Product Design* (Portland, OR: Productivity Press, 1990), and Yoji Akao and Shigeru Mizuno, *Quality Function Deployment: The Customer-Driven Approach to Quality Planning and Deployment* (Tokyo: Asian Productivity Organization, 1994).

tion from customers about their current concerns and issues. The average does not change much over time—most of the change is observed in the variation around the average.

2. **Limits on its validity.** Often data is collected using sampling techniques to establish the sense of the market regarding specific issues or satisfaction in general. In this approach, the sampling process puts a limit on the validity of the information. This is indicative of the power of the test and is typically described as "margin of error" within which the sample size does not provide enough resolution to distinguish among comparisons.

Not only should the margin of error be published with the data, but when comparisons are made and the distinction is within the margin of error, it is inappropriate to draw conclusions other than to say the sample size is insufficient to determine a statistical difference. If it is important to draw the distinction, then a larger sample size is required to increase the power of the test.

3. **Use of incorrect demonstration methods.** Customer-satisfaction data is often plotted as bar charts to show the averages of a satisfaction index as it changes over time (month to month). But this is not an appropriate use of a bar chart, which is more appropriately used to illustrate data accumulation, not the midpoint in a range, because when a bar chart is used to indicate average, 50% of the information is above the bar and 50% is contained within the bar. This misrepresents the central tendency.

A box plot or similar graph that shows information about central tendency and spread in customer-satisfaction response is a superior graphical format to the bar chart for displaying summary data and trend analyses.

4. **Measures present, not future, market performance.** Customer-satisfaction data is not directly related to future market performance. A customer might be satisfied with a product, but the product itself might not deliver a high degree of value for the customer's foreseeable future.

Measures of brand value consider the potential for future diversification of product lines to meet emerging customer requirements and reflect on historical performance in areas of importance to customers.

At the business level of performance, customer loyalty becomes a key measure because it establishes benefits of customer retention through sustained satisfaction that drives future purchasing decisions and thereby creates brand value.

Some of the benefits of customer retention are:

▶ It is less expensive to maintain your current customers than to replace defecting customers and repair reputation lost from losing customers.

▶ Loyal customers tend to increase their spending per transaction because they are satisfied that the value they achieve by doing so is superior to their alternative choices.

- Enhanced brand reputation within industry and among customers occurs because retention decisions result in superior feelings about a company and generate much stronger referrals to others.

- Productivity gains occur because closer relationships with customers lead to improvements in ordering information as well as better knowledge of delivery requirements that can be used to optimize production.

Should customer loyalty rather than brand value be used as an overall metric? From one perspective, customer loyalty is weaker than brand value: Loyalty is focused on a specific service relationship or product-line value, while brand value describes the relationship of an organization with its customers—the sum of all experiences as well as the anticipated experience with new or extended products.

Loyal customers might repurchase a specific product, but that choice might not extend to their purchasing decisions for all products the company produces.

Calculating brand value

Brand value is not just a singular asset in a company's asset tree. It represents a complex, interconnected, and dynamic result of the work the organization accomplishes from a market perspective. Brand value is also built into the value of the intangible assets of an organization. This increases the value of its shares and drives market capitalization.

Brand value changes as the earning stream from a brand is influenced by how well organizations manage their brand and external factors in the competitive market. Because these factors change continuously, brand value changes.

Thus, while brand value is a dynamic indicator of performance and provides a way to monitor the ongoing effect of decisions made by the management team and the competitive response, it is not a good way to identify a particular performance gap. Indeed, short-term actions to improve a brand might destroy its long-term value. A full suite of customer-satisfaction measures must be used to support the top-tier metric of brand value to ensure long-term strength is not being eroded by short-term actions that are not advantageous to customers or markets.

While brand value is a performance metric that management must monitor, it is in too immature a stage of development to be used as a monitoring statistic, and a predictible decomposition of the measure to sub-measures is not feasible.

Six Sigma and better reporting

Six Sigma logic supports management's need to deliver shareholder value by developing deeper insights than those of a purely financial measurement system. One such insight might be the inefficiencies in the hidden factories of their business.

Six Sigma performance measurement systems break down the top-tier enterprise performance metrics into their component logical relationships and cascade these measures into front-line performance measures to report work at the operational level. Six Sigma projects apply $Y = f(X)$ analysis to break down the top-tier metrics that influence the targeted customer at the business Y level—say, shareholder value—and then apply the similar MECE (mutually exclusive, completely exhaustive) logic to break down the top-tier metric into its components.

By choosing top-tier factors critical to the quality judgment of customers, the organization remains aligned with the market forces that determine its ultimate success. By cascading these metrics to levels that have line-of-sight visibility to all business areas, the organization ensures logical linkages to actions that can drive the return on business a CEO seeks.

The two sources of capital that can cause a business upset are investment capital (from shareholders) and capital generated by operations (from customers). To ensure both sources are satisfied, an organization must consistently perform on its value propositions by providing return on business that meets expectations of the capital source. This requires return on investment for shareholders as well as appropriate value for customers (total cost of ownership as a function of perceived value for the product, whether product is considered durable goods or a service provided).

Accounting for accounting

If "value creation" is a job for design and "value delivery" is a job for operations, then it follows that "value capture" is a job for accounting. How does accounting contribute to business knowledge about cost and value? Accounting measures of cost and value are the standard yardstick by which business success (profit) is measured. Managers believe that if the costs as measured during an accounting reporting period are up, then profitability will decrease—and that the converse is true. This viewpoint reflects a classical approach to accounting; however, there are alternative ways to look at issues regarding cost and value in business.[18, 19]

The logic of managerial accounting

As a prelude to further discussion, it is essential to understand the concept of management accounting that binds together the three business disciplines of marketing, engineering, and accounting. Although I typically think

---

[18] One caveat about this section—I am not an accountant, but just attempting to paint a picture of the issues and concerns that managers and engineers should have with the methods of accounting and how they affect the decisions that we make about product profitability through our pricing for value based on cost considerations.

[19] The first draft of this section was prepared as a reading assignment for graduate-level industrial engineering students in a course on the subject of value engineering that I taught at Oklahoma State University. Many thanks to my students—Tom Ukens, Frank Horn, Sam Ledbetter, Tokunbo Omaniwa, Khaali Salim, Mark Nadig, and Kalli Clark—for their most valuable ideas and insights. In addition, David Luther did much to straighten out my muddled thinking in this section.

of management accounting as the way that business "takes stock of itself," it does have a more formal definition. The National Association of Accountants (NAA) has defined the process of management accounting as the "identification, measurement, accumulation, analysis, preparation, interpretation, and communication of financial information used by management to plan, evaluate, and control within an organization and to ensure appropriate use of and accountability for its resources. Management accounting also comprises the preparation of financial reports for non-management groups, such as shareholders, creditors, regulatory agencies, and tax authorities."[20] So, how does it work? Typically, management accounting focuses on determining costs and improving work in a way that reduces cost.

The examination of product-related costs is the crux of a sound cost-management system of accounting. Fundamentally, such a system works like this: All costs are described, measured, and managed based on their nature (i.e., fixed or variable). Fixed costs are those that do not vary with product volume (e.g., the cost of production equipment), while variable costs are costs that change with product volume (e.g., the price reduction in parts that occurs as a function of volume produced or step-functions of cost increments, such as those that occur when an entire production line must be added to meet volumetric demands). Fixed costs are managed as a group based on asset type, while variable costs (product costs and profit margins—sometimes called profit contribution) are then managed on a product-by-product basis. Personal and organizational performance targets and budgets are then based on accomplishments against both of these factors independently, with overhead costs acting as a control function. Such a decision to divide the cost categories allows product pricing based on learning-curve results that are much more obvious when fixed costs are removed from the product cost and treated separately. This approach of isolating the three cost categories (fixed, variable, and overhead) and managing them as separate business factors has been taken by many companies in order to more efficiently control their cost-driving business factors. When this is done, the answers to business questions are much different than when actions are taken to control these costs using a textbook-standard cost management system.

Decisions that are made about funding individual projects are typically based on a return-on-investment analysis that assesses the profit potential from alternative applications or uses of the organization's assets. The analysis that is done to create this financial ratio of return on investment is summarized in a tree diagram that is called a DuPont analysis because it originated in the DuPont chemical company in the 1930s (described in chapter 3). This analysis forms the basis of most investment decisions made by organizations.

---

[20] Management and Accounting Web, www.maaw.info/ARTSumDefinitionofManagementAcc.htm. This site was accessed on 2 March 2005. It cites James R. Martin's definition from the National Association of Accountants, *Journal of Management Accounting*, January 1981, pp. 58–59.

Standard cost accounting

Standard cost accounting was developed in the early twentieth century. It describes the generally accepted practices for accounting for cash flows in a business, including the reconciliation of the income received with the expenditure of funds to determine the profit that is achieved by employing the assets of an organization. The standards for cost accounting are based on average performance of the organization (e.g., average labor hours expended to produce a product, average cost of materials, average time to produce, etc.). The problem with standard cost accounting lies in how it accounts for indirect cost (also called overhead, burden, or allocation). In order to determine the profit, it is necessary to consider labor and material costs (which are easy to determine), as well as to distribute the indirect costs among the many products that consume them (e.g., everything from utility costs to the costs of supervisory labor). Accountants distribute these costs using relatively simple formulas based on labor contents, product volume, or product revenue, which then distorts the actual pattern of consumption for these services. However, today labor is a relatively minor cost (especially when compared to its dominant cost contribution at the time that cost accounting was "invented")[21], and most factories are flexible enough to produce a wide variety of products, so these approximations do not provide a good method for distributing indirect costs. In addition, they don't spotlight actionable improvement areas, as they do not directly specify the cost of non-value, which should be eliminated from products and processes as waste.

Cost of poor quality

The concept of cost of poor quality (COPQ) was developed between the 1950s and 1980s as a means to improve the definition of non-value in business processes. COPQ accounts for the cost of things gone wrong and the cost of prevention for anticipated failure opportunities. COPQ makes a point-in-time calculation of the sum of failure cost, appraisal cost, and prevention cost. COPQ is most typically indexed against sales (e.g., presented as a perentage of revenue) and can be tracked from one accounting period to another, but it is not typically monitored on a regular basis. The biggest concern over COPQ is that it is not tied directly into the organization's accounting system, so it is typically done as a one-time study to calculate a point-estimate of performance—and therefore not used as a measurement for ongoing monitoring of performance. While COPQ often stimulated positive action, it did not become ingrained in the standard cost-accounting process; therefore, COPQ did not gain acceptance by the accounting community.

---

[21] While labor is no longer a dominant cost factor, that doesn't mean it can't be a cost driver that makes a significant performance difference for a company—especially when American labor costs can be orders of magnitude greater than a foreign worker's cost. Indeed, labor costs, tax advantages, regulations, laws and trade agreements, and financial-exchange rates are often drivers of the decision for plant location—especially in the current environment, where profit margins have been squeezed to the limits, allowing no room for "emotional" or "patriotic" reasons to prevail in this decision.

Activity-based cost accounting

Activity-based cost (ABC) accounting was described by Harvard Professors H. Thomas Johnson and Robert S. Kaplan in their 1987 book *Relevance Lost*.[22] It was developed as an alternative to standard cost accounting in order to provide a more relevant approach to understanding product cost so that its price (market or exchange value) could be determined better. Since most of an organization's costs are incurred to support the production and delivery of products (either goods or services), then it naturally follows that these costs should be attached to the products that incur them. In recognition of this, the ABC methodology was extended in the 1990s to include all aspects of the cost structure in an attempt to distinguish between the value-adding costs and non-value-adding costs so that the latter could be minimized, thereby enhancing business profits.

Throughput cost accounting

Throughput accounting is a management accounting system that is based on Eliyahu Goldratt's Theory of Constraints (TOC); it developed into an accounting method under the work of Thomas Corbett in his 1998 book *Throughput Accounting*.[23] It is erroneous business thinking to use transfer prices to generate an accounting of the internal profit of an organization. Speaking about this practice, the eminent business thought leader Peter Drucker said: "The only profit center is a customer whose check doesn't bounce." Thus, throughput accounting applies the TOC process constraint concept in the value delivery chain to focus on its role as a cost driver. It is the constraint that determines the throughput of a business system and the value that an organization is able to produce. By improving the performance (throughput) at the point of constraint, a company is able to better meet its goal: to make money both now and in the future.

Where did "standard cost accounting" originate and why?

Standard cost accounting originated due to the need to evaluate the cost of production and estimate the cost of new product development more effectively. The publication of a series of three articles by engineer G. Charter Harrison in 1918 marked the birth of cost accounting.[24] The factor that motivated Harrison to develop this method was the need to define the breakeven point achieved for production in the payback of the investment for product development. Although standard cost accounting was born at this time, it had to wait some time until its technology diffused to mainstream business applications. Standard cost accounting was popularized when corporations (like General Motors under Alfred Sloan) needed to standardize profit calculations to comply with the newly imposed income taxes during the administration of Franklin Roosevelt in the 1930s.

---

[22] H. Thomas Johnson and Robert S. Kaplan, *Relevance Lost: The Rise and Fall of Management Accounting* (Boston: Harvard Business School Press, 1987).

[23] Thomas Corbett, *Throughput Accounting* (Great Barrington, MA: North River Press Publishing, 1998).

[24] G. Charter Harrison, "Cost Accounting to Aid Production: Standards and Standard Cost," *Industrial Management—The Engineering Magazine*, vol. LVI, no. 5, October 1918. [Note that this magazine is a forerunner of *Industrial Engineering*, published by the Institute of Industrial Engineers.]

When trying to decrease the total life cost of a product, it is necessary to learn its design cost, production cost, material cost, service cost, and the cost of obsolescence at the end of product life.

Cost is an outcome of design—a symptom of the choices made—the root cause is the design process. However, the standard approach to cost analysis does not focus on the illumination of the root cause, just in pointing out that the cost and schedule are deviating from the plan (in accounting terms, this is called "variance analysis"). The standard cost accounting methods of variance analysis are used to determine if there is a management problem in a particular design effort. In this approach, the following key indicators are used for performance monitoring:

Where:

BCWP = budgeted cost of work performed

ACWP = actual cost of work performed

BSWP = budgeted schedule of work performed (months)

ASWP = actual schedule of work performed (months)

then:

[1]   cost variance = BCWP – ACWP

[2]   schedule variance = BSWP – ASWP

[3]   cost performance index (CPI) = BCWP / ACWP

[4]   schedule performance index (SPI) = BSWP / ASWP

[5]   schedule slip rate (SSR) = SPI × 100%

This slip rate indicator is important to new product development because time is always a cost, as it cannot be replaced once it is lost due to delays or revisions in the product requirements (as it is in the design process). When time is the cost of failure to progress, then project slippage is always the result.[25]

However, these indicators are aggregate indicators of performance for a budget center as established by the cost accounting process. The costs that are reported as actual costs include both the direct and indirect accounting costs—what is actually spent on the project, as well as other costs that are allocated to the project (e.g., overhead).

---

[25] See chapter 3 for the formula and graphical presentation method for slip rate.

In standard cost accounting, costs are allocated to things (e.g., transactions) using a standard set of cost allocation rules for usage, which are based on an agreed assignment of overhead cost to budget centers. Budget centers are allocated to the major steps in a production process as well as to the products that flow through them. The cost of the functions in a product is the accumulated costs of the materials, labor, and process costs required to deliver the functionality. However, process costs are distributed across a number of budget centers (e.g., the warehouse budget center takes on the cost of receiving parts; the sub-assembly cost centers take on the costs of making each of the sub-assemblies; and the production line takes on the cost of final assembly, testing, and packaging; while master scheduling, production engineering, material movement and expediting support, management information systems, supervisory costs, and purchasing costs are all assigned to overhead and allocated across the identifiable cost centers of the production line to determine product cost). The final cost of goods sold (COGS) is the net effect of these two ways of managing costs. Production cost (or COGS) is typically illustrated using the following breakdown of its components:

Breakout of Calculation for Cost of Goods Sold

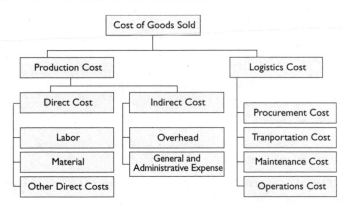

Three of these cost elements need further sub-categorization for clarity by providing a more complete description:

Other direct costs:

▶ Tooling

▶ Sub-contractors

▶ Travel

▶ Testing

▶ Design support

▶ Etc.

Overhead:

▶ Employee benefits

▶ Depreciation

▶ Insurance

▶ Supplies

▶ Energy (fuel and power)

▶ Security

▶ Taxes

▶ Etc.

General and administrative expense:

▶ Executive salaries and benefits

▶ Legal

▶ Finance

▶ Sales

▶ Marketing

▶ Research

▶ Product design

▶ Etc.

How can we decide about the lifetime
financial value of an improvement project?

There are a number of different methods used for this task. Some of the more frequently used methods include:

Breakeven analysis

Breakeven analysis is used to determine at what quantity the total costs of two alternative functions, designs, or products are equal and beyond which one alternative becomes more attractive than the other as judged solely by its cost. It is also used to determine the quantity of product that must be sold in order for the product to contribute profit to the bottom line. The application of breakeven analysis includes analyzing the cost of any change in a product from an old design to a new design in order to determine the incremental sales required to "pay back" the additional fixed and variable cost of the change. Fixed costs are those costs that do not change appreciably with changes in production rate, while variable costs are those costs that are a direct function of the unit volume of production.

Breakeven analysis uses the ratio of fixed and variable cost between the two alternatives to determine the production volume at which the two options are equal. The categories of fixed and variable cost include a number of considerations:

Fixed cost:

▶ Design

▶ Tooling

▶ Testing

▶ Publications

▶ Research

▶ Setup

▶ Overhead

▶ G&A

Variable cost:

▶ Labor

▶ Materials

▶ Packing

▶ Inspection

▶ Shipping

▶ Storage

▶ Energy (fuel and power)

▶ Maintenance

Variable costs are expressed in cost per unit that recurs as production continues (this is sometimes called recurring costs, as compared to fixed costs, which are considered non-recurring). Fixed costs are normally expressed in a lump sum using the monetary unit for organizational decision making (typically in U.S. dollars or euros). The following symbols are used in this equation:

F_1 = fixed cost of alternative 1

V_1 = variable cost of alternative 1

F_2 = fixed cost of alternative 2

V_2 = variable cost of alternative 2

X = breakeven volume of production units

By setting the two options to the breakeven point, the following equation is solved:

[6] $X = (F_1 - F_2) \div (V_1 - V_2)$

This equation is used for comparing two design alternatives; however, if comparing a change to an already-existing product, then the fixed costs must be considered as already incurred, and they should not enter into the decision, as they are "sunk" costs and cannot be recovered. Therefore, when doing an after-the-fact comparison (X_a) for a change proposal to an existing product, then F_1 must be set to zero, and the equation to use is:

[7] $X_a = F_2 \div (V_1 - V_2)$

Note that breakeven analysis deals only with cost consequences of design alternatives and does not address profit, which is a function of the total volume sold; the sales velocity determines how soon a profit expectation is realized (see payback analysis).

Net present value

Breakeven analysis considers all costs and revenues as current; however, to account for any costs or sales cash flows that are not in the current timeframe, an adjustment must be made to these terms. Fundamental to this adjustment is the performance of the cash flow concept. A cash flow represents an initial investment (cash paid out or investment made) followed by a periodic return (e.g., sales revenue) that offsets the initial investment so it accumulates into a "return on investment" (ROI). (See the illustration below, where these cash flows are represented relative to a cash-neutral position with cash investments shown as "down" arrows and cash outlays as "up" arrows.) The interest expense incurred as a cost of capital to obtain these funds (and thereby generate a return) is netted from the return prior to calculation of the cash receipt; this method is used to calculate a net present value (NPV).

Cash Flow Analysis

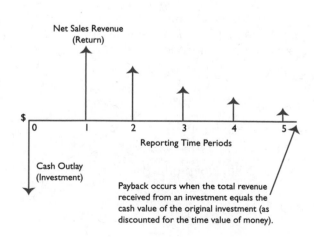

Net Sales Revenue (Return)

Cash Outlay (Investment)

Reporting Time Periods

Payback occurs when the total revenue received from an investment equals the cash value of the original investment (as discounted for the time value of money).

Thus, NPV recognizes that future cash flows are not as "valuable" in the present as the cash on hand. Thus, the value of future cash flows must be "discounted" to reflect this difference. This discounting factor (called cost of capital, interest rate, or cost of money) is typically fixed for all company investments and might include the effect of both interest cost and inflation. When the interest rate is fixed, then net present value of a cash flow is calculated by:

[8] $NPV_i = F_n \div (1 + i)^n$

   where:

   F_n = The difference between cash receipts and the expense to generate this cash in a given reporting period (n) of N reporting periods.

   i = The interest rate for cost of capital in the nth reporting period

When the interest rate is variable in these periods, then the formula becomes:

[9] $NPV(i_n - n) = F_0 + (F_1 \div (1 + i_1)) + (F_2 \div (1 + i_2)) + ...$

Note that positive NPV represents a positive surplus of cash returning to an organization, and this means that the decision should be to fund such a project, if the project priority is strategic and there are sufficient funds for the investment.

Internal rate of return
The internal rate of return (IRR) of a project is another discounted measure of investment worth or value similar to the NPV methodology. IRR is the rate of interest that equates the current value of the entire cash flow series (also called the future value) to zero. This relationship for IRR (i^*) is represented by the following formula:

[10] $NPV (i^*) = \sum (F_n \div (1 + i^*)^n) = 0$ (for n = 0 to N)

According to the decision rules used in most businesses, a project should be accepted if its IRR is greater than its cost of capital. This choice represents the same decision criteria used in calculating EVA.

Cost/benefit ratio
Another way to evaluate the goodness of an investment is to compare the sum of the cash generated to the total investment cost. This ratio is called the cost/benefit ratio (even though the total benefit might be more than financial, the calculation is limited only to the market's vote for the project—total sales activity by customers to acquire the product's benefit). The cost/benefit ratio divides the investment into two components in order to evaluate the ratio properly: the initial capital expenditure (n = 1 to m) and the annual expenses that are incurred in each reporting period subsequent (n = m + 1 to N). After a number of periods, the initial investment has been paid back (at reporting time "m"), and this term is no longer required in the equation; however, the annual costs remain for the projected manufacturing

life of the product. The benefits achieved in the period can be calculated as net benefits (period revenue minus period costs), and then this measure is a *profitability index*, as it shows the net benefit expected per dollar invested. The formula for this cost-benefit ratio is:

$$[11] \quad R = ((\sum_{n=0}^{m} (F_n \div (1+i)^n) - (\sum C_n (1+i)^{-n})) \div (\sum_{n=m+1}^{N} C_n (1+i)^{-n})$$

$$\text{where:} \quad \sum_{n=0}^{m} C_n (1+i)^{-n} > 0$$

Payback period

Payback period (n_p) is the number of reporting periods that it will take to recover an initial investment outlay. The payback period is the smallest value of n that satisfies the equation:

$$[12] \quad \sum_{n=0}^{n_p} F_n \geq 0$$

The decision rule for accepting or rejecting a project with payback period is to compare the computed payback period to the maximum acceptable period. If the maximum value is greater than the one calculated, then the project should be accepted; otherwise, the project should be rejected. Payback period is a popular measure because it focuses on the time that a firm can be "made whole again" by recovering its initial investment outlay. It operates as a constraint on project performance (no project payback period more than the maximum desired payback time) rather than a figure of merit (e.g., projects must exceed a 12% IRR).

Breakeven time

The lifetime cash flow of a project has two major patterns: a period of negative cash flow balance and a period of positive cash flow balance. The crossover between these two patterns occurs at the payback period. An alternative way to look at this decision about product investment was developed at the Hewlett-Packard Company.

HP combined these concepts into a measurement system that it calls "The Return Map," which introduces measures of performance for determining and tracking the impact of time to market and product-schedule adherence on the gross profitability of the product. This methodology introduced three sub-measures of product development performance: breakeven time (BET), breakeven after release (BEAR), and the return factor (RF). BET was developed at Hewlett-Packard in the late 1980s in order to make better decisions about funding alternative R&D project investments. BET is a discounted cash-flow analysis of the investment stream that is applied to a project and determines the time that it takes to pay back this investment once product revenues are developed (initially calculations are based on market forecasts, shifting to

$\mathcal{D}$esign for Six Sigma

revenue stream when sales revenue returns to the company).[26] BET is broken down into two components: time to market (TTM) and BEAR. TTM runs from the time a project receives first funding (has a unique accounting code) to the time it is presented in its initial commercial market (product launch), and this describes the initial area of negative cash flow. TTM focuses the product team on managing to schedule, rather than managing to costs, because analyses done by HP indicated that the highest profit levels are generated by products that meet their market "window of opportunity," which is best measured in the domain of time rather than in the domain of costs. Further, this study indicated that overspending by up to 50% of the R&D budget had less effect than just small slips in schedule on the lifetime profitability of the product. BEAR tracks the revenue stream from the time of manufacturing release of the product to the market (marketing calls this product launch) to the time that the revenue generated equals the total investment made in the product. The desired behavior is clear: A short BEAR means that the new product will contribute to business profitability sooner. The final indicator in this system is the return factor (RF). RF, an ROI-like summary measure, is the ratio of the net profit generated at a point in time to the total investment made in the product. The higher the RF, the better the R&D investment.

HP combined these measures into a graphical view that indicates the relationship among BET, BEAR, and RF as follows:

Breakeven Time: The Return Map

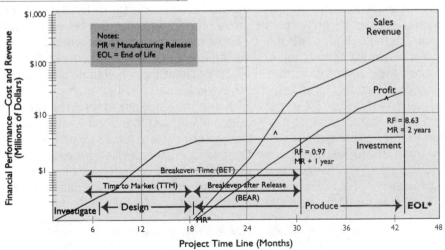

---

[26] BET originated out of an internal 1985 R&D study that HP conducted of best practices for project scheduling. Most of the teams at that time were using slip rates (days lost from the original schedule) to keep track of development timing. However, a team of managers from some HP divisions doing just-in-time manufacturing were seeking a more time-based approach that incorporated investment, return, and market forecasting considerations. This team, led by HP San Diego Division controller Gloria Kingzet, was responsible for developing the BET metric and Return Map measurement concept. After HP CEO John Young "went public" with these tools in a February 1989 cover story in *Fortune* magazine on "Speed to Market," these ideas came into the mainstream of business thinking. These concepts were documented in a book by McKinsey consultant Donald G. Reinertsen: *Developing Products in Half the Time* (New York: Van Nostrand Reinhold, 1991).

One difficulty with this family of measures is that a series of products might be interrelated through designs that use common sub-assemblies (either software or hardware). When this is the situation (it is becoming more common to develop a family of products), then the calculations should include the entire series of products, as a positive ROI might not be achieved until the nth product has been introduced. Earlier products, if considered on their own merits, might fail the investment hurdle rate. However, when the product family is considered, then the full effect of the return on the investment can be observed.[27]

What are the problems inherent in standard cost accounting?

Standard cost accounting uses averages to describe expense and income as linear functions of production volume and thereby predict the breakeven point for operations. The difference from this standard cost is called a "cost account variance," and it is typically analyzed to determine what the difference is due to (a component of cost, such as a labor or materials variance, or a component of sales, such as a price, volume, or sales administration variance). However, as these are averaged data, the presence of variation should be expected (even predicted) and use of the average only complicates the situation when all variances must be explained—in normal conditions, half of the data observations should be above the average and half below it! However, standard cost accounting systems interpret these "cost accounting variances" as the causes of profits and losses!

Further, the job of cost accounting should be to identify the difference between planned and actual performance into components that can be assigned to specific managers for performance accountability and improvement—creating responsibility centers rather than cost centers. The problem with this use of accounting variances is that they do not distinguish signal (real change) from noise (random change), and they make judgments based on generalized data as if it were fact—not just a central tendency among the data observations. Statistical analyses produce likelihood functions—which can be used to infer future behavior, but they do not dictate future results. As Dr. W. Edwards Deming so often pointed out to managers, asking for explanations of action taken to change random behavior (this is the effect of reacting to cost variances of standard cost accounting) will lead to performance insanity from chasing random causes, rather than root causes, of problems.[28]

---

[27] For more information about these measures, see: Charles House and Raymond Price, "The Return Map: Tracking Product Teams," *Harvard Business Review*, January–February 1992.

[28] In cost accounting, a variance is a difference between an actual value and a standard or budgeted value. The act of computing and interpreting variances is called variance analysis. Unfortunately, the accounting definition of variance has no relationship whatsoever with the statistical definition previously developed by Sir Ronald A. Fisher (in 1919 versus 1964, when the term *variance analysis* was introduced in accounting). In statistics, variance means a statistical measure based on the squared length of the variation vector. An analysis of variance (ANOVA) deconstructs the variance into its component terms based on both short-term (within sample) and long-term (between samples) data observations. This method defines the process for analyzing components of variation. The accounting definition means only the difference between actual and standard values. The difference between these two definitions for analysis of variance is as great as Mark Twain's comment: "It is the difference between lightning and a lightning bug." The real problem is practical: Senior managers regularly (typically this ritual occurs at month end) ask for explanations of this random variance.

Statisticians know that the first place where change can be observed is in the tails of a data distribution. The problem with standard cost accounting is that it uses the central tendency for making decisions and is totally insensitive to what is happening in the tail of the distribution for any of its performance measures. Thus, it looks at only one component of variation—mean to mean shift over time—and not at the within-sample variation, where change is first observed. What are the situations where this weakness can affect a decision? Consider "new data" that is being collected when a product is launched or the changes that occur as a product approaches obsolescence. In either case, the use of "standard" or "average" cost distorts the picture of what is happening.

Additionally, the allocation of indirect and logistics cost by simple formula to all units of production creates distortion in the understanding of actual profitability for individual products. This distortion occurs in two ways: first, as a result of averaging, the cost of poor quality is baked into the recipe for the product production, thereby obscuring a clear vision of what improvement could occur; second, by distorting life-cycle cost decisions about the product.

By simplifying the accounting system and averaging performance for indirect cost components, many of the costs of poor quality are "lost" from management visibility. Where is the cost of additional labor for sorting bad parts? It is accounted for in the same cost variance in which overtime hours are accumulated when additional products must be produced to keep up with sales. However, one of these expenses is good for the bottom line, while the other only offers a reduction in profit! What is it that management sees in its performance indicators? Management observes a variance from standard cost of labor with no clear knowledge of the cause of this variance. In a similar way, the cost of parts might be inflated to account for failures; inventory might be inflated to allow for material buffers due to poor quality; procurement costs might be increased to account for expediting and dealing with problem suppliers, etc. Also, the accounting system does not really get at customer value—it assumes that value is cost-driven. But what is the cost of a dissatisfied customer, the loss of brand reputation, or the effect on a dealer of excessive warranty claims? These costs are unknown and might even be unknowable, unless an organization really understands what it is that the customer really values! Price is only a surrogate for value as customers use it to judge the worth of alternative decisions; however, it should not be confused with the total criteria by which customers judge value. Customer judgments are based on the job that they want to get done—how to use the product to their advantage—and the degree of satisfaction that they have with the product for meeting their expectations to fulfill this task. How does the standard cost-accounting system calculate this?

Regarding the second concern, consider the product that is no longer "young" in its life cycle. Based on its age, it has probably already returned the investment that was made to create it, and it no longer requires much in the way of ongoing materials support—its production is operating more or less on automatic pilot. Yet it is being burdened with these other expenses in exactly the same way as a product at launch. As the product gets a bit older, it might be necessary to use additional expediting to get parts that are no longer in full production—or even make a "lifetime" purchase of parts to ensure that they are available for as long as the product is being produced and supported (in some firms, support lasts for ten years after final production). If the standard cost-accounting system applies the same allocation formula to all of these products, then it will overemphasize the profitability of the "mature product" by underestimating the cost of maintaining its material availability. Also, the potential profitability of the new product is being allocated costs for R&D investment payback, and this might make its profitability look different than that of the mature product. Concerns about the way product costing is performed have led to the development of cost of poor quality, activity-based costing and management, and throughput accounting.

How did the cost of poor quality come into existence?

In 1956, Dr. Armand V. (Val) Feigenbaum wrote an article in the *Harvard Business Review*[29] where he introduced the concept of the cost of poor quality. He then included this concept of quality economics in his book *Total Quality Control*.[30] This concept was popularized through its inclusion in Dr. Joseph M. Juran's *Quality Control Handbook*[31] and the subsequent adaptation by Philip B. Crosby in his book *Quality Is Free*[32], where the cost of non-conformance is related to the production of value. The primary reason this method was developed was to account for lack of visibility of waste in standard cost accounting. These methods sought to correct the standard cost-accounting system by overlaying a "quick fix" that would add this missing component to provide a more business-like basis for quality management.

What are the core concepts that define the cost of poor quality?

In the definition of cost of poor quality (COPQ), there are three major components:

▶ **Failure costs**: the cost of things that don't conform to requirements as well as the costs associated with evaluation, disposition, and consumer affairs (this is corrective action taken to repair the tarnished reputation) aspects of failure. Included in this cost category are all material and labor costs (fully loaded), and if the problem is significant enough to affect brand reputation, then there should also be a figure for the cost of lost credibility. Specific cost items include:

---

[29] Armand V. Feigenbaum, "Total Quality Control," *Harvard Business Review*, November–December 1956.

[30] Armand V. Feigenbaum, *Total Quality Control*, 3rd edition (New York: McGraw-Hill, 1991). [Note: The first edition of Feigenbaum's book was published in 1951.]

[31] Joseph M. Juran, Dudley H. Hill, and Blanton A. Godfrey, *Juran's Quality Control Handbook*, 5th edition (New York: McGraw-Hill, 1998). [Note: The first edition of Juran's handbook was published in 1955.]

[32] Philip B. Crosby, *Quality Is Free* (New York: Mentor Press, 1979).

- Engineering analysis
- Redesign
- Engineering change order
- Purchasing change order
- Documentation change requests
- Scrap
- Rework
- Warranty payments
- Product liability
- After-sales service corrective actions
- Consumer affairs or repairs to customer relationships

▶ *Appraisal costs*: the costs incurred while conducting inspections, tests, and other planned assessments to determine whether the product as it is produced conforms to its customer requirements. Customer requirements include both engineering specifications and performance expectations of both customers and markets. Specific cost items in this category include:

- Prototype inspection and test
- Tooling tryout and qualification
- Production specification and conformance inspection
- Supplier surveillance and auditing
- Receiving inspection and test
- Product acceptance testing
- Process-control inspection
- Packaging inspection
- Final test and conformance inspection
- Status measurement and reporting

▶ *Prevention costs*: the costs of all activities undertaken to prevent defects in the design and development, purchasing, and production aspects of product creation as well as continuing customer-focused "due diligence" requirements for measurement and preventive actions that must be taken as a normal part of doing business, including:

- Design reviews
- Product qualification
- Drawing assessment and quality control
- Engineering quality orientation
- Employee quality orientation

- Employee suggestion system
- Quality improvement program
- Supplier qualification
- Supplier quality training
- Specification reviews
- Process capability studies
- Tool, measurement system, and documentation control
- Measurement system calibration
- Production operator training
- Acceptance planning
- Quality audits and cost of quality certification
- Preventive maintenance
- Six Sigma program overhead (Black Belt and team expense)

Thus:

[13]   COPQ = failure costs + appraisal costs + prevention costs

What are activity-based cost analysis and activity-based management?

Activity-based management applies the methods of ABC to recognize the unique impact on cost structure of each product, customer, brand, and distribution channel. All of these factors make different demands on an organization's resources and therefore cannot be accurately consolidated into a single cost structure. Cost cannot be controlled at the macro level (as implied by an allocation system, with its emphasis on the balance sheet and income statement); therefore, ABC focuses on the facility-level expenses. ABC creates a hierarchy of activities and assigns costs to each activity that incurs them. The activities available for assignment include four categories:

▶ **Unit activities**: tasks performed at a specific production location or operation for a single part or product component (e.g., the activity of machining a part, welding two parts, or inspecting a sub-assembly).

▶ **Batch activities**: activities that are performed on a number of parts simultaneously (e.g., setting up production equipment to process parts (like changing the mold in an injection molding machine).

▶ **Product activities**: work that is required to develop the overall capability to produce a product (e.g., receiving inspection, material handling, process engineering, etc.).

▶ *Facility activities*: any activities that sustain operation of the entire production facility (e.g., plant management or utilities).

ABC unit, batch, and product activity costs are allocated to a product while the costs of facility activities are kept separate as a different slice of the financial performance picture. To clarify how costs are really consumed and how value is actually produced, ABC develops pseudo profit centers by grouping all costs according to the activities and separating the "blurred overhead" into discretely attributable sources of variation—those factors in the business that are responsible for developing these costs (e.g., brand identity, marketing channel support, customer service, production, etc.).

ABC can be applied broadly to improve the management of an entire enterprise through the careful questioning of business considerations that drive costs by comparing the profit made to support various brands, distribution channels, customers, or geographic regions. Once the relative profitability of each is known, then ABC focuses on improving those that are less profitable. For example, consider two of these profitability investigations:

▶ *Brand profitability*: Discrete costs associated with branding include the costs of unique packaging, promotion, advertising, and the support system for maintaining the brand reputation in the market (e.g., brand managers and brand research). In order to know if a brand is profitable, all the unique costs must be identified and compared to the revenues earned by the brand. By performing this analysis of brand profitability across brands, management can better understand how market dynamics affect their product portfolio.

▶ *Customer profitability*: Begin by calculating the profit contribution from major or key customers (customer sales revenue minus product-related expenses) and then subtract the costs of sustaining this unique customer (e.g., technical support or marketing and promotional support), which are independent of volume and mix of the products sold. These costs include travel and engineering costs required to support customer demands, costs of calling on the customer and maintaining customer information to support their operations and marketing, and all the administrative support costs of maintaining the customer (e.g., assessment of credit ratings and financial support for their payment performance).

Once costs have been understood using this approach, there are two types of management decisions that are available when applying ABC for management improvement: product re-pricing and reduction of resource consumption.

▶ *Re-pricing products*: Raise the price on those products that make heavy demands on support services from the company (e.g., material support like expediting), and lower the prices on the higher-volume products that have been subsidizing the rest of the products (by the Pareto rule, 80% of the profit is from 20% of the products of an organization). If a re-pricing strategy is successful, then it should result in a product mix that generates more revenue for the same resource consumption while making fewer contingency demands on the use of resources.[33]

▶ *Reduce resource consumption*: Perhaps more important, companies can seek to improve the performance of their resources by decreasing the number of times that activities are performed (thereby reducing transaction volumes) by combining product options, changing the approach for supporting individual customers, or reducing the resources required to support the current products and customers (e.g., by redesigning products to use more common parts, reducing the base of suppliers, or customizing products at the final stage of production so that less work in process inventory is kept at "unique" product levels in their bill of materials). Another consideration might be the application of quality improvement programs that reduce setup time costs, eliminate defects, or facilitate the flow of the factory to increase efficiency, or the adoption of new information systems to integrate the stream of data in the order-fulfillment process.

How does the ABC approach improve on standard cost accounting?

In order to discover what actions are most appropriate to improve selling margins and also reduce operating expenses, managers need to understand the patterns of resource consumption at the micro-level of work activity within the organization. This is the point where positive action can be taken to reduce costs and thereby improve selling margins. ABC provides an activity-level, in-depth, micro-viewpoint of what the organization does to consume resources or generate cost. Unlike traditional standard cost accounting, ABC directly prescribes actions through its links into the activities, thereby allowing an improved level of decision-making. Costs are not intrinsically either fixed or variable. ABC helps managers understand the sources and costs of variability more thoroughly than standard cost accounting, which tends to blur the sources and costs of variability. As a result of the improved visibility of variability, managers have the opportunity to make better decisions about the application of scarce resources. However, some have questioned: "Does ABC-based thinking go far enough?" This question has led to the development of the concept of throughput accounting.

What is throughput accounting?

The Theory of Constraints (TOC) views any company as a system. One of its most fundamental concepts is the recognition of the important role that the system's constraint plays, and because of this concept, throughput accounting does not allocate costs to products. In a controversial shift from standard cost accounting, one of the basic ideas of throughput accounting is that if we want to make good decisions, we should not calculate the cost of products.

---

[33] The basis for re-pricing is given as products making heavy demands on support services. Not always is this a good reason to re-price. There must be a look into the reason for the resource demand change before changing prices. I have witnessed cases where price increases are recommended, only to start a slow death spiral of successive price increases until the product is no longer saleable. In these cases, the price increase was a self-fulfilling prophecy. In reality, the component was priced out of the market, and if it had been priced more competitively, the volume would have gone up, reducing the net individual cost. Standard cost accounting does not point out these deficiencies.

TOC uses a chain analogy to exemplify the principle of constraint. If we pull a chain, where will it break? The chain will break at its weakest link (and the chain has only one weakest link). If we want to increase the chain's strength, what should we do? We should strengthen its weakest link, this system's constraint. Strengthening any other link before strengthening the weakest link would be a waste of time and resources, because the weakest link determines the maximum performance of the entire chain. Therefore, a system's constraint dictates its performance. If we want to increase a system's performance, then we have to identify and explore its prime constraint.

When a company has a constraint in its production process, it has to decide which products are more important to the company, as it does not have enough capacity to sell everything the market wants. This constraint is the time available for production at the constraint resource. To increase the company's throughput, it must maximize the use of this time.

The company wants to sell the products that have the highest throughputs and, at the same time, sell the products that use less time on the constraint. A problem occurs when comparing two products—one with a higher throughput and another that uses less time on the constraint. How to decide which one is best for the company? To solve this problem, the performance measurements must take into account the need to maximize the company's throughput. The conflict is that on one hand we have the product's throughput, and on the other hand we have the minutes it uses of the constraint. To decide which one contributes the most to the company's bottom line, it is necessary to divide the product's throughput by the time it uses on the constraint, finding the product's throughput per time of the constraint. But this measure identifies only the most profitable product when the company does not have enough capacity to sell everything the market wants.

When the company has more capacity than the market demands, the constraint is not the company's available capacity. In this case, the criterion of comparison between products should be throughput per unit, because there is no resource limiting the company's performance. In this case, any product's sale whose price is bigger than the total variable cost, and that doesn't increase operating expense, contributes to the increase of the bottom line.

According to Goldratt, a company's goal is to make money now and in the future. To form a bridge between net profit (NP) and return on investment (ROI), the TOC uses three indicators. To judge if a company is moving toward its goal, one must answer "Three simple questions: How much money is generated by our company? How much money is captured by our company? And how much money do we have to spend to operate it?"[34] These measurements are intuitively obvious. These questions are converted to formal definitions as follows:[35]

---

[34] To get an idea of how these three questions show whether a decision takes the company toward its goal, read chapter 4 of Eliyahu Goldratt's book The Goal.

[35] Eliyahu Goldratt, The Haystack Syndrome: Sifting Information out of the Data Ocean (Croton-on-Hudson, NY: North River Press, 1990), p. 18.

▶ **Throughput**: the rate at which the system generates money through sales—all money that enters the company minus what it pays to its vendors. This is the money that the company has generated. The money paid to the vendors is money generated by other companies.

▶ **Investment**: all money the business system invests in purchasing things that it intends to sell. This measure and the conventional accounting measure "assets" might be mistaken, but they are very different when applied to work in process and finished-goods inventory. "What value should we attach to a finished product stored in a warehouse? According to the definition given above, we are allowed to assign just the price that we paid to our vendors for the material and purchased parts that went into the product. There is no added value by the system itself, not even direct labor."[36] The value given to the work in process (WIP) and the finished-goods inventory is their totally variable cost (TVC). One of the objectives here is to eliminate the generation of "apparent profits" due to the cost-allocation process. With this methodology it is not possible to increase short-term profits by increasing WIP and finished-goods inventory (delaying the recognition of some expenses that will certainly decrease profits of future periods).

▶ *Operating expense*: all money the system spends to turn investment into throughput. "Taking added value out of inventory does not mean that we do not have these outlays of money."[37] There is no added value to the product. "Operating expense (OE) is intuitively understood as all the money we have to pour into the machine on an ongoing basis to turn the machine's wheels."[38] Wages, from the salary of the company's CEO to the direct labor, rents, energy, etc., are not classified by TOC as fixed, variable, indirect, or direct cost. OE is simply all other accounts that did not go into either throughput or investment. The increases or decreases in OE are analyzed on a case-by-case basis, where its impact on the bottom line is taken into account.

How does throughput accounting evaluate cost and value?

Simply stated, cost is not calculated in throughput accounting, and value is a function of the return on investment. To calculate the throughput per unit of each product, we need to subtract the TVC from its selling price. TVC is the cost that varies for every extra unit produced (in many cases, this is only the cost of raw material). TVC describes how much money the company generates from selling one additional unit of the product. In order to calculate the company's total throughput, all we need to do is add the total throughput of each product (which is the throughput per unit multiplied by the sales volume).

---

[36] *Ibid.*, p. 23.

[37] *Ibid.*, p. 29.

[38] *Ibid.*, p. 18.

TOC says that these three measures are sufficient for us to make the bridge between NP and ROI and the managers' daily actions. The formulas describing this relationship are:

When:

T = total throughput

OE = total operating expense

I = total investment

then:

[14] net profit (NP) = T − OE

[15] return on investment (ROI) = (T − OE) ÷ I[39]

Using these three measures (T, I, and OE), we can describe the impact a decision has on a company's bottom line. The ideal is a decision that increases T and decreases I and OE. Throughput per time of the constraint or the throughput per unit should never be the only measurements taken into consideration to evaluate a decision. In all decisions, it is necessary to quantify its impact on the company's NP and ROI. But any decision that has a positive impact on ROI is a decision that takes the company toward its goal. The final judgment about the goodness of a business decision should be made using the ROI criteria.

How does this TOC method differ from standard cost accounting and ABC?

A fundamental tenet of standard cost accounting is the amortization of costs in the pricing of goods—leading, in part, to the practice of locally optimizing all equipment for maximum output to improve cost/performance (e.g., to maximize the equipment utilization performance measure)—which generates excess inventory and waste, since the system is constrained at some point from production, and work in process must stand idle at this bottleneck, adding further cost and not producing any value.

While ABC seeks to improve the way that costs are accounted for in the product price and used in decision making, it still uses the same basis for calculations as standard cost accounting—averaging performance to obtain a central tendency for estimating costs. ABC also develops costs for the entire business system in order to determine its cost-effectiveness—thus, decisions are optimized locally at each process step, rather than at the equipment level in standard cost accounting, to obtain an effective business system.

---

[39] Note that Goldratt's use of ROI differs greatly from that of standard cost accounting, where the return is calculated as revenue minus costs to produce the revenue, and investment is the initial capital investment to produce this stream of revenue. Mark Twain's lightning-bug analogy does indeed strike twice!

On the other hand, throughput accounting turns cost accounting inside out by taking costs out of the equation. This occurs because throughput accounting reportedly corrects the misaligned focus on local optimization by standard cost accounting (at the machine level) and ABC (at the process level) by emphasizing globally optimized throughput of the entire facility, based on the TOC holistic perspective of production as a unified system governed by a single constraint. Thus, efficient production at this constraint regulates the value produced in the entire production facility (when it has been analyzed for its most profitable product). However, while TOC applies a simple, empirical rule to determining the location of a constraint, in a complex system, the use of statistical methods (particularly analysis of variance) can be helpful to determining the sensitivity of the entire system to performance at the constraint—especially with a fragile system, where the constraint changes location as a function of the production characteristics of products in the facility.

Expressing shareholder value

What is the opportunity for applying a variation-based financial measure of success? One approach to stating profit in shareholder terms when the business is capital-intensive and therefore uses return on capital employed (ROCE) as its principal indicator of performance is as follows:

$$[16] \quad ROCE = \frac{\text{Net sales after taxes}}{\text{Capital employed}}$$

Every organization should work out its own unique approach to define a related efficiency-loss function for its shareholders' investments based on the specific business model it uses to evaluate profitability.

Another definition of return on capital is after-tax operating income (which is also called net operating profit after tax) divided by capital invested (the sum of interest-bearing debt and equity) and excluding long-term tax liabilities.

Thus, ROCE is not inflated by the unpaid tax liabilities (which must be paid before returns are provided to investors), and it represents a more shareholder-friendly perspective on the profitability of a firm. A common-sense definition of ROCE is "the economic value of a capital investment when it is performing at its normal level of process capability."

While this performance measure indicates return (revenue) as a function of investments, it contains an implicit assumption that the financial measurement system ignores: The level of observed performance does not represent the optimum design efficiency, so the return achieved for a given capital investment represents a loss from the design performance that was purchased when the equipment was new.

This means that when management relies on ROCE as an indicator of performance, it is looking only at actual achievement and ignoring the need to close the gap to the equipment's designed level of performance. Capital should be more efficiently employed, but diminishing performance often conspires against the process, creating an implicit bias against sustaining optimal performance. Management simply has no idea that using the standard cost basis of measurement contained in ROCE will not lead it to achieving the performance it was entitled to obtain based on the original equipment design.

How can management estimate what this achievable level of capital efficiency is and evaluate the potential gap in capital effectiveness if this gap is closed? One way is by calculating a different ratio, $ROCE_{ADJUSTED}$, in which a ratio of capital efficiency is used to estimate the loss of performance from the initially purchased or original performance design:

$$[17] \quad ROCE_{ADJUSTED} = \frac{1}{\text{capital efficiency index}} \times \frac{\text{net sales after taxes}}{\text{capital employed}}$$

Net sales is from the annual cash flow due to a specific capital facility, and the capital efficiency index is a slip ratio that indicates a reduction from the initial capability of the capital equipment when the equipment was first purchased or last upgraded, therefore:

$$[18] \quad \text{capital efficiency index} = CEI = \frac{C_{pk}}{C_p}$$

CEI is the performance percentage loss in performance from the design process capability (C_p) measured using the actual or achieved process capability (C_{pk}) for short-term process performance in a system that is operating under conditions of statistical control.

How should $ROCE_{ADJUSTED}$ be interpreted? The CEI illustrates the magnitude of impact in the loss of the initial performance (the original design capability, which is also called the "nameplate performance" for some types of capital equipment) as reduced to the current operating performance—the achieved performance resulting from process variation.

When CEI is multiplied by ROCE, it indicates potential financial effectiveness of the original capital investment. It must be noted that $ROCE_{ADJUSTED}$ changes when specifications are tightened—whenever the customer asks for more or better in new generations of products, and as production processes become better when technology improves and allows the specifications to get tighter.

These shifts mean $ROCE_{ADJUSTED}$ does not remain fixed and must be constantly updated. It becomes a critical business assumption subject to review during annual planning cycles. Changes in $ROCE_{ADJUSTED}$ document the fact that there is great value in challenging process specifications to improve and continuously updating business metrics to reflect the current ability to deliver the results that customers seek.

When interpreting the CEI, remember the design or purchased efficiency represented by C_p (process capability is the ratio of the specified performance to the process variation) is the best level at which a process should be expected to perform on a consistent basis. Degraded performance results in the C_{pk} (which has been shifted from the C_p based on long-term degradation functions, such as corrosion or wear effects as observed in sampled data).[36]

As process performance is optimized and the C_{pk} approaches the value of C_p, the ROCE result approaches the level that should have been anticipated in the initial capital budget investment decision. Losses due to the difference between C_p and C_{pk} represent a rough-order magnitude estimate of the financial improvement that could be obtained by improving performance of this capital equipment to the level at which it was initially designed. Two examples might help make this concept more understandable.

Example 1.
An organization purchased a capital facility for $10,000, and its nameplate design capability was 2.0. Today the facility is operating at a C_{pk} of 0.67 while contributing $2,500 to annual sales. The potential ROCE ($ROCE_{ADJUSTED}$) would be 75%, which is significantly greater than the 25% return calculated for ROCE using the standard financial ratio definition.

The gap between these figures represents potential improvements in capital efficiency that could be available if the process were operating within its design parameters. The CEO should find out what is inhibiting this result.

Example 2.
The process yield on a piece of capital equipment operating on a single shift was 97%. However, the design capability of the process advertised a throughput of 5,000 units per hour, while the 97% yield had a throughput of only 1,782 units.

The process yield was based on the performance against forecast, which was in turn related to standard production volume used in cost-accounting analyses. This approach to calculating expected performance means a forecast is anticipating achievement of the average past performance observed in calculating the cost-accounting standards.

If this rate of throughput is compared to the original design capability, this result does not show the same high performance indicator as the classical process yield. Instead, it shows the achieved performance is degraded from the design capability, and the actual performance of this equipment is only 35.6% of its original design capability. Management will perceive the ROCE for this equipment as only a small fraction of what it could actually be able to contribute to overall business performance.

---

[36] The best information about process-capability studies is contained in the book by Davis R. Bothe, *Measuring Process Capability* (New York, McGraw-Hill, 1997).

This nonproductive contribution is masked by standard accounting practices used to calculate performance expectations and does not indicate the real potential of a system to deliver value. If this equipment represents a production bottleneck, its potential for improving $ROCE_{ADJUSTED}$ might be significant for the entire business process as it paces the stream of value-adding activities. Improving its performance will directly benefit productivity and increase the value of the entire business.

It is clear that $ROCE_{ADJUSTED}$ can be a useful eye-opener for CEOs, providing feedback on the implementation of their past capital-investment decisions and pointing them toward areas where process inefficiencies are currently being lost without their knowledge. This metric can help transition a hidden factory into a visual factory.[41]

What further developments must be made to improve standard cost accounting?

One major fallacy in modern business is the assumption that the value of a product to a customer is determined by the cost incurred in making the product. The value of a product to the customer is only the value as judged by that customer.[42] Once this stark tenet of business is accepted, then value engineering can begin its work to resolve the chronic issues facing organizations of poor value (this is an external business focus) and high cost (this is an internal business focus).

Based on the perspective presented in this book, the next steps required for improvement of accounting appear to be clear—integrating the statistical approach to variance analysis, but using financial and time-based measures rather than quality measures as the indicator of throughput. Quality is a "must be" attribute in this system—perhaps Philip B. Crosby was right when he focused on the "Zero Defects"[43] concept as a means to productivity improvement—this approach will abbreviate the considerations for costing as well by eliminating the source of variation due to quality problems!

---

[41] There are many different performance measures that are used in accounting to evaluate different aspects of business performance. However, one metric that is critical for assessing the short-term strength of an organization is working capital. Working capital is the total cash that is available for operations (e.g., paying suppliers, employees, and investors—it represents the liquid assets that are available for production of further revenue that can be applied to the cost of operations). Working capital is calculated as current assets in excess of current liabilities. The monitoring of working capital is perhaps the best accounting indicator of the effectiveness of an organization's managerial performance, operational strength, and capacity for growth.

[42] Companies using enterprise requirements planning systems (such as those from SAP or Oracle) have an additional problem in that their accounting is driven in a specific way, which is not always suitable for the products they produce or for supporting activity-based cost analysis and value estimation. The tendency is to make the accounting system fit all product lines and divisions to the detriment of real cost analysis. In many of these systems, someone with proper access and authority is required to manage account codes and break down accounts into their component elements. This does not make it easy to determine function costs or value. The result is that engineering often maintains its own financial records to compare costs and justify projects without any confirmation that this system adequately reflects the official accounting system.

[43] For a description of Philip B. Crosby's approach to Zero Defects, see his 1979 book *Quality Is Free*.

Chapter 5
Engineering Value into Designs

*"There is only one valid definition of a business
purpose: to create a customer."*

~ Peter F. Drucker

In the foreword to this book, a three-step model for producing quality was presented as the framework for developing the concepts of design for Six Sigma. How does the concept of engineering value into products fit into this framework, and what work is actually done to support the development or enhancement of value in products and processes? Peter Drucker once observed: "An adequate information system has to include information that makes executives question [their business assumptions]. It must lead them to ask the right questions, not just feed them the information that they expect."[1] In order to learn what information is essential to stimulate business growth, let's look inside the model for quality from the engineering perspective and examine its performance drivers, and then we might be able to ask four "right" questions:

▶ How do you know if you are doing this right?

▶ How do you know that the features and functions that have been designed into your products actually address the customer's needs in an effective manner?

▶ How can you design your work processes so that they produce a consistent output relative to the design specification?

▶ How do you integrate the cross-functional business processes to allow the different functional areas to collaborate in a process organization?

---

[1] As quoted in Gregory H. Watson, "A CEO's Obligation Is to Drive Return on Business," *Six Sigma Forum Magazine*, August 2002.

The steps in the three-phase model for delivering quality[2] address three key issues: understanding what customers want; making customers a commercial promise; and delivering on this promise to customers. Each of these steps is part of the proposition of adding value to the job that customers need to get done. In the first step, technology that can enhance a customer's work is identified and evaluated for commercial worthiness. In the second step, innovation is applied to match the technology to the customer's job and create a promise about performance in the customer's environment. In the third step, quality is the result of things done correctly—promise-keeping once the goods have been delivered. Across these three steps, the value proposition for customers is developed, defined, and delivered. Thus, technology and innovation are the drivers of quality performance results.

The first question to address inquires about customers. How do you know if you are doing this right? Harvard Professor Clayton M. Christensen suggests that there are three categories of customers that must be considered to determine if you have an appropriate customer value proposition. He recommends investigating those customers who are overshot (customers who historically have bought all new products, but have stopped purchasing further improvements in either function or performance), undershot (customers who purchase a product but are very frustrated with its limitations and are willing to pay more to get what they want), and non-consumers (people who lack the resources to purchase your current product, but have a similar job that they need to get done from ad hoc resources, or they pull together a lesser solution and force themselves to be satisfied).[3] All three of these categories produce strategic vulnerability in an organization's value proposition for product leadership, and each also represents a different opportunity for adding value.

The second question inquires about the nature of products that are developed to do the customer's job. How do you know that the features and functions that have been designed into your products actually address the customer's needs in an effective manner? This second question is embedded within the first question. This means that answers must be discovered for the following questions: Which customers are most important (and what is the standard for judging importance)?; What are their needs (and how will you discover what is necessary for them)?; Which needs have priority (and how do you assess priority across different customers, requirements, and applications)?; and How effectively have these needs been addressed in the design?

The third question inquires about the nature of the processes that produce these products. Products are produced in processes, and processes have variation in input materials, process operations, and people skills. How can you design your work processes so that they produce a consistent output relative to the design specification? In other words, can you make a predict-

---

[2] This three-phased model for quality is presented in the foreword to this book, where it is more fully described.

[3] Clayton M. Christensen, Scott D. Anthony, and Erik A. Roth, Seeing What's Next: Using the Theories of Innovation to Predict Industry Change (Boston: Harvard Business School Press, 2004), pp. 4–5.

able product? The secret in creating predictable product is to produce it in a predictable work process. Predictable work processes aren't achieved by accident; they are the creation of a robust design effort—a work process design that accepts variation in the inputs without transferring this variation to the outputs. When such a design has taken place, then the revised work process is capable of producing consistent results.

The fourth question asks about the operation of the overall system. How do you integrate the cross-functional business processes to allow the different functional areas to collaborate in a process organization? Work processes do not operate in a vacuum. They operate within the context of an overall management or business process. The basic structure of an organization contains at least three cross-functional processes: the product-creation process, the product-delivery process, and the management process. The product-creation process goes from concept to commercialization; the product-delivery process goes from order to cash; and the management process goes from vision, to plan, to implementation, to the post-mortem review. Other cross-functional, global processes could include a shared services center of excellence or supply chain management.

One of the basic quality tenets is that all work is a process and that every process can and should be improved. Processes are a sequence of work activities, procedures, or tasks that are coordinated to achieve common objectives or produce desired outputs.

What work does an organization do?

The process for answering these four questions defines strategic work for a business. How do you know if you are doing strategic work? First, the different types of work must be identified. Work can be segmented into five distinct categories:

▶ **Value-added work**: increases worth of a product or service and adds real value or worth to the output of the work process; transforms raw material or information to meet customer requirements and is something the customer is willing to pay for!

▶ **Necessary work**: required to keep the organization operating.

▶ **Rework**: required because something was not done right the first time.

▶ **Unnecessary work**: all other tasks not identified above.

▶ **Not working (but being paid)**: can be either authorized (vacations and holidays, illness, breaks, training, etc.) or unauthorized (waiting time, idle time, breakdown time, setup time, etc.).[4]

Work can also be segmented according to essential or strategic work. Essential work accomplishes the routine tasks required to manage the business on

---

[4] Idle time is not necessarily bad—too high a utilization rate is what will lead to an exponential increase in overall cycle time.

a daily basis. Based on the breakdown of work categories above, essential work includes value-added work, necessary work, and authorized "not working" time. On the other hand, non-essential work involves rework, unnecessary work, and unauthorized "not working" time. Strategic work prepares the organization for the future. The basic characteristics of strategic work are described in chapter 1 and are summarized in the figure below:

Strategic Work

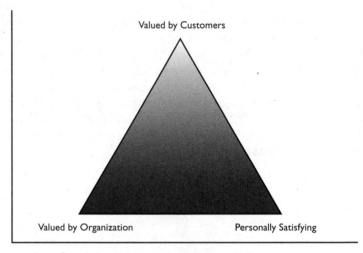

Requirements:
- Management Commitment
- Skilled People
- Strong Support Infastructure

In product design, strategic work involves the three elements of value production: value creation, value delivery, and value capture. Value creation is the process of identifying customer needs, product functions, and production processes that can be combined to deliver a value proposition to customers that meets their needs better than alternative choices. Value delivery is the process of realizing these values in a product that is delivered to customers and functions according to design and customer need in the customer's environment. Value capture is the process of building long-term business relationships that produce both brand value and shareholder value. "In a CEO's world, two factors dominate and drive long-term organizational strength: first, value as delivered to shareholders; second, value as perceived in its market."[5]

In this strategic work, value itself has several grades of meaning. The economic value of a process is a function of the transactions that it accomplishes. The more transactions that add value to a product or service in a unit of production time, the higher the value-adding capability of the process.

[5] Gregory H. Watson, "A CEO's Obligation Is to Drive Return on Business," *Six Sigma Forum Magazine*, August 2002.

Efficiency occurs when the volume of transactions of process throughput (production units that have valued functions designed into them) increases, and, at the same time, the cost per transaction decreases. This measure of value is mostly internal, but it transfers as a value function to customers through product-pricing decisions. The other components of value are brand value and shareholder value, which involve both an irrational, subjective component and a rational and more objective component. Neither of these two measures is a perfect predictor of organizational performance. Thus, the focus of value production through design engineering is on the value created by organizational throughput—both in product value and through cost-effective, efficiently operating work processes. Here, design includes both product design and process design as accomplished by a manufacturing engineering technology support organization.

What essential and strategic work occurs in an engineering design project?

What is the strategic work of the engineering design process? The process of value creation, value delivery, and value capture is usually translated into a new product development process or sometimes called a concurrent engineering process. This approach to product design, development, and delivery consists of a series of phases and decision gates that are described in chapter 2 as the product line management (PLM) process. Major phases where this process creates value are product planning, product development, and product management. Key physical outputs include:

▶ *Conceptual design*: Value is added through the alignment of the product concept to the real-world requirements of customers with differentiation from competitors' products. Market and commercial sources of risk are reduced through research of customer product-related concerns, issues, and desires and then sorting the design concepts that result according to customer-oriented performance criteria.

▶ *Laboratory prototype*: Value is added through demonstration of the readiness of advanced technology for full-scale production and by performance demonstration of the functionality required for customers. Technology risk is reduced through an assessment of its reliability growth and elimination of the major potential failure modes from the product design.

▶ *Production prototype*: Value is added by demonstrating its production readiness with full-scale production version tooling, production-ready assembly lines along with production of a sufficient product volume to satisfy market launch, lifetime reliability testing, and regulatory compliance testing. Production risk is reduced through the exercise of the full-scale manufacturing capability in a dress rehearsal for product release to the production environment.

▶ *Production product versions*: Value is added by servicing customers with a product that is ordered, on time, and with the right quality and the proper support services to create an exceptional customer experience on installation and first use. Commercial risk is reduced through careful product-launch planning and setting the proper expectations for the initial customer experience.

▶ *Cost-reduction product version(s)*: Value is added to the production version by reducing product cost while enhancing reliability, maintaining functionality, and reducing customer complaints. Production risk is reduced by eliminating problem parts, reducing the part count, consolidating functions, and replacing suppliers that have irreparable problems.

Mid-twentieth-century Austrian economist Joseph Schumpeter defined innovation as the planned abandonment of the past and creative destruction of the familiar way of doing things. For a Six Sigma company, the product-creation process is innovation at work—it is the planned abandonment of past products and technologies to embrace newer ones that deliver more value to customers. Innovation is a critical success factor for the product-creation process, and innovation itself will also follow a process!

Improving the product-creation process requires that the management team take a tough look at their work processes. They must determine what the customer values, how much time is spent producing the customer-desired value, how much time is spent in other essential activities, how much work in process exists between the process steps, the cycle time of the process flow as compared to the order cycle time from customers, and the best match of product features, functions, and form to meet the cross-section of targeted customers or market niches. Throughout this entire process, management should seek to understand how value is added to the product by the process and how value is destroyed by the process. This is the starting point for creating profound knowledge. As illustrated in the figure below, the greatest opportunity for potential savings, or value addition, occurs during the

Opportunities for Potential Savings

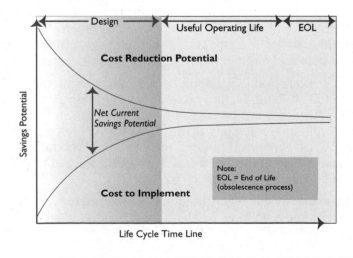

Ðesign for Six Sigma

design phase of a product's total life cycle. Thus, getting the product right in design provides the highest potential return on investment for business resources expended to continuously improve.

What is value addition?

Value addition is the incremental increase in the worth of a product or service that occurs at a single process step due to the actions that have been designed into that step. For instance, in a mechanical production process, the steps of cutting, polishing, and finishing can be considered to be value adding because each enhances the customer's image of the product. In the service industry, steps like order-taking, inquiry response, and service delivery are all steps that a customer values and help make up a definition of the worth of the service process. However, activities like material movement have no intrinsic value to the customer and do not add to their perception of the worth of a product. The material movement steps add cost to a product without adding value, and therefore they should be minimized in the production or service-delivery process. The value stream of a product is the sequence of activities that define a product and create its value as perceived by its customer.[6] Creation of exceptional customer value should be the overarching product-design goal!

What is value?

In value engineering, value is judged from the viewpoint of a consuming customer. Value is the customer's utility function combined with the esteem value that is based on brand and feelings—which combines into the exchange value (price) of the product. Customer-perceived value ("Was this worth what I paid for it?") is a function of the customer's expectation combined with their perception of the experience that they had in using (consuming) the product. In the world of Six Sigma, this concept of value identifies the critical-to-satisfaction (CTS) functions of a consuming customer and bases a product's value proposition on the ability to fulfill these functions.

Six Sigma designates functions as CTS when they are essential work for getting the customer's job done. Six Sigma defines the relationship between the function as delivered to the customer and the internal work required to produce that function. This internal work is considered to be critical to quality because it creates the quality characteristics of the CTS function. In this way, internal work can be observed as adding value directly in the production of an external function that customers perceive as value-adding.

---

[6] For more detail on lean methods and value addition, see James P. Womack and Daniel T. Jones, *Lean Thinking* (New York: Simon & Schuster, 1996).

What is value-adding work?

Value is added to a product from its very beginning with the conceptual design of the product or service. It is essential to know what customers really want: What job are they trying to perform, and how will your product or services support them to achieve that in the most economical way? Value is added in two ways—first, by enhancing the perceived-value (worth what is paid for it) perception of the consuming customer, and second, by decreasing the cost component of the product or service.

How is value lost?

If a product function is "too good," then it has passed the point of diminishing returns, as the customer will probably not want to pay for any extra capability that is beyond their need. (In the language of Christensen, this customer is overshot—served with more value than they are willing to pay for.) This creates a value loss in terms of cost to produce the extra capability that takes the product beyond the "good enough" level of performance. If a process step has too much waste (scrap, rework, inventory, testing, etc.), then it is costing the customer too much, and the function that the process step is adding to the product is also costing too much. Also, if the functional performance of a product feature is well beyond the customer need (sometimes referred to as "gold-plating"), then there is a value loss to the customer. Thus, value can be added to a process by delivering the functionality and features that customers want as well as by improving the performance of processes that produce the function so that they do not consume too much cost.

How is value added to a product or service?

Value is added by choosing the right function, designing it at the lowest cost to meet the functional requirements of customers and to achieve a performance advantage over similar competing products (this produces a sales point that is worthy of advertising), and producing the function with a reliable, low-cost process.

How do Six Sigma methods affect value?

Six Sigma can be summarized as a business improvement approach that seeks to find and eliminate causes of mistakes or defects in business processes by focusing on outputs that are of significance to customers. The concepts underlying Six Sigma deal with the fact that process and product variation are known to be strong factors affecting product-production lead times, product and process costs, process yields, and, ultimately, customer satisfaction. One of the most important aspects of "Black Belt" work is to define and measure variation with the intent of discovering its causes and to develop efficient operational means to control and reduce variation. The heart of the fresh approach that is implicit in Six Sigma lies within packaging of the toolkit relative to its rigorous problem-solving approach, the dedicated application of trained business analysts to well-structured process or product improvement projects, and the attention to bottom-line results and sustaining those results over time.

What is value engineering?

Lawrence D. Miles, a purchasing engineer with General Electric, developed the initial concept of value engineering (VE) during World War II as a means to substitute scarce materials while at the same time delivering all of the functional value that was required in the equipment design.[7] Subsequently, this methodology has been taught and promulgated widely; however, the biggest consumer of value engineering appears to be the U.S. Federal Government, which has mandated its use on military and construction projects.[8]

Value engineering has been historically defined as:

▶ An organized effort to analyze the functions of systems, equipment, facilities, services, and supplies in order to deliver the essential functions at the lowest life-cycle cost consistent with required performance, quality, reliability, and safety.

▶ A method for enhancing product value by improving the relationship of worth to cost by studying function and its application in product design and development.

▶ The application of value-analysis methods to assess existing products and provide required functions at the lowest overall cost consistent with achieving the required acceptance or performance for customers.

▶ Analysis of the value of product functions assessed using customer perceptions in the marketplace to improve cost-effectiveness in product design and development.

How should value engineering be conducted on Six Sigma projects?

There are a number of core concepts of value engineering and related methodologies that also have a definite place in the Six Sigma toolkit. The objective of the following list is to expose business leaders to the toolkit and its application without getting into the detailed "how to" level of description for actually using or creating the tool.

---

[7] Lawrence D. Miles, *Techniques of Value Analysis and Engineering*, 3rd edition (Lawrence D. Miles Value Foundation, 1989). (This book is available from SAVE International—www.value-eng.org.)

[8] See further: The Government Performance Results Act of 1993, Office of Management and Budget Circular A-131, and Federal Acquisition Regulations Part 48.

▶ **Work breakdown structure**: A work breakdown structure divides work into overall categories of things to get done on a project, followed by the division of each of these categories into detailed, more specific elements, until the final component is an individual task that can be reported as a project deliverable. The sub-elements of each category in the breakdown are numbered using a detailed outline format (see Appendix B for an example of a work breakdown structure).

▶ **Value stream map** (VSM): VSM is a process-mapping methodology that was first developed for lean process analysis because it focuses attention on where value is created and destroyed in the sequence of operational steps by tracking progress of work, cycle times, and inventory held at the work-activity level of a process.

▶ **Customer requirements analysis**: A customer table summarizes findings from a customer requirements analysis and serves as a base document from which the product-design specification and QFD matrices can be developed. An example of a customer table for requirements analysis follows:

Customer Needs Table

Customer Name	Voice of the Customer	Customer Use: Who?	Customer Use: What?	Customer Use: When?	Customer Use: Where?	Typical Use: How? How Much?

Expected Quality	Reworded Needs or Wants	Reliability Expectation	Function and Ease of Use	Safety Issues	Customer Value (Cost/ Price)	Special Customer Requests

▶ **Functional analysis using the theory of inventive problem solving** (TRIZ): In a TRIZ analysis of a technological system, a Substance-Field (Su-Field) is used to model the activity. Every system is created to perform some functions. The desired function is the output from an object or substance (substance 1), caused by another object (substance 2) with the help of some means (type of energy field). Substances are objects of any level of complexity. They can be single items or complex systems. The action or means of accomplishing the action is called a field. Su-Field analysis works best for well-formulated problems, and the model for a Su-Field is represented by a triangle (see the figure below).[9]

Su-Field Model

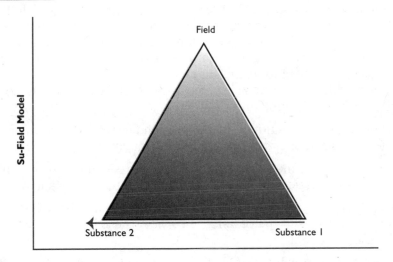

The Su-Field model follows the same format as the basic function model used in value engineering, where the originating source of an action (or energy field) is called the subject (substance 1), the recipient of this action is called the object (substance 2), the action (field) is labeled as a verb, and the subject and objects are labeled as nouns (see the following illustration).

Function Model

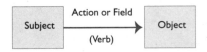

TRIZ and the value-engineering tool of function analysis accomplish similar tasks, and the TRIZ Su-Field methodology can be used to generate function definitions for integration into a product model using the function analysis system technique (FAST—see below).

▶ **Function analysis**: A function is the result or purpose that an activity is intended to perform. It is that which makes an item or service work or sell—in other words, an item's function is why the customer buys the product or service. A function must be expressed in a measurable parameter in order to obtain a value for it in later analysis. The most common approach to classifying functions is to list the physical parts of the project, steps of a proce-

---

[9] John Terninko, Alla Zusman, and Boris Zlotin, *Systematic Innovation: An Introduction to TRIZ* (New York: St. Lucie Press, 1998), p. 113.

dure, or items in a set, and attempt to define the functions associated with each part or step. An activity is the sequence of actions that are required to perform a function or set of functions. Functions and activities are defined hierarchically, and the total of the function values (costs, weight, space, etc.) for any tier must add up to the values of the function of which they are a subset. Functional analysis defines the functional hierarchy first. Next the methodology assigns cost targets (along with any other factors that need to be controlled (e.g., weight, volume, part count, resultant performance, reliability, maintainability, etc.). Functions can also be defined by their type and prioritized by their cost as a percentage of total cost. The categories or types of functions include:

Basic function: A basic function describes the fundamental reason the product or service exists and operates in its prescribed manner.

Secondary function: The method used to execute a basic function or a function that supports the basic function (can be either wanted or unwanted).

Required function: Required functions are customer requirements that must be satisfied in order to sell the product or service. These functions are considered *secondary* functions.

Critical path function: Any function that is on the "How" or "Why" logic paths of a FAST diagram (see below) is called a critical path function. If this function is also a basic function, then it is called a major critical path function.

Item-to-Function Cost Breakdown

Item or Component	Function			Current Cost	Cost Basis	Percent Total	Cost Rank
	Noun	Verb	Type				

▶ **Functional analysis system technique (FAST)**: This analysis methodology is at the heart of value engineering—it is a methodology for analyzing how product functions are combined to deliver the total value proposition to a customer. A FAST diagram describes "what" functions or actions a product performs, while a process diagram describes "how" they are performed. Both perspectives are required for a complete analysis of capability. Thorough analysis of a product results in the elimination of unnecessary functions and streamlining of the design to those functions that are essential to the customer's requirement. The FAST diagram provides a logical description of the interrelationships among product functions. The FAST diagram can be read and interpreted from the perspective of either an engineer or a customer. As the FAST diagram is read from left to right, increasing levels of detail are exposed, from high-level abstraction to specific tasks of the function at the "atomic" level of work. As these non-verb phrases are read, they are interpreted as "how" the function delivers its output, with the answer being the next functional level in the decomposition of the actual work performed on this horizontal plane. Work at the basic function level is connected on the horizontal plane, while secondary functions are organized on a vertical plane. The customer viewpoint of a FAST diagram occurs when the diagram is read in the opposite direction (from right to left), and the non-verb phrases are then interpreted as "why" the result occurs, with the answer being the next function on the horizontal plane. There should be congruence between the engineer and customer viewpoints in order for the FAST diagram to be logically consistent; stability of these two interpretation paths is a key quality indicator that the diagram has been successfully completed. A FAST model is built using the engineering viewpoint and tested using the customer viewpoint (see the figure below):

Function Analysis System Technique

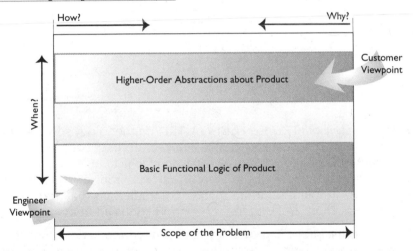

Along this horizontal pathway for interpreting the FAST diagram, two logical conditions can be modeled—functions can be coupled by "and" logic for dependent functions and "or" logic for coupling independent functions. The logic for "and" and "or" is found on the vertical path. The vertical dimension of the FAST diagram answers the logical condition of "when," which provides a definition of enhancements rather than sequence of actions (a FAST diagram does *not* imply a temporal sequence of action). If a "when" function is of a higher-order abstraction or is an independent function, then it is placed above the basic function flow. If the "when" function is a subset, then it is placed below the functional flow as a sub-activity. In a FAST diagram, the continued existence of functions in a design is justified only by the "how," "why," or "when" logic.[10]

▶ *Alternatives generation*: Following the definition of functions and their logical analyses using the FAST diagram, the next step in the value-engineering process is to define alternative designs for the function. This is a process that requires the use of systematic innovation (which can be another application for TRIZ of the use of a creative problem-solving analysis) to generate alternatives for the product functions.[11] The objective of alternatives generation is to develop as many ways to deliver the function as can possibly be imagined, not to pass judgment on their efficacy. Thus, this team exercise focuses on "opening options," not on "sorting" or gaining "closure" by making a choice before each option is fully understood.

Functional Alternative Analysis

Function		What else will do the job?	Evaluation	
Noun	Verb		Cycle Time	Cost

▶ *Conflict resolution with TRIZ (see chapter 6)*: TRIZ methodology specializes in the elimination of conflicts or contradictions that occur between two functions in a system. A contradiction is a situation in which an attempt to improve one function or feature of the system detracts from another function or feature. TRIZ problem solutions resolve contradictions that are the cause of the problem. There are two types of contradictions addressed:

1. *Trade-off contradiction* (also called a technical contradiction) means that if something good happens, something bad happens, too (e.g., performance increases but product weight is adversely affected at the same time).

2. *Inherent contradiction* means that I want that one thing that has two opposite properties (e.g., want the product thick for strength, but thin for weight).[12]

---

[10] FAST methodology is described in: Thomas Snodgras and Muthich Kasi, *Function Analysis: The Stepping Stone to Grow Value* (Dayton, Ohio: SAVE International, 1996).

[11] Michael Brassard and Diane Ritter, *The Creativity Tools Memory Jogger* (Salem, NH: GOAL/QPC, 1998).

[12] Kalevi Rantanen and Ellen Domb, *Simplified TRIZ: New Problem-Solving Applications for Engineers and Manufacturing Professionals* (New York: St. Lucie Press, 2002), pp. 5, 27.

▶ **Total life-cycle cost**: The total cost of ownership for a product, including all of the costs related to acquire, use, enjoy, maintain, and dispose of a product (this also includes the material overhead costs for purchasing and material management, as well as the risk associated with the purchase). The cost that is used in a VE analysis should include the costs of acquisition, operations, maintenance, and obsolescence. These costs associated with a product are broken down by function for further analysis (see the figure below):

Product Cost Breakdown

Sub-Product Categories	Functional Description							Cost per 1000	
	A	B	C	D	E...	---->	N	$	%
1									
2									
3									
4									
5									
...									
N									
Cost of Function									
Percentage of Total									
High Cost Function									

▶ **Activity-based cost analysis (see chapter 4)**: It is important to use actual costs in the product-cost analysis. The preferable approach would be to use activity-based cost results rather than the standard costs derived from managerial cost accounting. By using the ABC methods for product costing, distortions due to the use of standard cost-accounting methods are avoided and a more realistic expectation can be set for product-design decisions.

▶ **Function cost analysis**: The next step in the value-engineering process is to do a function cost analysis, which performs a cost breakdown of the complete product by functional sub-assembly into its component cost structure. This tool also sets the initial expectation regarding the "worth" of functions by comparing the product function with an analogous function of known value

Function Cost Analysis: Value Determination

Function			Current Cost	Cost Basis	Function Comparison		Value Index (Cost/Worth)
Noun	Verb	Type			Comp Basis	Worth	

(e.g., uses analogy to identify a different approach for delivering the same function at a known price) and calculating a value index that helps to define where to focus a value-engineering project for cost reduction.

▶ *Risk analysis in product design*: Functional analysis should not result in a diminished product from the customer's viewpoint—the objective is for customers to perceive enhanced worth. Thus, in any value-engineering effort, it is strongly recommended to do a risk analysis using Failure Mode and Effects Analysis (FMEA) to expose potential risks in changes to the product's functional design. By doing an FMEA at this stage of a value-engineering project, engineers can appropriately address risk issues in the design and ensure that the "trade-off" analyses that are done using TRIZ do not increase product risks in other areas.

▶ *Financial value assessment*: In conducting a value-engineering cost analysis of the alternative designs, two financial indices are used to make comparisons:

1. **Value index**: This index evaluates the relative worth of various product functions. It is calculated as the ratio of the cost to produce a function (at the expected production volume using an ABC-based cost) to the customer-perceived worth of that function. A design objective should be to drive this value close to unity.

2. **Savings index**: This index evaluates the relative savings from alternative value-engineering projects by calculating a savings-to-investment ratio for all of the functional changes that are being considered. Savings are estimated for the same period for all alternative functional designs (e.g., using a one-, two-, or three-year forecast or outlook to set expectations), and investment combines both recurring and non-recurring costs in a probabilistic risk assessment.

▶ *Pugh concept selection matrix*: The late Professor Stuart Pugh provoked much of the thinking in design for Six Sigma, but he is best known as creator of the concept selection matrix that bears his name.[13] The Pugh concept selection matrix is a decision prioritization matrix that is used to compare alternative design concepts against a set of evaluation criteria. Each of the alternatives is rated using pairwise comparison to a baseline case (usually the current product) for each of the criteria listed among the critical design parameters. A tally of each alternative is made for the number of times the alternative is superior, the same, or inferior to the base case, and the summary of these ratings is presented at the column bottom for each of the alternative concepts.

---

[13] Pugh's work is contained in three volumes: Stuart Pugh, *Total Design: Integrated Methods for Successful Product Engineering* (Reading, MA: Addison-Wesley, 1991); Stuart Pugh, *Creating Innovative Products Using Total Design* (Reading, MA: Addison-Wesley, 1996), and Stuart Pugh and Bill Hollins, *Successful Product Design: What to Do and When* (Boston: Butterworth, 1990).

Pugh Concept Selection Matrix

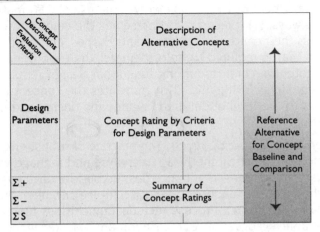

Concept Descriptions / Evaluation Criteria	Description of Alternative Concepts		Reference Alternative for Concept Baseline and Comparison
Design Parameters	Concept Rating by Criteria for Design Parameters		
Σ +	Summary of Concept Ratings		
Σ −			
Σ S			

▶ **Alternatives analysis (see chapter 3):** There are a number of different methods and techniques that can be used to evaluate relative goodness among functional design alternatives: Pugh concept selection matrix, multi-voting, nominal group technique (NGT), and the analytic hierarchy process (see chapter 3). What is common in each of these methods is that a set of criteria (which can be either implicit or explicit) are compared across alternatives, and the alternative that rates highest relative to the other choices is selected for implementation. A number of other methods can be used to clarify and summarize the choices. For instance, a decision matrix can be constructed to present the advantages, disadvantages, cost, and concerns among the alternative concepts. Such a decision matrix can also be used to record the outcome of the final decision process for ranking alternatives (see the example below).

Decision Matrix

Concept	Advantages	Disadvantages	Countermeasures	Ranking
Comparison of the sorted concepts should first summarize the options, then work on obtaining closure.				

- **Quality function deployment (QFD)** (*see chapter 2*): Another helpful tool for supporting value-engineering decisions involves the use of QFD matrices. QFD helps in three ways: (1) it records and preserves the voice of the customer as they express their concerns, desires, wants, hopes, and needs regarding the capability that is required to help them get their job done better; (2) it identifies potential conflicts among functional design requirements for resolution (e.g., using TRIZ); and (3) it translates the conceptual function characteristics to the level of detailed engineering design and production implementation.

- **Robust engineering design** (*see chapter 8*): The practice of robust engineering is the application of statistical methods to analyze and manage variation in critical design parameters—to enhance desired performance (signal) while decreasing the sources of undesired variation (noise). Some of the methods involved in a robust design process include Taguchi loss function, multi-vari analysis, analysis of variance, regression analysis, designed statistical experiments (DOE), Taguchi analysis for critical parameter analysis and statistical tolerance development, and statistical process control. These methods aim at variation reduction and selection of appropriate customer specifications in order to establish robust production-process capability.

- **Value-engineering change proposal (VECP):** In value-engineering work that is done on contract to the U.S. government, a value-engineering change proposal (VECP) is required to initiate a value-engineering improvement project. A VECP proposes changes to an existing product, design concept,

Value-Engineering Change Proposal

Value-Engineering Change Proposal		Proposal No.:
Item Name:	Specification No.:	
Function:	Drawing No.:	
Present Unit Cost:	Proposed Unit Cost:	
	Projected Savings:	
References:		
Present Method:	Proposed Method:	

Additional details or drawings can be appended to this VECP form to describe what is being changed, as well as the relative advantages and disadvantages of proposed changes.

Estimated Cost to Complete:	$	Labor Hours	Elapsed Time
Engineering			
Drafting			
Tooling			
Materials			
Testing			
Other			
TOTAL			
Estimated Gross Savings - First Year			
Estimated Implementation Cost			
Net Savings - First Year			
Net Savings - Succeeding Year			
Savings-to-Investment Ratio			
Team Members:			
Date Submitted:			

or production process that result in savings that are shared jointly between the contractor and the government. The format for a VECP, as specified in content by the Federal Acquisition Regulations (Part 48), is presented on page 200.

▶ **Business controls (see chapter 9):** A final tool for the value-engineering kit is a suite of business controls that the organization can use to effectively apply the results of the value-engineering project in its operations. All work output must become part of the daily management system if it is to be integrated into the normal work pace and turned into daily routine. As Jack Welch, former GE CEO, observed: "Six Sigma is not about sloganeering or bureaucracy or filling out forms; it finally gives us a route to get to the business control function, the hardest thing to do in a corporation."[14] Effective business control is the essential element of any management process. It first requires that managers lead by example. No management system can endure leaders who do not apply the same principles to themselves as they apply to their people. Effective business control also requires that an organization manage by process. Organizations that do not use process management become introspective and self-seeking and lose their competitive edge. Effective business control also requires that its people monitor measurements. It is not just the act of measuring that is essential; it is the use of good measures to learn about the business and choose direction more carefully. Effective business control also requires managers to evaluate progress. Performance management without effective decision making results in frustration for the entire organization. It is only when measurement systems are used to identify and effect change in routine operations that people actually believe that such methods can make a difference. Finally, effective business control means managers adapt their personal behavior to this environment. Excellence comes only by execution. Excellence is not merely the product of a good process map, measurement system, or self-assessment scheme—excellence is the result that comes when leaders lead by example and hold others accountable for following that example.

In addition to the value-engineering project measures indicated above, what are some of the performance measures that highlight value in business operations?[15]

---

[14] This quotation is taken from the General Electric Company official web site.

[15] A note of explanation for small and medium enterprises (SME) is appropriate. The product-creation effort that is outlined is complete; however, it is scaled for a large enterprise that has the resources to consider value engineering without delaying the project schedule. For an SME to apply value-engineering methods, the design process must be streamlined so the "overhead" from applying this methodology doesn't overburden the project resources. Asking the basic value-engineering questions as proposed by Lawrence D. Miles (see his previously cited book, *Techniques of Value Analysis and Engineering*) might be sufficient: What is it? What does it do? What does it cost? What else will do the job? and What does that cost? Answering these questions can lead a team through the entire value-engineering process without getting embroiled in the bureaucratic structure that has engaged many government-based value-engineering efforts. This approach is Ockham's Razor applied to value engineering!

What are value-related measures of process performance?

Some process-level performance indicators (see chapter 4) that will help to identify the components of a work-process value stream include:

◗ Customer satisfaction with product features and performance (competition-based)
◗ Fixed and variable cost of production
◗ Warranty cost
◗ Labor variance for rework and testing
◗ Cost variance due to expedited shipping
◗ Buffer inventory
◗ Work-in-process inventory
◗ Production setup time
◗ Production cycle time
◗ Ratio of on-line to off-line production
◗ *Takt* time—matching production rate to the rate of incoming orders
◗ Scrap and rejected production material
◗ Lost production productivity
◗ Customer productivity loss
◗ Order line item fill rate
◗ Order turnaround time

What are the new design principles for engineering value into products?

What design rules should be implemented to support the best practices of engineering for customer value? Here is a preliminary set of design rules for consideration in the development of an applied value-engineering method:

◗ Product development decisions should encourage organic growth as measured by both brand value and shareholder value.
◗ Value should be measured from both the functional and process perspective and compared to management risk so the resultant product is truly cost-effective.
◗ Innovative product designs should resolve any performance trade-offs or inherent contradictions in the simplest manner, using readily available resources.

- Designed functions should be traceable to their origin at the voice of the customer.

- Designed function development should be traceable from its origin to its point of implementation.

- Products should be designed so they are robust and not sensitive to any sources of unwanted variation that will degrade their functional performance.

- Product prototypes should be tested to the point of complete failure so designers know the ways that customers can experience failure in critical functions and so countermeasures can be developed and implemented in the design.

- Effective business and statistical controls are necessary requirements in order to transition a product to full-scale production.

How should value-engineering results be reported?

The results of a value-engineering project should report two different types of project-performance measures: overall cost reduction, and improvement

Cost Improvement Pareto Presentation

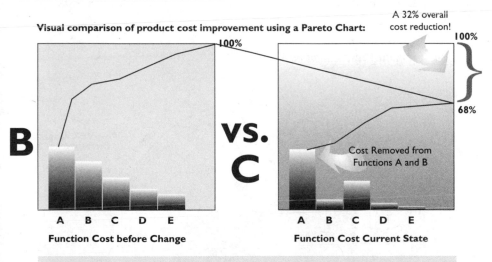

Visual comparison of product cost improvement using a Pareto Chart: A 32% overall cost reduction!

- "B vs. C" Pareto analysis illustrates results of process change on performance, comparing pre- and post-change outcomes.

- A "before" Pareto indicates dominant causes and those that have been the focal effort of the improvement (causes A and B above).

- The "Current State" Pareto is drawn to the same scale as the "B" Pareto, and all of the same causes are indicated. An estimate of the overall effect of the changes is provided by comparing results of the current state (after change) to the cost magnitude before the change.

by value dimension for the key elements of value. The first report should include a Pareto analysis that shows the leading opportunities for value enhancement in a "before" the project initiation condition, and the total cost indicated as the 100% baseline. The second Pareto chart should show the value reduction for these functions and the total cost that has been removed from the project based on a single VECP. This overall picture of improvement can be illustrated on a "B vs. C" (before versus current state) Pareto analysis, as illustrated in the figure on page 203.

The second type of performance chart is a radar diagram (also called a spider chart), which illustrates the dimensions of improvement that have been obtained for this specific value-engineering project. There are eight dimensions for comparison that are typically used in this diagram. One dimension should remain constant—the basic or core functions should not be diminished as a result of a project. In addition, there are four dimensions that should be reduced: total life-cycle cost, number of parts that are included in the bill of materials, weight of the item, and physical volume of the item (the space that it occupies). The final three dimensions should all be improved as a result of a value-engineering project: performance of the functionality that is delivered, reliability of the product performance, and efficiency of the item's ability to operate (either consume fewer resources while delivering the same productivity, or increase productivity for the same level of resource consumption). Cost improvement by these basic value dimensions is illustrated in the figure below:

Cost Improvement Presentation by Function

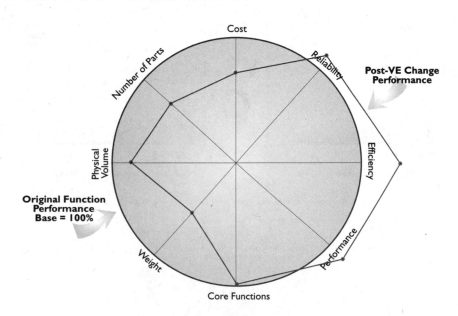

Let's consider an example: the medical diagnosis process for breast cancer.[16]

The process begins with a self-examination that lasts just three minutes. Upon detection of a "suspicious" lump, a woman makes an appointment with the doctor for an assessment. Of course, she has to wait three weeks for the doctor's appointment. The appointment itself lasts 15 minutes, but she has to sit in the waiting room for almost 45 minutes because the doctor is late from his rounds. Of the 15 minutes that the appointment consumes, the examination lasts only 2 minutes, and the advice to obtain the mammogram lab test takes less than 30 seconds. The rest of the time is spent talking about social matters. She has to wait two days to get the mammogram that took only 10 minutes to conduct, and she is pleased that she waited only 10 minutes to have the test. Although the technician interprets the results, they are sent back to the doctor, so she has to wait until the next week to see him—another five days without knowing the results. Sure enough, at the doctor's next 15-minute appointment (waiting-room time down to 35 minutes on this visit), she learns that the lump is indeed suspicious, and it requires an ultrasound test to clarify the diagnosis. Later that afternoon, an ultrasound time slot is open, and she obtains the examination in just 25 minutes (with only 5 minutes of waiting). Again the technician interprets the results and sends her back to the doctor—a three-day waiting period, after which she has another 15-minute appointment (after 50 minutes of waiting) to learn that she should really have a biopsy to classify the tumor that was indicated on the ultrasound. Back to the hospital laboratory on the following afternoon (waiting only 14 hours) for the 20-minute biopsy and a return to the doctor in four days for a 15-minute session to hear the good news that it is not cancerous! Count the time spent in this process:

Examination/test time—value-added: 123 minutes

Waiting time (at doctor's office and hospital)—non-value-added: > 115 minutes

Waiting time (between appointments)—non-value-added: >35 days

What could be done to make the process lean? Why wait between tests? If the technician is able to interpret the results, is the doctor's follow-up visit providing any value-add? It is providing information, but the value was already produced at the time of the examination, when the technician interpreted the results. The delivery of the information generated by the examination is just delayed—a value-reducing step. Is there some way that this process could be done better to add value?

Consider the following process redesign, which eliminates most of the "between-appointment" waiting-time buffers:

---

[16] This example is paraphrased from a TV news broadcast that I saw in Toronto, Canada, in 2004. Unfortunately, I didn't capture any of the specifics to make this a truly real-world case study.

Self-examination: 3 minutes (go immediately to walk-in clinic)

Doctor's confirmation: 15 minutes (go directly to mammogram)

Mammogram: 10 minutes (go directly to ultrasound)

Ultrasound: 25 minutes (go directly to biopsy)

Biopsy: 20 minutes (go to doctor's office and wait for lab results)

Doctor's conclusion: 15 minutes

What happened to the time? The total value-added process time is just 88 minutes (down because the duplication in reporting is eliminated); the total waiting time is down to less than 8 hours (down because the process is flowed from one test to the next, and the technician is empowered to send the patient to the next stage). This is indicative of the type of improvement that is available in many processes when the flow of work is considered.

What do these observations imply for value engineering?

Of course, this focus on process efficiency has an increase in value-add to the patient/customer; however, does the "price-worth-what-is-paid-for" actually change? True, there are fewer doctor's appointments.[17] However, value engineering looks at the function (e. g., mammogram test, ultrasound test, biopsy, etc.) and assigns cost to these functions. None of these costs changed! However, the customer perceived a great increase in value because many of the personal cost components that were borne by the customer have been eliminated, and the customer's peace of mind is enhanced because of the faster "time to diagnosis." One problem with value engineering is that it focuses at the function level and not at the entire process. If the analysis is limited to the functions, then, these two processes would be considered to have equal value. However, if the cost is considered as a loss to society[18] (e.g., the customer's lost time), then the second process is greatly improved from the customer's perspective! In the process of value engineering, the customer's perspective of value must be the focus, and the way that value is interpreted must be from the customer's viewpoint, not an internal organizational viewpoint. This case study illustrates the need to blend both functional cost analysis and process-cost analysis together to get the full picture on the value that is delivered to the customer by the entire product (not just from a couple of the core features or functions).

---

[17] Of course, this also points out that there are two sides to this coin—what is cost reduction for the patient and the insurance company is income reduction for the doctor and medical system. As illustrated in this example, the use of value-engineering principles to interpret this process can lead to a more customer-centric perspective to health care!

[18] Genichi Taguchi introduced his quality-loss function to describe the economic loss associated with variation from the typical (normal customer expectation) and equated the costs as the total costs that are borne by society for the occurrence of this loss. Thus, losses should also include the impact on your customer's processes, as well as their direct cost and economic losses associated with lost productivity or production throughput! See chapter 8 for more on Taguchi's methods.

What is value engineering's unique contribution to Six Sigma?

The uniqueness of value engineering is its application of functional analysis. There are two opportunities to apply functional analysis in Six Sigma. First, use functional analysis in the DMAIC (Define-Measure-Analyze-Improve-Control) process to help identify the relationship between the critical-to-satisfaction (CTS) and critical-to-quality (CTQ) factors and to link these factors to the cost-value proposition that they offer to the customer. Second, use functional analysis in the DMADV (Define-Measure-Analyze-Design-Verify) process for design as a tool to analyze alternative functional designs and integrate cost factors into the criteria for selection of the best alternative.

The DFSS challenge for value engineering

While value engineering's contribution to Six Sigma is relatively straightforward, there is a stronger implication in the opposite direction. Value engineering is deeply challenged by Six Sigma thinking because traditional value engineering focuses almost exclusively on functions and ignores the process component of cost. On the other hand, Six Sigma seeks cost reductions in both of these dimensions.[19] Examining an opportunity for cost reduction based solely on a functional analysis is shortsighted and will not lead to the lowest total cost, as process-related cost is not integrated into the total solution. Additionally, value engineering should be integrated with advanced accounting tools and methods to ensure that a distorted picture of value is not used for product-level business decisions, as discussed in chapter 4. It is clear that the value-engineering methods belong in the Six Sigma toolkit, but it also appears that value engineering as a stand-alone discipline is in need of upgrading and that the Six Sigma methodology can point in the direction of some much-needed change.

---

[19] However, Six Sigma is also challenged by value engineering in that efforts to reduce variation beyond a certain level will result in non-value-adding work, as the customer would not perceive any additional advantage—Six Sigma must always focus on performance relative to customer requirement. This is particularly true when seeking to reduce process costs.

Chapter 6
Planning Innovative Design Developments

"You have to relentlessly communicate change from the top, because the resistors in the middle will spin it differently. Change takes relentless persistence."

~ John F. "Jack" Welch

Design applications of innovation[1]

Innovation requires planning; it is more than just a spark of creativity, an instantaneous spark of brilliance. Planning is one way to induce new ideas within an organization and apply these ideas to see things differently and do things differently. Economist Joseph Schumpeter has defined innovation as the *planned* abandonment of the *familiar* and the *creative destruction* of the past in order to embrace new ways of doing things.[2] Planning aligns the activities of an organization to its strategic direction—and, by persistent pursuit and constancy of purpose, the organization prevails in delivering the objectives that it has defined. However, there is a danger in the symbiosis of innovation and strategy in that either can overpower the other so that the organization fails to achieve its overall growth objectives. Allowed free rein, innovation can go out of control and produce more ideas that diffuse the organization's market strategy and dilute product development resources away from the focused development of the most commercially viable products that can ensure the sustained success of the organization.

Few companies are in business for the singular purpose of sowing innovation; rather, most are targeting development of specific product lines. While the diversification of products is desirable as long as the diversity is related to customer needs, there are also core competencies that must remain the focus of corporate management, or else over-diversification can lead to resource thinning beyond acceptable levels. On the other hand, strategy

---

[1] This discussion builds on the description of innovation presented in chapter 2.

[2] Joseph A. Schumpeter, *Capitalism, Socialism, and Democracy* (New York: Harper, 1950).

applied with a domineering hand can and will lead to squelching true innovation, leaving an organization's technology locked into reheated versions of old product ideas and knowledge due to overkill in the control function.[3] Both of these conditions can be fatal to an organization, which must grow to sustain itself. In the end, distraction resulting from unfocused innovation can kill competitiveness just as easily as stagnation resulting from lack of innovation, and just as fast. Organizations must manage the introduction of both sustaining technology and disruptive technology innovations to ensure that they remain competitive. But what opportunities are there for managing innovation, and how can it be done?[4]

Russian Nobel Laureate Albert Szent Györgyi said: "Discovery consists of looking at the same thing as everyone else and thinking something different."[5] Innovation is required to see things differently; interpret things differently; translate the language of the market to the language of the engineer and back to the language of the user; define the functions of a product; design alternatives that are able to deliver customer-desired functionality; resolve conflicts among engineering implementation options for functional designs; and implement appropriate processes that deliver these functions into a capable production process (a process that is designed so that it satisfies the conditions of a predictable factory).

In Six Sigma, the design goal is "ideality based on customer requirements"—one that was endorsed some time ago by Philip B. Crosby as "conformity at the level of zero defects to the standard of the customer's requirements." How is an ideal function defined, and what DFSS tools can be used to ensure its appropriate design?

The pursuit of ideality through DFSS

The ideal function that meets customer requirements will provide flawless execution of the design against the customer's functional requirement, a Six Sigma design capability. Pursuit of this goal provides opportunities for innovation—achieving ideal performance capability in a condition or function where there is a real customer need.

Seeking an "ideal solution" requires the combination of both brain hemispheres, as the total human capability must be engaged—contributions and

---

[3] Robert A. Burgelman and Leonard R. Sayles, *Inside Corporate Innovation: Strategy, Structure, and Managerial Skills* (New York: The Free Press. 1986) p. 80. Also, proper applications for business controls are discussed in chapter 9.

[4] This theme is derived from the work of Harvard professor Clayton M. Christensen in his three books: *The Innovator's Dilemma* (Boston: Harvard Business School Press, 1997), *The Innovator's Solution* (with Michael E. Raynor) (Boston: Harvard Business School Press, 2003), and *Seeing What's Next* (with Scott D. Anthony and Erik A. Roth) (Boston: Harvard Business School Press, 2004). In a collection of provocative articles, Xerox Chief Scientist John Seeley Brown provides a good background for Christensen's concepts: *Seeing Differently: Insights on Innovation* (Boston: Harvard Business School Press, 1997).

[5] As quoted by John Terninko, Alla Zusman, and Boris Zlotin, *Systematic Innovation: An Introduction to TRIZ* (New York: St. Lucie Press, 1998), p. ix.

insights are required from both the logical mind and the emotional mind because the process is not completely a rational one. The "ideality" of a function is a measure of how close it is to perfection as indicated by first principles or the theoretical performance calculations. A perfect system (or ideal product) has all the benefits the customer wants, at minimal cost, and it does not produce any harmful effects. Therefore, a system increases in its "ideality" when it delivers more of what customers want or less of what they don't want—and is able to do it at a lower total cost of ownership (typically with less design complexity).

One methodology that is central to the discovery and definition of ideal solutions to design problems in DFSS is called TRIZ. What is this TRIZ tool? TRIZ (pronounced "treez") is an acronym derived from the Russian phrase "teorija rezhenija izobretatelskih zadach," which means "the theory of inventive problem solving." TRIZ was invented by the late Russian engineer Genrich S. Altshuller (1926–1998) and developed in collaboration with many colleagues inside Russia. Since 1985, it has been applied in numerous design projects around the world.[6]

What is the TRIZ methodology in a nutshell? This question highlights part of the problem with TRIZ: It can't be fit into a nutshell, and the methodology requires sound technical knowledge for it to be applied properly. This helps to explain why the TRIZ method is not better known by business leaders! This chapter defines TRIZ in a way that should be helpful to business leaders so they can appreciate how TRIZ can be used to contribute to better designs and see how TRIZ is an integral part of the DFSS methodology.[7]

TRIZ is based on the theory that "the patterns of technical evolution repeat across boundaries of science and industry" and that understanding these similarities provides an approach for solving what it calls "inventive problems." The power of TRIZ is that its insights, principles, and methodologies for innovation are derived from extensive study of what differentiates a great invention from an ordinary one. The ideas generated by the TRIZ approach apply heuristic rules that are observed as differentiating an invention as

[6] Genrich S. Altshuller, *And Suddenly the Inventor Appeared* (Worcester, MA: Technical Innovation Center, 1996); John Terninko, Alla Zusman, and Boris Zlotin, *Systematic Innovation: An Introduction to TRIZ* (New York: St. Lucie Press, 1998); Stan Kaplan, *An Introduction to TRIZ* (Southfield, MI: Ideation International, 1996), and Kalevi Rantanen and Ellen Domb, *Simplified TRIZ: New Problem-Solving Applications for Engineers and Manufacturing Professionals* (New York: St. Lucie Press, 2002).

[7] A number of web sites offer information, publications, and software that are related to TRIZ methods. Some of these web sites include:

Altshuller Foundation, www.altshuller.ru

Altshuller Institute, www.aitriz.org

Engineering.com, www.engineering.com

TRIZ Journal, www.triz-journal.com

Technical Innovation Center, www.triz.org

CREAX Innovation Suite™ 3.0, www.creax.com

Ideation Workbench™, www.ideationtriz.com

Knowledge Wizard™ 2.8, www.ideationtriz.com

Goldfire™, www.invention-machine.com

unique. So, to learn more about how TRIZ works, let's begin by asking: What is meant by an "inventive problem," and how is the TRIZ method able to solve such problems?

Overview of inventive problem solving

TRIZ is a methodology that generates ideas that can be applied to develop solutions; it does not directly resolve a problem. TRIZ provides the approach by which a problem can be more clearly understood and through which a design team can gain new insights and directions to pursue that result in problem resolution. The power of TRIZ is that it is derived from observations of what makes the difference between ordinary inventions and great inventions. TRIZ asks new questions like: What is the difference between good and bad ideas, solutions, and products? What are the good and bad features of this component or operation? What gets better and what gets worse if we leave this out? A good idea will resolve contradictions, increase the "ideality" of the system, and use idle, easily available resources to resolve a conflict. Bad ideas create conflicts and inhibit the performance desired by the product's customer.[8]

TRIZ is an engineering tool that supports functional design.[9] A function describes what a product does and is defined using a noun-verb combination, as represented by the following model. A subject acts on an object; this relationship is called a function—what a product does to deliver customer requirements (desired function).[10]

Function Model

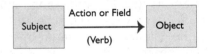

An inventive problem is one where there is a conflict between key design parameters (i.e., there is a definite contradiction between the technical performance observed in a design's functional parameters and the physical properties of the product). Removal of dependency from this interaction effect occurs by applying the inventive principles (also called separation principles) to overcome the technical or physical contradiction. The existence of engi-

---

[8] Rantanen and Domb, *op. cit.*, pp. 9, 43.

[9] This statement is meant to focus this discussion, not to limit the use of TRIZ to this one application. The author acknowledges that TRIZ can be used to assist in the resolution of a wide variety of problems, but the focus of this discussion will be on functional design in DFSS.

[10] Functional analysis is a methodology developed by Lawrence Miles—see the preceding chapter for more details on how functional analysis works. The Su-Field Model is a TRIZ approach to developing function definitions.

neering interactions and design-parameter contradictions indicates the need for a TRIZ analysis. The goal of this analysis is to create an ideal function by breaking the contradiction between these parameters by applying analogy to find solutions that were applied previously using current resources to resolve the conflict at the lowest total cost. A compromise in design capability to resolve the conflict is no longer a design objective.[11]

Parametric analysis can be used to identify conflicts among design parameters that arise due to technical or physical contradictions. A contradiction is a situation in which the improvement of one design feature results in a degradation of another one. Contradictions can be interpreted as "interaction effects" or "trade-offs" in the way that the design operates: When something good happens, something bad happens at the same time; for example, as an object gets stronger (a desirable condition), it gets heavier (an undesirable condition)—or it might be a matter of degree, as when something good gets better, then something undesirable gets worse. An inherent contradiction is one that has two opposite properties—one desirable and one undesirable (an example that is often used in TRIZ literature is the airbag—it must deploy quickly to save lives of car drivers or passengers, but it should also deploy slowly to minimize harm to children). The basic principle of TRIZ is that designed systems improve through the resolution of such conflicts. TRIZ resolves inventive problems by removing the conflicts among the design parameters so the function can approach its ideal state.

Parametric analysis will typically cross-plot the operating response characteristics of two functions in order to discover any interaction effects. For instance, as automobile velocity increases, safety of automobile operation decreases:

Parametric Analysis Showing Interaction

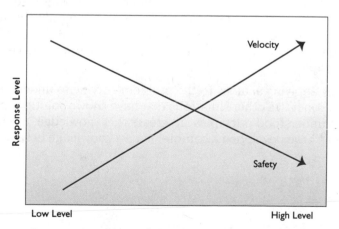

Interaction: A conflict between two useful features

---

[11] A contradiction is a situation in which an attempt to improve one feature of the system detracts from another feature (herein lies the conflict). This situation is also called an "interaction effect," and it would require a design-parameter trade-off to resolve the conflict using a traditional engineering approach.

Two basic principles in the TRIZ approach apply to such a problem. First, this problem, or one very much like it, has already been solved by someone, someplace; so, the true indicator of creativity lies in your ability to find that solution and modify it to fit your circumstances.[12] Second, don't accept compromises in the solution, but remove the source of the problem! Optimize the loss function for this problem.[13]

What is the basic TRIZ toolkit that is used to accomplish this objective?[14] One way to summarize the TRIZ methodology is to present it as a thought map (see the figure below).

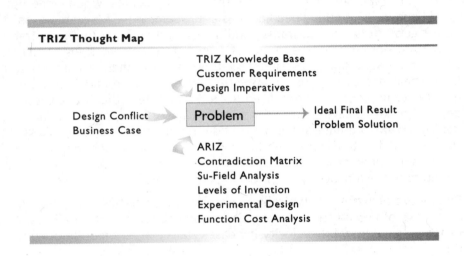

TRIZ Thought Map

TRIZ Knowledge Base
Customer Requirements
Design Imperatives

Design Conflict → **Problem** → Ideal Final Result
Business Case   Problem Solution

ARIZ
Contradiction Matrix
Su-Field Analysis
Levels of Invention
Experimental Design
Function Cost Analysis

The TRIZ methodology has a general approach for solving inventive problems: define the problem, state the contradiction, identify the resources, describe the ideal solution, determine the gap to the ideal state, evaluate the knowledge base to discover analogies, and then ask how resources could be used differently.

TRIZ works by applying analogy to the problem—trying to understand how a current situation is like other situations that have known solutions or operate according to understood principles. To create this knowledge, Altshuller and his colleagues have developed a comprehensive knowledge base of scientific

---

[12] In its benchmarking process, Xerox called this practice "creative imitation."

[13] For a description of the Taguchi Loss Function, see chapter 8.

[14] See chapter 5 for related concepts in value engineering, and chapter 8 for experimental designs.

effects, inventive principles, and design parameters.[15] Once an analogy can be established, then a solution is already at hand. "TRIZ does not give the team the detailed design solution, but it points the team to focused and clear directions for innovation. TRIZ innovation methods can work only to the level of knowledge and experience of the people involved."[16] In other words, TRIZ helps a design team to think and see more clearly.

What is the TRIZ toolkit, and how does it work?

The elements of the TRIZ toolkit include:

▶ **Levels of invention:** Based on Altshuller's exhaustive study of Russian patents and inventions, he identified five levels of invention that describe their innovative content and suggest a design approach:[17]

1. Apparent or conventional solution (32%): Solution by methods well known within specialty.

2. Small invention inside the current paradigm (45%): Improvement of an existing system, usually with some compromise.

3. Substantial invention inside the current technology (18%): Essential improvement of an existing system.

4. Invention outside the currently available technology (4%): Requires a new generation of design using science, not technology.

5. Discovery of the unknown (1%): Requires a major discovery with new scientific knowledge.

The first three levels of inventive problems typically have solutions that can be transferred from one discipline to another (this is 95% of the inventive problems!), while TRIZ works best for the middle three levels (or two-thirds of the total inventive problems). The level of invention that a product achieves depends on the ability of the design team to remove conflicts! This research is the basis for the optimism about the potential applications for TRIZ.

---

[15] The pure comprehensiveness of their work is intellectually daunting to anyone first introduced to the TRIZ methodology. Surely Ockham's Razor could be applied to this knowledge base? (The Razor is a practical principle of the scientific method proposed by William of Ockham in the fourteenth century: "Pluralitas non est ponenda sine necessitate," or "entities should not be multiplied unnecessarily." Practically, the Razor can be interpreted as "keep it simple, stupid" [the so-called KISS principle] or phrased more subtly: Don't add concepts unnecessarily beyond what is required to explain the observed phenomena.) However, that would nullify the strength of the knowledge base—when faced with the potential need to resolve any kind of problem, there is no way to know beforehand what knowledge or information will be required to stimulate the analogous thinking that leads to a solution that will resolve it! Indeed, the true strength of TRIZ lies in its approach to stimulate the creative thinking of knowledgeable experts so that they can call on their collective experience to interpret the knowledge bases and, through the guide of the TRIZ approach, find the inventive solution that creates an ideal final result.

[16] Subir Chowdhury, *Design for Six Sigma*, p. 112.

[17] The TRIZ methodology grew out of a comprehensive analysis of over 50,000 patents to discern the underlying patterns of invention that occur. By grouping these observations in different ways, a set of knowledge bases were developed (e.g., TRIZ techniques such as the thirty-nine design parameters or the forty inventive principles).

▶ **TRIZ** *problem statement*: Defining a problem means clarifying the contradiction (conflict) by finding an alternative for providing a desired function without adding harmful effects (in design-parameter performance, cost, or resultant harmful effects, such as an impact on the environment). When the conflict is properly resolved, then the problem has been solved!

A conflict occurs when a desired function A requires a function C, which damages B or causes an undesired function B. The logic of the situation is that function A requires function C, and function C causes function B, which is a harmful effect. A problem occurs in that the ideal final result (IFR) for C must be delivered without incurring the harmful effect of B. The following statements are derived from this conflict:

▶ Find an alternative to C that provides or enhances A but does not cause B.

▶ Find a way to eliminate, reduce, or prevent B under the condition of C.

▶ Find a way to enhance C.

▶ Find a way to resolve the contradiction: C should provide A and not cause B.

▶ Find an alternative way to provide A that does not require C.

▶ Find a way to enhance A.

▶ Find a way to eliminate, reduce, or prevent B under the condition of C.

▶ Find a way to benefit from B.[18]

Resolving the logical problems described by these alternatives leads to solution of the problem.

▶ **Ideality**: The ideal performance that can be expected from a function's design—and an ideal design provides the desired function without any resources! The design objective is to reduce the capability gap between the current design and the ideal system to zero. Ideality is defined as the sum of the useful effects divided by the sum of the harmful effects, which includes cost, space occupied, noise emitted, energy consumed, and waste (process waste as well as environmental waste or pollution). If the harmful effects are computed in financial terms, then this function is the optimization of a function's value calculation as derived from value engineering. The ideal solution excludes secondary functions and all unnecessary design elements (waste, derived resources, substance modification); applies self-service to operations; replaces elements, parts, or the total system or changes the principle of operation; and effectively uses available resources. When the harmful effects can be estimated in financial terms, then the function for ideality can be expressed as follows:

$$\text{Ideality} = \frac{\text{Functionality}}{\text{Cost}}$$

---

[18] Note adapted from Terninko, p. 67.

▶ *Patterns of evolution*: The patterns of evolution are the theoretical foundation of TRIZ—they describe the basic laws or patterns of development that govern the maturing of technological systems. These patterns were identified by Altshuller and applied to engineering development as the basis for resolving engineering problems. These patterns can be used to consciously develop specifications for technology functions and inventive problem solving, replacing the inefficient one-factor-at-a-time (OFAT) parametric searches for functional relationships. The eight basic patterns of evolution in the maturing of engineering design are that:

1. Evolution occurs in stages (the S-curve phenomenon).

2. Evolution moves toward increased ideality.

3. There is non-uniform development in maturity of the system elements.

4. Evolution moves toward increased dynamism and controllability.

5. Increases in complexity are followed by simplification (reduction).

6. Evolution with matching and mismatching components.

7. Evolution toward micro-level and increased use of fields.

8. Evolution toward decreased human involvement.

▶ **ARIZ (***Algorithm for Inventive Problem Solving***)**: ARIZ is an analysis approach for using the TRIZ toolkit to resolve an inventive problem. There are three TRIZ methods to solve inventive problems, which ARIZ organizes into a systematic approach that has three alternative ways to resolve problems once it has been thoroughly defined:[19]

1. Resolving conflicts using a contradiction matrix (for problem solving)

2. Substance-Field analysis (for system enhancements)

3. Effects database of scientific phenomena (for required functions)

ARIZ asks questions that integrate the different elements of TRIZ and begins with the assumption that the nature of the problem is unknown. ARIZ is a logical approach to the reformulation of the problem through application of the various knowledge bases that have been developed for resolving conflicts. ARIZ applies ideality to understand the ideal solution to the problem; contractions to evaluate first technical and then physical elements, using the thirty-nine design parameters and forty inventive principles; and specification of the system resources, scientific effects, and Su-Field modeling, with the seventy-six standard solutions to stimulate solution ideas. The ARIZ approach has nine steps, which are divided into the following three phases:

I. Restructure the original problem.

1) Analyze the system.

2) Analyze the resources.

---

[19] For more on ARIZ, see Pentti Soderlin, "Thoughts on ARIZ," *TRIZ Journal*, April 2003.

3) Define the ideal final result (IFR) and formulate the contradiction.

II. Remove the physical contradiction.

4) Separate the physical contradiction.

5) Apply TRIZ knowledge base of effects, standards, and principles.

6) Change the "mini-problem" (subset of the system-level problem).

III. Analyze the solution.

7) Review the solution and analyze removal of the contradiction.

8) Develop maximum usage of the solution.

9) Review all the stages in ARIZ in "real-time" application.

▶ *Contradiction matrix*: This tool (also called the Altshuller Matrix) is perhaps the best known in the TRIZ method. The most frequent problem in using the contradiction matrix is translating from the problem statement to the language used in the matrix; for this reason, there have been many different "reformulations" of the matrix for different types of applications (e.g., software design, chemical design, etc.). The matrix is formed to define the relationships of the conflict for each of the thirty-nine design parameters to assess relationships between the improving conditions (shown in the rows) and worsening conditions (shown in the columns). Each cell in the contradictions matrix is evaluated using a pairwise comparison of these two conditions, according to the criteria of the forty inventive principles, to determine how they could potentially apply to resolve the contradiction.

Contradiction Matrix

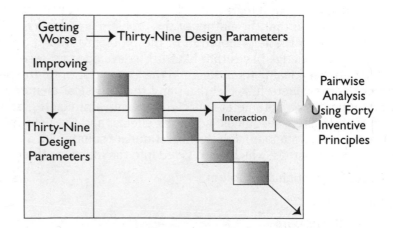

The entire matrix operates as an idea generator that is enhanced by the expertise and capability of the people who are involved in the assessment. Contradiction analysis uses the matrix to help interpret and understand the nature of the conflict. The contradiction matrix is interpreted from top to bottom as well as from left to right to determine the relative priority of potential solution opportunities. All potential solutions to the conflict are evaluated based on decision criteria (which include both design and business considerations), and the best solution is chosen (this is a good application for the Pugh Concept Selection Matrix).

▶ *Thirty-nine design parameters*: This set of design parameters was developed in Altshuller's research on patents. The parameters represent design considerations that should be evaluated when creating a function, and they include the following thirty-nine components:

1. Weight of moving object
2. Weight of non-moving object
3. Length of moving object
4. Length of non-moving object
5. Area of moving object
6. Area of non-moving object
7. Volume of moving object
8. Volume of non-moving object
9. Speed
10. Force
11. Tension, pressure
12. Shape
13. Stability of object
14. Strength
15. Durability of moving object
16. Durability of non-moving object
17. Temperature
18. Brightness
19. Energy spent by moving object
20. Energy spent by non-moving objects
21. Power
22. Waste of energy
23. Waste of substance
24. Loss of information
25. Waste of time
26. Amount of substance
27. Reliability
28. Accuracy of measurement
29. Accuracy of manufacturing
30. Harmful factors acting on object

31. Harmful side effects
32. Manufacturability
33. Convenience of use
34. Repairability
35. Adaptability
36. Complexity of device
37. Complexity of control
38. Level of automation
39. Productivity

▶ **Forty inventive principles**: Likewise, the inventive principles were developed by Altshuller, and they are recommended principles that can be applied to remove the problem. These inventive principles provide clues to identify potential solutions for conflict resolution and include:

1. Segmentation
2. Extraction
3. Local quality
4. Asymmetry
5. Combining
6. Universality
7. Nesting
8. Counterweight
9. Prior counter-action
10. Prior action
11. Cushion in advance
12. Equipotentiality
13. Inversion
14. Spheroidicity
15. Dynamicity
16. Partial of overdone action
17. Moving to a new dimension
18. Mechanical vibration
19. Periodic action
20. Continuity of useful action
21. Rushing through
22. Convert harm into benefit
23. Feedback
24. Mediator
25. Self-service
26. Copying
27. An inexpensive short-lived object instead of an expensive, durable one
28. Replacement of a mechanical system
29. Use of a pneumatic or hydraulic construction
30. Flexible film or thin membranes

31. Use of porous material
32. Changing the color
33. Homogeneity
34. Rejecting and regenerating parts
35. Transformation of physical and chemical states of an object
36. Phase transition
37. Thermal expansion
38. Use strong oxidizers
39. Inert environment
40. Composite materials[20]

▶ **Resources:** Resources are information, energy, materials, objects, proper-ties, or anything that can be readily made from the system's resources or resources that are on hand.[21] Resources are often ignored because they cannot be seen to be discovered. When looking at the problem, some re-sources are invisible, like the air that the Finnish company Fiskars uses to increase the driving force of its axe design by using a hollow handle that actually weighs less than the solid handle, but delivers more force (effec-tive weight) when used. Such a resource is invisible because we are not accustomed to thinking of air as part of the axe design, but the air can be used as a resource to solve the problem, once it is seen differently! Such an unseen resource is idle in the design system, and it is not being used effectively because it has not been discovered. Using these resources differently can help remove the contradiction and achieve the ideal final result. An ideal final result is the solution that resolves the contradiction with compromise.

▶ **Substance-Field (Su-Field) Model:** The method for building a functional model of the problems related to existing or new technological systems is the Su-Field. It recognizes that each system is created to perform a certain function and that the definition of this function is an action performed on one sub-stance (the subject) that typically has a result on another substance (the object). Typically, a function represents an action toward a certain object (identified as substance 2 in the figure on the next page) by the subject (identified as substance 1 in the figure), and this action is accomplished by some means (or energy) (identified as a field in the figure).[22] Thus, a Su-Field can be seen as a TRIZ "function generator." It works best for prob-lems that are well structured.

---

[20] Detailed definitions of the items in these lists (the thirty-nine design parameters and forty inventive principles) are found in the TRIZ literature cited in footnotes 5 and 6 of this chapter; therefore, their descriptions are not repeated here. The lists are included so that business leaders can observe how comprehensive the TRIZ methodology is.

[21] Resources could include any of the following: substances and things, modified substances and things, voids, in-teractions and the energy to make them happen, form, features or properties, space, time, information, harmful substances and interactions, people's skills and abilities, etc.

[22] An observation about the TRIZ use of "field" is necessary (courtesy of Ellen Domb): TRIZ is quite broad in the way it interprets "field." While in classical physics a field refers to phenomena such as gravity, electromagnetism, or nuclear fields, TRIZ calls any form of force or action a field, such as mechanical fields (e.g., strength of material, pushing, or pulling), acoustic fields, and gradients (thermal field and pressure field, etc.).

Su-Field Model

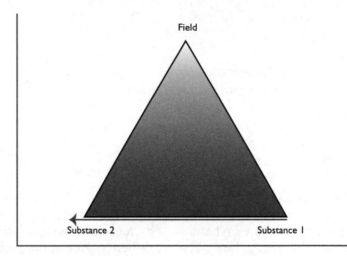

There are four basic models of Su-Fields, which are defined by a logic table that evaluates system completeness and the effectiveness of the result: A design system can be either complete or incomplete, and the outcome of the design can be either effective or ineffective (to the point of being harmful). The "truth table" diagram of this logic (below) shows these relationships graphically:

Function Completeness vs. Effectiveness

	Complete	Incomplete	
Effective	Effective Complete Design	Inefficient Incomplete Design	Requires either completion or new design.
Ineffective	Ineffective Complete Design	Harmful Incomplete Design	Requires that the conflict be eliminated.

Requires design improvement to achieve ideal function.

There are four steps in building the model of a Su-Field:

1. Identify the three elements of the design system and how they operate with respect to each other. (Note that the field is either acting on both of the substances or is integrated with substance 2 as a causal system.)

2. Construct the model and evaluate its completeness and effectiveness of making improvements as required (see the truth table above).

3. Consider solutions for the Su-Field based on the seventy-six standard solutions.

4. Develop a design concept that implements the solution.

▶ *Seventy-six standard solutions*: The third step in a Su-Field analysis considers the set of standard solutions from the TRIZ knowledge base. Although they are formally called the seventy-six solutions, there are actually eighty-six solutions. These standard solutions are helpful for resolving conflicts that arise in level-3 inventive problems, where often the problem-resolving ideas are known in another industry but need to be reformulated and transitioned in order to resolve the current problem situation. This approach is helpful in 18% of the inventive patents (see levels of invention above). Some of the thought leaders in the TRIZ community have subsequently grouped the seventy-six into the following five categories:[23]

1. Improving the system with little or no change (13 standard solutions).

2. Improving the system by changing the system (23 standard solutions).

3. System transitions (6 standard solutions).

4. Detection and measurement (17 standard solutions).

5. Strategies for simplification and improvement (17 standard solutions).[24]

This methodology requires definition of the required function (this is the job of the function-generation process of the Su-Field analysis) to determine the desired capability. The standard solutions are used to stimulate thinking and present new concepts so that the design team can find a suitable effect that is able to produce the desired result. Once an effect has been identified, the next step is to formulate that concept into the design by replacing substance 2 with a new substance 3 in the Su-Field or applying a different field. Note that almost any harmful function can be converted into a useful function either by reversing the field (i.e., changing heating to cooling) or making the field adjustable (e.g., adding temperature-regulating capability).[25]

▶ *Effects database of scientific phenomena*: Once a required function has been defined, then a third problem-resolution approach is to browse the effects database of scientific information to generate new ideas (invention level 4). The effects database of scientific phenomena summarizes objective laws of nature (e.g., laws of thermodynamics and heat exchange) to apply them to

---

[23] These standard solutions are best analyzed; the set of standard solutions is more fully described in the series of five articles by John Terninko, Ellen Domb, and Joe Miller that appeared in the year 2000 volume of the *TRIZ Journal*.

[24] John Terninko, Ellen Domb, and Joe Miller, "The Seventy-Six Standard Solutions with Examples—Part I," *TRIZ Journal*, February 2000 (www.triz-journal.com).

[25] For a more complete description of this approach, see John Terninko, "Su-Field Analysis," *TRIZ Journal*, February 2000.

a specific technical situation as required by the function to be improved. The scientific effects database can be searched in order to build the analogy necessary for "ideation," or the process of creating ideas from all of the different effects that have been found can be initiated, and these ideas can be screened for relative usefulness (e.g., applying the Pugh concept selection matrix or the contradiction matrix) and improved to resolve the problem.[26]

Other design methods that support TRIZ

As Dr. Ellen Domb, editor of the TRIZ *Journal*, observed in a 2003 TRIZ tutorial: "It's hard to keep up: Knowledge expands exponentially, but the exponent keeps on increasing!" There are a number of other methods that apply to the solution of inventive problems and have been cited as potentially complementary to TRIZ. A few of the more frequently described complementary techniques are value engineering and function analysis, systematic innovation, Pugh concept selection matrix, axiomatic design, and Taguchi methods. TRIZ also can be applied as a tool in the application of other methods (e.g., in the gap-resolving problem of benchmarking studies, where "creative imitation" is required to transfer knowledge of the observed best practices into an adaptation that works in different cultural situations and business environments). In addition, there are many implications for TRIZ from the development of Stephen Wolfram's research into rules for creating cellular automata that do not appear to have been considered based on the open literature that is available today.

From this discussion, it can be observed that there are three methods that have not been discussed elsewhere in this book: systematic innovation process (SIP), axiomatic design, and Wolfram's cellular automata.[27] How do these three methods relate to the TRIZ methods, and what promise is held for future developments?

▶ *Systematic innovation process* (SIP): The approach to innovation through the use of tools has been turned into a process by the integration of a basic toolkit that can be applied systematically to consider new ideas, assess their potential against current issues, and select an approach for application in a problem. GOAL/QPC is a leader in this field and offers seminars and a toolkit that encourage a creative approach to problem-solving.[28]

The approach to systematic innovation that applies to building new technology is one that engages the creative energies of the organization in a collaborative way to solve problems by engaging the organization in a "creative dialogue" that generates new ideas, analyzes their applications, and chooses an approach or direction for the resolution of the issue. This approach con-

---

[26] Searching for matches to scientific phenomena is most efficiently accomplished using software like the TechOptimizer™.

[27] Value engineering and function analysis are described in chapter 5, while the Taguchi methods are described in chapter 8 and appendix C, so they will not be described here.

[28] Michael Brassard and Diane Ritter, *The Creativity Tools Memory Jogger* (Salem, NH: GOAL/QPC, 1998).

sists of two phases. The first SIP phase is the logistical phase of defining the problem; identifying the resources, tools, and logistics to be applied to the problem; and organizing the "creative dialogue" event.

<u>*Systematic Innovation Process*</u> (As opposed to random acts of brilliance!)

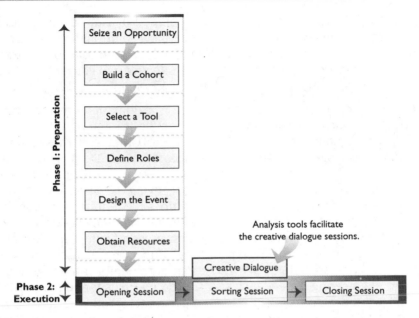

The second phase is conducting the creative dialogue, which follows a three-part approach (both the phase I and phase II models are shown below); opening, or the process of generating ideas for consideration; sorting, or the assessment of logical relationships among the ideas generated; and closing, or the actual choice of the best approach for implementation. While the first phase is conducted by the manager-facilitator, the second phase is the work process of a team specifically constructed to address this problem.

<u>*Phases of Creative Dialogue*</u>

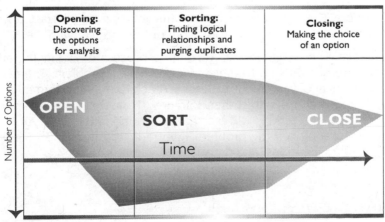

The tools chosen for use in the SIP process are relatively simple compared to the TRIZ toolkit and are accessible for team members from all organizational levels. These tools include brainstorming, brain-writing, interrelationship and affinity diagrams, multi-voting, nominal group technique, and the Pugh concept selection matrix.

▶ *Axiomatic design*: Axiomatic design was developed by Nam P. Suh and provides a more detailed approach for engineering a solution that can be more tightly coupled to the use of TRIZ.[29] There are four main concepts in axiomatic design that are applied to create more effective and efficient functional designs: domains, hierarchies, zigzagging, and two primary design axioms.

   ▶ **Domains**: Four domains are considered in axiomatic design: customer domain, functional domain, physical domain (design parameters), and process domain (production process "control variables"). These domains roughly translate into the four matrices of the QFD house of quality, where the QFD "A" matrix describes the customer domain (voice of the customer versus voice of the design, specifying the customer needs in a conceptual design document that describes the required functionality), and the QFD "B" matrix describes the functional domain as documented in the functional requirements and system constraints, etc. Axiomatic design maps the relationship between functional requirements (FR) and design parameters (DP) into a matrix to demonstrate their logical and engineering dependencies. A second matrix is formed to illustrate the dependencies between the design parameters and the process variables (PV). Functional requirements are the minimum set of independent requirements that completely characterize the functional needs of the design solution in the functional domain. (Some typical functional requirements include: the resulting product must work [do its job]; be safe, economical, and reliable; and meet the needs of its customers.) Design parameters are those elements of the design solution in the physical domain that are chosen to satisfy the specified functional requirements. Constraints are bounds on acceptable solutions. Process variables are the elements of the process domain that characterize the process that satisfies the specified design parameters.

   ▶ **Hierarchies**: The output of each domain evolves from abstract concepts to detailed information in a top-down or hierarchical manner.

   ▶ **Zigzagging**: The designer goes through a process of zigzagging among these four domains in decomposing the design problem. The result is a hierarchical development process in each domain performed in conjunction with those in the other domains. (Note that a similar approach has been suggested in TRIZ by zigzagging among the three ARIZ alternatives to approach the problem [contradiction matrix, Su-Field with its standard solutions, and database of scientific effects].)

---

[29] Nam P. Suh, *The Principles of Design* (London: Oxford University Press, 1990).

▶ *Primary design axioms*: Two design axioms describe the relationship that should exist between the functional requirements and design parameters, provide a rational basis for evaluation of proposed design alternatives, and form the basis for selection of the best alternative. The *independence axiom* presents a design rule to maximize the independence of the functional requirements.[30] The second design axiom is the *information axiom*, which says that to maximize the probability of success for the design project, the information content of the design should be minimized. This is an application of Ockham's Razor to the design process: The design should be as simple as possible while still meeting the customer's requirements. The process of axiomatic design should make good use of regularity in the design process and reuse modules of design wherever possible in order to keep the design of the product simple.

▶ *Stephen Wolfram's new science*: Stephen Wolfram is the scientific guru for a new age in science: programmer, mathematician, and inventor.[31] Wolfram is often credited with development of chaos theory and cellular automata.[32] By using a computer program that he designed (called Mathematica), Wolfram has been able to generate a set of some 256 simple rules that generate counterintuitively complex results that are experientially observable in computer-based systems called cellular automata. Cellular automata are the algorithms, rules, and models that tie together reality into its patterns of behavior. The linkage of Wolfram's New Kind of Science (NKS) and TRIZ has not yet been made, but it suggests a fourth possible application of ARIZ to address level-5 inventive problems.[33]

---

[30] See further the description of orthogonality as presented in chapter 8 and appendix C.

[31] Wolfram is the "boy wonder" of science in the same way Bill Gates took this role in computer science.

[32] See the web site www.wolfram.com and also his book: Stephen Wolfram, *A New Kind of Science* (Champaign, IL: Wolfram Media, 2002)—especially pages 820–823 and 1192–1195, where he discusses engineering implications—for an in-depth description of his discoveries.

[33] In an e-mail dated January 24, 2005, Jason Cawley of Wolfram Research offered the following comments: "The main point here is that past engineering has tended to work exclusively with systems whose behavior was simple, because predictability of behavior—even micro behavior—was considered essential. As a result, truly complicated outcomes could be achieved only by using quite complicated arrangements of parts or subsystems. And as the internal complexity of these subsystems grows, the problem of integrating the various bits becomes more and more difficult. Basically, the human designer has to do all of the work, putting in every specific linkage within the overall resulting system. The result, for a complicated target behavior, can be a mess.

"What NKS suggests is to look for rules that are simple, rather than components whose behavior is simple enough to predict. They are not the same, because simple rules can already give rise to arbitrarily intricate behaviors. Regularity is needed only at the level of the underlying rule—what any given one does can be as unpredictable as you please. Then one "mines" the space of simple rules looking for the sorts of behavior one wants. Instead of designing a system component-by-component to have a given behavior, one scans possible rules for the overall behavior one wants.

"What makes this possible is the simplicity of the rules and the computational tactics that simplicity allows. Rules that are simple enough can be enumerated, formally simulated on a computer, and exhaustively searched. You can try literally all the possibilities, in many cases. For slightly more complicated rules, you can still try huge samples. You don't have to know beforehand which exact rule will work, because you can just simulate them directly and see what they will actually do.

"You aren't looking for the best possible X for doing Y, just for some X(i) that happens to do Y fairly well, for large portions of the space of parameters. Sometimes you will want to mix a few others—X(j), X(k)—for outlier regions of the parameter space. (Sensitivity analysis is obviously part of this exploration of problem parameters.) One is after a "good enough" "cover" of the space of tasks—not one best. All with the characteristic that they are simple at the level of the rule, but not necessarily simple at the level of the behavior that results from repeated use of that rule.

"This has some useful side effects. Simple rules are computationally tractable (unlike, for example, large systems of arbitrarily complex equations). Simple rules can generally be instantiated by simple components, whose local interactions just have to follow the rule in question. Since it is purely formal, the outcome can be simulated easily before anything is actually built. Also, as a side effect of formalism, the individual details of the problem or of special components will rarely matter. The result will tend to be general. Last, since each is tractable, one can readily scan a wide variety of candidate solutions.

"Some of these elements have been used already in methods like ant algorithms and swarms, in combinatorial chemistry, and the like. [See the note "searching for technology" on page 1193 of the book and the notes following it for more instances.]

"One can also try applying the same sorts of methods to systems engineering or overall process design, rather than the search for particular underlying technologies or subsystems. We talked to some people doing so. They are using methods akin to Petri nets to model their problem or system, then getting NKS-ee about enumerating all the possibilities and just simulating them to see how they typically behave."

Chapter 7
Building Reliability into Products

"The most important figures are those that are unknown and unknowable. What about the multiplying effect of a happy customer, in either manufacturing or service? Is that in your figures? What about the multiplying effect of an unhappy customer? Is that in your figures?"

~ W. Edwards Deming

Intoduction

Reliable products don't just happen; they are engineered through a disciplined design and development process to ensure progress toward achieving maturity in functional performance and stability, or consistency of performance, throughout the phase-gate development sequence. The job of design for reliability (DFR) is to grow product longevity throughout the R&D process by enhancing the probability that a product will continue to perform as it has been designed over time once it has been delivered to customers for use in their environment to do the job that they have for the product.

Reliability is the dimension of quality performance that represents the delivery of enduring value to customers. In expressing the meaning of reliability with the same model that was presented in the foreword to this book, reliability represents the enduring consistency in delivery of explicit and implicit promises made to customers about the performance of a product or service. Applying this model, reliability is a subset of quality, but it might be understood differently in different industries. For instance, when reliability is assessed in a service operation, the meaning is very closely related to "consistency of performance delivery" rather than to the duration of product life. Even in the product industry, there are differing ideas about reliability as applied to durable goods, consumable goods, and software.

We will consider reliability in the context of its contribution to customer value. It has been said that "customers buy the first time based on quality and come back to buy again based on reliability."[1] Timo Hannukainen, vice president of quality for Nokia Mobile Phones, once remarked to me that "quality occurs when our customers come back, but our products don't!" Reliability delivers on the product or service customer promise that addresses the time from the initial time of purchase through the operation of the product or service in its useful operating life. This implies that reliability is an important factor in developing a long-term brand reputation for products and services, thereby making reliability a significant contributor to the competitiveness of an organization. In highly competitive markets, reliability might be the most significant differentiator, as Tom Peters implies: "With an explosion of competitors, many of them new and without track records, reliability, rather than overly aggressive promises, is the most valuable strategic edge, especially for the mid- to long-haul."[2]

Reliability engineering makes use of measurements taken in the controlled environment of an engineering laboratory as well as in the uncontrolled field environment. For many engineers, the field environment does not determine the product reliability, but the only failures that are of interest are the ones they are able to replicate in their controlled environment. Over-reliance on such internal data is one assumption that can get a company into significant trouble—reality must always be observed from the eyes of your customer. Jim Harrington observed: "You know you are in trouble when your data look good and your customers are frowning."[3] Ross Cooley, vice president of North American sales for Compaq Computer, calls such customer frowns part of the "street noise" that he uses as an early indicator that there are problems with a product. Thus, an organization's emphasis on reliability management should deliver sustained performance in the customer environment, not just in the engineering laboratory. However, the ultimate purpose of reliability analysis is to make decisions relative to engineering system design in the face of uncertainty. We must remember that all systems are prone to failure no matter what approaches to design for reliability are implemented, and system failure will always cause a loss to be incurred by customers. The product-design objective should be to postpone the failure and minimize this loss!

This chapter will concentrate on product reliability, rather than service or software reliability. It will also focus on a managerial explanation of reliability rather than an explanation for engineers.

---

[1] H. James Harrington, *Reliability Simplified: Going beyond Quality to Keep Customers for Life* (New York: McGraw-Hill, 1999), p. xvii.

[2] Tom Peters, *Thriving on Chaos* (New York: Alfred A. Knopf, 1988), p. 96.

[3] Harrington, *op. cit.*, p. 81.

Perhaps one good way to begin a discussion of reliability is with Murphy's Law—USAF Captain Edward A. Murphy made the following observation of a missile system failure: "If there are two or more ways of doing something, and one of them can lead to catastrophe, then someone will do it." A more popular version of Murphy's Law is "If something can go wrong, it will." Over the years, several corollaries to Murphy's Law have been expressed: Nothing is as easy as it looks; everything takes longer than you think; every solution breeds new problems; and nature always sides with the hidden flaw. An insightful cynic once observed: "It is impossible to make anything foolproof because fools are so ingenious!" Sometimes conditions present themselves so that it seems Murphy was an optimist! Certainly, Murphy's Law presents a wonderful context for a discussion of reliability engineering![4]

Detection of reliability is distinct from that of quality. Customers perceive quality but experience reliability.[5] Some people differentiate between quality and reliability by describing quality as the performance that is observed in the initial customer experience with a product or service, while reliability is the customer experience that comes from sustained operation. The automotive industry makes this distinction clearly, offering recognition to manufacturers for "initial quality" and also giving dubious recognition to those products that don't perform over time—the "lemons" of production that are not able to deliver the sustained performance desired by customers.

The objective of reliability management is to prevent failures before their natural (expected) time. Reliability management cannot, however, reverse the laws of nature. For instance, the second law of thermodynamics says that all processes and physical things have a tendency to decay and disintegrate (moving from order to disorder), increasing the entropy or the state of randomness and disorder of their system—the energy that is not available for productive work. Thus, in the world of products we can observe that all products will fail and that failure is a matter of timing and the conditions of use where the product operates. All electronic equipment is designed to operate for a specified period of time under a targeted set of operating conditions that are defined by a combination of customer requirements, cost targets, and the inherent reliability of its component parts. Reliability is the ability of a system to operate effectively within the time frame of its expected useful operating life. Prevention of reliability problems should occur during the product design, where engineering approaches can be applied to grow confidence in product-performance estimates of reliability based on the testing strategy.

---

[4] Richard Rhodes, *Visions of Technology* (New York: Simon & Schuster, 1999), p. 187.

[5] Harrington, *op. cit.*, p. 2..

It is clear that all business decisions are made under the condition of risk, and one of the primary objectives of reliability management is the elimination or mitigation of technical risk through the product design and development process. One specific business decision is addressed by reliability management: Is the risk of a specified set of product failures so remote with respect to the possible loss that the product should be launched into the market for customers to experience this performance in the real world? While there are many different types of risk that can be addressed by managerial decisions (see the figure below), reliability focuses on five of these risks, which tend to dominate the application of a product or service in the ultimate user environment:

▶ *Technological risk*: conditions that induce failure modes in the product over time.

▶ *Performance risk*: conditions that decrease ability to consistently deliver the performance customers expect.

▶ *Safety risk*: conditions that increase the likelihood of injury or accident during customer operation of the product.

▶ *Liability risk*: conditions that increase the likelihood of product liability due to performance problems from the producer's legal perspective.

▶ *Regulatory risk*: conditions that decrease performance for specified consumer-protection risks as specified by government regulations.

The purpose of reliability management methods is to first expose the potential for risk, determine if the risk can be "engineered" to an acceptable level, and then to provide a systems response to known risks, which can combine prevention, anticipation, detection, and repair into a coordinated "reliability strategy" for a product. This reliability strategy includes components in the design of the product, production of the product, and the service of the product once it is in customers' hands.

<u>*Reliability Methods*</u>

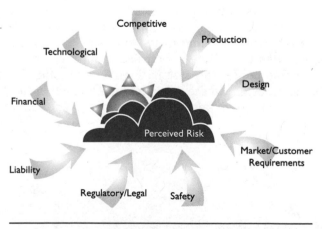

Reliability methods are used to engineer a total system response to known risks.

Risks are realized at different points in the life cycle of a product. Customers experience two broad categories of failure: 1) failure upon initial installation and 2) failure during a product's normal operating use. A definition of a product's useful life is characterized according to three types of failure that are observed in all products: infant mortality, random failure, and wear-out. As a cumulative distribution for their probability of occurrence in the range of a product's useful life, these three failure modes appear to represent what has been likened to a "bathtub"—a shape that has a very steep decline in the range of infant mortality, the service life represented by the bottom of the tub, and the wear-out period illustrated by the opposite side of the tub. These three regions describe what is often called the traditional "bathtub" reliability curve. These regions are also named after the pattern observed in actuarial tables for assessing human mortality risk in the insurance industry (e.g., infant mortality, random accidental mortality, and end-of-life mortality). These conditions can be described as follows:

▶ **Infant mortality**: These early failures occur due to "weak" parts that have been made at the lower limit of their operating characteristics curve. These units have latent defects that are realized within a short period of time after their initial operation. As they are discovered, this population of problems is quickly dissipated—usually by a production tactic of environmentally stressed burn-in (decreasing hazard rate).

▶ **Steady-state failure rate**: This occurs when the device or product is operating in normal conditions and subject to random failures that experience a constant failure frequency, or a slowly increasing failure rate (steady-state hazard rate).

▶ **Product wear-out**: This occurs when the hazard rate rises and the remaining units fail as physical limits for device or product operation are approached at the product's end of life (EOL) (increasing hazard rate).

In reliability, another condition precedes these three states: dead on arrival (DOA). DOA failures occur during initial product testing, either within the confines of the production areas or upon initial delivery in the chain of custody to the final customer. In many organizations, DOA failures are considered part of the original product quality and are not included in the reliability calculations because their costs are assessed against production, rather than against field warranty claims. All subsequent failures that occur during the operating life are usually combined into a product's field failure rate (FFR), and the expenses for repair of these failures during the promised performance life (the warranty period) are reimbursed using an organization's warranty account. (It should be observed that warranty costs come directly out of gross operating profit and that any savings in warranty cost become contributions to profitability.) These regions of reliability are shown in the next figure as a bathtub curve preceded by a DOA spike:

Bathtub Curve

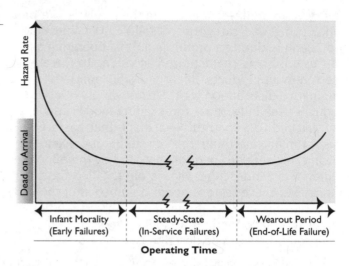

Discovering product reliability

Reliability engineering seeks to avoid the phenomenon that Dorian Shainin called "Dutch books"—where the sum of all the results accounts for less than 100% of the total performance. The analysis tools used for reliability engineering seek to eliminate the possibility of an incomplete analysis of factors (or the situation where a missing factor from the analysis triggers the critical failure mode—the "red X" of Shainin's statistical engineering process). In such a "Dutch books" condition, any decision based on such data would give rise to certain loss, no matter what actually occurs, since not all factors have been accounted for. In order to ensure a proper accounting of failure opportunities and potential failure modes, reliability analysis begins with explicit definitions of expectations and reasons for failure to achieve these expectations:

▶ **Reliability function**: Describes the cumulative probability function for a particular product by identifying probability of failure as a function of time (operating time in the life cycle) based on occurrence of specified failure modes in a targeted operating environment.

▶ **Failure**: Termination of product operation or performance degradation in a product's required reliability function; results that occur that are unexpected, undesired, or lead to the wrong application of a product function.

▶ **Observed failure rate**: A ratio of the total number of failures in a sample taken during a stated period in the product life to the cumulative observed time on that sample. The observed failure rate is an average that can be used as a quick estimator of product reliability.

▶ **Failure classification**: Sometimes it is helpful to classify the severity of failures in order to prioritize the corrective action process (see the severity rankings in the definition of FMEA [Failure Mode and Effects Analysis] later in this chapter). In the user environment, these ratings can be simplified into a four-class system based on the effect on operations: "mission-critical" for any failure that stops the customer from being able to complete their work; "severe" for failures that inhibit customers from effectively performing their desired tasks; "nuisance" for all failures that bother customers but do not prevent them from doing productive work; and "suppressed" for all remaining failures, as well as any failure that is not detectable by the customer except in a rare operating condition. The use of these failure codes helps to classify failures that are observed in operation. Another classification system adds the ability to duplicate these failures under the controlled laboratory conditions of a test facility—and adds the category of no fault found (NFF) or cannot duplicate (CND) for those reported failures that are not repeatable in the laboratory.

▶ **Hazard rate**: This is the instantaneous rate of failure for units of a population of products or devices that have survived to a specific time. This measure represents a conditional probability of failure—the probability that a failure will occur now (or in the next operating cycle), given that a failure has not occurred up to the present time. This type of analysis uses a *Bayesian* statistical model (a conditional probability function) to calculate hazard rate—the rate at which defects occur. Simplifying assumptions include: the product specification will identify the intended life; the product is not operated beyond its design limit for wear-out; and design engineering and product testing have eliminated failure that can be expected due to infant mortality considerations. *Thus, failure analysis tends to focus on the variation of hazard rate that occurs during the intended service life of the product.* Reliability can be understood by studying the hazard function that describes the rate of failure in the next observable time period given that no failure had occurred previously. The bathtub curve provides a generic description of a product's cumulative hazard function across its operating life.

▶ **Reliability**: The ability of a device or product to perform its required functions under its stated operating conditions for a prescribed period of time. Intrinsic reliability is the performance a system achieves based on the inherent capability of the devices that are included in its overall product design.

These definitions help to set the framework for talking about increasing the reliability of a product by decreasing its inherent hazard rate for specifically classified failure opportunities as measured by its probability of failure through a reliability function. Of course, it must be observed that this performance can be enhanced through a proactive reliability strategy that combines designed-in reliability with maintenance activities that are mitigated by a service strategy that anticipates and corrects potential failures *before* they are experienced by customers and *prior* to the impact on performance that results in any losses.

Reliability analysis applies statistical methods to estimate performance and to infer appropriate settings for general customer expectations of system reliability—a figure of merit that measures the central tendency or trend for performance that can be expected under a specified set of operating factors or environmental conditions. The following section defines various measures that are used to express the figure of merit for system reliability. Measures of system reliability must include considerations of how equipment is being operated as well as whether or not the equipment is repairable. For instance, one prime indicator of system reliability is the mean time to failure (MTTF), which should not be confused with the mean time between failures (MTBF). The expected time between two successive failures is the MTTF when a system is not repairable. However, when the system is repairable, the metric is called MTBF. The consideration of both product reliability and maintainability is included in the development of the service strategy for any particular product. Product service is preventive maintenance that anticipates the occurrence of a "highly probable" potential failure mode and eliminates the failure by making a repair "prior to" its occurrence.

Some reliability indicators that have been traditionally used to describe performance include:

▶ **MTTFF** (*mean time to first failure*): The average time for observation of the first system failure from the time of initial installation.

▶ **MTTF** (*mean time to failure*): The average time observed to the first operating failure (for a non-repairable system) or between failures (in a repairable system). This statistic is also known as mean time between failures (MTBF) for repairable systems.

▶ **MOT** (*mean operating time*): The average time of system operation during which all functions are performed within their individual specified limits.

▶ **FIT** (*failures in time*): An FIT is a unit of probability of failure at 10^{-9} in the next hour of the operation of an electronic device given that it has survived up to the time of assessment. This is used to characterize the nearly constant failure rates that occur during the steady-state portion of the bathtub curve.

▶ **Maintainability**: The ability of a device or product, under stated conditions of use, to be retained in, or restored to, a normal state in which it can perform its required functions after the performance of a sequence of planned maintenance activities using prescribed procedures and resources.

▶ **MTTR** (*mean time to repair*): The total corrective maintenance time divided by the total number of corrective maintenance actions during a given period of time.

▶ **MRT** (*mean repair time*): The average time that a system is "down" or inoperable following a failure event. The downtime between occurrence of a failure and the completion of the repair also called the average repair time, or just repair time.

▶ MTTPM (*mean time to preventive maintenance*): The average time from installation of a product to its initial scheduled preventive maintenance intervention.

▶ Availability: The ability of a device or product (applying a combination of design reliability, maintainability, and maintenance service support) to perform its required function at a stated instant of time or over a stated period of time.

▶ Intrinsic availability: The operating time of a system divided by the sum of the operating time and the active repair time (this does not include waiting time).

▶ A_o (*operational availability*): The uptime of a system (the time interval during which the system/equipment is either being operated or ready for operation) divided by the total of operating time and down time (the time interval during which the system/equipment is in a state of failure or inoperable).

▶ Operational reliability: The probability that a system is ready when it is needed multiplied by the probability that it will function for a specified length of time.

▶ Operational readiness: The equipment or system uptime divided by total calendar time of the period observed.

▶ System effectiveness: A function defined by the Markov sequence of operational availability, reliability, operational readiness, and the performance capability of the functional design in its intended application and operational environment.

These indicators should *not* be used without questioning by management, as they might lead to the wrong product decisions being made! For instance, increasing the MTBF of a product might not result in an enhanced total customer experience! The MTBF is an average—half the expected failures occur before this point in time, and half occur after this point in time. Better questions to ask are: What failures do customers care about, and what is the probability that these failures will occur? In a Six Sigma product development strategy, the *mean*, or average, time to failure is not as significant an indicator of performance integrity as is the time to first failure for those things that matter to the customer as experienced by the customer during the product's useful life. The job of a DFR approach to Six Sigma design is to apply its toolkit to keep these harmful experiences from happening to customers!

The tools of reliability

Over the past decades, a number of tools have been developed to help address these concerns about product reliability. Some of the reliability tools fit together naturally in a sequence of analysis methods: The Bayesian approach can be used as a natural companion to the fault tree analysis for estimation of probability for sequential system failure using conditional probability logic. The reliability block diagram provides the logical structure for developing a fault tree analysis. The failure mode and effects analysis provides understanding of relationships between failure modes and the dependent events in order to structure a logical sequence of system failures. System structural analysis helps establish "weak points" in the product design, while reliability allocation helps design teams to coordinate their reliability-improvement activities across the components and subsystems. Fault tolerance, redundancy in design, design derating, and reliability testing can be used to improve reliability during the design process, while analysis of field data can be used to validate laboratory tests and detect the occurrence of predicted failure modes. What are these tools, and how are they used?

▶ **Design review checklist:** These checklists are used at the various decision milestones of an organization's design process (sometimes called a tollgate or decision gate system) to ensure that appropriate reliability tests have been successfully performed with corrective actions taken at the most appropriate point in the product development process, based on project review findings for successful product development programs.

▶ **Functional specification (FS):** The functional specification describes the function and its critical operating parameters, redundancy features that can ensure continued operation during its failure conditions, protection features that keep error conditions from generating extensive problems or that inhibit minor failures from causing system failure, and key instrumentation features that aid in measurement for detection or provide operational control.

▶ **Functional analysis system technique (FAST):** A FAST diagram is used to illustrate the relationships among the functions of a product and to specify the logical inter-relationships among the various functions that deliver value to customers.

▶ **Reliability block diagram:** A diagram that provides a graphical representation of the system's engineering subsystems, illustrating how they are connected to deliver the functions.

▶ **FMEA and criticality analysis:** An analysis of the functions of a product, the ways in which these functions can fail, the causes of these failures, the detection opportunities for these failures, and the impact that these failures could have on customers.

▶ **Fault tree analysis:** A system-level analysis of the failure potential for multiple event failures in complex interdependent systems (e.g., nuclear power plant or airplane).

▶ **System structure analysis:** A system-design-level analysis method that identifies critical pathways for multiple event failures in order to ascertain where redundancies in design and more robust tolerances for critical design parameters would result in improved system-level reliability.

▶ **Reliability allocation:** The allocation of failures by sub-module or subsystem to create a budget that will deliver the overall system target for reliability. Combined with design rules that systems that are similar to those in operation deliver improved performance over prior generations, this allocation process is particularly helpful for understanding how much failure can be tolerated in new technology areas.

▶ *Fault tolerance:* The ability of a product or system to tolerate fault conditions without passing on the effect to the user. There are three levels of fault tolerance: warning about an impending failure mode; maintaining a safeguard mode of operation during the time of failure that provides functionality at a reduced level of performance but permits corrective action; and shifting the full operation to a redundant operating system to maintain full functionality.

▶ *Redundancy:* Redundancy exists when there is more than one approach to execute a given product function. The approaches for performing the function do not need to be identical.

▶ *Redundancy, active:* That redundancy whereby all redundant items are operating simultaneously rather than being switched on when needed.

▶ *Redundancy, passive:* That redundancy wherein the alternative means of performing a function is inoperative until it is required and is activated upon detection of a failure in the primary means of performing the function.

▶ *Operating characteristic* (OC) *curves:* An operating characteristic curve plots the full-spectrum performance (for the design characterization of a product feature) against another factor to illustrate the operating envelope response (for definition of the normal performance range) for a specific critical product feature. An OC graph can also be used to illustrate the power of sampling plan (probability of acceptance on the Y axis) for rejecting various percent defectives (on the X axis) for a family of curves representing various sample sizes.

▶ *Design derating:* Reliability performance can be improved by selecting component parts for performance characteristics on critical operating parameters so that the parts never reach stress-level conditions. This approach explicitly provides a performance "buffer" that overdesigns or "guard-bands" a specified design factor (say by 30% to 40%) so that the stress conditions that lead to failure are less likely to occur. Rather than designing a product to just maintain its normal performance under operating conditions of maximum stress, this approach adds a further "design margin" that acts like an insurance policy against the failure condition that is being protected against. However, this approach also costs more than another alternative that is favored by Six Sigma (robust design) because it will increase cost that customers might not perceive as value (which is one of the problems with failure—when it doesn't occur, customers aren't aware of what was done to prevent the failure). This is another form of the philosophical question "If a tree falls in the forest and there is no one to hear it, does it make a noise?"

▶ *Reliability testing:* Reliability testing is a "check and balance" done by designers on behalf of customers and shareholders alike. Reliability testing implements a design-maturity development strategy that uses a set of tests to demonstrate the sustained capability of a product to meet or exceed its expected performance from both a customer-requirements perspective and a fiduciary-responsibility perspective. Reliability testing is conducted to optimize the design of a product and its production processes; deliberately induce product failures to establish the performance limits of a product; or demonstrate the achievement of a specified level or duration for sustained, acceptable performance. Poor product testing destroys shareholder value because it does not protect fiscal resources from excessive risk of failure—this protection is really an insurance policy for the capital invested by shareholders in the company. What tests will provide an adequate assessment of risk and should be performed to achieve these objectives? Some of the more routine reliability tests include:

- Shock, vibration, and drop tests for both the product and its packaging.
- Product stress testing (vibration and thermal tests, sometimes called "shake and bake").
- Moisture, humidity, and dust exposure.
- Thermal shock—hot and cold temperature cycling.
- Functional testing to demonstrate sustainable performance of mechanical functions (e.g., keyboard, connector plug-in, hinge-case operation, power-cycling, etc.).
- Electrostatic discharge (ESD) testing.
- Electromagnetic interference (EMI) testing.
- Endurance testing to demonstrate useful product life and estimate product reliability.

There are several important benefits of reliability testing. Such testing delivers:

- Stability in product design
- Consistency of product operation
- Predictability of product performance
- Availability to customer demand

▶ *Environmental stress screening* (ESS): Represents the qualification testing approach where the product design goes through a battery of environmental screening tests just prior to launch in order to demonstrate adherence to specifications for environmental factors (this methodology is replaced by HALT, HASS, and HASA).

▶ *Highly accelerated life testing* (HALT): Accelerated testing regimes are used to obtain information about failure modes and the useful life of a product during the design phase of product development, prior to launch in the marketplace. It is a useful tool for designers to identify potential weaknesses in parts, materials, and processes that can be easily corrected prior to high-volume shipment in order to make a product more durable. In HALT, the product is evaluated in extreme conditions that are beyond its normal operating envelope in order to ensure performance

▶ **Highly accelerated stress screening (HASS):** A test regime that is used during the full-volume production to verify sustained reliability performance as characterized during HALT. HASS places the system under the highest possible stresses (well beyond the normal operating levels) in order to achieve the time compression required for an effective screening of product performance.

▶ **Highly accelerated stress audit (HASA):** HASA provides a testing regime that uses a sampling plan to monitor reliability life during a post-production audit (as compared to HASS, where 100% of a product is screened).

▶ **Beta testing:** Testing that is conducted in the situation of the customer's operating environment and done with the cooperation of customers. This testing can be either supervised or unsupervised by the design team. The objectives of beta testing are twofold: to demonstrate product-performance capability in the customer environment, and to obtain feedback on unsatisfactory design parameters or operating modes for corrective action prior to release of the product for full production.

▶ **Reliability data analysis and interpretation:** Two distinct sources of information on reliability—one is from dedicated testing, such as accelerated life testing, and the other is monitored performance, either in the factory at the point of production or in the field during customer operation. Since field conditions do not always capture sufficient information and since dedicated tests do not always stress a product in the same way as the customer environment, both of these methods must be used to understand a system's reliability performance. In an accelerated test, some conditions are altered (e.g., temperature, voltage, humidity, power cycling, etc.) to stress operating performance at a corner case of its operating envelope. This stress is greater than normal, typical, or expected operating conditions and is applied to accelerate the occurrence of failure modes exhibited under these conditions. It is assumed that whatever failures occur in reaction to such extreme stimuli are representative of the failure modes that would also occur during normal operating conditions. This is not necessarily a valid assumption and must be validated to ensure adequacy of the testing process.

These tests and engineering methods are used to induce and observe failure modes in order to predict product performance in the hands of the customer. Data observations are summarized using deductive statistics, and predictions are made about future performance using inductive statistics to determine the probability of failure modes occurring. What statistical methods are used to support these engineering tools?

Statistical analyses are used to determine the expected value of product reliability. Most of these tests are concerned with the trend in central tendency for failure performance. Statistical methods are used to characterize observed failure distributions over time and to estimate the likelihood of failure as a function of time. These characterizations of failure are used to improve product designs, establish replacement-part demands, and plan for scheduled maintenance.

▶ *Reliability modeling*: Construction of probabilistic models illustrating risks in a physical system; these models are used to calculate end-to-end system reliability based on individual component reliability.

▶ *Poisson defect model*: Illustrates a distribution that occurs at a constant average rate for only one or two countable outcomes (e.g., success or failure). The Poisson distribution is used to show probability of failure for attribute data (applications in service applications and software quality).

▶ *Weibull distribution*: This statistical distribution provides a nonlinear expression for the hazard-rate function that includes special cases of several other probability distributions, including the normal distribution. As the hazard rate changes, the shape of the Weibull distribution describes three distinct areas of reliability described by the bathtub curve (when the hazard rate is decreasing, it defines the infant mortality; when it is constant, it defines the steady-state condition; and when it is increasing, the Weibull distribution defines the wear-out period at the end of life).

▶ *Markov chain*: A logical sequence of events that is dependent on the successful completion of prior events. Thus, the performance of the nth step is based on the successful completion of all $n-1$ previous steps. The transition probability for each sequential state in a Markov chain is the estimate of success for that stage multiplied by the probability of entering that state. For a total Markov system, the overall probability of success would be the product of success in each of the individual states.

▶ *Bayesian probability*: This conditional probability calculates the success for a current activity, given that the sequence of activities leading up to this event was successful. For instance, the probability of success for a sequenced event (striking oil, for instance) is conditioned on the fact that prior events have been successfully completed (e.g., drilling a well). If a well had not been successfully drilled, then a necessary precondition for the subsequent event would not have been met, and there would be no probability for its success.

▶ *Reliability as probability*: Reliability is presented as a probability of successful operation given a set of conditions (this would be 1 minus the failure rate). The calculation of system reliability must take into account the different performance effects of parallel and serial subsystem designs.

- **Reliability of serial systems:** The overall reliability of a serial system is the product of the reliability rate of its individual components. In this case, the performance of the whole system depends on its "weakest link"—the component or element with the lowest reliability.

- **Reliability of parallel systems:** When redundancy is built into a system, then the reliability of the system will improve. Reliability performance of the redundant stage can be estimated as one minus the product of the failure rate of the redundant components. Including redundant systems in a design is one way, albeit costly, to improve the performance of the overall system. However, this might be the only option available if there are no engineering alternatives based on the state of the art in the component design.

Since no one can say "for certain" what failures will occur when, probability theory and its application have become a significant part of the language of reliability—often to the detriment of reliability engineers who attempt to use these methods to explain their observations to management! What are more pragmatic ways to describe how poor reliability performance affects customers? How can these methods be translated into a language that managers understand—using financial terms?

Relationship of Correction Cost to Time of Detection

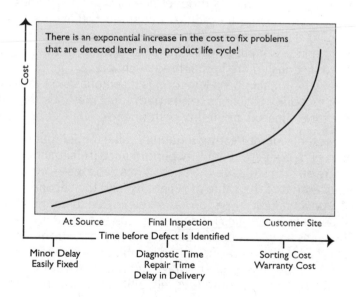

Product life-cycle considerations

There is a pragmatic operational problem for managers who seek higher reliability: No amount of good manufacturing can fix a poor design, while poor manufacturing can ruin the best design. Both design excellence and good manufacturing practice are necessary, as neither alone is a sufficient condition to sustain strong product performance. Typically there is a lot of "finger-pointing" and "blame shifting" that goes on between production and design teams (both of these activities are forms of the managerial sport called "root blame analysis") whenever a failure escapes from the confines of an organization to its customers in the field. The emphasis of reliability engineering is an economic interest to find and fix potential failures before they are ever released to the field for their useful life and incur the highest cost to repair. How big is the impact of potential failure cost on a product's profitability? In one study conducted by Ford Motor Company engineers, the cost of failure had an exponential relationship relative to the time at which the problem is first detected—they called this observation the rule of 10's (as shown in the figure on the previous page)—where, at each subsequent stage in the process development, the cost of corrective action increased by tenfold over that for the previous stage.

The economics of reliability

Dr. Genichi Taguchi, a Japanese telecommunications engineer with NTT, created an economic function that describes the relationship between performance to specification and the loss that occurs as a function of variation, which is now called the Taguchi Loss Function.[6] He observed not only that quality losses occur when a product does not meet specification and is scrapped or rejected (an internal failure), but products that meet the tolerance might also inflict a quality loss that is visible to the customer if the variation of their performance is great (an external cost of failure). Taguchi's methods for robust product design are highlighted in chapter 8. The most significant contribution of the Taguchi Loss Function is its emphasis on variation as the true cause of reliability problems, while traditional methods rely on average performance for estimating reliability performance.

Harrington presents an interesting reliability value model that identifies four unique zones of a product's reliability performance (this function is illustrated in the figure on the next page).[7] The chart has two axes—one describes the customer perception of the value of reliability, and the second shows a relative plot of product reliability performance referenced to its specification. The chart is divided into four zones for ease of interpretation. Performance in the first zone provides an inadequate reliability performance from the customer's perspective (less than 8% of the specified reliability), which indicates that the product is still in the development stage and not ready for commercialization. In the second zone, the product reliability is grown through reliability engineering during the design process. In this reliability-growth or product-maturing process, reliability increases from 8% of the specification to exceed the customer specification. For most products whose reliability is a critical quality element for competitiveness, meeting the customer specification for performance is an entry condition to the market; therefore, moving through

---

[6] Madhav S. Phadke, *Quality Engineering Using Robust Design* (Englewood Cliffs, NJ: Prentice-Hall, 1989), pp. 17–22.

[7] Harrington, *op. cit.*, p. 55.

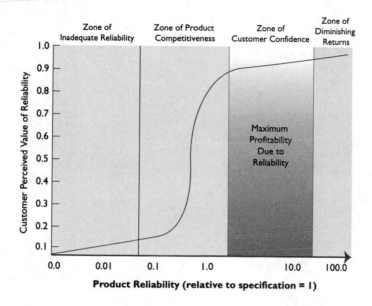

Product Reliability (relative to specification = 1)

this performance zone is only the "price of admission" for consideration in a competitive market. Profitability is generated by reliability only when the investment in reliability generates exceptional customer confidence that then warrants a price differential in the market, as observed in the third zone. However, there can also be a point of diminishing economic returns where exceptional engineering methods are used to achieve the highest levels of reliability (this occurs in mission-critical systems that impact life and death, such as in the design of aircraft or medical life-support systems) where the investment in the product's reliability is no longer motivated by financial return and consumer confidence. In this zone, investment in monitoring equipment and redundant systems is justified because reliability losses could result in unacceptable costs to society.

Harrington suggests plotting on this same graph the cost function for producing these reliability results. This would provide a value-engineering-related insight into the transition from reliability as a producer-borne cost to reliability as a contributor to the worth of the product (where worth is related to customer value and cost—see chapter 5). This would be capable of identifying the point of diminishing economic returns where investment in more reliability (beyond the level desired by consumers) results in decreased profitability to the producer.

Interrelationship Diagram

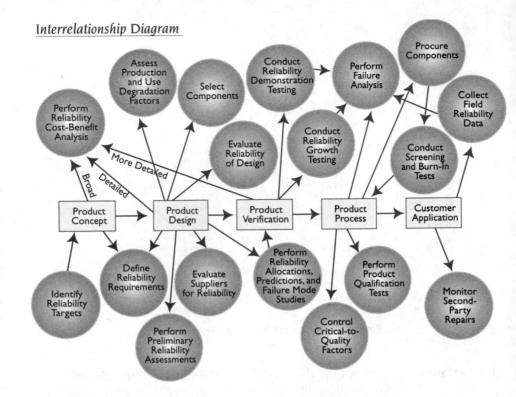

Reliability improvement strategies

A key question for managers is: How can reliability contribute to performance improvement throughout the entire product life cycle? One answer to this question is the interrelationship diagram, which illustrates the typical sequence of product-design activities intermeshed with the reliability activities associated with each of these steps (see the figure above).

The following sections of this chapter focus on how reliability is enabled and assisted across the elements of the design process and the production process, as well as through the service activities of the organization. This perspective demonstrates that a successful reliability strategy should not be confined to the design of products, but must be part of the production and service strategies of the organization as well.

Reliability in design

As illustrated using Ford's rule of 10's, the highest-payoff investment for improving product reliability occurs during the design phase of new product development. Since it is best to influence reliability during design, the reliability engineering toolkit focuses strongly on catching problems early by concentrating on safety margins, degradation in strength of materials, and protection against extreme loads in order to achieve designs that will be failure-free. Some elements in this reliability toolkit include:

- **Red-flag conditions**: These are manufacturing conditions that provoke errors or mistakes in the production of a product. These conditions must be avoided during the design process, and the use of product-design rules is a key way to ensure that known operating conditions that cause failure will be avoided in new product developments.

- **Product-design rules**: The set of lessons learned about product design that have been captured in post-manufacturing release design reviews (sometimes called post-mortem project reviews—they are conducted after the project is dead). Many companies assemble these rules in a "book of knowledge" that is required reading for new project managers. Design rules can cover a variety of topics, such as common part selection, production tooling development, new-part qualification procedures, initial product burn-in requirements, supplier qualification process, etc. In many of the high-technology companies, these design rules have been specifically established to ensure a successful transition across modules in a multi-generational product development program.

- **Reliability prediction**: There are two basic approaches for prediction of product reliability. One is the traditional approach taken using the MTTF statistic, which seeks to estimate the average time to failure for a complex product and then tests the product to ensure that the observed rate of failure exceeds this average (using a statistical test of difference). There are several problems in applying this approach, not the least of which is the fact that there is a bias to design all parts to achieve a different level of reliability than might be required by the consumer market because all of the standards used in these calculations are based on engineering data. A second approach is used in Six Sigma analysis of failure estimation, where the standard of performance is the targeted useful life of the product that is being designed, and only those product components that fail to meet this standard become the target of special engineering attention. This Six Sigma approach has the benefit of being linked to the market and ensuring that the reliability value proposition is aligned with the demands of customers.

- **Reliability growth and testing**: Reliability growth and testing is used to ensure that initial designs make consistent progress in improvement of reliability performance across different prototype builds and engineering tests. The output of reliability growth is typically plotted on what is called a Duane curve, which describes the trend in improvement of reliability relative to the product's reliability design target. This curve was derived by J. T. Duane based on his empirical observations of reliability improvement. Duane observed that the total test time divided by the total failures ($MTBF_\theta$) plotted against total time on log-log paper resulted in a straight line that estimated MTBF improvement or growth. The slope of this line indicates the rate of MTBF growth and is therefore useful for estimating improvement that occurs from eliminating failure modes in the design process.[8]

---

[8] Patrick D. T. O'Connor, *Practical Reliability Engineering*, 3rd edition (New York: John Wiley & Sons, 1991) p. 292.

▶ **Reliability qualification testing**: These tests demonstrate the achievement of the initial design criteria for reliability in the environment as required by the product specification. A product is considered qualified when it passes all required tests. Many large procurers of high-technology equipment have their own set of conditions or batteries of tests that they use for demonstration of performance according to their specifications—these acceptance tests are typically specified in the initial contract terms and conditions.

The next best thing to ensuring reliability in design is to ensure reliability through the process of production.

Reliability in production

The focus of reliability improvement during production is to ensure that three objectives are met: the product continues to perform according to its initially demonstrated reliability; that any changes to the product do not decrease its expected reliability; and that improvement opportunities include both cost reduction and corrective action when product reliability does not equal competitive performance. To achieve these objectives, several different operational methods can be employed:

▶ **MTTF/MTBF** *validation testing*: This off-line HALT process is a continuation of the design testing to ensure that any changes in the product that occur as a result of continuous improvement during production engineering make a positive contribution to the expected product life. This test differs from the HASA test, as it is triggered by a change to the product or packaging design.

▶ **Production reliability audit**: Two types of audit testing can be accomplished at the end of the production line. One is based on sampling to ensure that the product still meets pragmatic goals for reliability (e.g., it is able to be shipped reliably without initiating any conditions or failure modes leading to a DOA event). The second is an audit of products using the HASA to ensure that a random selection of products still meets the expected reliability performance.

▶ **Field product testing**: This testing extends beta testing with partner customers to evaluate how the product contributes to the customer application (while at the same time identifying shortfalls that might imply the need for product revisions in the next variant that is designed).

▶ **Surrogate customer testing**: This testing occurs at the end of the production line and entails two levels of testing. In one, the product is received by a surrogate customer and installed in a typical workplace to emulate the customer experience and study it for potential problems. The second is a follow-on assessment where the surrogate customer then objectively completes a customer-satisfaction survey regarding their experience. The results of this survey must deliver the targeted level of field customer satisfaction and also have a high correlation to the actual level of satisfaction that is measured during the normal customer-survey process (this should be over a 90% correlation).

▶ *Poka-yoke mistake-proofing*: This is a fail-safe process for avoidance of inadvertent errors in work processes. Poka-yoke also provides for detection and prevention of errors (mistakes at the operator source) before they become defects (released to the customer) by using warning (when something is about to go wrong), control (managing to ensure that errors are not possible), and shutdown (to prevent a mistake that is about to be made). Poka-yoke is related to reliability engineering, as it operates as an effective part of an overall strategy for managing potential failure modes (listed in priority order for elimination of known problems):

1. Eliminate the occurrence of the failure mode.

2. Reduce the severity of the failure mode.

3. Reduce the occurrence of the failure mode.

4. Improve the detection of defects for the failure mode.

5. Provide a means for customers to detect failure during use of the product.[9]

▶ *Five S's*: A set of standards for conducting disciplined work that achieves order and then ensures consistency in performance. This system was developed in Japan and consists of five activities that create a disciplined work environment: *seiri* (sifting or removing unneeded materials and equipment); *seiton* (sorting or arranging materials for ease of operator use); *seiso* (sweeping, or a campaign of cleaning up the workplace to make it "spic and span"); *seketsu* (standardizing, or the process of maintaining the agreed-upon work standards); and *shitsuke* (sustaining the 5S culture in the daily routine management processes).[10]

▶ *Warranty failure rate*: The total number of failures for products that are still covered by their warranty agreement observed during a reporting period divided by the total number of products produced that are still within their warranty period.

▶ *Field failure rate analysis*: Collection, analysis, and interpretation of information from the point of sales, service, and use is critical for understanding how well business and engineering processes deliver product reliability. The ability to capture such information varies greatly with the type of product and its application. Some products lend themselves to close relationships with customers or end users, thereby permitting close observation and data collection, while other products do not even lend themselves to identification of the ultimate end user (e.g., a consumer product sold through a mass-merchandising chain, where low response to product registration will typically inhibit knowledge of the end customer and their product ap-

---

[9] For a good summary discussion of poka-yoke, see Nikkan Kogyo Shimbun Ltd., *Poka-Yoke: Improving Product Quality by Preventing Defects* (Portland, OR: Productivity Press, 1988), pp. 3–28.

[10] For an in-depth introduction to the 5S methods, see Hiroyuki Hirano, *Putting 5S to Work* (New York: PHP Institute, Inc., 1993).

plication). In this second type of situation, there are two tactics that can be employed to improve an organization's level of information—one is to improve the response rate for product registration through the offer of a value proposition that customers find "irresistible," while the second is to regularly track a sample of products through the production process to the end customer and to interview these customers when their expected product use approaches a statistically valid "usage experience" (as measured in hours of use or events processed, depending on the product). Both of these tactics can be done concurrently and will improve understanding of the customer experience among the installed base of customers—valuable information for managers, product designers, and producers!

The last resort for managing a product-reliability program is to prevent failure by using a service program that anticipates failure and performs a program of planned preventive maintenance to ensure continuous operational availability and reduce the probability of system breakdowns.

Reliability in service

Once a product has been put into use, two related activities can increase its productive life. The first of these deals with the maintenance of products; the second deals with the servicing of products. Maintenance differs from service in that operators or employees of the organization conduct maintenance, while technicians representing OEMs (original equipment manufacturers) conduct service. The first four activities described below refer to maintainability, while the last two activities are included in design for serviceability (DFS).

▶ *Corrective maintenance* (CM): The actions performed as a result of device or product failure to restore the device or product to its specified operating condition.

▶ *Preventive maintenance* (PM): The actions performed in an attempt to retain the performance of a device or product in a specified operating condition by providing systematic inspection, detection, and prevention of incipient failure. There are three basic reasons for doing preventive maintenance: to prevent or mitigate a failure, to detect the onset of a failure mode, or to discover a hidden failure that is not detectable during normal operations. These are the initial considerations for conducting PM. A second decision criterion is the cost-effectiveness of conducting PM—if the entire operation must be halted to do the required maintenance, then a firm might choose a less expensive action that maintains production and schedule either a system-wide shutdown to allow many tasks to be consolidated into a single time frame (thereby mitigating the production lost time) or make a decision to run the operation to the point of failure.

▶ *Reliability-centered maintenance* (RCM): While many maintenance programs focus on what can be done and when it can be done, RCM emphasizes what should be done to preserve the function of the system. In order to accomplish this, RCM first identifies the failure modes that prevent the functions from performing properly and prioritizes the functions based on their failure modes—selecting only functions that meet both of the decision conditions defined above for a preventive maintenance task. RCM ignores non-critical functional failures and focuses on the most critical equipment operations for PM. RCM follows a seven-step process:

1. System selection and information collection.

2. System boundary definition.

3. System description and functional block diagram.

4. System functions and functional failures.

5. Failure mode and effects analysis (FMEA).

6. Logic (decision) tree analysis (LTA).

7. Task selection.[11]

▶ **Total productive maintenance (TPM)**: TPM is that set of activities for restoring equipment to its optimal operating conditions and changing the work environment to maintain those conditions. The TPM approach is aligned with a Six Sigma approach to problem solving because it seeks to eliminate all chronic problems from operating equipment through an evaluation of all potential causes of failure. TPM analysis follows an eight-step process:

1. Clarify the operational definition of the defect phenomenon by eliminating any preconceptions, observing and analyzing the facts at the site of the operation, sorting and stratifying the phenomena thoroughly, and comparing good products with known bad products (pairwise analysis) to identify all significant differences. This is similar to Dorian Shainin's statistical engineering process for components search and "B" (better) versus "C" (current) comparisons.

2. Conduct a physical analysis of the system (e.g., What are the basic operating principles, operational standards, and physical analysis of interacting elements and quantifiable changes that are related to the function?) to observe both *how* the phenomenon occurs and *where* it occurs.

3. Identify constituent conditions in the 4M categories (i.e., machines, man [people], methods, and materials) that are either logically necessary or sufficient conditions for the physical phenomena analyzed in the prior step to occur.

4. Study the 4Ms for causal factors to identify relationships (sequential and correlations) among the constituent conditions identified in the previous step, where a constituent condition is considered the "effect" and the 4M elements are identified to determine the potential "causes."

---

[11] Anthony M. Smith, *Reliability Centered Maintenance* (New York: McGraw-Hill, 1993), p. 55.

5. Establish optimal conditions (necessary and desirable) and standard values, returning to basic principles to study and validate all standards related to equipment functions and characterizing each action to clearly identify the boundary conditions between normal and abnormal operation, either by examining all standards or by conducting analyses and experiments.

6. Survey the causal factors for abnormalities to measure the gap between the current state of the causal conditions (steps 3 and 4) and their ideal values (step 5).

7. Identify abnormalities (any factor that is either abnormal or on the boundary between normal and abnormal) that should be addressed.

8. Propose and make improvements, with emphasis placed on restoration of the optimal conditions and then improving equipment by solving hardware problems, updating obsolete technologies, and preventing recurrence of problems by mistake-proofing the standard work.[12]

▶ *Spare parts provisioning and logistics planning*: When the expected failure point of a product is known at its component level, then a prediction model, based on probability of failure for all the component parts, can be used to determine the stocking strategy for spare parts at product launch and during full-scale production. If an effective logistics plan is not put into place for spare parts, then sales organizations might require that parts be taken from production lines to satisfy customer demands for repairs—while reducing the output of products to the market.

▶ *Planned service interventions*: A final application of reliability in the production environment is to estimate the failure profile of a product in order to establish appropriate service intervals as a function of its operating life—perhaps even using known failure-acceleration factors in an on-site survey that would increase the frequency of service based on the actual customer usage.

Design for serviceability is the final element in a complete DFR program. When this program is designed effectively and executed efficiently, then it leads to competitive advantage—products that are perceptibly better than the competition's. A reputation for reliability is a key ingredient in the management discipline of product leadership.

Competing through reliability-enhanced reputation

Organizations that wish to compete on reliability performance must engage all three of these methods for ensuring reliability: reliability is produced during design, during production, and in service! Reliability, like quality, is such an essential ingredient that it must be ubiquitous—it must be included in every aspect for developing the customer experience with your products and services. How does management ensure high reliability?

---

[12] These steps were derived from chapters 2 through 5 of the book *P-M Analysis: An Advanced Step in TPM Implementation*, by Kunio Shirose, Yoshifumi Kimura, and Mitsugu Kaneda (Portland, OR: Productivity Press, 1995).

One essential activity to ensure reliability that managers must do is to conduct a self-assessment of the current state of their organization's reliability performance. This is done through the application of two tools: One is a set of performance measures that help to give systematic customer insights into your reliability performance, and the other provides criteria (checklist) for evaluating how well your reliability procedures incorporate recognized best practices. Neither of these tools is valuable, however, without the proper leadership and organizational attitude toward reliability.

Measurement system

Because reliability is the sum of many details, no single performance measure can be used to describe "the current state of reliability" in an organization's performance. Reliability has an impact on financial performance, service levels for operations, customer satisfaction, and such soft measures as employee motivation and job satisfaction. It is essential that measurement systems include a suite of metrics that provide a comprehensive understanding of the current state of an organization's performance from both financial and market viewpoints.

Some of the more important performance factor relationships that need to be evaluated in assessing the current state of reliability include:

Field failure rate (FFR)

This is directly proportionate to actual warranty costs—there are two very important considerations that must be made in this analysis. First, warranty costs should include only repairs conducted during the warranty period. Many of the high-technology companies have been observed to use the warranty budget for rewarding sales partners for performance or for buy-back of obsolete inventory. The actual cost of repairing failures must be related to the reported FFR in order to establish a meaningful relationship. Note that reduction in actual warranty cost becomes a direct contribution to the profitability of a product—working on reliability drives bottom-line performance!

▶ FFR by product is inversely proportionate to the profit contribution of the product.

▶ FFR is directly proportionate to unscheduled maintenance or service calls.

▶ FFR can be directly proportionate to reported customer complaints.

▶ FFR is inversely proportionate to overall customer satisfaction with a product or service.

Other indicators of reliability are warranty rate (warranty expense as a percentage of sales revenue), customer complaint rate (customer complaints as a percentage of units sold), and the ratio of unplanned service calls to total service calls. When management monitors a set of standard reliability measures over time, then it can focus its product development efforts on chronic areas that require improvement to achieve sustainable advantage. One way to achieve breakthrough performance in reliability is to observe best practices and implement those practices that will lead to enhanced reliability and competitive differentiation.

What do customers do when things go wrong with a product or service? First, we must recognize that for many people failure is an emotional catalyst that drives them from their normal mental domain of sane rationality to a more distraught emotional condition—with anger at the end of the scale! Upon hearing of a customer problem, the first reaction of most companies is denial: "It's less than a one percent problem" is a comment that has been overheard in insensitive companies. So, the first response is often not embraced by real listening to the voice of the customer! Contrast this "avoidance" response to the attitude of the more mature Japanese companies, where a single customer complaint is considered to be more valuable than gold—an incomparable gift—because it provides insight into a problem that the company could not detect using its internal management processes. Another response of companies is to seek an immediate countermeasure, as if this Band-Aid will completely rectify the issue. Often when customers get into problems with a company's product, the response is a "finger-pointing exercise" where responsibility and accountability for the problem shift on emotional whims until a resolution can be made—this is an exercise in root blame analysis! Deeper responses tend to couple good active listening to "street noise" from customers with follow-up data analysis and a combination of the immediate corrective action and longer-term preventive action to prevent recurrence.

The best companies find these problems and drive preventive action into their corporate product development archive in order to prevent recurrence across many product generations—this is a source of product development design rules for reliability engineering. Richard Moss, a manager of reliability in the Hewlett-Packard corporate quality office, developed such a set of rules in the late 1980s. These rules were outlined in speeches presented at the Annual Reliability and Maintainability Symposium and have been modified over time. The basic rules represent an operational definition of preventive problem solving for product design—also known as design for reliability—and are summarized as follows:

▶ Deliver the performance expectations that have been set for customers and validated as significant expectations by sound market research.

▶ Design products to minimize risk of failure from part, process, and product perspectives.

▶ Design products for robust performance in the ultimate user (that customer who places their hands on a product to use it) environments.

▶ Involve suppliers early in the design process to ensure a systems approach for the use of their parts in the design and to ensure that supply-chain processes are robust and do not contribute potential problems from the ultimate customer perspective.

▶ Stabilize the requirements early in the design process to eliminate last-minute changes that are counterproductive.

- Predict product reliability for design alternatives to ensure that new product designs are better than products previously delivered to the market.
- Test product to the point of failure to identify and then prevent these failure modes from being delivered to the market.
- Foolproof the production processes to prevent operator error and eliminate the escape of mistakes to customers as well as to stabilize the production flow.
- Minimize engineering changes to reduce the risk for introducing new product failures and test each change to ensure that it meets the *original* product specification requirements.

Leadership through reliability

Businesses will continue to compete for customers, one customer at a time. If your customers' experiences are not positive, then they will consider alternative sources of supply for your products or services. For hardware products, the formation of a "brand image" takes time, as this represents the cumulative experience across products that define a brand. However, it doesn't take much time to damage a corporate brand image. Peter Drucker has said that "you can't send a repairman to the battlefield."[13] Like quality, reliability is most effectively delivered in the design of a product or service. If this is not done, then an organization relinquishes competitive advantage to other companies who pay attention to this detail! It is the obligation of leadership to ensure that reliability is effectively managed across the entire product life cycle, that this dimension of product performance is specifically defined for those characteristics that customers expect to "endure," and that this performance is monitored and reported regularly in operating reviews to ensure that reliability receives an appropriate level of attention throughout their organization.

[13] Gregory H. Watson, editor, *Drucker on Quality* (Milwaukee: WI: ASQ Quality Press, 2002).

Chapter 8
Experimenting to Create Robust Performance

"Leadership takes a major step forward when they stop asking for explanations of random variation."

~ W. Edwards Deming

Experimentation for performance explanation

This chapter gives a management perspective of statistically designed experiments and how they can be used to improve product and process designs. It focuses on how engineers can use a sequence of statistical tools to manage development of their projects to demonstrate growth in product-design maturity and prepare the process to produce the product. Statistically designed experiments can be employed throughout the design process to ensure that the design progresses through its developmental milestones and that the performance of the design's functions become more defined as the mechanisms for consistent delivery of outcomes are specified.[1]

Dr. Genichi Taguchi developed his methodology of robust engineering in the 1950s at Nippon Telephone and Telegraph because he observed that problems in the design of telecommunications equipment (and his ideas apply to other engineered systems) are caused by variability in the design's function and that engineers must focus on the function itself in order to improve its quality. The methodology of robust design is built on the framework of experimental design that was developed by Sir Ronald Alymer Fisher at the British Rothamsted Experimental Station in the 1920s to address the

---

[1] Appendix C provides a more technical description of these concepts without going to the level of probability theory and mathematical statistics required to fully demonstrate all the concepts.

efficient design of agricultural scientific experiments in the field. Dorian Shainin, an engineering consultant, also contributed to the understanding of experimental design through his approach to what he called "statistical engineering" as he applied the tools and methods of experimental design to front-line engineering problems in the last half of the twentieth century.[2] The experimental concepts that these men defined converge under the umbrella of the scientific method to provide a systematic approach for explaining and managing variation in engineered products and processes.

Robustness as a design objective

Engineered systems are designed by human beings to deliver functions that transform energy by applying the laws of physics or chemistry to achieve the result desired by an end user (who we are calling the targeted customer).[3]

What is a "robust design" and why is it important? Dr. Taguchi defines robustness as "the state where the technology, product, or process performance is minimally sensitive to factors causing variability (either in the manufacturing or the user's environment) at the lowest cost."[4] A robust design is one that delivers the performance promise made to customers, despite the presence of unwanted variation. Robust designs are relatively insensitive to the effects of unwanted variation—changes in the inputs are not transferred into changes in the outputs. The critical design factors in a robust design act like variation "sinks"; they soak up variation from the inputs. This performance capability is made possible through discoveries about the way that process- and product-related variables behave as they are manipulated during an effective strategy of designed experiments. Dr. Taguchi recommends that robustness be measured with a signal-to-noise ratio (SNR) and that maximizing SNR should be the primary objective of robust design. What does this mean?

---

[2] There are a number of excellent books on this subject, but I am going to recommend only the four that I tell Six Sigma Black Belts are the most useful. Anyone seriously interested in this subject should read the first half of the book: George E. P. Box, William G. Hunter, and J. Stuart Hunter, *Statistics for Experimenters: An Introduction to Design, Data Analysis, and Model Building* (New York: John Wiley & Sons, Inc., 1978). Two other good DOE books are: Douglas C. Montgomery, *Design and Analysis of Experiments*, fourth edition (New York: John Wiley & Sons, Inc., 1997), and Mark J. Anderson and Patrick J. Whitcomb, *DOE Simplified* (Portland, OR: Productivity Press, 2000). Two practical references for applied statistical thinking are: Roger Hoerl and Ronald Snee, *Statistical Thinking: Improving Business Performance* (Pacific Grove, CA: Duxbury, 2001), and Mary G. Leitnaker, Richard D. Sanders, and Cheryl Hild, *The Power of Statistical Thinking: Improving Industrial Processes* (New York: Addison-Wesley, 1996).

[3] Fisher and Taguchi are like England and the U.S.: "two countries separated by a common language." In order to have a more cohesive body of DFSS knowledge, a common language has been attempted to speak about all these methods and tools defined in this book. The author believes that it should not be the work of businesspeople who are trying to serve their customers better to correct the language difficulties and technical problems of those who have preceded them. This is a more proper job for academics and consultants! When the ideas of Shainin are added to the mix, the complexity of thinking goes beyond most practitioners! This chapter (with its accompanying appendix) attempts eclecticism by bringing these ideas into a more coherent unity.

[4] Genichi Taguchi, Subir Chowdhury, and Shin Taguchi, *Robust Engineering* (New York: McGraw-Hill, 2000), p. 4.

Performance information can be divided into two components: signal and noise. The signal is the force that triggers the energy transformation, and it represents the energy that is transformed to do the work required by a function (sometimes the signals have been called "black noise" to recognize that they are an identifiable and desirable component in the spectrum of system effects). On the other hand, "white noise" is energy that has been transformed to anything other than the desired function—it might or might not have the same source as the "black noise," and it represents degradation in the customer's ability to detect and apply the signal to achieve the intended purpose of the engineered system. In an ideal engineered function (as described also in TRIZ), all the energy is transferred from the inputs to the response. If this ideal transfer function were consistently achieved, then there would be no loss in input energy transformed into undesired results or unintended functions (e.g., defects, scrap, rework, customer complaints, warranty claims, etc.). While all systems have some degree of loss in their energy-transfer function, it is true that the larger the loss, the less efficient the system and the more problems in its use by customers. Fault-free performance is achieved only when all of the energy in the input function has been transferred to achieve the desired response. One foundation for understanding variation is to examine the components of variation at their highest level as signal and noise.

An engineered system reaches its "ideal function" when all of its energy (inputs) is transformed efficiently into creating the desired outputs with no losses that reduce efficiency or create a poorly performing function (e.g., energy transformed into friction, scrap, rework, or complaints). Ideal functions are created through a process called robust design.

The vector difference between a pure signal and its observed effect is noise. In order to improve performance of a function toward ideality, the negative impact of noise effects must be eliminated. The measure of goodness used for improvement must comprehend both the controllable signal and the impact of noise on the system.

The Vector Difference

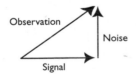

The measure of goodness for this transfer function is the signal-to-noise ratio, or SNR. This ratio is an index that measures robustness in the quality of a function's design as a ratio of the energy-transfer function to achieve the desired functional performance compared to the variability of the desired function. Variation decreases the desired function in two distinct ways—it either causes the total performance to shift from the nominal or desired level of performance, or it distributes energy so that less signal is concentrated in the desired range of performance.[5] The engineering problem is one of sorting out and eliminating the noise effects while at the same time enhancing the signal so that it is more clear and coherent. To do this, engineers must identify the sources of variation that affect product performance and control them to remove the unwanted effects of variation.

Thus, observations are composed of both signal and noise. An observation can also be considered as a function of the measurement of common-cause and special-cause effects of variation on the "true signal" at a point in time. As data is collected over time, special-cause variation and measurement effort can be separated and identified—with just signal average and common-cause variation remaining. Statistical methods such as control charts, measurement systems analysis, and analysis of variance can be used to identify, separate, and manage these components of variation.

Another way of explaining this problem uses a vector to describe all combined effects. A vector is a set of numbers that is treated as a single entity. A vector defines both magnitude and direction of a signal and is depicted as an arrow connecting one point in space to another. One way to interpret a vector is that it combines signal and noise components of an observation in order to identify the underlying relationship. Such a relationship between an original "ideal signal" that would occur at an event and the impact of observations over time could be illustrated as a vector in the following way:

Impact of Observations

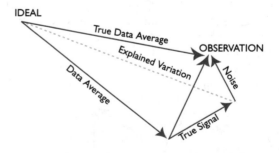

[5] The author's personal frame of reference for thinking about this comes from his Navy experience in anti-submarine warfare. Acoustic frequencies radiating from submarines represented the desired signal that was to be detected. Maximum energy has transferred to the ocean at the interface between the hull of the submarine and the ocean, and then it dissipates at that point through a variety of mechanisms. In an engineering sense, the problem is to increase the gain on this signal so it is detectable in the presence of noise (the ocean environment with its conflicting signals, such as noise from merchant ships). A basic approach to this problem is to focus the acoustic search on the exact frequency of interest (the nominal value) and to decrease the bandwidth of the search so that it matches the frequency of the submarine's original source of energy (the width of the frequency). In this way, the observer has maximized the available SNR and provided an optimal detection capability. This is the same principle that is being applied in DFSS in a commercial environment.

How can these vectors be explained? One vector is the raw observed data (signal embedded with both noise and variation), and the other represents a constructed function (this is a corrected signal that is derived by combining the vector differences in the data signal for components of both noise and explained variation based on a statistical analysis). Average data is used so that the individual data observations do not add to performance misperceptions. Over time, the trend in performance, rather than singular observations, can estimate both central tendency and variation (it includes signal, noise, and explained variation), and this distribution will provide the best basis for drawing predictive information about future performance results.

The problem with this perspective is that S-N viewpoints of observed data also include variation—common-cause variation that is not distinguishable from noise at the time of the observation! These statistical tools help distinguish among the different types of variation in the following ways:

▶ Control charts can be used to identify and separate special causes of variation that might be related to product or process properties from common-cause variation that is due to the design capability of the product or process.

▶ Measurement systems analysis (MSA) deconstructs the variation into observed signal (combined with all sources of noise and variation) and variation due to the measurement system (operator, methods of measurement, and the equipment used for measuring).

▶ Analysis of variance (ANOVA) deconstructs the variance into its component terms based on both short-term (within sample) and long-term (between samples) data observations. This method defines the process for analyzing components of variation. An ANOVA-based viewpoint looks at this differently in terms of three components: true signal, explained variation (special-cause variation), and noise (including measurement error, unknown signals or factors, and common-cause variation).

The process of design is successfully concluded when a robust design approaches the performance capability of its ideal function. To accomplish this, the designer must complete a threefold job: 1) identify the appropriate signal level for performance based on an understanding of the environmental noise; 2) define a set of feasible options for design performance that can satisfy these design criteria; and 3) choose the option with the highest SNR that yields the greatest robustness at the lowest total cost.

Designing robust functions

The basic approach to achieve functional ideality is to apply engineering analysis in order to specify nominal design values for the critical functional parameters. Taguchi recommends the use of parameter design to accomplish this engineering task. In his approach to parameter design, he specifies both control and noise factors. Control factors are critical design parameters that allow an engineer to effectively specify and maintain nominal performance and cost. The control factors are used to optimize and manage the combined product and process robustness. Noise factors influence performance by contributing unwanted variation from known or unknown sources that can be either controllable or uncontrollable in the process.

Also important in this analysis are the interaction effects between control and noise factors that describe how the control variables can be changed to "manage" the effects of noise. Once the relationships among the critical parameters are known, what is the strategy that an engineer should follow to minimize the variation? They should set the targets for performance (nominal values) to achieve the maximum SNR. Practically speaking, robustness means performance consistency at the nominal value! The second element of a robust design is the cost component. In order to understand how cost is involved in the process, Taguchi referenced his definition of quality to what he called a loss function: Quality is "the loss a product causes to society after being shipped, other than any losses caused by its intrinsic functions. Quality design in the product design is particularly important because, although variability can be reduced in production, deterioration of the product or unsuitability for its environment cannot."

Thus, the lowest total-cost parameter design is defined using the Taguchi loss function (TLF), which identifies the cost impact of variation from "nominal is best" parametric design in the SNR:

$$TLF = L = kE(Y - T)^2$$

where:

    L = quality loss suffered at Y-value

    k = quality loss coefficient (cost of variation)

    E = expected value of Y

    Y = observed value of Y

    T = target value of Y (nominal or ideal value)

The Taguchi loss function ("nominal is best") can be illustrated as follows: The loss function is not a single equation, but a family of equations that define how to set the target value of Y based on design rules that apply to the function. The equation above is for the decision rule "nominal is best," but other rules also can be applied, like "smaller is better" or "larger is better."

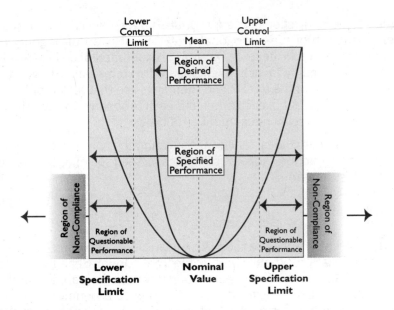

The equations for these two rules are found by modifying the basic equation for a target value of Y that defines the ideal state of the function. Thus, the two equations are as follows:

To apply the "smaller is better" rule, set $T = 0$ in the nominal TLF:

$$TLF = L = kEY^2$$

To apply the "larger is better" rule, use the reciprocal of Y^2 above:

$$TLF = L = kE/Y^2$$

Thus, there are two components to the quality loss—one due to the deviation of the mean from the nominal target value, and a second due to variation in the performance level. The graphical description for each of these functions is illustrated in the figure below.

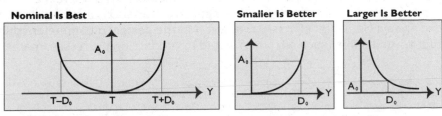

T = Target
A_0 = Cost of Repair or Replacement
D_0 = Functional Limit

In Taguchi's method, choosing appropriate targets for critical design parameters is the job of the orthogonal array![6] What is an orthogonal array? Orthogonal arrays are the heart of a system of experimental design developed by Fisher and applied by Taguchi to engineered systems. An orthogonal array balances the design of the factors and their levels so that all factor levels are statistically independent of each other and each is observed across the entire experimental sequence an equal number of times.[7]

Any deviations from the ideal function that cannot be controlled in either the design or the production process must be assessed for financial risk using the Taguchi loss function.

Sources of variation and "Theory O"

So far, this description has begged the question of the source of observed performance deviation. Where does it come from? Dorian Shainin described a process that he called "variables search" and developed a graphical multi-vari analysis method as a prelude to conducting designed experiments in order to screen a large number of variables for the magnitude of their contribution to the total observed variation. He used this process to search for a "Red X"—an unknown design parameter that influences performance of a customer's critical-to-satisfaction factor (the Y or response variable in the experiment that defines the customer's ideal function, where Y is a combination of both X and an error term using the function $Y = f(X) + f(\varepsilon)$).

This error has several sources. First, there is error that is intrinsic to the system itself. Because this type of error has equal probability of producing a measurement higher or lower numerically than the "true" value, it is called random error. Second, there is non-random or systematic error, due to factors that bias the result in one direction. No measurement, and therefore no experiment, can be perfectly precise. At the same time, statistics provides some standard ways of estimating—and, in some cases, reducing—these errors. Thus, it is important to determine measurement accuracy and precision of a factor when stating quantitative results and to quote the measurement error. Any measurement without a quoted error is a meaningless number, as the magnitude of the true signal is not known compared to the influence of all the combined measurement errors. The comparison between observations and theory is made within the context of experimental errors. There are three sub-categories of this second variation source: 1) variation due to customer abuse or environmental effects; 2) variation in the designed parameters due to unit-to-unit shifts (such as those related to production processes, materi-

---

[6] For an executive description of Taguchi's work, see Genichi Taguchi and Don Clausing, "Robust Quality," *Harvard Business Review*, January–February 1990. For a more in-depth perspective of the technical aspects of the Taguchi methods, see Genichi Taguchi, *Introduction to Quality Engineering* (Tokyo: Asian Productivity Organization, 1986), and Genichi Taguchi, *System of Experimental Design*, vol. 1 & 2 (Dearborn, MI: American Supplier Institute, 1987). Other excellent references on the Taguchi method include: Glen Stuart Peace, *Taguchi Methods* (New York: Addison-Wesley, 1993), and Ranjit K. Roy, *A Primer on the Taguchi Method* (New York: Van Nostrand Reinhold, 1990).

[7] Orthogonal arrays are more completely defined in appendix C.

als, etc.); and 3) the natural degradation of functional characteristics over time as the product deteriorates from usage over time.

Engineers must ask: How many standard deviations are the observed results from the theoretical (ideal) prediction? Have all the sources of systematic and random errors been properly estimated? This approach helps to indicate the presence of any unusual or extraordinary observations in the data.

Have you ever wondered why organizations make the decisions they do? One reason is Theory O, or theory opinion: Organizations make decisions based on the collective strength of the opinion that they hold on a particular topic based on their shared set of experiences related to that topic. But experience is the undesigned observation of what happens. Experience is the victim of circumstances, and from experience is born "Theory O."[8] Management judgments made based on experience include the effects of opinions, gut feelings, suspicions, circumstances and superstitions and can represent facts as well as the hopes, wishes, dreams, desires, and hallucinations of the author. Such subjectively based assertions must have a factual foundation in order to make a sound contribution to performance improvement. Theory O postulates that the best starting point for understanding performance is to collect these experiences in the form of hypotheses and to test these experiential hypotheses against facts. Typical decision processes begin and end with the experience of an authoritative individual that is converted into a conclusion imbued with "truth"—and therefore unquestionable by the organization's analysts. But what if the basis for this experience is wrong and its effect on decision-making is detrimental? What if the critical assumptions are flawed or the experience doesn't represent the generality? Shouldn't experiences be tested first, before accepting them as the basis or root cause of problems?

Sir Ronald Fisher once commented: "That's not an experiment you have there—it's an experience!" To go beyond collective experience as a decision factor about process variation, one must apply the principles of the scientific method. An experimental approach can permit the uncovering of causal systems and allow business leaders and engineers to improve on the quality of their educated guesses.

How does the scientific method address causation?

Albert Einstein postulated that "the scientific method can teach us nothing else beyond how facts are related to, and conditioned by, each other." However, Aldous Huxley disagrees: "The essence of science is prediction, not correlation." So, exactly what is the scientific method, and how does it help to discover relationships among functional parameters in the midst of variation and noise?

Sir Francis Bacon (1561–1626) is generally considered the father of modern science and deductive reasoning. In his *Novum Organum*, Bacon described a

---

[8] Gregory H. Watson, "Comments on Quality: Oh No! It's Theory O!" *Quality Progress Magazine*, October 2000.

new method that would kindle a light in nature—"a light that would eventually disclose and bring into sight all that is most hidden and secret in the universe." The method that Bacon proposed involved the collection of data, its judicious interpretation, and conducting experiments to learn the secrets of nature by organized observation of its regularities.

The objective of engineering, in contrast to science, is to apply scientific knowledge in the practical domain of life. One of the great modern engineers was Thomas Alva Edison (1847–1931), founder of General Electric and inventor of (among over 1,000 patents) the incandescent light bulb with a filament that was practical enough to be used. "Never waste time inventing things that people would not want to buy," he said. He exhaustively applied parametric analysis (one-factor-at-a-time [OFAT] analysis) in order to discover (from some 50,000 options) which filaments provided the longest life in a light bulb. Without an army of technical assistants, Edison's "experiments" would have taken forever! However, such experimentation might not be efficient, as it takes a long time and requires significant investment to pursue. Another approach is required to resolve concerns more rapidly at lower total system cost.

Bacon and Edison provide just two "lights" along the development pathway of what is often called "the scientific method" and serves as the logical basis of Six Sigma analysis and design methodologies. The scientific method describes a generic way to analyze situations using hypothesis-based deductive logic. While not all scientific discoveries come by application of the scientific method, the approach is invoked to prove a result once the discovery has been made. There are five basic steps that can be said to describe the scientific method:

▶ Observation and description of a phenomenon (or group of phenomena).

▶ Formulation of hypotheses to explain these phenomena (typically the hypothesis describes both a causal mechanism and a statistical relationship).

▶ Demonstration of the hypothesis' validity by conducting objective experiments.

▶ Projection or application of the hypothesis to predict the existence of other related phenomena, or to predict quantitatively the results of new observations.

▶ Performance of experimental tests of the predictions by several independent experimenters using independent, properly performed experiments.

The key question that is addressed in such scientific experimentation is: How much signal (knowledge) is available from the field of noise (experience)? Experimental tests might lead either to the confirmation of the hypothesis or to the ruling out of the hypothesis.[9] Thus, planning the experiment is critical

---

[9] Thomas Kuhn, *The Structure of Scientific Revolutions* (Chicago: University of Chicago Press, 1962).

to the process of knowledge building. The scientific method has a significant advantage over Theory O in that it offers an unprejudiced analysis that can be replicated by another researcher because the results using this method are repeatable.

In planning an experiment, the designer applies this scientific method. Experiments are an attempt to increase the "internal validity" of observations by understanding how something that was changed caused something that is observed. In addition, experimental designers also want to build "construct validity," which means that the specific change that was made led directly to (was the actual cause of) the observed outcome. What inhibits an experience from achieving validity? The principal answer to this question is: causality. Causality is a way to explain unwanted deviation in a subject. If a problem represents a deviation from your expectation, then it is most appropriate to ask: What are the sources of the variation that caused this deviation? What does it take to establish such a causal relationship?

Four criteria provide the evidence of a highly probable causal relationship. First, there must be a logical relationship among the factors—the factors must be part of a logical chain that can be described by $Y = f(X)$. Second, there must be temporal precedence between the factors—the cause must happen before the effect. Third, there must be a relationship between the factors such that not only is the cause always present before the effect, but the strength of the cause is related to the strength of the effect (co-variation between the cause and effect). Finally, it is important to establish that there is no other plausible alternative explanation for the observed effect—there is no external situation that is not part of the experiment that creates an influencing effect on its outcome (for instance, if you are studying the influence of a particular drug on smoking behaviors, an external variable might be the issuance of a new report on smoking by the Surgeon General). This type of effect is sometimes called a "missing variable," and it is appropriate to conduct a "variables search" for such a Red X! This is especially true if the variable has a co-linear behavior—in other words, its influence changes in the same direction as the experimental effect.

To establish internal validity, it is important to determine if any plausible alternative explanations of the observed variation have any validity. In order to do this, the four criteria for causality in the primary variables can be assessed through design of an experiment. One simple way to accomplish test validity is to establish a control group—a group that is comparable to the treatment group, with the difference that they are controlled and are not given the specific treatment, but are exposed to all external "historical threats" to internal validity (e.g., both groups have equal access to the Surgeon General's report). By using a control group, experimenters can block external variables, and their effect is taken out of the experimental design. This is one reason why the experimental design is so important—it is the best way to eliminate the effect of a "missing variable." This approach to the scientific method is the process of conducting designed experiments.

Professor Douglas C. Montgomery describes designed experiments as "a test or series of tests in which purposeful changes are made to the input variables of a process or system so that we can observe and identify the reasons for changes in the output response." Indeed, experimental design is the vehicle of the scientific method that provides an unambiguous, objective way to establish causal relationships among factors being studied. A designed experiment structures an analysis by demonstrating how all of the major parts of the experiment fit together—the samples or rational subgroups being tested; measures of performance for the groups and their response to the planned intervention or treatment; treatments or the programmed change in relationship among the factors being modified to determine the response (outcome); methods of assignment of individuals to groups; the sampling method used for selecting individuals; and the statistical tests that demonstrate causal relationships among factors.

Designed experiments combine various statistical approaches as an analytical engine to discover sources of variation that make a difference in SNR response: hypothesis testing logic, sampling theory, data-collection methods, regression analysis, analysis of variance, and tests of difference and goodness. Designed experiments should produce robust functions! How does this analytical engine work?

▶ Hypotheses translate practical questions into statistical questions. In this manner, the "real-world" problem is represented in an approach that supports the process of scientific investigation.

▶ Sampling theory is applied to ensure that representative samples are taken and that variation is not induced in the data observations from non-random acts induced in the data-collection process. Sampling theory also ensures that the results are statistically significant because of the structured, objective approach to collecting data.

▶ Data-collection methods ensure rigor in the process of making observations and the recording of events in the process. Observations of experimental outcomes are performed using measurement systems that have been demonstrated to be adequate in terms of their tolerance for recording significant process differences at a level of confidence that is adequate to the experimental objective (at appropriate levels of precision and accuracy).

▶ Regression analysis describes mathematical relationships of experimental factors as they change across levels, as well as the effect of interactions among all of the various experimental factors.

▶ Analysis of variance is used to define the goodness of the model (the combination of experimental factors) as well as to describe how well the model explains the observed variation in the response variable.

▶ Tests of difference define the significance of the observed result. Experiments can use a number of statistical methods to determine significance by interpreting values calculated for R2, p-values, F-test, mean squared error, and significance of the coefficients of the model factors.

▶ Tests of goodness of fit for the model are done by looking at the residual data that is "left over" after the variation has been decomposed and explained. In general, the residuals should be normal (indicating the presence of only "white noise"), should not exhibit any coherent pattern, and should be symmetrically distributed around zero (indicating the presence of an undetected signal or a variable that should be considered). The residuals should have a constant variance across their range of values; otherwise, the model might not fit equally well across the entire performance range of data.

Principles of experimentation

Fisher's basic approach to design of experiments (DOE) has been incorporated into the methods of Shainin and Taguchi and is applied in both the Six Sigma DMAIC and DMADV processes. In order to understand the methodology (a detailed description is contained in appendix C), some background is necessary to describe the most important experimental factors. Experimental factors are variable engineering parameters whose relationships are studied during an experiment. A factor has a finite number of different levels that describe its performance. Each level is the same in some quality or quantity. It is not necessary that the independent variables be measured on an interval or continuous scale; however, if factors are measured on an approximately interval scale, then some flexibility is gained in the analysis. These factors can be described in the following ways:

▶ *Treatment factors*: Quantitatively or qualitatively different levels of experience. In a very simple experiment, there are two levels of treatment: none (also called the control condition), and some change, called the experimental condition. The treatment factors are the principal focus of the experiment, and they have two main attributes: Any of the subjects can be assigned to any one of the levels of the factor (random assignment), and different levels of the factor consist of explicitly distinguishable stimuli or situations in the environment of the subject (e.g., high and low settings, etc.).

▶ *Group factors*: A factor in which the subjects are arbitrarily assigned to a given group that differs from other groups only in that different subjects are assigned to it. If each group has some distinguishing feature other than the subjects that are assigned to it, then it would no longer be considered as a group factor.

▶ *Trial factors*: If each subject is scored more than once under the same condition, and the separate scores are included in the analysis, then a trial factor exists. If the different scores for a subject are found under different levels of a treatment, then the factor would be called a treatment factor rather than a trial factor.

- **Blocking factors**: If subjects are grouped according to some pre-existing subject similarity, then that grouping is called a blocking factor. The experimenter has no choice but to assign the subject to one or the other of the levels of a blocking factor (e.g., sex of the participant). Blocking confuses causal inference. However, if the blocking factor accounts for differences in performance, it might add power to the experiment and explain some of the differences between the performance of groups that make it more likely to find additional treatment effects (for instance, to include sex as a blocking factor, because otherwise gender differences would be included in the error variance). In some cases, the blocking factor is quantitative, in which case a median split can be used (e.g., assigning individuals who have scores above the median in one group and those with scores below the median to a second group). Variations of this procedure can be used to assign individuals to three or more groups.

- **Unit factors**: The entity from which a score is taken (e.g., person, organization, group, activity, process, or function).

- **Error factors**: Not a factor that is included in the experimental design, but the result of all other factors that have not been explained in the analysis (both measurement error and factors that are not included in the design).

- **Fixed factors**: An experimental design factor where the results of the factor generalize only to the levels that are included in the experimental design, but not to external or untried performance levels. In addition, any procedure might be able to select the levels of the factor. If the experiment were replicated, then the same levels of that factor would be included in the new experiment. In general, it is not possible to determine a fixed factor prior to an experiment; therefore, screening experiments can be conducted to better understand how the factors relate to each other.

- **Random factors**: An experimental factor is considered random if the results of the factor generalize to levels that were included in the factor as well as to levels that were not. The levels of the factor used in an experiment are selected by a random procedure. If the experiments were replicated, then different levels of that factor would be included in the new experiment.

Why conduct a designed experiment? First, experiments are an effective approach for studying complex systems. By fixing the response of blocking factors and structuring the performance level of treatments, it is possible to observe an "effect" in a response variable. Second, increased effectiveness in the capability of the process or the functionality of a product is the result of the experimental efforts and comes at a reasonable investment in data acquisition and analysis. Third, clarity in the problem-solving framework is achieved through the explicit structure of an experimental design, where each factor must be defined and characterized in order to create a detailed test plan for conducting the experiment. Finally, designed experiments enable the use of the scientific method to thoroughly investigate the problem at hand.

Taguchi focuses his approach to designed experiments by using orthogonal arrays to help manage SNR at the lowest total loss to society through a three-phased sequential design process:

▶ **System design**: This represents the conceptual definition of the product and establishes the product technology, the system configuration, and relationships of subsystems to the customer requirement. This phase of the design process sets the conditions that define the functional parameters, noise factors, and the transfer function by which energy is transformed into results. All these components influence the quality loss of the product from its ideal functional state.

▶ **Parameter design**: This process optimizes performance of the transfer function by choosing the nominal values for the design parameters by reducing the effect of the noise factors on them—creating a design that is insensitive to noise.

▶ **Tolerance design**: The final phase of the design process establishes appropriate variation levels for the design parameters.

No matter what type of factor is present, there are two basic relationships that describe the most common types of experimental designs (however, not all experiments fit so neatly into these two categories): crossed and nested designs.

Crossed and nested experimental designs

Crossed or factorial designs: In a crossed experimental design, each level of each factor is evaluated against each level of the other factors. In a crossed design, the dominant sources of variation are observed between the factors. For instance, if an experiment is evaluating the influence of caffeine on performance, then each subject would be tested with and without caffeine to influence performance. The distinguishing feature in a crossed experimental design (also called a factorial design) is that each subject will have more than one observation (e.g., both with and without caffeine), and one of these observations will be under the influence of the experimental treatment or effect. Crossing subjects with treatments has two advantages. First, this typically requires fewer subjects than a nested design approach because each of the subjects participates more than once in the experiment. Second, crossed designs are more likely to result in an observation of a significant effect, given that the effect is real, because the differences between subjects are eliminated from the error term. However, crossing subjects with treatments also has some disadvantages. First, the experimental designer must be concerned with carry-over effects (for example, people who are not used to caffeine might still feel the effect on the second day, when they are tested for the "without caffeine" condition). Second, the first measurement taken can influence the second one (e.g., if the treatment consists of a score on a test and learning occurs while taking the test). Third, the assumptions required for more complex factorial designs (more than two treatment levels) might be restrictive. Finally, it is not possible to cross a blocking factor with other factors (e.g., once a male, always a male—well, almost).

Nested designs: An experimental design is nested within a factor if each meaningful level of that factor occurs in conjunction with only one level of the other factor. These experimental designs are sometimes called hierarchical designs. In a nested experimental design, the dominant sources of variation are within the factors. Nested designs appear in those aspects of our society that are organized in a hierarchy (business processes, organizational structures, etc.). It is also possible to nest treatment conditions within other treatment conditions (for example, studying food consumption might nest food that is classified as either high or low cholesterol in the experimental design). While any experimental factor can be nested within any other factor, nesting is much more critical when it comes to subjects of the experiment. For example, if a subject is nested within one factor, then they appear only under that one combination of factors within which they are nested. These effects are sometimes called the "between subjects" effects. If a subject is crossed with some combination of other factors, then each subject sees all combinations of factors with which they are crossed—these effects are called the "within subjects" effects. Subjects are necessarily nested within blocking factors (by definition). Treatment factors can be either nested or crossed with subjects. For instance, the effect of caffeine on alertness while performing a test could be studied by dividing the subjects into two groups: one that receives a beverage with caffeine and another that does not. This design nests subjects with caffeine. If the subjects appeared under both caffeine conditions, then the subjects would be crossed with caffeine.

Dealing with noise

In addition to the structure of the data, experimental designs also specify strategies to deal with noise. The more typical experimental strategies and their applications are summarized below:

▶ *Randomization*: When a noise variable is "unknown" and uncontrolled, then by randomizing the data-collection process (order of collecting the data—both the runs and the actual sampling process when repetition is made), its effect can be effectively distributed across the entire data set, because the sample was selected so that each item in the population had an equal chance of being selected (there is no systematic pattern in the data-collection process).

▶ *Repetition*: Repeating data observations allows an estimate of short-term variation and is achieved by taking several observations with the same setting of the design factors.

▶ *Replication*: Replicating the design factor settings allows an estimate of long-term variation by varying combinations of treatments and then observing the combinations again after resetting the experimental factors.

▶ **Blocking**: When a noise factor is known and controllable, then unwanted variation can be blocked to remove its effect from the analysis and focus on variation that influences the experimental outcome. Blocking ensures that background variables do not contaminate the effects of the experimental variables. Blocks should be chosen so that variation between the experimental blocks is greater than the variation within blocks (e.g., the blocks are relatively homogeneous).

▶ **Center points**: An experiment can also include center points (halfway settings between the high and low levels). Center points help to deal with noise by forcing the process to reset itself to the nominal operating conditions within the time frame of the experimental design. This is particularly helpful in screening types of experiments where the process is running close to the limits of its normal operating envelope. By distributing the center points symmetrically throughout the design runs, the process is forced back to its nominal settings, thereby reducing problems that could be encountered when operating near its performance limits.

▶ **Star points**: An experimental design can be augmented by adding star points that are located beyond the range of the factor levels. These star points help to show how gracefully the experimental factors degrade in performance outside the range of desired performance. While star points do not directly contribute to managing noise in experiments, they do provide the benefit of demonstrating the fragility of the level settings that can be affected by noise. If the area beyond the DOE hyper-cube is particularly sensitive to variation, then a Taguchi experiment using outer arrays might help to make the function's performance more robust to this type of variation.

▶ **Outer array**: Provide information about what happens at the corner cases of the DOE hyper-cube. The outer array provides statistical knowledge about effects of variation for setting parameter levels and their tolerances. An outer array contains noise factors that are beyond the control of the experimenter (it is also known as the noise matrix).

A basic rule in the design of an experiment is to "block what you can and randomize what you cannot block!"

Process sorting and variables screening

Which variables are most important in the design of functions? To answer this question requires an in-depth understanding of the customers' environment for using a function as well as knowledge of the performance of competing products. A process for design function analysis was covered previously (see chapter 5), so the focus here will be on how to conduct a parametric analysis of designated product functions. By the term *parameter*, we mean a measurable functional response of either attribute or variable data that is either a controllable or uncontrollable design factor.

Parametric Analysis (PA) was defined by Professor Stuart Pugh as an analysis, primarily from published product data, that seeks out relationships between parameters for particular product functions with the objective of finding correlations or other relationships among them. Pairwise cross-plots of performance for hundreds of product-related factors are developed whereby product performance is shown with respect to that of the leading competitors. PA is a natural precursor to hypothesis testing, as it provides a factual basis for creating hypotheses. The process that Pugh recommends to perform parametric analysis is as follows:[10]

1. Gather as much information as possible about competitive products.

2. Group the data so that it is comparable within the range of product applications.

3. Group the data so that it applies to products at the same generic level.

4. Start with logical relationships and cross-plot as many parameters as possible, looking for patterns among the data (e.g., comparisons that evaluate price against performance factors, price versus size factors, performance factors versus other performance factors, performance factors versus size, etc.)—plotted both as raw data (all companies on the same plot) and difference data (own company to industry leader) to demonstrate competitive gaps.

5. Use the data in its raw state; don't try to transpose or index the data so that any useful combinations of parameters will have a natural meaning.

6. Question why plots are exhibiting strong or unexpected relationships.

7. Place promising plots in a common work space and compare them collectively. Is there any missing logic or new explanations about performance differences?

8. Look for exceptions to strong patterns that can occur because a) the plot is wrong, b) the particular model is exceptional (then ask why?), or c) the product models are not of the same generic base.

9. Draw conclusions from the plots—this is not an academic exercise.

10. Correlate the findings and conclusions with traditional market research.

11. Use information gained to influence the product's functional design specification.

Clyde Creveling, Jeff Slutsky, and David Antis present an approach that builds on the work of Pugh and develops a complete system of parametric analysis that permits what they call critical parameter management (CPM).[11] CPM delivers functional performance for a set of critical design parameters and creates on-target nominal designs that fulfill their objectives despite the

---

[10] Adapted from: Stuart Pugh, edited by Don Clausing and Ron Andrade, *Creating Innovative Products Using Total Design* (New York: Addison-Wesley, 1996), pp. 161–165.

[11] Clyde M. Creveling, Jeffrey L. Slutsky, and David Antis, Jr., *Design for Six Sigma in Technology and Product Development*, pp. 256–330.

presence of "white noise" and uncontrollable variation. What is the process that they recommend? They basically follow the three-phased Taguchi process (described previously in this chapter) by following these four phases:

▶ *Critical parameter identification*: CPM identifies critical functional responses of the product and uses design and manufacturing capability indices (Cp) to track the maturing capability of the product-creation process to fill the system-level and sub-system-level requirements that ultimately satisfy the customer (specifically, the gap between Cp and Cpk distinguishes short-term and long-term performance).

▶ *Operating envelope specification*: Nominal set points and operating envelopes for critical parameters are identified and optimized through application of designed experiments.

▶ *Statistical tolerance analysis*: Functional specifications are developed that define both the nominal set-points and their performance tolerances based on statistical analyses.

▶ *Statistical process control*: The product-design specification, production operating procedures, and control plan identify the process for managing variation during the full-scale production by applying statistical process control to critical parameters.

Conducting a designed experiment

Since a poorly designed experiment is difficult to analyze, emphasis must be placed on both developing and implementing a well-designed plan or experimental strategy. In order to have an effective experiment, three activities should be part of this plan development: anticipation of what the data will "be like" when it is collected in order to test how the data will be analyzed; anticipating what you will do with the data once it is collected; and estimating how much data is needed to draw conclusions at the confidence level that is desired. Planning a designed experiment typically follows a logical progression of activities:

▶ Make a statement of the problem.

▶ Determine the objective of the experiment.

▶ Determine the response variable to be studied (Y).

▶ Collect relevant background information.

▶ Select the factors (X's) and factor levels to be studied.

▶ Select the experimental design.

▶ Determine the sequence of runs (apply randomization, replication, and repetition).

▶ Determine the number of resources (sample size) the experiment requires.

▶ Conduct the experiment and collect the data.

- Analyze the results and confirm.
- Assess results, make conclusions, and document your results.
- Formulate recommendations based on the experiment.

How are these steps combined into an experimental process?

1. *Define the problem.*

Defining the problem is accomplished by completion of the Define phase of a Six Sigma project: identifying the design capability being addressed, current baseline performance, cost performance, process capability, customer satisfaction, potential response factors, and treatment factors, and assessment of the measurement capability of the system. It is clear that variables data (measurements) are preferable to attribute (categorical) data. In the problem statement, the theoretical or ideal performance of the process should be expressed in the most complete statistical terms available.

Problem identification. Follow the basic approach to Six Sigma problem solving as taught in the DMAIC Define and Measure phases. First, determine the factors that are critical to satisfaction (CTS) from the viewpoint of the customer of the process. These CTS factors have a relationship to the key process output variables (KPOV) of your process. This relationship is formulated by the expression $Y = f(X)$, where Y is the desired performance response (a KPOV that is CTS to your customer, probably because it is critical to quality [CTQ] for their requirement of your process output). This causal chain is the fundamental reason that there is a relationship between the function and your customer. It is important that the rationale for this causal chain is clearly understood and that its performance is monitored to enable your result to "live up to" your customer's expectations (either implicitly inferred from an ill-stated need or explicitly derived from a well-thought-out specification of hypotheses).

Process verification. The Six Sigma DMAIC toolkit applies deployment diagrams, thought process maps, failure mode analysis, cause-and-effect fishbone diagrams, and critical-to product and process trees to decipher this relationship ($Y = f(X)$) between your customer's CTS and your process CTQ. Typical process diagrams indicate how the process flows when all is going well. Additional information to discover includes such process information as those points where data is sampled, measurement control can be executed, inspections and tests occur, decisions are made, bottlenecks occur in the process flow, inventory is accumulated in buffers, scrap is being produced, and rework is being performed. This information tells what the process does when it is not operating according to plan. Touring the process in person is required to verify that the flow, with these points of interest, is verified.[12] While gathering this information, it is also helpful for the implementation

---

[12] An excellent article that describes a structured walkthrough of a work process is: Benson P. Shapiro, V. Kasturi Rangan, and John J. Sviokla, "Staple Yourself to an Order," *Harvard Business Review*, July–August 1992.

phase of the experiment to look for a "multiplier" or "leverage" effects in the process, where improvements that are identified during the experiment can be extended to other areas (i.e., look for leverage factors like similar production lines, manufacturing equipment, service areas, processes, etc.).

Measurement management. In addition to understanding what to measure and where it is measured, it is also important to understand how measurements are taken and how well they are taken. To develop this understanding, it is necessary to characterize how the measurements are made by examining and evaluating the measurement process. How is this examination conducted? To answer this question requires a review of the DMAIC Measure phase, where the measurement process is evaluated to determine if it is sensitive enough to detect significant changes in the variables. Reviewing some of the steps taken to conduct an MSA in this process will help to determine if you have already developed an adequate understanding of how good your measurements are:

▶ Identify measurement control points and key measures in the process.

▶ Identify which process factors (input and in-process variables) have the most significant contribution to variation in the measurements.

▶ Identify "customers" of the measurement process and determine their requirements for use of the measures (what decisions they make, need for accuracy, precision, stability, etc.).

▶ Determine how well-calibrated the measurement equipment is and when the accuracy was last examined or tested.

▶ Determine the discrimination capability of measurement equipment (precision of the measurements relative to customer requirement for data preciseness).

▶ Conduct a measurement study (e.g., measurement systems analysis) to determine if the measurement system is capable of detecting a change in the process that is significant from the customer's perspective.

▶ Determine what process is used for monitoring measurement system effectiveness and determining how well that process is operating.

2. Set the experimental objective.

After defining a problem, the purpose of the experiment should be succinctly defined in a written experimental objective. Experimental objectives are usually stated about the effects of inputs (X's) on outputs (Y's), and they are developed in a way that is analogous to a hypothesis statement. For example, experiments could determine:

- Effects of material variation on product reliability.
- Sources of variation in a critical process.
- Effects of less expensive materials on product performance.
- Impact of operator variation on product quality.
- Cause/effect relationships between process inputs and product characteristics.

Typically, experiments are conducted to achieve specific analytical objectives in an efficient manner—to gain the maximum amount of knowledge in a minimum number of experimental trials. The four most common analytical objectives of experiments are:

- *Screening*: Sort out X's that have little parametric effect on performance of the Y.
- *Modeling*: Define the equation $Y = f(X)$ by identifying the factors that contribute the most to shifting the average, affecting the variability, and eliminating those that have no effect.
- *Optimizing*: Determine the optimal settings of the X's that achieve the desired Y performance at the minimal cost.
- *Validating*: Confirm the results of the DOE selections in a full-scale production environment.

3. *Identify the factors and levels.*

The knowledge gained to this point in time of the DOE should be summarized to allow a clearer plan to be developed. Consider the knowledge gained from both graphical analysis and statistical analysis: thought map, $Y = f(X)$ analysis, deployment map, FMEA, CNX fishbone, process capability analysis, and historical data, such as trend analysis and SPC (statistical process control) charts. No factor should be eliminated by "Theory O" because sometimes a factor that "everybody knows is *not* important" turns out to be *most* important or contributes to an interaction effect that was not previously understood.

Define the output variables:

- Is the output qualitative or quantitative?
- Is the experimental objective distribution centering or variation reduction?
- What is the current performance baseline (mean, sigma, and Cp)?
- Is the output variable under statistical control?
- Does the output vary over time?
- How much change in the output do you want to detect (experimental sensitivity)?

- Is the output normally distributed?
- Is the measurement system adequate?
- Are you concerned about multiple outputs?

Selecting inputs and the output (response variable):

- Build on the characterization analysis (FMEA, CNX fishbone, process thought map, capability studies, etc.).
- Identify factors related to measurement error (operators, machines, shifts, suppliers, etc.).
- Identify factors due to noise (barometric pressure, ambient temperature, relative humidity, material characteristics).
- Identify controllable inputs (where physical control can be exercised to set a level or fix performance in some way) and key process outputs.

Determine the baseline performance:

- What is the ideal performance? Use descriptive statistics and time-series analysis to characterize current, historical, and theoretical performance levels.
- How is the process performing relative to customer-defined control limits and internal specification limits?
- What is the stability of the process performance over time? Is the process operating under statistical control?
- If the process is not operating under control (does not exhibit stability in its performance), what efforts can be made to identify and remove any special causes of process variation?
- What has been the historical experience in managing this process? Do any of the variables indicate particular performance trends?
- What is known about the effect of process variables on CTQ parameters or process-performance characteristics?
- Are any of these variables measured regularly, monitored by automated process controllers or data-acquisition systems, or control-charted or tracked in some way by operators?
- Based on historical performance, will the process need to stabilize itself after an adjustment in level occurs during the experiment? Has the time for process stabilization been determined?

Identification of factors (X's):

A factor is one of the controlled or uncontrolled inputs into a process whose influence on a response (Y) is being studied in the experiment.

▶ Factors might be quantitative (variables data, such as temperature, time, etc.).

▶ Factors might be qualitative (attribute data, such as different machines, operators, clean/not clean, etc.).

Which factors are included in the experimental design? Base your decision about which variables to include based on the learning and insights from process characterization:

▶ Process thought map

▶ CTS/CTQ matrix, critical-to-product/process tree, and $Y = f(X)$ analysis

▶ C/N/X fishbone

▶ FMEA

▶ Multi-vari analysis

▶ Hypothesis testing

▶ Objective: literature review, engineering knowledge, or scientific theory

▶ Subjective: customer/operator/supplier brainstorming inputs

Identify any other variables that have a potential influence on the experimental result that cannot be reasonably adjusted in practice. Decide if they should be included in the experiment as a blocking variable (held constant at some level) or if they should be measured but permitted to vary naturally.

Choosing the levels for each factor:

Answer some important questions about these factors: How many levels per factor must be analyzed? How far apart can these levels be set? How closely must these factor levels be controlled? As a rule of thumb, variations in these levels should be set differently based on the performance objectives of the experiment. If you are doing a screening experiment, then these levels should be set close to their maximum limits to induce variation and ensure that effects are observed. If you are conducting an optimization experiment, then these levels should be set so that they are less than 5% of the total range of factor performance and centered on the nominal value.

4. *Select the experimental design.*

Some of the considerations included in the experimental design are:

▶ What data should be collected?

▶ Should the design be nested or crossed?

▶ What are the factors for consideration?

- How many levels will be evaluated?
- What blocking variables will be used to separate unwanted effects from desired effects?
- How many runs and how many observations per run are required?
- What is the most efficient fractional plan?
- How can replication be achieved?
- Are center points available to calibrate the design against current performance and determine linearity of the results?

5. Determine the experiment's resource requirements.

Determine the number of resources (sample size) the experiment requires:
- Based on the need for statistical confidence and the estimated cost of sampling and data analysis, what is the desired sample size per run?

Determine the sequence of runs (apply randomization, replication, and repetition):
- How will randomization of the design be achieved?
- Will repetition of runs be used to calculate the mean and standard deviation of the experimental results?
- Will replication be done to determine the error in the experiment?

Consider logistical, programmatic, and schedule issues:
- How long will it take to complete each experimental run?
- How expensive is each run? What are the sampling costs? Are there any changes in process output that might render it unmarketable? What is the cost of testing or analysis?

6. Perform a trial experiment.

Remember: One lost run can invalidate a whole experiment! Enlist the co-operation of the people involved in the process (including maintenance and support personnel). Carefully explain what the experiment is about and the importance of doing it according to the specified plan (especially why you are making their life so difficult by randomizing the sequence—they have a penchant for un-randomizing runs to make their life easier!). Do they see any problems in the way measurements must be collected? (For example, will data collection itself create a bias or inaccurate result, as in sampling from the top of a stratified data set?) Can the factor levels be attained and held stable for the periods specified? How long will it take the system to become stable to ensure that the desired Y effect is observed? Include the comments of the process participants in any revisions to your DOE plan.

7. Perform the experiment.

Conduct the experiment and collect the data:

Perform the experiment according to the design. Record all relevant data and any incidents that occur during the experimental run. Runs *must* be carried out at the planned settings. DO NOT adjust non-experimental factors during the experiment. Any factors that require adjustment should be included in the measurement. Making adjustments to any variable that is not in the experimental design during the progress of an experimental run will invalidate the experiment. The experimenter must be at the scene of the experiment while it is being conducted. Remember: Experiments are not a spectator sport!

8. Analyze the results, confirm outcomes, and draw conclusions.

▶ Plot the data in every useful manner (in addition to graphs of the main effects and interactions, consider regressions and ANOVA presentations of the data).

▶ A confirmation run is essential to ensure that the results are representative of the performance.

▶ Follow-up experiments might be required if curvature is found in the data.

▶ Assess results, make conclusions, and document your results.

▶ Formulate recommendations based on the experiment.

9. Document the experiment and present the results.

Describing Analysis Results:

The analysis of the experiment should present the ANOVA table summary, the results of the regression equation for the model, and the more significant graphical analyses, such as the following four items:

▶ *Main effects plot*: the plot of change in average effect from one level to another of a single experimental factor.

▶ *Cube plot*: the plot of response averages for all corners of a full factorial 2^3 DOE.

▶ *Contour plot*: a hyper-cube of three-dimensional responses of nonlinear factors in central composite design (CCD) or response surface model (RSM) experiments.

▶ *Pareto chart of effects*: a chart of the effects ranked by magnitude and compared to a statistical test for significance.[13]

---

[13] The Minitab (version 14) software package provides all of these graphical outputs as analysis options of the Analyze DOE functional output.

While interaction plots and residuals analyses are also available graphically, these graphs are more difficult to interpret and are normally used just for analysis and not provided for management examination. However, they should be included in an appendix to the final report.

Just as in scientific research and sound engineering practice, an experiment should not be considered complete until it has been properly documented. Four items define the proper documentation of a designed experiment:

▶ Initial proposal and experimental plan.

▶ Logbook of the experimenter, defining a day-to-day account of the experiment and the record of results for all actions taken.

▶ Formal experimental report that presents the experimental design, data-collection plan, and analysis methodology and presents the final results of the study along with the recommendations. The files included with the experimental report should preserve the data collected in its entirety.

▶ If a peer review of the experiment is conducted, then the conclusions of the peer review should also be included in the experimental record.

While the final report should include all elements of documentation of the experiment, the executive summary should be an abridgement of this information containing only the following elements:

▶ Statement of the problem

▶ Objectives of the experiment

▶ Background to the business situation

▶ Method of the experimental design and data collection

▶ Results of the experiment

▶ Conclusions and recommendations to management

The second form of documentation is the "oral story" of the experiment, which is the presentation or briefing of the experiment that is given to its sponsor. It presents the experimental design, findings of the data collection, and recommendations on actions to be taken.

Barriers to effective DOE:

Not all experiments can be successfully conducted, and the biggest barriers come from the attitudes and opinions of management. The most frequently occurring barriers to the use of DOE occur because of the following factors:

▶ The problem is not well-defined.

▶ The objectives of the experiment are not clear.

▶ There is inadequate knowledge of potential causal factors.

▶ The results of the experiment are not clear.

- It costs too much money to collect sample data and initiate the experiment.
- The experiment will take more time than is available to make a decision.
- Management lacks understanding of DOE strategies.
- Analysts lack understanding of DOE methodologies.
- Confidence in the approach has not been developed in the early stages of analysis.
- There is a general lack of management support for analysis methods.
- Management feels a need for "instant pudding" results.
- There is a lack of adequate coaching/support for conducting the DOE.

Some barriers can be overcome by taking a different approach to experimentation by employing simulation analysis when the problem takes too long, is too big, costs too much, or requires a large-scale methodology that is impractical.

Simulation as an experimental alternative

What is simulation, and why is it an alternative to experimentation? Simulation is the process of building a mathematical model of a real-world system and then conducting probabilistic experiments by varying model inputs to observe the system response. A discrete event simulation model is used to evaluate business processes, as the stimulus for performance comes from the arrival of customer orders or other discrete events. A dynamic event (also called stochastic) simulation model is used to model continuous measurement systems that vary as a function of time and probability—which occurs frequently in modeling of engineered system functions.

How is it done? Both types of simulation models are built in a similar way and can be used to construct models that simulate the performance of the real-world process and can be evaluated with a designed experiment on the simulated data. In general, the following steps define this process:

1. **Map and model your process.**
- Gather historical process-performance data and create the process map.
- Fit the data to probability distributions to improve model accuracy.

2. **Validate your process map and model.**
- Conduct simulations.
- Log the simulation transactions to validate behavior.
- Compare reported data with operational performance data.

- Conduct a statistical test of differences.

3. Baseline the "as-is" simulation model performance.

4. Prepare the map and model for DOE.
- Modify the process map to show alternatives.
- Modify the process parameters (process X's).
- Ensure that result (process Y's) variables exist.

5. Conduct DOE.
- Choose appropriate factors and levels.
- Choose appropriate model design.
- Chose appropriate response factors.

6. Create the "to-be" process map and simulation model.
- Eliminate non-optimal path alternatives.
- Replace scenario attributes in activities with optimal values.

7. Conduct a DOE confirmation run.

When should you conduct simulation? Simulation can be used to estimate system errors, set the operating parameters for system optimization, validate process operations, and improve process performance. Some of the conditions under which a simulation could be used include:

- When it is unsafe to run a process at the experimental performance levels.
- When a system is already running at its design limits.
- When it is too costly to conduct experiments in the real world.
- When it is impractical to conduct experiments due to operating requirements.
- When the system performance does not stabilize rapidly after process upsets.

However, it must be remembered that simulation does not provide a realistic result if the model has not been validated in real-world conditions. Simulations provide estimates of performance that are helpful only if the model reflects reality!

DOE and SPC are preludes to the final act of DFSS: establishing and maintaining a state of control. Walter Shewhart said in his 1939 book, *Statistical Method from the Viewpoint of Quality Control*: "The idea of control involves action for the purpose of achieving a desired result." So, now we turn our attention to execution of the design and the development of a system of business controls.

Chapter 9
Controlling Product Realization

"Different processes are afflicted by different diseases."

~ George E. P. Box

Product realization commercializes design output

New product development projects develop an organization's future value and deliver opportunities for its future financial success. There is considerable risk to an organization if the projects it commissions to "create the future" cannot be executed to coincide with market rhythm (where rhythm combines "time to market" with "timing to market"). R&D projects that effectively complete design in the product-creation process are deemed "commercially ready" and are considered ready for transition to the product realization process.

The management challenge is to manage project risks and deliver results on schedule while at the same time seizing opportunities offered by the mistakes of competitors who do not have a clear vision of customer need that is commercially viable.[1]

Larry Bossidy, former CEO of AlliedSignal and Honeywell, said that "execution is the gap between what a company's leaders want to achieve and the ability of their organizations to deliver it."[2] He asked executives to create a discipline of execution: "Leadership without the discipline of execution is incomplete and ineffective."[3] Bossidy is echoing the words of management guru Peter F. Drucker: "The most time-consuming step in the process is not making the decision, but putting it into effect. Unless a decision has degenerated into work, it is not a decision; it is at best a good intention."[4] A more folk-like way of expressing the same idea would be to say: "Just because people can read the words doesn't mean that they can sing the music."

From a product development viewpoint, there are two key decisions: The first is to initiate a product development project; the second is to transition the product for commercialization, ensuring that the product is ready for its consumers and better than its competitive offerings. Following the first decision, management writes the words, but after the second decision, the orchestrated organization sings the music!

This chapter will demonstrate how methods associated with lean enterprise and Six Sigma analysis help to deliver the discipline of execution and how policy deployment can be used as a control plan for delivering consistent business performance. Bossidy describes three processes as key to execution excellence: the people process, the strategy process, and the operations process. The approach that we will take in this chapter is to understand potential problem areas from both their risk and opportunity viewpoints; describe the strategy process for integrating measurement and objectives alignment so that people can be held accountable for their work; and defining people processes necessary for implementing this approach to design for Six Sigma.

Requirements for accountability for quality

One prerequisite for business control is the ability to hold people accountable for the execution of the work that they are asked to do. Accountability should be bidirectional—people should be accountable to their customers for meeting the performance expectation that is set by their company, and they should be accountable to their management for execution of the re-

---

[1] This chapter continues the discussion of chapter 3 and emphasizes those project management considerations that should be completed at the time a product is released to manufacturing for full-scale production as a commercially ready item for consumption.

[2] Larry Bossidy and Ram Charan, *Execution: The Discipline of Getting Things Done* (New York: Crown Business, 2002), p. 19.

[3] *Ibid.*, p. 34.

[4] Peter F. Drucker, *The Effective Executive*, p. 114.

sponsibility with which they are entrusted (this is the principle of steward-ship). What does it take to do this? What are the requirements for holding people accountable for the quality of their work? There are three necessary and sufficient conditions that must be met for management to be able to properly hold individuals accountable for the quality of their work outcomes. In his book *The Practice of Management*, Peter Drucker outlined an approach to self-control or self-regulation of work performance that leads to effective work outcomes. Three sequential conditions must be met for people to be effective:[5, 6]

▶ First, they must know their job. People must have knowledge of the job that they are being asked to do, be trained in the methods that are required to do it effectively, and have a clear expectation regarding targeted require-ments and their performance (capability).

▶ Second, they must know the performance requirements for their job. People must have knowledge of the standard of performance that they are being asked to attain (which, in turn, should be derived from their relationship with customers and the job that customers need to get done using their products or services), and an objective measurement system must be in place to ensure that the data is being collected objectively to evaluate this performance (responsibility).

▶ Third, they must have the ability to self-regulate their work to affect its outcome—the ability to observe work-process measures and to make deci-sions about what corrective actions are required to keep the process oper-ating according to the required standard of performance (authority).

Drucker observed that when performance measures are applied in a man-agement-induced, control-oriented work environment, they are not nearly as effective as when they are applied in a self-regulated or self-managed improvement-oriented work environment. Business systems that have not taken into account these basic requirements in design of work not only incur a significant risk of non-performance from their people, but they also become a de-motivating factor among the entire workforce. If people do not believe that they can influence the quality of their work, why bother? A good busi-ness-control system will measure and assess the business risks incurred and address how to engage the workforce to ensure that a discipline of execution is embedded into their jobs and ensure that the conditions for accountability are met. While it is important to measure performance, it is even more impor-tant to improve based on insights gained from using these measurements! Thus, excellent control is achieved by emphasizing improvement rather than

---

[5] Peter F. Drucker, *The Practice of Management* (New York: Harper and Row, 1954). See chapter 6, titled "Management by Objectives and Self-Control," which places particular emphasis on the distinction that Drucker draws between control and improvement measures.

[6] Control is not used here in Drucker's meaning as "domination"; rather, it is used in the sense of work-process management, where it refers to a state in which process parameters are regulated (or self-regulated) so that the process performance or outcome is predictable within an expected range based on its design capability.

control! However, in the face of performance measurement and taking action, there is always a risk of doing the wrong thing or making the wrong choice. How should risk be assessed?[7]

Managing risk and seizing opportunities

Controlling business risk is only half of the management problem—the second half is seizing the appropriate opportunities. Risk must be controlled, and controls tend to restrict freedom of decision-making and inhibit the ability to grow without restraint because controls slow down decision-making. Opportunity management, on the other hand, must understand the types of opportunities that should be seized; when these opportunities are detected, it must allow an organization to move and choose its way as soon as the path is opened. Managing risk results in a "protective" way of thinking about work. However, on the obverse of the risk coin is the opportunity—but care must be taken to choose the right opportunities. Thus, if the business becomes over-controlled, then it will stifle its ability to find the next generation of technology. Business leaders must remember that risk exists in everything we do. It can't be eliminated—either in business or in personal life. Thus, business controls cannot imply eliminating risk. Instead, business controls must help limit unwanted events and reduce their consequences while emphasizing the need to improve performance and response to customers. Effectively managing risk means finding a balance between business controls that are either so lax that business is hurt financially or operationally so stringent that they cost more than the benefit they create—either in actual or lost-opportunity costs! Achieving this balance results in a flexible business-control system that is able to respond appropriately to a dynamic work environment. Overly rigid business controls will constipate the flow of ideas and improvement in a business and cause it to slow down and miss opportunities to capture new markets or develop new products. Over-control results in delayed decisions and "wishy-washy" thinking that inhibits market-leading choices that induce competitive advantage. To eliminate such "core rigidity" from taking over your company's business mind, an appropriate analysis and response to business risk must be achieved.

Controlling a business begins by first understanding its risk. This assessment process should begin by management's conducting a risk analysis to determine if the business controls are capable of producing products in a flawless manner (operating as a predictable factory), and if not, determining where the problems occur. Business controls should be analyzed to evaluate how well they are operating in the face of business risks and to determine the severity and probability of specific consequences of the occurrence of potential risks. Such a risk assessment should include the following components:

---

[7] The types of risks that a business faces were previously discussed in chapter 7, so this subject will not be duplicated here.

- **Risk scenario** (*What could adversely affect the business?*): Assessing risk begins with developing risk scenarios for business processes or product functions that are identified as high risk based on a preliminary risk screening by management. The preliminary risk screening assigns a broad risk level (high, medium, or low) to both core business processes and key product functions. Medium- and low-risk business processes and product functions are assessed after the total risk analysis has been done for these high-risk items. Risk screening determines the potential for events to adversely impact a business in the absence of any business controls. This determines risk-priority areas for more stringent control. Risk scenarios are managed by designing and applying business controls as countermeasures to deal with the initiating situation as well as the risk consequences.

- **Risk category** (*What type of risk would affect the business in this situation?*): Assigning a risk category to the scenario helps to focus on the dominant type of risk that is generated in the scenario. Is it risk from new technology, market risk, or tooling risk that is the dominant "lurking problem" for the business? Some of the categories of risk to consider include product-related risks due to:

  Technology—conditions that induce failure modes in the product over time due to design, technical capability, or producibility of the product's functions.

  Performance—conditions that decrease ability to consistently deliver the performance customers expect.

  Safety—conditions that increase the likelihood of injury or accident during customer operation of the product.

  Liability—conditions that increase the likelihood of product liability due to performance problems from the producer's legal perspective.

  Regulatory—conditions that decrease product performance for specified consumer-protection risks as required by government regulations.

- **Risk severity** (*How seriously could business be affected?*): Determining the risk severity provides a guide in deciding what threats need the greatest emphasis by management for business controls. A severity rating for each risk consequence category is selected based on what would happen if the business controls failed. The following risk-severity factors can be used in the risk screening to determine how severe the impact would be:

  Third-party effects (suppliers, distributors, technology partners, or customers)

  Organizational change requirements

  Complexity of operations affected

  Computer system changes required

  Information sensitivity regarding the affected area

  Number and nature of locations affected

  Expense exposure from the failure

  Liquidity of assets affected by the results

  Other risks associated with the failure

Impact of the Effect of the Problem on the Customer

Severity Evaluation Criteria	
Severity of Effect:	Ranking
Minor Unreasonable to expect that the minor nature of this failure would cause any real effect on the overall performance of the product, or on a subsequent process or operation. Customer will probably not notice the failure.	1
Low Very limited to local process, no effect on downstream processes or customer. May require local rework.	2 3
Moderate Failure causes customer dissatisfaction in the form of annoyance. Failure noticed by customer requires correction. Customer notices slight performance degradation.	4 5 6
High Loss of some product function but not of system performance. Product inoperable or fails to meet performance criteria.	7 8
Extreme Potentially hazardous effect. Possibly safety-related. Product safety or liability hazard.	9 10

A severity ranking number is assigned based on a scalar judgment, where the scale is anchored by comments that relate to the impact of the effect on the customer or on the business. Each ranking level maps into the anchor scale to include both a high and low level for each severity category. In this way, severity is a surrogate indicator for importance of the failure mode.

Likelihood of the Problem's Cause Occurring

Occurrence Evaluation Criteria			
Probability the Cause Will Occur:	Possible Failure Rate (D-PPM)	Process Capability	Ranking
Remote Failure is unlikely. No known failures associated with almost-identical processes.	<1 in 10^8 (<.002)	$Cpk \geq 2.0$	1
Very Low Only isolated failures associated with similar designs.	<1 in 10^6 (<1)	$Cpk \geq 1.67$	2
Low Occasional failures associated with similar designs.	<1 in 20K (<50)	$Cpk \geq 1.33$	3
Moderate Previous designs have experienced problems or occasional factory out-of-control conditions.	1 in 3,000 1 in 1,000 1 in 400	$Cpk \geq 1.0$ $Cpk < 1.0$	4 5 6
High Processes not in statistical control. Similar processes have experienced problems.	1 in 40 1 in 20		7 8
Extreme Failure almost inevitable.	1 in 8 1 in 2		9 10

Detection Evaluation Criteria			
Probability of Controls Detecting the Problem:	Probability of Shipping a Failure	Defects (PPM)	Ranking
Very Effective The control will detect a design weakness prior to production release.	I in 10,000 I in 5,000	100 200	I 2
High Controls will have a good chance of detecting design weakness. Will be detectable after release but before installation at customer.	I in 2,000 I in 1,000	500 1,000	3 4
Moderate Controls might detect design weakness before installation. Will be detected prior to shipment to customer.	I in 500 I in 200 I in 100	2,000 5,000 10,000	5 6 7
Low Controls not likely to detect design weakness and must wait for larger volume. Controls will probably not detect failure.	I in 50 I in 20	20,000 50,000	8 9
Very Low Controls cannot or will not detect failure.	I in 10	100,000	10

▶ **Risk probability** (How likely is the risk scenario?): What is the likelihood that a consequence will occur? Are there any conditions that drive the event (operating like a Markov process and driving the conditional probability of the bad event higher)?[8]

▶ **Risk detectability** (How likely is the business-control system to identify the risk in a timely manner?): How well will the current systems of business controls work to detect the initiating condition that drives the specific failure mode identified?

▶ **Risk consequences** (What threats are associated with the risk scenario, or how could the scenario unfold?): Risk severity and probability can be determined for each of the following categories of risk consequences, considering the effectiveness of the business controls that have already been put into place:

1. Customer loyalty, end-user satisfaction, and market share
2. Brand image and corporate reputation
3. Proprietary information or data integrity (loss or inappropriate disclosure)
4. Regulatory and contractual violations or ethical controversies
5. Financial loss (both for short-term expense and long-term capital costs)

▶ **Risk countermeasures** (What actions can be taken to eliminate, mitigate, detect, or otherwise safe-proof the risk scenario and reduce the effect of the

[8] A Markov process is one where the sequence of events act like a chain—the probability of each event contributes to the success of the whole as a series. Thus, the overall probability of success is the product of the successful transition across the states or sub-processes that make up the elements of this chain of events. In Six Sigma, this idea is expressed as "rolled throughput yield."

problem on the business?): This process is called *poka-yoke* in Japan—error-proofing to make it impossible to make mistakes (defects) that are passed on to customers.

For many engineers, the idea of risk assessment is synonymous with the Failure Mode and Effects Analysis (FMEA) methodology, which calculates the priority risks among potential failure modes using the three factors of severity, probability of occurrence, and detectability. The risk priority number (RPN) calculated for each failure mode is the product of these three estimated factors for each failure mode. However, the RPN is approximate at best, as the FMEA methodology suffers from several problems:

▶ Severity is typically assigned based on a consensus ranking by a team of "experts" who assess risks for their domain of knowledge rather than on examination of the current customer complaint or field failure data. One of the biggest mistakes in the risk assessment process occurs when severity is not assessed from the viewpoint of targeted customers and the impact that the failure mode has on the job that they need to get done. This can occur when the FMEA is developed by a team of engineers without adequate customer input so that customer importance is not included in the severity consideration.

▶ Probability of occurrence is often based on "engineering estimates" that have been derived from reliability testing. However, when products have not been tested to the point of failure, then not all failure modes will be "estimate-able," and the result will not be inclusive of the total life experience with the product. In addition, in many complex products it is not possible to evaluate all conditional failure modes that can be generated through functional linkages (for example, in many software programs there are functional combinations that might never be tested after their initial acceptance in the design due to the size and complexity of the architecture).

▶ The detection capability of controls is a function of measurement capability, but impact of measurement-systems analysis is not part of the detectability definition.

▶ Detectability is also a part of the corrective action or risk countermeasures that are invoked to reduce the impact of risk (e.g., in poka-yoke[9]). As a result, including an indicator for detectability in the RPN equation confuses the objective of the risk assessment by confounding problem identification with its solution.[10]

▶ The mathematics of the RPN calculation can be difficult to interpret. If there is no discipline in creating the components of the RPN, then the product would be the same as the product of wishes times hopes times dreams and would equal nothing in the real world except perhaps an hallucination! This

---

[9] Poka-yoke was described, along with other lean enterprise tools, in chapter 2.

[10] In the prior discussion of detectability, the impact of the effect has been reduced by clearly identifying a focus on the effectiveness of "current" business controls, rather than on the construction of new business controls as part of the countermeasures to be put into effect to help manage the dominant risks.

illustrates another example of the hidden potential impact of "Theory O" on business decision-making![11]

One way to manage these problems is to tighten the operational definitions that are identified in these problem areas. Another way to improve the process is to describe risk by a criticality analysis, which cross-plots the residual risk for relevant risk consequences using just severity ratings and probability of occurrence. A third approach to improving the use of this type of analysis is to use AHP[12] to integrate the calculation of the consequences of the failure mode (severity, probability, and detectability) by using relative-importance weighting of these categories of the RPN calculation for each of the different failure modes that are compared in order to develop the corrective action strategy for introducing risk countermeasures.

The discipline of execution is embedded in management control

The objective of any management system is to deliver desired results. When desired results are delivered in a consistent, predictable manner, the business is considered to be operating in a state of control. In such conditions, the people all know what to do, how to do it, how to evaluate their work output, and how to correct their work processes in order to maintain performance and prevent errors or defects from occurring. In addition, their work has been designed to flow seamlessly from one activity to another, without excess loss of time or money, while maintaining the required quality of their combined output.

Such states of control do not normally happen without heroic efforts of the entire system of the business: people at all layers (from executives to front-line workers), integration of work-process design (from supplier through process to the customer), and alignment of the management measurement system (from the business Y to the work-process X). These are the components of a management system that is built to execute—it is based on work disciplines that control performance. Control in this case does not mean dictating a single approach to working. Indeed, many control systems are adaptive and change based on the information provided by their measurements to define the current environmental state so that the system can intelligently choose the alternative course of action it should employ in operations. Such an adaptive control process is required to meet the ever-changing performance demands that are placed on businesses today. What should be included in such an adaptive control system?

An adaptive approach to business control

How is this system of management created? A daily management system must define both how the process organization works and how the functional

---

[11] This is another instance of the measurement problem addressed by Stevens (chapters 4 and 8).

[12] The AHP (Analytic Hierarchy Process) methodology was described in chapter 2.

organizations deliver support services to the business processes. This requires that the organization map its business architecture across the end-to-end customer delivery process and link all of the functional processes to this business process. This type of process map is called an enterprise model, and it spotlights those different points where progress is measured and where control must be exercised. The enterprise model also identifies work processes whose activity should be documented in a standard operating practice or work procedure. How can this tool be used to make daily management processes more disciplined and yet adaptive?

Effective implementation and execution of a comprehensive daily management control system results in the delivery of consistent, predictable performance. Controls are used to ensure constancy of purpose in the organization's strategic direction and repeatability of performance in its mission-critical areas. To achieve this result requires that two aspects of the management process must be effectively designed, integrated, and implemented: statistical controls and business controls. What does this imply? The organization needs to examine each of these capabilities independently and then determine how they fit together in a practical and efficient daily management system that can provide the stability to pursue the organization's vision while at the same time provide the flexibility to adapt to changing circumstances.

Statistical thinking seeks to minimize variation in the way that work is performed. We can choose to work and manage our work processes so that the outcomes are highly predictable (possessing minimum variation). Effective statistical control is achieved only when a process is consistently operating close to its targeted customer performance requirement over a sustained period of time and observed process variation is less than the customer's tolerance for quality changes in performance (i.e., there are no observed special causes of work-process variation that can be explained by assignable causes). DFSS identifies business concerns that are causing significant problems and transforms them into statistical problems.

Statistical problems are resolved by identifying the factors that shift the average performance or reduce process variation. By breaking down the work-process measurement system from the business Y to the X-factors of the work process (measured in quality, cost, and time parameters), the relationship of the measurement system to the statistical problem can be established. Identifying which of these X-factors should be the focal point of business improvement is the analytical objective of a Six Sigma project. This objective is achieved by following the Six Sigma "drill down" logic that traces the controllable factors in the problem to those that are the high-variation contributors to the business outcome "sigma" and determining how to manage the work-process factors of the daily management system to minimize this variation. By discovering the sources of variation and determining how to control them, the gap between statistical control and business control is bridged in a way that achieves practical control.

Practical control comes from eliminating the root cause of a problem and integrating business and statistical controls. This is the formula for sustainable success. Once a business understands how to operate under statistical control, then its business controls perform even better!

Effective business control is the essential element of any management process. It first requires that managers lead by example. No management system can endure leaders who do not apply the same principles to themselves as they apply to their people. Effective business control also requires that the organization manage by process. Organizations that do not use process management become introspective and self-seeking and lose their competitive edge. Effective business control also requires that its people monitor measurements.[13] It is not just the act of measuring that is essential; it is the use of good measures to learn about the business and choose direction more carefully.[14] Effective business control also requires that managers evaluate progress. Performance management without effective decision making results in frustration for the entire organization. It is only when measurement systems are used to identify and effect change in routine operations that people actually believe that such methods can make a difference. Finally, effective business control also requires that managers adapt to their environment. Excellence comes only by execution. Excellence is not merely the product of a good process map, measurement system, or self-assessment scheme—excellence comes when leaders lead by example and also hold others accountable for following that example. How do each of these three factors relate to the creation of a system for business control?

Leading by example

One key emphasis of managerial leadership is the design of the organization's system of management. This system defines opportunities for statistical common causes of process failure in executing fundamental business controls. The common-cause system includes both the organization's assumptions about how it works and its vulnerabilities to critical inflections in its business environment. Leaders must provide the vision (a context that motivates employees to seek performance beyond their local process) and strategic direction (the definition of the specific pathway that the organization will pursue to attain its vision). For organizations to want to follow this "leadership direction" it is essential that leaders be role models by establishing trust in

---

[13] Your attention is redirected back to chapter 4, in particular the section regarding problems with measurement systems. Measurement systems must be aligned to market issues in order to deliver commercial success. Internal measures must be defined relative to their impact on external measurements of success. Without such an alignment, it is not possible to build a "predictive" performance-measurement process that can achieve a state of sound business control.

[14] This assumes that management applies beneficial performance indicators for the organization—putting service above self and not just taking a "What's in it for me?" approach. The rational habit of many managers does not take this approach; see the classic 1971 HBR article by Thomas H. Fitzgerald, former vice president of human resources for the Chevrolet Division of General Motors: "Why Motivation Theory Doesn't Work," and the study by Robert Jackall, Moral Mazes: The World of Corporate Managers (New York: Oxford University Press, 1988).

their organizations—acting with integrity and putting personal service to the organization beyond self-interest. The actions of the top management team must be consistent with the organization's strategies, beliefs, and values. To lead by example means that business leaders are role models for the type of behavior that is desirable throughout the entire organization. Failure to establish this degree of trust reduces to the objection that many organizations have to strategic change: lack of management commitment.[15] Executive commitment means that leaders:

▶ Allocate time for activities that are within their responsibility.

▶ Display a positive attitude toward improving the organization.

▶ Be visible and involved in planning and evaluating work performance.

▶ Assess the readiness of the organization and its employees to accept their own responsibilities for daily management activities.

▶ Verify that employees are applying the necessary control steps in their daily work and that they are reacting appropriately to out-of-control conditions.

▶ Lead the business unit in conducting self-assessments of current-state performance.

▶ Express meaningful appreciation in a fair manner to all employees who have made the desired behavior or organizational performance change (this means not just reward, but also personal acts of recognition that the memory of both the organization and individuals will hold dear as part of its cherished history).

The most critical change that organizations must endeavor to undertake is the transition from a cost-based, functional view of management to a values-based, process view of management. This shift in emphasis is fundamental in transitioning to an evolving value proposition where customers are the most crucial determinant of sustained business success, whether it is a product leadership strategy, marketing agility strategy, or an operational excellence strategy. What does managing by process really mean?

Managing by process

Processes are collections of activities that define how work is done and the set of tasks that, taken together, deliver value to customers. In functional organizations, the emphasis is placed on satisfying the functional manager: keeping the boss happy by giving other people work to accomplish. This internal focus feeds a hierarchical organization that emphasizes layers of reporting rather than focusing on the customer. Process organizations also have functions, but their use is as a collaborative "center of functional excellence" that works with peer organizations as a "boundary-less team" that

---

[15] In a 1988 *Harvard Business Review* article titled "Can Organizational Culture Really be Managed?" Thomas H. Fitzgerald points out that visionary light in an organization is perhaps like the physical properties of light—it will diminish in intensity to the inverse proportion to the distance squared—or in layman's terms, it shines much brighter in the boardroom than it does on the shipping dock.

operates independently of the functional organization and is totally focused on meeting the needs of customers. What are the characteristics of a process organization? First, it keeps a clear line of sight to the requirements, wishes, hopes, aspirations, dreams, or desires of its customers. It succeeds through customer intimacy—knowing what the customer wants and providing that output in a flawless manner. Flawless execution of the customer requirement is a cornerstone of process operations. To achieve this level of performance, process organizations must master the basic skills of process management:

▶ Making process steps visible and understanding clearly what is required for each segment in the customer delivery chain.

▶ Measuring performance of the process at each critical junction point capable of characterizing performance: input, within process, and output or results measures.

▶ Managing to optimize flow across the process by eliminating bottlenecks and decreasing setup and waiting times across all activities.

▶ Evaluating progress to ensure that the common direction is being maintained and that the rate of progress is satisfactory in all areas.

The beginning of managing by process is charting work processes to design the map by which work flows across functions in response to demand signals from customers or markets. Charting processes identifies all of the key inputs, outputs, process steps, and performance measures. Such workflow analysis can be conducted at different levels of abstraction, depending on the objective of the mapping exercise. At the highest level of abstraction, the need is to have a simple working model that explains how the business operates. A block diagram is capable of meeting this requirement. If it is necessary to describe how work flows across functions, then a deployment diagram is required. If the mapping of measures to process flows is the critical need, then a thought process map is the appropriate tool. Each of these tools helps to characterize processes, determine how to sequence the activities, and establish the relationship among the process variables that delivers achievement of optimal performance. Analysis is needed to both define the necessary and sufficient set of process measures and establish appropriate performance levels for these factors. Once performance levels have been established for the critical process parameters, then the business objective should be to define those conditions that will keep performance at the optimal level. These conditions are the fundamental aspects of the business control system used for daily management.

Workflow charting helps to design and document work processes as well as to build business literacy. A workflow chart is a blueprint for the entire business process. It is constructed from the customer's perspective. That is, the customer's requirement describes the goals of the process. Once a business model has been designed to document the workflow, then it is essential to shift the responsibility of the management team to using the measurement system to generate action that keeps the organization aligned toward its business objectives. Process owners are responsible for measuring and improving the key areas of routine business control by:

▶ Monitoring periodic progress toward achieving results against the set of expectations, benchmarks, and performance indicators that establish the desired performance-operating envelope.

▶ Evaluating progress to ensure proper stewardship of resources and to ensure that the desired results are consistently obtained (building a predictable factory out of the work processes and using the measures of business fundamentals to demonstrate appropriate stewardship and progress).

These responsibilities require a robust measurement system for process monitoring.

Monitoring by measurement

In order to monitor workflow performance well, it is essential to have a system for measuring routine work that is aligned to the organization's performance objectives.

Tracking based on specific performance indicators gives the most immediate feedback on how well business goals are being met as well as the effectiveness of the daily management system. These fundamental day-to-day or month-to-month indicators help spot problems before they become major business issues. The performance indicators are either results indicators or process measures that help to pinpoint improvement opportunities that will better meet customer needs.

Results measures (Y variables) evaluate the process output of work and describe how well a process is doing with respect to meeting customer expectations or business goals. Often, external benchmarks are used for comparison to ensure that these goals remain competitive and that expectations are refreshed relative to changes in market conditions and competitors' moves.

Process measures evaluate either the input performance to a process or the in-process performance while a transaction is being conducted or while a transformation is in progress. Input measures describe how well suppliers are meeting an organization's expectations as a customer and indicate how well the daily management system is working at the interface with the supplier. In-process measures indicate potential defects in the system, places where the process is inefficient (too much time or resources consumed), or where some significant opportunities exist for performance improvement (defect, cost, or cycle-time reduction). The process measures provide the earliest warning of potential customer problems.

Tracking these measures provides insight into the degree to which expectations are being met and processes are making progress toward achieving their performance objectives. The design of this monitoring system must take into account the requirement for consistency in measurement and action (deconflicting, measurement-driven actions) as well as simplicity of the measurement structure so that required action is clear at all levels. Even when the measurement system is operating effectively, it is still essential for management to monitor its performance and conduct regular self-assessments. The purpose of these self-assessments is to ensure that the results produced are reflective of real-world conditions (the current state of performance) and that there are no changes in underlying process or business assumptions that would require a departure from the current strategic direction.

Performance management applies three cornerstone business principles: ownership, stewardship, and accountability:

▶ *Principle of ownership*: Ownership is a principle that describes the way an individual cares for a resource. Owners will establish a system of business control for preservation of capital and risk management methodologies for defining and operating within their personal comfort zone for potential loss of capital (or any owned asset) in order to achieve their desired level of return.

▶ *Principle of stewardship*: Stewardship is a principle that directs a person to take responsibility for the management of resources that have been entrusted into their care by an owner. Corporate stewardship implies that the value of capital investments is preserved and enhanced by the actions of management. Stewardship impacts all business issues (e.g., social, health, and environmental ramifications of the production methodologies as well as the use and eventual disposal of products). The primary roles in ensuring stewardship in the life cycle of a product typically involve manufacturers, retailers, service providers, consumers, and government. Stewardship acts on behalf of these participating communities to preserve value and exercise due diligence in the management of the organization's resources to achieve purposeful ends.[16]

▶ *Principle of accountability*: Delegation of authority and resources from an owner to a designated steward brings accountability for how the authority is used and how the resources are deployed or consumed.

These business principles drive the need of organizations to evaluate their progress.

Evaluating progress

Evaluating progress contains two dimensions: It uses the measurement system to evaluate results, and it conducts self-assessments of the process for executing daily work processes. Included in this process is the activity of stewardship. Stewarding is an accountability process whereby measurement of compliance is reported and improvement actions are identified. Stewardship focuses on management of financial, physical, and process resources to achieve the targeted performance requirements. Two types of evaluation are

---

[16] For more information about this subject, see Peter Block, *Stewardship: Choosing Service over Self-Interest* (New York: Berrett-Koehler, 1993).

used: operational reviews, which look over performance measures to ensure that work is being carried out and that it is meeting the plan (shortfalls or overachievement both require explanation and potential actions), and current state analysis, which ensures that all work processes are in compliance with business requirements and regulatory constraints.

Managers need to establish a local culture that reinforces and sustains the daily management system in order to achieve performance objectives and compliance with all constraining business and regulatory requirements. Performance assessment is best conducted when it is a normal part of the daily work activities.

Standards of work performance

Once the dimensions and magnitude of business risks are known, then effective work processes and product standards can be designed to manage this risk. A conscious design is required to create a system of business controls to govern routine, daily operations of organizations and to align these controls to the performance expectations of customers. This business-control system must balance the need for strong process discipline to keep undesirable change from diluting performance capability that has been built into the process with the need to continuously improve the process in order to maintain parity with the ever-growing expectations of customers for higher levels of performance from products and services. Thus, the critical success factor in the management of a change process is the ability of the management system to adapt to the changing requirements of customers or the opportunities presented by technology to create a differentiable advantage with respect to competitors. However, any change that impacts business controls must be managed using a change management process to ensure that undesirable risk is not introduced into the business.[17]

Elements of business control

Daily management combines several activities: conducting standard work, monitoring standard work to ensure controls compliance, using measurement and statistical controls to trigger alerts that compliance with standard operating procedures is not occurring, training front-line employees in the skills required to do their jobs and refreshing their ability to perform this work, and evaluating both the process and the people to ensure that timely preventive action is taken that keeps the entire work system operating according to customer needs. The objective of this control system is to increase the value of shareholder investment while at the same time satisfying cus-

---

[17] Engineers can use FMEA at a number of different points in the design process: at the system level of the product, at the assembly level, and/or at the part and manufacturing process level. This use of FMEA analysis applies the methodology to the management control system of the business rather than focusing on product-specific technical issues.

tomers. This requires strengthening long-term capability while delivering the expected short-term performance. In order to maintain this balance between short-term and long-term performance, it is essential that the daily management system be strengthened by periodic strategic efforts that deliver the long-term strength. This is the objective of a strategic change project–selection process or the application of DFSS to business-process improvement based on the Recognize phase that precedes the choice of DFSS or DMAIC projects for business improvement. Former GE CEO Jack Welch observed (as quoted in the first chapter) that Six Sigma provides a way to design the business-control function. Developing adequate business controls is very difficult and requires a focused organization with disciplined execution. What are the elements of a business-control system? There are six elements that need to be defined in business-control systems:

1. Policy

2. Process

3. Standards

4. Measures

5. Execution

6. Review[18]

Each of these six elements will be discussed in turn.

1. Policy

Control systems must answer questions that keep a business on track: "An adequate information system has to include information that makes executives question [their business assumptions]. It must lead them to ask the right questions, not just feed them the information that they expect."[19]

Policy is a general rule or operating principle that describes a management-approved approach to do business based on how it chooses to control its work and manage risk. Once the right policies have been determined, then an organization has a template to handle similar situations by pragmatically adapting this policy to the concrete situation that it faces. Truly unique business situations that run counter to the critical assumptions of the organization's business model require the full attention of the senior management team to evaluate how these situations challenge and threaten its policies of operations through change imposed from externalities.

---

[18] The system described below is a composite management system based on the author's experience as an executive at Hewlett-Packard, Compaq Computer, and Xerox, as well as his consulting experience at over a hundred firms. It roughly parallels the Japanese management system called policy deployment, management by policy (MBP), or *hoshin kanri*, its Japanese name. A form of this system was implemented in the U.S. federal government in the Government Performance and Results Act of 1993 (GPRA).

[19] Peter F. Drucker, "The Information Executives Truly Need," *Harvard Business Review*, January–February 1995, pp. 54–62.

Development of guiding policy is the responsibility of the board of directors and is provided to the management team through the CEO. The business management team sets strategic direction and reports the progress toward their specified direction using a "balanced scorecard" that describes the organizational performance from the perspective of each of the organization's unique stakeholders. Strategic direction is deployed to operational managers by a cascade of objectives and performance indicators using a customer dashboard—an action-oriented measurement system defining linkages between internal performance measures and external success measures of value delivery to the stakeholders. Operational results are reported to business management to enable self-regulation of performance, ensuring that objectives are met, and acting to achieve the desired business results. Policies consist of targets (what needs to be accomplished by the organization that is of strategic importance) and means (the approach by which the organization seeks to accomplish the targets). Guiding policy from the board of directors consists of a target-setting process that senior management completes by defining the means to accomplish these targets during the strategic direction-setting process. Basic policies for corporate excellence amplify the organization's mission or purpose by describing how the organization should act. Some of these high-level policies could include:

▶ Preserve shareholder value.

▶ Continuously innovate to remain at the leading edge of technology.

▶ Deliver satisfaction to customers.

▶ Provide a productive working environment for employees.

▶ Allow supplier partners to make a fair profit.

▶ Do no harm to the environment.

▶ Act as a good citizen in local communities.

▶ Conduct activities demonstrating high moral and ethical values.

To these aggregate policies at the corporate level, additional policies for operational excellence can be added to increase reliability of the management system by continuously improving the consistency of its operations:

▶ Decrease the requirement for working capital.

▶ Decrease non-value-added cycle time from work processes.

▶ Decrease cost of failures, defects, errors, and missed opportunities.

▶ Enhance the workforce productivity of current resources.

▶ Enhance return on capital employed by increasing asset efficiency.

Policies guide how organizations manage their work processes and set the context for the measurement system and standards of performance.

2. Process

All work is accomplished through processes—some formal and some informal. While the degree of formality might differ, processes tend to have a number of ingredients in common: inputs (information and materials), output (results), resources that are consumed to transform the inputs into outputs (plant, equipment, and supplies), and control signals that tell the process how to perform (a build plan or some other form of a demand response that is linked to customers). In addition to the process basics, there are four other components to processes that get lesser attention than these more obvious ones:

▶ *Checkpoints*: Checkpoints designate points in calendar time or process flow at which the organization must assess its performance. For instance, there are design-review checkpoints in the product-creation process to ensure that progress is being made on the projects. There are also financial checkpoints to ensure that value is being delivered and captured through monthly, quarterly, and annual financial reports on fiscal progress. There are physical checkpoints associated with the flow of products and related to management of inventory and materials required to produce products. Each checkpoint is monitored and reported in the daily management system.

▶ *Check items*: The items that are monitored at a checkpoint are called check items, as they represent the most important factors that affect the outcome of the work process. In Six Sigma language, check items are the X's in the $Y = f(X)$ transfer function of the equation that describes the flow of progress from input to the output of the total business system.

▶ *Control point*: Control points are special checkpoints in the sequence of work activity where corrective action can be taken or countermeasures can be put in place to resolve a concern or issue that has been identified at a checkpoint. The control point is more inclusive than a checkpoint in that it not only measures performance for an actionable business parameter but has a means to regulate the performance outcomes (e.g., the issuing of materials to a production line controls both the volume of flow through the line as well as the mix of the products that will be built).

▶ *Control items*: Control items are used to verify if results agree with established process goals—Does the work demonstrate progress in accomplishments that will enable the final achievement of targets? Control items must be predictive of the final results—those X's that explain the variation in the critical business metrics as established through a thorough analysis of the business processes and product-creation efforts.

What are value-related measures of process performance? Some of the process-level performance measures to consider for process check or control items include:

▶ Customer satisfaction with product features and performance (competition-based)

- Fixed and variable cost of production
- Warranty cost
- Labor variance for rework and testing
- Cost variance due to expedited shipping
- Buffer inventory
- Work-in-process inventory
- Production setup time
- Production cycle time
- Ratio of on-line to off-line production
- *Takt* time—matching production rate to the rate of incoming orders
- Scrap
- Lost production productivity
- Customer productivity loss
- Order line item fill rate
- Order turnaround time
- Taguchi loss function[20] for critical design parameter performance

3. Standards

There are a number of standards that an organization can use to ensure adherence to its business-control system: financial standards, delegation of authority for decision-making, quality systems (e.g., ISO 9000), organizational design and reporting systems (as observed in organizational charts and position descriptions), standard operating procedures for cross-functional work, work procedures for functional work, product and part specifications for design and testing of products, and maintenance of the operational facilities. Of the standards that organizations find helpful, four deserve special comment:

- **Standard work**: The idea of standard work is fundamental to ensuring long-term performance. Standard work means that the routine work of the organization is done in a standard manner—it is performed consistently in the best way that is possible. This definition implies that the "best way" is known; it is documented for people to understand; the workers have been trained to follow the procedures; and improvement opportunities that deliver improved efficiency, effectiveness, or economy in performance are introduced as soon as they are proven. Some of the characteristics of

---

[20] Genichi Taguchi introduced his quality loss function to describe the economic loss associated with variation from the typical (normal customer expectation) and equated the costs as the total costs that are borne by society for the occurrence of this loss. Thus, losses should also include the impact on your customer's processes as well as their direct cost and economic losses associated with lost productivity or production throughput! For a more thorough discussion of the TLF, see chapter 8.

standard work include a consistent path for material flow, visual alerts to work-process variation, and documented processes with measurement control points. Tools applied to support standard work are largely derived from the lean enterprise efforts developed initially at Toyota in Japan and include visual management, 5S housekeeping, statistical process control, and *poka-yoke*.

▶ *Knowledge mapping and management*: How is standard work created and then deployed to the organization? One way this is accomplished is through transition of work designed in the product-creation process to the product-realization process. This is a role of quality function deployment (QFD) in the design process. QFD defines the critical functions that must be delivered to customers and translates the "what" must be accomplished in the design into the "how" it is executed as the design progresses from the conceptual phase (where functions are created) to the operating phase (where parts are made and products are assembled) to embed these functions into the product. As the design progresses across the product development stages, the language used by the people changes, and QFD helps to translate the meaning of the customer requirements from one discipline to the next and preserve the true meaning of the customer's voice. Thus, QFD maps the knowledge gained during design in the product-creation process into the product-realization process in order to preserve the information required to execute the business-control function in the daily management system as documented in the quality management system.

▶ *Quality management system*: The quality management system that is most often used in business is based on the ISO 9000 standard. It defines work that is done at the process level and the control mechanisms that ensure the appropriate outcomes are achieved. The content of the procedural documents describes the detailed business controls of the work process. These work instructions should include information such as:

▶ Document-control information, such as identifying information, date of issue, revision level, management review and approval responsibility, process owner, linkage to other business-control documents, etc.

▶ Business-control purposes that the procedure is designed to accomplish.

▶ The scope covered by the work process procedure, including exceptions that are not covered by the procedure.

▶ References that are specifically referred to within the procedure (e.g., how to create and interpret control charts, how to conduct standard product tests, etc.).

▶ Operational definitions of terms unique to the procedure.

▶ A step-by-step written description of the work process, using the work-process flow diagram as the model (one procedure step for each activity box on the flow diagram).

▶ Requirements for records storage and retention prescribing the critical business records (identified on the flow diagram) are specified by name, format, storage location, retention period, authority for disposal, and disposal method.

▶ The quality-control plan for the procedure should also be included, as this is the place in the daily management system where the control plan is executed.

▶ *Quality-control plan*: Quality-control plans should be developed prior to product introduction in order to document the business controls that are implemented for supporting a new product in the daily management system. There are three stages in developing a quality-control plan: identifying the critical parameters that must be placed under control in the daily management system, creating a measurement specification to define the control items and data-collection system, and defining the countermeasures for response when potential out-of-control conditions can occur. An example of the components of a quality-control plan is presented in the following figure. The final quality-control plan is recorded in the work procedures of the quality management system where the control point is managed.

Stages in Developing a Control Plan

Critical Parameter Identification

Process	Task	Activity	Critical to Satisfaction		Quality Characteristic	Specification Requirement		
			KPIV	KPOV		LSL	Target	USL

Measurement System Specification

Measurement Method	Measurement Capability	Sample Size	Sampling Frequency	Who Measures	Where Recorded	Last Calibrated

Response Characterization

Action Limit	Decision Rule	Countermeasures	SOP Reference

4. Measures

When productivity gains are recorded in the daily management system (e.g., less time is spent in "hidden factories" for rework, on-line repair, inspection and testing, etc.), then the work processes are producing more throughput. This productivity increase has one detrimental side effect—there is less time to fix problems during the normal *takt* or beat of the cycle. As a result, robust process control becomes more important, and gaining profound knowledge about how processes work to prevent upsets and quality defects becomes a critical success factor. Six Sigma methods have integrated the techniques of lean thinking with statistical understanding of variation in processes to create exactly the profound knowledge that can lead to better-designed work processes. But how can management know where to focus its work-process improvement efforts? The answer to this question lies in the measures of performance that management reviews to ascertain the continuing goodness in execution of its business. So, how should management review its performance?

The fundamental measurements of the daily management system are indicated in terms of quality (How good is the result?), cost (What did it cost to produce this output?), and time (How long did it take to generate the output?). How stable are these performance indicators for quality, cost, and time across a product's life cycle? If one considers a simplified product life cycle as consisting of just four periods, then some observations can be made about the measure of these three performance elements and their relative priority across product life cycles. Change between life-cycle stages creates turbulence in the performance of the business and requires a shift in priority for management attention. Different measures, emphasis, and strategies are required at each life-cycle phase. Specific measures for quality, cost, and time will change from business to business, as will their relative priority across the product's life cycle. An indication of how these measures operate synergistically is shown in the figure below:

Life Cycle Performance Measurement

R&D	Launch	Maturity	End of Life
Time to Market	Responsiveness	Field Failures	Obsolescence Cost
Product Features	Show-Stoppers	Cost Reduction	Warranty Cost
Project Cost	Production Ramp	Product Availability	Risk Probability

▶ **Business-control measures**: A business-control measurement system must be capable of describing and diagnosing business problems. It must operate at the strategic level of the business to describe the overall performance, and it must be connected to the operating level of the business so that a "line of sight" is clear between the strategic and operational measures of business performance. A Six Sigma business-control system should be developed so that operational measures of performance are predictive of strategic performance. In this way, people who are managing their work at the operational level of the organization understand how their work contributes to the strategic direction. When line of sight from the strategic level exists to the operational level, then a diagnostic pathway has been developed for analyzing business-performance problems. Such a measurement system operates at three levels:

(1) The first job of business-control measures is to provide valid insights into the relative competitive position of the organization—the measurement system should provide at least three levels of information. At the top level is a general indicator that a gap might exist using an overall metric that indicates there might be a gap in the overall level of performance of the organization from its potential performance—for example, as obtained from using a metric like $ROCE_{ADJUSTED}$ and a combination of brand value with a table that defines current state of customer satisfaction by product line.

(2) The second level of the measurement system must provide evidence that indicates both the magnitude of performance inefficiency and the location of gaps in the management system. This evidence must be presented in financial terms and should come from the accounting system. Also, the evidence of performance problems should be unambiguous and define the problem while diagnosing potential solutions. In addition, this information should be referenced to the competitive position and provide a compelling argument that the competition is moving faster. This evidence must not be hearsay or anecdotal, but factual and based on data analyses; it must show that at least one major competitor is making moves to disrupt the market, creating chaos and turmoil among your organization's targeted customers. This evidence then leads the way for sound managerial judgment as to its interpretation. Some of the performance indicators that can provide the context for this judgment include:

▶ Warranty cost trend as a percentage of revenue.

▶ Capital efficiency index (CEI) by major capital facility.

▶ Revenue vintage chart, which is a trend analysis of annual sales grouped according to the date of product introduction.

▶ Compound annual growth rate in gross profit.

▶ Compound annual growth rate in brand value.

- Competitive comparisons for business factors such as market-share growth, profit margin, customer satisfaction, productivity, sales overhead (sales and administrative expenses), and product and service quality.

(3) The third set of measures should initiate a drill-down analysis to discover potential areas for business improvement, and the organization's follow-up diagnostic analysis should address questions like:

- Do we have a problem today with productivity and quality?

- Are we doing better than the competition?

- What can we do to gain competitive advantage in our industry?

- How big are our problems, and where are they occurring—for example, are our biggest improvement opportunities in research, operations, or administration?

- Will improvements through innovation remove the problem, or do we need to improve the discipline of our current work-process operations?

- *Balanced scorecards and customer dashboards*: The balanced scorecard (BSC) was described in chapter 4 with respect to the accounting system. It incorporates the first of two important criteria for building a business-control measurement system. This criterion is the need for balance in measurements to ensure all perspectives are reflected in assessment of performance. A second criterion is failed by most BSC systems: alignment to ensure the organization has a linked response between corporate metrics of success and operational actions that deliver success. Both of these concepts are foundations for building a Six Sigma customer dashboard. The Six Sigma customer dashboard extends the idea of the balanced scorecard concept and focuses on building a predictive measurement system to assess value that is delivered to customers by employees in order to generate return for shareholders. The customer dashboard maintains statistical connectivity of the strategic drivers of business value to the front-line operations that deliver work that produces this value through the $Y = f(X)$ transfer function.

An example of a scorecard used in DFSS is illustrated on the next page. It measures the set of critical parameters for a single critical-to-satisfaction factor in a new product development.

Hewlett-Packard embedded its daily management system into a process measurement system that it initially called "Business Fundamentals Tables." Other companies refer to the set of measures that translate strategic goals into operational measures of work (in units such as quality, cost, and time) as either a customer dashboard or a balanced scorecard. These systems are used to monitor the daily operations of a business and to report to management on the progress in the process for developing and delivering value to customers. This measurement process must operate in close to real time to

New Product Development Scorecard

Functional Performance Scorecard									
Parameter	Measure	LSL	USL	Mean	Standard Deviation	Process Capability	Target Level	Forecast Level	Sigma Level

Total Opportunities	
DPU (customer view)	
DPMO (product view)	
Sigma Level	

permit process owners to take appropriate corrective action that will limit the "escape" of defects, errors, or mistakes to external customers. Such measures of control for core work processes can be called "business fundamentals" because they must operate under control for the business to achieve its fundamental performance objectives.

5. Execution

Larry Bossidy describes execution as "the gap between what a company's leaders want to achieve and the ability of their organizations to deliver it." Execution is the systematic process of rigorously discussing the what's and how's, prodding the processes for knowledge and questioning the way things have been done, and then tenaciously following through and ensuring accountability. Execution involves understanding the business environment, assessing the organization's capabilities, linking strategy to operations and the people who are going to implement the strategy, synchronizing the work of these people and their functional disciplines, holding people accountable for the quality of their work, and, finally, linking rewards to outcomes. It also includes mechanisms for modifying business assumptions as the environment changes and upgrading the company's capabilities to meet the challenges of an ambitious strategy. Bossidy uses the analogy of farming to describe the importance of execution: The business must both plant the seeds and harvest the crop in order to enjoy the fruits of its labor.

Bossidy defines three processes that ensure effective business execution—the strategy process, the operations process, and the people process—and places his priority on the people process as most important, saying, "An organization's human beings are its most reliable resource for generating excellent results year after year." It is the people who perform the follow-through that has been defined in the strategy process and deployed to the operations process. While the business leaders are overseers of the transition from strategy to operations, it is in the disciplined execution of the operations that performance is achieved. Without follow-through, plans are a worthless exercise.

To ensure follow-through, a business leader must know the organization's capabilities, insist on realism in reporting and measuring performance, and create follow-through mechanisms such as a meeting, telephone call, or e-mail that holds the employee accountable for their required action. Then leaders must consistently enforce accountability, sending the message to the rest of the organization that they too can expect follow-through actions in the future. Excellent follow-through behavior must be promoted by rewarding those who get things done in the organization. Business leaders should use this approach to coach their people to get things done—coaching provides the difference between giving orders and teaching people how to get things done. Coaching is the business leader's enabling behavior for encouraging effective execution by the workforce.

6. Review

The review process is the organization's opportunity to "get things right" before their work meets the ultimate test of the consuming market. Reviews provide a formal or informal occasion for assessment of different aspects of the business performance in a results-oriented "performance management" system. There are three types of reviews that management conducts: business review, design review, and operations review. As Peter Drucker once commented, "Feedback has to be built into the decision to provide a continuous testing, against actual events, of the expectations that underlie a decision."[21] These reviews can be conducted in two ways. One is through self-assessment by local managers, where they assess their opportunities for improvement against a set of standard business excellence criteria (e.g., Malcolm Baldrige National Quality Award criteria) to determine areas for improvement compared to accepted best practice in management. The second way these reviews can be conducted is through evaluating the performance measures of the daily management system through operating reviews that focus on the results produced by the work processes to determine areas where the results are not aligned with expectations for performance. New products are assessed in design reviews to determine the growth in maturity of their readiness for joining the normal work process and transitioning to routine business operations of the production environment.

---

[21] Peter F. Drucker, The Effective Executive, p. 139.

The review process seeks to identify conformance to plans (e.g., "Is there any shortfall or overachievement in targets?"). When a nonconformity is identified, then the root cause of the deviation is discerned to determine an appropriate response to the out-of-control type of condition. Both corrective actions and countermeasures are identified to realign the process and ensure that process integrity and stability are achieved in the business-control system. Actions taken in response to out-of-control conditions are:

▶ Emergency countermeasures to alleviate the immediate issue, concern, or problem.

▶ Short-term corrective action to prevent the specific problem from recurring.

▶ Long-term preventive action to remove the root cause of the problem and mistake-proof the process, thereby providing a permanent solution for preventing the problem from recurring.

Key aspects of these reviews include:

▶ **Business review:** Business reviews are conducted to determine the achievement of the organization relative to the following elements of its plan:

  ▶ Change-project objectives
  ▶ Business-planning objectives and corporate commitment
  ▶ Business improvement plans
  ▶ Economic plans and projections
  ▶ Customer requirements and expectations
  ▶ Competitive performance analysis
  ▶ Business excellence self-assessment

When gaps in performance capability are observed, then the management team must make the strategic decision of the action to pursue.

Questions addressed during a business review include:

  ▶ What results have been demonstrated?
  ▶ Which results were expected, and which were unexpected?
  ▶ What does this outcome do for customers?
  ▶ What have we done well that our competitors have done poorly?
  ▶ What have we done poorly but our competitors seem to have mastered?

Additional considerations can be included in a business review, such as the use of the criteria from the Malcolm Baldrige National Quality Award, to evaluate how well the organization has defined its business model, how thoroughly the approach to business has been deployed, and how effective this approach has been in terms of the results achieved.

▶ *Design review:* Periodically, the progress of design projects must be evaluated to determine the percentage of completion, performance against targets, shortfalls from expected performance, and causes for both under-

and over-achievement. Specific action must be identified to compensate for performance deficiencies and prevent recurrence of such problems in future change management projects.[22] The fundamental considerations to be included in design reviews are listed in the following figure.

Product Development Process Review

Review	Review Items	Focus Areas
Concept	• Market Surveys • Product History Files • Customer Focus Groups • Customer Requirements Table	• Customer Importance • Competitive Differentials • Parametric Analysis • Technology Readiness
Definition	• Preliminary Design Specifications • Product's System Architecture • Preliminary Engineering Drawings • Laboratory Prototype	• Functional Design • Regulatory Requirements • Growth in Design Quality • Functional Performance
Design	• Final Design Specification • Detailed Engineering Drawings • Production Tooling • Production Prototype	• Demonstrated Robustness • Production Readiness • Supplier Readiness • Transition to Control
Production	• Field Performance Information • After-Market Customer Survey	• Product Reliability • Customer Satisfaction

▶ **Operations review**: Operations reviews are conducted by reviewing the measures of the daily management system in comparison to targeted performance, external benchmarks, and the original design-process capability to determine improvement areas and performance against competitors. The purpose of the operating review is to ensure follow-through in execution of the business plans.

Implementing design for Six Sigma

The traditional approach to implementing Six Sigma begins with applying DMAIC for solving problems—reacting to the current organizational issues and chronic problems. DFSS approaches Six Sigma in a less reactive way by seeking to create a future that is predictable and capable of delivering customer requirements consistently.

---

[22] One approach to Six Sigma design reviews was presented by D. H. Stamatis in a series of articles that appeared in *Quality Digest* (starting in April 2002). Stamatis does not use the DMADV model for DFSS—instead, he proposes DCOV: Define, Characterize, Optimize, and Verify. There is no essential difference in the model that he presents—Define and Characterize are no different from the DMA steps of DMADV, and optimization occurs in the Design step of DMADV; however, it is not clear where the design emphasis is in DCOV. By separating Design into a phase of DMADV, the DFSS process is able to focus on the business front end to design and also introduce a multi-generational product plan in the context of an overall product-line management approach. Stamatis does present an assessment tool, modeled after the Malcolm Baldrige National Quality Award, that could be customized to an organization's design process for evaluating design maturity.

DFSS works on developing a predictable quality level for products and processes by emphasizing the "right the first time" approach to product and process design. But because DFSS systematically integrates engineering design methods that are already being used by an organization with statistical methods to permit prediction of the final quality levels and improvement of the design quality prior to manufacturing release of the product, the DFSS methodology takes a much longer time to adopt than DMAIC. When implementing DFSS, an organization quickly discovers where it has systemic weaknesses in its design and development process infrastructure, such as the following:[23]

1. Insufficient methods to solicit and understand true customer requirements.

2. Design procedures that are informal and variant from project to project.

3. Missing reliability tests or parametric capability demonstration tests.

4. Measurement and/or test equipment that is not capable of meeting requirements.

5. Inadequate engineer training in tools and methods related to Six Sigma.

DFSS is more than adding a few analysis methods (e.g., robust engineering, DOE, QFD, TRIZ, etc.) to the current design process. DFSS is a disciplined enhancement of the engineering design and development process that must be adapted to each organization using a systems engineering approach to its business, products, and technologies in order to appropriately address the most significant design elements that apply to its competitive market. DFSS is a comprehensive operating philosophy that applies statistical thinking to understand the impact of variation on all of the components of design and seeks to achieve sustained control over production processes through the appropriate considerations of variation in the design process.[24]

What are the "first steps" toward developing a DFSS capability? First, an organization needs to learn what is unique regarding its approach to product design and discover which of the DFSS methods are most important for application in its environment. A good way to do this is to follow the five steps presented on the next page:

---

[23] Maurice L. Berryman, "DFSS and Big Profits," *Six Sigma Forum Magazine*, November 2002.

[24] For additional advice on implementing Six Sigma, see the author's responses to fifty most "frequently asked questions" regarding Six Sigma in: Gregory H. Watson, *Six Sigma for Business Leaders* (Salem, NH: GOAL/QPC, 2004).

Conduct awareness training for the senior engineering team on the tool content and methodology of DFSS.

Evaluate the performance of your most recent product development projects regarding their project and market success and develop a set of lessons learned based on your investigation.

Evaluate your current design process for its degree of integration of the tools and methods related to DFSS and determine the most important DFSS tools or methods that should be integrated into your design process.

Conduct a self-assessment (see appendix A) to identify the current state of your readiness to pursue design for Six Sigma and the priority of any gaps in your design capability that must be addressed.

Develop a plan for "gap closure" and choose a specific design project as the pilot for implementation.

The last step in the journey to design for Six Sigma is the hardest: Execute your plan one project at a time![25] Best wishes on your journey!

---

[25] While this book has focused on DFSS as applied to product development, the same style of thinking can also be applied to the design of business processes and services. An important principle of DFSS is to design products and the processes that produce them at the same time.

Afterword
Charting the Direction of Six Sigma

"Statistical thinking will one day be as necessary for efficient citizenship as the ability to read and write."

~ H. G. Wells

Perspective for creating history

Mankind is unique among nature in that we can create our own history. We preserve knowledge through recorded communications and transfer this knowledge through education and training for use by future generations. People are capable of continuous learning, across individuals and organizations. Learning is adaptive and collaborative. It is a process whereby lessons are generated by both our successes and our failures—as well as through the success and failure of others—and, in this way, we gain an ability to steer our future direction more soundly by avoiding repetition of historical catastrophes while building on past successes. We can plan to achieve new outcomes based on our understanding of opportunities and the perspective gained from history. Thus, wherever behavioral patterns exist, it is important to understand how these patterns are created and what they imply—to a Six Sigma thinker, these patterns can identify potential root causes of business failure and become important guidelines for our planning.

Adaptive learning helps us discern meaning in continuously changing systems that are undergoing transformation. This is a persistent challenge for most businesses—a continuously changing environment that requires its working processes to learn and adapt to rapidly shifting market and technological conditions so that the business can maintain its progress toward achieving its performance objectives.

Change is being accelerated by the global technological shift toward interconnectivity. As the world moves from relationships based on "atoms" (where value comes from physical products) to one based on "bytes" (where value is a function of services or software provided to support products whose functions have become more generic), customization becomes deliverable concurrently by mass-production processes. Today, this phenomenon occurs in the cellular phone industry, where both after-market custom cases and user-programmable ringing tones and games allow the phone to become truly unique and personalized. But how will value be delivered in the future as we learn more? Will the knowledge of customer needs become so complete that appropriate insights are always gained into customer requirements and value becomes taken for granted? Will flawless execution of work become possible so that customers consistently receive the value that they desire—not just require? These two conditions define a utopian state that is potentially closer now than it has ever been before—thanks to the opportunities provided by design for Six Sigma.

To understand the changing forces that will be affecting our future, we must first discuss the current state of Six Sigma efforts from a historical perspective, answering the question "How did we get here?" Then we can assess the trends that will influence the movement toward the future state of the application of Six Sigma philosophies and methods.

Current state of Six Sigma

Where is Six Sigma heading? To answer this question, we need both the historical perspective of where Six Sigma has been and a current-state assessment of where it is today.

The bits and pieces that define Six Sigma have developed over the years through the individual efforts of talented people who have invented tools and gained insights into how business processes work. Six Sigma is quite literally the product of decades of work by a community of people and has been honed into a set of core processes and key methods through its application in a number of "thought-leading" organizations. Without either the individual efforts of the methodology's pioneers or the collective efforts of the methodology's integrators, Six Sigma would not exist. Both owe a debt of gratitude to the other: The organizations owe the individuals a deep appreciation of the laborious effort involved in thinking through and documenting new approaches to problems so they can be applied in a practical way—and the individuals owe these organizations a debt of gratitude for taking these (sometimes too academic and obtuse) methods and applying them pragmatically to solve their real problems and create a real competitive advantage.

It is proper to ask if Six Sigma is "done" yet. However, when the tools and methods that define Six Sigma are surveyed, it is clear that much more needs to be done before there is a "holistic" theory and application that can be pragmatically applied. What do we observe that is incomplete or in need of further development? It seems to me that there are three areas where Six Sigma is challenged: completing the integration of the business-improvement tools that are available; operationally defining what is meant by design for Six Sigma (appendix B of this book is another step in this direction); and developing software and support tools that provide more comprehensive integration of the tools so that end-to-end project management can be expedited further.[1]

Leveraging learning for the future: More integration!

Where is Six Sigma today? I believe that it is evident that Six Sigma is becoming integrated into the business systems of many of the world's leading organizations, even as lean thinking and "just-in-time" methods are being incorporated into today's Six Sigma toolkit. It has been applied in all categories of industry, as well as by governments and small businesses as well as multi-divisional organizations. Six Sigma has taken the best ideas, methods, and tools from previous quality approaches and merged them into a unique system that engages the entire business (rather than a single function), and a related operating philosophy and organizational culture have been developed and adapted by leadership teams of numerous organizations as a core dimension in establishing their way of working. The formalization of toolkits, bodies of knowledge, and skill-based certifications are only the beginning steps toward this integration. Coming in the near future will also be more software products that support Six Sigma (even Microsoft is getting into this business with its Six Sigma project management tool Accelerator), as well as statistical standards that specify the toolkit more thoroughly; ISO TC69, the technical committee focused on statistical matters, has formed a Six Sigma Technical Advisory Committee to review the need for standards to better support Six Sigma. I believe that eventually the ISO 9000 quality management system standard and the Malcolm Baldrige National Quality Award criteria might more explicitly ascribe to a more Six Sigma–focused approach to business improvement.

The resultant business-systems integration will be centered on an organization's people dimension and using a process model of its critical business processes and the measurement control points to link balanced-scorecard metrics to indicators of actionable operating conditions that drive the routine performance and produce the desired output of the entire business value chain. Such business-system integration will not be driven by selection of an enterprise resource program (ERP) with preset process definitions, but it will

---

[1] Several years ago, in connection with the ASQ Futures Study, I wrote an article for *Quality Progress* magazine that provides some insight into this type of integration, which should become available in the future: Gregory H. Watson, "Digital Nails and Electronic Hammers: Tools of the Next Generation," *Quality Progress*, July 1998, pp. 21–26.

represent a choice for doing business that is identified and desired by management (process definitions, measurement systems, and people systems, which are then embedded into the ERP). While the current generation of ERP systems can provide consistency of operation across a business, their generic solutions to operational problems might not provide competitive advantage if all the competitors are using the same process. Competitive advantage will come when the organization chooses its direction—one that is different from its competition, yet aligned with realities of the desired customer experience—and then focuses its energies and talent on making this choice work well.

In addition, customer service will be a growing dimension in Six Sigma as the world becomes more and more technologically capable and customers can directly reach out to all competitors in a particular market. In the final analysis, all organizations are service organizations, and all customer relationships require personal attention. Future business leaders will learn that customer relationship planning (CRP) is more than a software package that identifies customers and their buying patterns, and that customer-satisfaction measurement requires more than doing a survey to determine the average response to a couple of questions. Organizations will perceive each customer as a unique individual with a set of needs that must be identified, addressed, and then reviewed to ensure that they experience the level of service that they require. The focus of technology on behalf of the customer will be the true driver of sustainable competitiveness in the coming century. Six Sigma thinking will be the operational stimulus for this transformation.

While the current emphasis in business is on application of "fashionable" technology, technologies will become increasingly integrated as a convergence occurs to create a personal electronic appliance[2] that is able to deliver application-specific required knowledge electronically to the point of need. In the near future, technology will enable quality—placing solutions into the hands of workers at the time that they are needed—and anticipating problems through smart monitoring of all process-performance parameters that contribute significantly to the customer-perceivable output. To achieve this integration, organizations will become knowledge-based learning centers in their efforts to maintain a competitive edge.

For business improvement to be driven to the next level of performance, it must be comprehensively applied and assimilated into the entire business system equally at the grass-roots level of organizations and the strategic apex of senior leadership and their process of management. Continuous learning must be a value of the organization of the future—leaders must create an environment where everyone is a learner, everyone is a teacher, and everyone takes responsibility to mentor those who need development. Such a proactive human-focused business environment can be developed only when both the "hard, analytical disciplines" and the "soft, psychological disciplines"

---

[2] By this term I mean the convergence of technologies for laptop computers, personal data assistants, mobile phones, electronic books, and the variety of electronic entertainment devices for playing games and music.

merge into a unified approach for managing results through people. How will the future migrate from the current state to establish the context for this integration?

Future Six Sigma methodology extensions

Today there is a lot of activity that extends the Six Sigma body of knowledge and seeks to integrate other proven improvement technologies with this methodology:

▶ Many of the tools that are now being integrated into Six Sigma processes for problem solving are associated with Japan's lean management processes. Indeed, numerous organizations are finding that the use of lean tools prior to a Six Sigma analysis can help clarify the issues that must be resolved and make the sources of variation even clearer.[3]

▶ Another very significant direction of Six Sigma is the integration of the concept of the balanced scorecard, but with a distinctive "Six Sigma" flavor to ensure statistical connectivity between top-tier metrics of business performance and the front-line measures of operational activities. In this system, the top-tier metrics are all "critical to satisfaction" for an organizational stakeholder (first customers, then shareholders, employees, government, and so on), while the lower-tier measures are all "critical to quality" for the host organization.

▶ Many organizations are using Six Sigma as a means for defining and implementing their internet strategies in addition to their new product development efforts.

▶ In addition, the next set of methods to be integrated into the Six Sigma toolkit have already been developed and proven in other fields. Some tools that are awaiting operational definition and inclusion in the DFSS body of knowledge include general linear model (GLM), auto-regressive integrated moving averages (ARIMA), adaptive learning systems, applied optimal estimation and Kalman filtering, D-optimal experimental designs, discrete event simulation, stochastic modeling, and multi-variable statistical control charts.

Some proponents of Six Sigma believe that this methodology will generate the ubiquitous "total" aspect of TQM—ensuring that quality management finds its way into all parts of the organization. Indeed, some companies have integrated their business-excellence models with Six Sigma change management to define the "Recognize" stage of Six Sigma, which defines opportunities for improvement through both DFSS and DMAIC. Other organizations have integrated their ISO 9000 quality management systems with the Six Sigma DMAIC "Control" stage to ensure that process monitoring and routine management are implemented and sustained. No matter how the future

---

[3] Gregory H. Watson, "Cycles of Learning: Observations of Jack Welch," *Six Sigma Forum Magazine*, vol. 1, no. 1, November 2001, pp. 13–17.

unfolds, it is clear that the Six Sigma initiatives of the 1990s have helped to establish a "total quality" way of doing business that has attracted the attention of the world's top managers—a feat that is difficult to achieve and one that signals an enduring impact on business thinking.

Innovation: The next focus of business leaders

Innovation is the dimension of quality that comes from the creative destruction of our past ways of delivering value based on our knowledge of the true requirements of customers and the ability to formulate the market promise. Operational quality is achieved through performance consistency in delivery of our promises to customers. Together, these factors are combined by the human dimension in a way that enables an organization to unfold the power of technology to achieve a competitive advantage. Together, these dimensions of quality will define the new value-delivery proposition of the future and drive future organizational performance.

Organizations are like weak casks trying to contain the powerful bubbling effects of fermenting wine, except in the case of organizations, the wine comes from both rapid technology development and social transformations. Organizations also badly need progress in cask and barrel technology to provide reinforcement for their growth. In plain terms, organizations must be reinforced to make them able to manage continuous and turbulent technological and social change. Too many companies considered as quality champions have slipped back to performing business as usual. In general, this was not because of technology, but because a pragmatic approach to quality was not really integrated into their business. Business leaders must act as organizational architects and be innovative in sculpting purposeful designs of their resources that anticipate future needs and are congruent with their organization's values.

There is no doubt that, for any organization, a culture that pursues a common vision and shared values can be an advantage over a haphazard approach that advocates living for the day and everyone for their own self. These elements of a quality culture, like any cultural concept, are factors contributing to differentiation in the future. DFSS and lessons learned from it will not spread in a uniform fashion around the world (indeed, rarely has any philosophy or method been taken at face value in all global cultures).[4] Indeed, some nations and cultures will be more receptive to the cultural factors embedded in DFSS that encourage quality results than others, and the scene will change over time in unpredictable cycles, as all cultural seasons do, and DFSS will take on a unique mantle in all its applications.

---

[4] In his lifetime study of innovation, Everett Rodgers (see his book *Diffusion of Innovation*) observed that there are many different rates of acceptance of new technology and that people can be grouped according to their willingness to accept new technology. I believe that the same categories could be applied to both nations and cultures to define their willingness to adapt to change. The question requires more study, as categorization of cultures would need to be made and the basis for cultural acceptance of change would need to be established. Perhaps this would be a good doctoral dissertation for some enterprising graduate student!

One thing we know, however, is that the future will not be sluggish—it will be fast-paced and complex as markets produce alternative technologies and applications diverge from the traditional knowledge base. This means that rapid choices must be made in the face of many types of risk—not just financial risk, but also operational risk, market risk, and technological risk. Managing in this complex web of interrelated opportunities for both success and failure will become a strain on business leaders. The complexity of the environment will force leaders to address new or emerging issues, such as quality in governance and ever-improving management of organizational change. It seems as though organizations have become proficient at defining the changes that they want to make, but fail during the implementation.[5] Business excellence will be observed through the actions taken by organizations as all these dimensions of quality are addressed simultaneously. The manager of the future must become a "circus ringmaster" as well as the "change master" as defined by Rosabeth Moss Kanter.[6]

Technology is not the only stimulus for change in the future. A second stimulus will be the increasing emphasis placed on finance in interpreting the meaning of operational performance. Nowhere is this more evident than in the Six Sigma initiative of General Electric. As quality becomes expressed more like a management concept in the language of finance (note that the "cost of poor quality" is still the language of quality but that most financial management systems do not recognize this subject as a meaningful topic), it will become an imperative to learn more and embrace the changes that will be generated as the financial management community is encouraged to provide more realistic and actionable reporting systems. Perhaps the important role played by finance in Six Sigma initiatives will help to define the proper system of change that must be initiated in the accounting systems of corporations.

Perhaps the next major catalyst for change in the future will be the combination of environmental and social responsibility of organizations. Organizations produce value targeted toward three different dimensions: value for markets and customers, value for shareholders and investors, and value for society. In this final area, there are no real measurement systems that define the overall "balanced scorecard" for performance. Many small indicators are used to determine if an organization is fulfilling its responsibility to employees, communities, government, and the public in general (including the future generations of mankind). Will there be an indicator for the social value-added contribution of a firm as there are for market value-added (MVA, or the brand value-added contribution) and economic value-added (EVA, or the shareholder value-added contribution)? How will the acceptance of these influences on business affect DFSS? Who knows? But, in any case, it is clear that

---

[5] Perhaps that is why AlliedSignal/Honeywell CEO Larry Bossidy and business consultant Ram Charan wrote their excellent book, *Execution: The Discipline of Getting Things Done* (New York: Crown, 2002).

[6] Rosabeth Moss Kanter, *The Change Masters* (New York: Simon & Schuster, 1983).

there will be an impact as environmental and social change ripple through the specification of requirements for new products.

Top management will not be credible business leaders if they do not convert their myopic focus on "the bottom line" into a focus on "a multiple bottom line" that extends their scope of attention from financial results to people- and society-related results. Perhaps the almost-exclusive focus of many American companies on shareholder value will become a big obstacle on the road to sustainable excellence. Conversely, many European countries focus more on stakeholder value than on shareholder value—and that, too, is an obstacle to excellence. "Society" as a stakeholder is going to become particularly important whenever the interest of mankind in a global world is at stake—not just protection of the environment and social responsibility, but also in the areas of bio-genetics and international relations. Mastering these changes will become more and more a quality-related issue, and the tools of DFSS must be brought to bear to protect humanity from the risk of disruptive changes to the environment.

Customer satisfaction should be the final goal of business activities and the ultimate enabler of enduring competitiveness—this is different from stakeholder satisfaction. Stakeholder value focuses on intrinsic characteristics of an organization—the ability to display creativity within the framework of restrictive conditions that are imposed by society. It is compliance or obedience-based. However, customer satisfaction is based on extrinsic characteristics and is the aim of work; it is achievement based. While the importance of stakeholder satisfaction will rapidly increase in the near future, it must be emphasized that achieving stakeholder satisfaction is nonsense if we have not first achieved customer satisfaction. The key lesson in DFSS is that the customer truly does own the balance of power and that it is the responsibility of enlightened business leaders to use and continuously refresh their kit of "blunt instruments" to improve the value that customers receive from current and future products and services.

Appendix A
Evaluating Your Readiness for DFSS

"It looked as if some of the tolerances were assigned much closer than should be necessary, and I started to try to find out how they had been fixed. To accomplish this, on every occasion when I met an engineer I asked him how he decided on the tolerances in his branch of the subject.... I concluded that in designing a new machine the chief engineer drew it freehand with dimensions to the nearest inch, and sent it to the draftsman to work out the detail to the nearest thousandth, who then gave it to his junior engineer to mark in the specific tolerances.... The junior assistant, anxious not to get himself in trouble, would, as a general rule, think of the smallest number he knew and then halve it."

~ Charles G. Darwin

How can you determine if your organization is ready for DFSS?

Design for Six Sigma (DFSS) is the deliberate act of designing new products, services, or processes for consistent delivery of Six Sigma levels of performance (this means flawless execution of work to deliver your customers' requirements) for those characteristics that are critical to satisfaction of targeted customers. The essence of DFSS is prediction of the design quality up front and driving quality measurements for predictability of improvement in the early design phases. DFSS requires a cultural change in the new product design and development process, as well as related project identification, budget allocation, and project management processes. DFSS quantifies risk throughout the process and signals a shift toward probabilistic thinking throughout the process—as compared to using "rules of thumb" or safety factors to ensure that problems don't occur.

How can you know if your company is ready to take on this challenge? Perhaps the best way to decide is to conduct a self-assessment of your practices to see how prepared you are for the next step. Once this self-assessment has been done, then the management team needs to determine where to focus improvement efforts: on the management processes for product development or on the engineering processes for design of new products.

There are three important considerations to keep in mind while conducting a DFSS self-assessment: First, determine the organization's generic capacity for change, which signals its readiness for adapting major change initiatives into its culture; second, evaluate the performance of the current product development process to determine its relative effectiveness and efficiency in delivering economic product solutions to customers; and third, analyze the extent of the application of best practices for managing new product development, from concept creation through the consistent execution of operational processes that prepare the final deliverables for customers. Let's look at the details of these three change considerations:

First: Determine your generic change capacity

John Young, former CEO of Hewlett-Packard, once encouraged his employees to "learn to love change." He went on to say that if they "don't learn to love change, then look for a job in the beer industry, because the electronics industry is all about change." That was in 1988, and of course, with the advent of light beer, iced beer, and flavored beers, today's beer industry no longer merely honors the historical brewing recipe! It has become a victim of drastic change also!

In some organizations, the continuous improvement model (called the Deming Cycle, Plan-Do-Check-Act-Cycle, or PDCA Cycle) implies "Please don't change again!" However, some leaders have observed that the more an organization changes, the more flexible it becomes to adapting to new ideas and incorporating them rapidly into its key business processes. Such flexibility equals sustainable competitiveness in a dynamically changing business environment. Thus, some "radical" executives have incorporated a chaos-based approach to change—encouraging frequent change as a means to create a dynamic organization that is capable of adapting to shifts in the business environment and competitive situations. A significant readiness factor for Six Sigma is the degree to which such change initiatives have been successfully incorporated in the past. Reviewing these past change efforts can often enlighten the top team about what it must do to improve the organization's ability to accept such changes in the future.

When reviewing past change initiatives, pay particular attention to the types of problem areas that were encountered throughout the implementation. Problems can occur when change is not managed properly. Some symptoms of poorly managed change initiatives can include the following:

- **Myopia**—The narrowness of vision that keeps management from seeing opportunities and threats from non-traditional sources.

- **Not invented here**—The feeling that nothing is of value or has merit for an organization unless it was first "invented" or developed within the organization.

- **Unintended consequences**—Getting something that you didn't want, instead of the result that you planned for.

- **Confusion**—The lack of clarity that occurs when different parts of an organization have a different understanding of the direction in which senior management wants to go.

- **Internal competition**—The focus on competition among internal business units, which is unhealthy because it averts the organization's focus away from the market forces of customers and competitors.

- **Repetition of mistakes**—Making the same mistakes that had been committed during a prior change initiative. This symptom typically occurs when the management team does not do a "post-mortem" analysis to find out what "went well" and what "possible improvement opportunities" are available from previous initiatives. Corrective action should be taken to keep from having the same mistakes repeated in new change initiatives.

- **Resistance to change**—This is a general symptom of an ineffective change initiative and typically indicates that one or more core concern areas have not been properly addressed in the change management planning.

- **Gamesmanship**—This trait occurs when managers believe that they can change the way the change initiative operates so that it fits their basic personal need not to change. One of the key symptoms of gamesmanship is the lack of acceptance of "standards" for measuring success in deployment of an initiative. Whenever local managers re-create elements of the change initiative, they build a local standard that no longer is part of the organization-wide management language.

- **False start**—This occurs when an initiative begins in part of an organization without the support of the top management team and must be "restarted" with the full support and active engagement of the senior management team.

- **Settling**—This occurs when the organization is not able to replicate the success that has been achieved in other organizations and decides to "accept" a lesser level of success by declaring "victory" even though it has not achieved its initial goals. Execution of a change initiative is hard work and requires constant review by top management to ensure that the desired objective remains as the target for the organization.

How many of these symptoms of "change disease" has your organization experienced?

When analyzing your historical capacity to change, consider the strength that your organization has developed over time in the following areas when evaluating a major change initiative such as Six Sigma. One way to evaluate the capacity for change is to rate significant change factors using a scalar measure that indicates the degree of acceptance that the organization has achieved. Conformity to major change principles can be assessed using a scale that indicates strong ability at one extreme, neutral at the center, and poor ability at the other extreme for the following criteria:

▶ *Propensity to experiment and adapt*—How willing is the organization to change the way it works—either in incremental steps or in major initiatives? Are managers open to experimentation with process improvements to see what works best?

▶ *Degree of success with last major change*—How much success was achieved with the last major change initiative? Did it meet its objectives? Did you learn from the success or failure of this initiative?

▶ *Access to information and resources*—Is information readily accessible to those who need it for planning or operating processes? Are enough resources allocated to ensure that management's priority projects and initiatives are effectively implemented?

▶ *Management tolerance for delay and failure*—Does management accept the fact that experiments are conducted to learn and might lead to success or failure and that the key reason to experiment is to gain profound knowledge? Will members of management tolerate any delays in programs in order to get them right, or do they force a solution with unproven or unknown consequences just to keep on schedule?

▶ *Level of interpersonal trust*—How much trust do employees have in the motives of the management team for change? Do employees believe top management is credible and that its members communicate with truthfulness when they speak about what will happen in the company and the rationale for the desired change?

▶ *Comfort level with change*—How comfortable is the organization with change? Do the employees accept change without question, or is there significant resistance to all change initiatives? Is this attitude consistent across all layers of the organization from top to front line?

▶ *Willingness to cooperate*—What is the degree of willingness of employees to take an active role in change initiatives and participate collaboratively to ensure that change is achieved in a timely and effective manner?

▶ *Management will for the new state*—How strong does the top management team feel about the desired change? Will the senior leaders commit to the initiative as a new way of working—part of their organization's "genetic structure," or DNA—or do they believe that if the organization gains "savoir faire," or knowledge, that it will be enough to carry them through to a new world? Change never happened by just gaining knowledge; management must know what to do with it and have a theory about how to apply that knowledge in order to achieve the desired performance. In the end, excellence is driven by execution, and execution occurs when the senior business leaders continuously ask the right questions that cause the organization to realize that the leaders have the will to change—that they won't let it go to seize another idea or management fad.

▶ *Leadership capability of teams*—Do the local teams in the business units have a solid leadership capability? Will your high-potential Black Belts challenge the leadership of the local process owners, or will they perceive the local process owners as peers?

▶ *Culture of continuous improvement*—Does the organization have a strong culture of continuous improvement, or has the organization been more focused on controlling all work to maintain process performance? Do people feel that it is their responsibility to continuously improve the quality of their work output?

▶ *Delegation of decision authority*—Has decision authority been delegated to the level that is appropriate—where data and process-performance knowledge allow the best decision to be made—or are such decisions closely held by senior business leaders?

▶ *Approach to standardization*—Does your organization accept work standards as the best way to ensure consistency in performance across shifts and work units, or do local business units seek to develop their own work procedures for common activities?

The following figure illustrates a form that can be used to record the results of this self-assessment of generic capacity to change. These performance fac-

Change Readiness Assessment						
Criterion	Low 1	2	Neutral 3	4	High 5	Score
Propensity to adapt and experiment						
Degree of success with last major change						
Access to information and resources						
Management tolerance for delay and failure						
Level of interpersonal trust						
Comfort level with change						
Willingness to cooperate						
Management will for achieving new state						
Leadership capability of local process teams						
Culture of continuous improvement						
Degree of delegation of decision authority						
Acceptability of work standardization						
					Total	

tors can help to enable the success of a change effort, and they will accelerate implementation of change. Incorporating these business improvement factors into all future change management initiatives will help to ensure a smoother transition and broader acceptance of a desired change.

Change-related lessons learned in Six Sigma initiatives

Six Sigma has been implemented in engineering companies since the mid-1980s, when it was initially developed by a group of companies involved in a semiconductor consortium. Both Motorola and Texas Instruments were successful in applying these methods. Since that time, there have been many lessons learned. Of the initial companies who were involved in the development of Six Sigma, four were not successful in making it work for the long term. These companies were observed to have four different failure modes that accounted for the root cause of the problems that they encountered during their adaptation of Six Sigma to their culture:

▶ **Lack of vision in deployment**—Intel did an exceptional job implementing Six Sigma within its fabrication facilities, and its current performance is about 0.5σ better than that of its closest competitor. However, Intel implemented Six Sigma only in production and failed to apply the Six Sigma methods to its business processes. Even a 5σ production line will not be able to satisfy customer deliveries if it is managed by a 2σ order-scheduling process—the variation in the planning process will cause the production process to operate out of control.

▶ **Lack of constancy of purpose from leadership**—IBM did a great job in its initial deployment of Six Sigma—until the CEO changed from John Akers to Lou Gestner. Gestner wanted to put his own imprint on IBM, so he systematically dismantled all of the programs that he associated with Akers—Six Sigma was one of these. Bad news for IBM customers, this change was accompanied by confusion in how to serve customers. After five years, IBM began to correct its error by bringing Six Sigma back as an operating discipline—unfortunately, it had already lost market share and position. Six Sigma is now helping to repair the company.

▶ **Lack of confidence in employees**—Harris Semiconductor executives were afraid of a backlash from employees over the "heavy statistics" associated with Six Sigma, so it was decided that Six Sigma would be implemented through a small team of degreed statisticians, rather than Black Belts selected from the company's best employees. In the case of Harris, the challenge for these statisticians was a career challenge, not a technical or a process challenge—there was no upward mobility available to them. So, Harris lost all of its trained statisticians to competitors who were more flexible in their way of working with staff professionals.

▶ **Lack of discipline in implementation**—Digital Equipment managers believed that an empowered employee would make better decisions. When the employees who looked into Six Sigma realized that they had already studied many of the analysis tools used in problem solving, management agreed to let the employees choose individual two- to three-day seminars to complete their Black Belt training. This choice effectively destroyed all of the integration in the Six Sigma problem-solving method, reducing the sequence to a set of independent tools without the learning structure of DMAIC. As a result, the Black Belts trained at Digital never achieved the same level of effectiveness as the Black Belts at Motorola and Texas Instruments did.

Since these early failures of Six Sigma, there have been several major trends observed in companies that have not been the most successful in implementing Six Sigma. In addition to an organization's ability to adapt to major change, there are five significant obstacles to successful change: leadership support, culture, communication, structure, and integration.

▶ *Leadership* can create major obstacles when support diminishes over time due to a shift in interest to other management topics or their decision to support other initiatives that move the organization in a different direction. DFSS overcomes this problem by encouraging active leadership involvement in project definition and review, as well as in recognition of the efforts of Six Sigma professionals. Another potential obstacle is lack of involvement and support from middle management. This was also a significant problem in deployment of many TQM programs. In Six Sigma, this obstacle is addressed by beginning training at the middle management level—those business leaders serve as project champions and process owners and have a significant role in implementing a Six Sigma initiative and in conducting business reviews of projects to ensure that bottom-line results are achieved and the benefits are captured.

▶ *Culture* creates obstacles to change that include elements based on fear of change—the unknown that will impact the way people work and their basic need for security in their employment environment. This obstacle is most often seen in the resistance to change, skepticism, and the atmosphere of mistrust due to fear of job loss by employees. DFSS conducts business leader seminars to define the policy for any reduction in work-force level that occurs due to Six Sigma projects and to craft the message that must be communicated about this policy to the organization in order to alleviate potential concerns with the fear of job loss (just two subjects of many in this workshop). It is important that management seek the means to motivate and inspire the work force to embrace Six Sigma as its normal way of working. Actively managing the change process through the use of a proven change model to outline the organization's deployment plan is another way that Six Sigma encourages the right atmosphere to encourage change.

▶ *Communication* is a significant component of any change initiative, and lack of a clear message coordinated across an organization is a critical element in the failure of many change initiatives. By developing a specific communication plan to describe the organization's business strategy, goals, roles, priorities, and expectations regarding DFSS, the deployment champion and steering committee can eliminate the uncertainty about change that comes from lack of knowledge.

▶ *Structure*—Obstacles to successful change deal with missing business systems, an organizational structure that does not support the change initiative, budgetary limitations, or lack of commitment of credible people to staff the initiative. In Six Sigma, the deployment plan addresses the structural engagement process to embrace Six Sigma in support systems as well as throughout the organization.

▶ *Integration*—or, rather, a lack of it—between initiatives for major changes that management supports, or the confounding of strategic direction due to lack of clear management priority among the change initiatives being promoted, is a significant problem. Six Sigma seeks to eliminate this problem by encouraging the executive sponsors to make key alignment decisions at the front end of the implementation process and to communicate their choice about alignment in their "elevator speech" about Six Sigma—a design feature of the executive seminar.

What do these lessons learned mean, and how can management anticipate these conditions and "mistake-proof" the implementation of a Six Sigma change initiative? Management must make careful plans to deploy Six Sigma, being sure to understand clearly the decisions that they make regarding the implementation as well as the implications that their choices can have on the effectiveness of their change initiative. Some specific problems noted with Six Sigma implementations include the following areas, which must have countermeasures included in the Six Sigma deployment planning:

▶ Misalignment with the organization's culture.

▶ Failure to convince leadership of the value of Six Sigma.

▶ Lack of management involvement.

▶ Black Belt candidates who are not capable of performing the analyses.

▶ Poor selection of Black Belt training projects.

▶ Insufficient communication of success stories.

▶ Unavailability of Master Black Belt coaches.

▶ Little integration with business-scorecard measurement or business strategy.

▶ Low priority for Six Sigma improvements.

▶ Inadequate resources allocated to support management of the Six Sigma initiative.

▶ Inadequate resources allocated for implementation of projects.

Management can customize a generic change-readiness self-assessment to contain as many of these warnings and criteria as necessary to fit to their current situation.

Second: Evaluate your performance in new product development

Given this extensive caution, how can you know if the proposed change is right? How can you learn if your organization is ready for such a change effort? These are the questions that can be answered during the DFSS-specific readiness assessment. This is done through the application of two tools: One is a set of performance measures that gives systematic customer-based insight into an organization's reliability performance, and the second provides criteria (checklist) for evaluating how well your new product development process incorporates recognized best practices. Neither of these tools is valuable without the proper leadership and organizational attitude toward quality and reliability.

How does this work? New product development consists of two major phases:

The measurement system for new product development should be designed from a viewpoint that is business-related. The principal function of a business's product-creation process is to ensure the long-range competitive advantage of an organization by the effective implementation of new technology applications. The product-creation process is the front end to the product-delivery process, where the detailed engineering work is performed: system design and testing, investment and production of tooling to support full-scale production, and preparation of marketing materials for the launch. The product-delivery process prepares a product for full-scale production and also commercializes the product for launch into its intended markets.

In order to meet the objective of the process, product creation must include several critical business subprocesses: strategic planning, competitive analysis, technology assessment, project management, research and technology management, intellectual property application, and technology transfer to product lines. The product-creation process contributes value to the total organization through the commercialization of technology into applications that fully align with the expressed and unexpressed desires of customers (and also potential customers). Thus, the mission or essential activity of this process is to develop for the business the intellectual capital required to both gain and sustain competitive advantage, while the mission of the product-delivery process is to deliver a commercially viable design to the market. Both phases of product development are essential in achieving sustained competitive performance.

New product development creates business value in two distinct ways:

▶ Through the direct delivery of technology into the organization's product lines.

▶ Through ensuring technology leadership in the marketplace.

How does new product development relate to the business objectives? The outcome of new product development must provide renewal of the current product portfolio as well as extensions of the product portfolio by providing innovative product concepts (the first commercial use of a concept or technology). In order to meet the long-range requirement for innovation, an engineering company must create strategic synergy in its strategy for technology investment between its internal and external opportunities, including both in-house research and development and external licensing options. To achieve excellence in new product development, an organization would experience a seamless flow of ideas from the level of physics, to product concepts, to product-line enhancement of features, to deliverable innovative new products. To optimize a high-technology business, an organization must seek synergy by combining its strategic plans for advanced development, business development, and research.

A basic objective in new product development is to produce a quality outcome. But to understand what this means, it is important to know what poor-quality outcomes would look like. To determine the meaning of "poor quality," consider the two types of defects that could exist in a research organization.

▶ The first type of defect is the result of a violation of the laws of nature (physics) or mathematics (statistics), errors in software, and/or problems in communication that cause confusion (these are special-cause defects).

▶ The second type of defect comes from the wrong investment of time in the pursuit of a technology that has no viable commercial application (this is an opportunity-cost type of defect—researchers' time could have been better invested in the pursuit of other technology that would have had a higher payoff). These are common-cause defects that result from the oversight of the management system and the decision-making process that governs the selection of projects, and from allocation of constrained resources against the objectives for business growth.

Poor-quality products embarrass a company due to the appearance of visible errors and vocal customer complaints that result in a lack of customer confidence in a product.

On the other hand, good products result in sustained competitive advantage and enhance the reputation of a company as a "technology leader" in its field. In order to distinguish between good and poor-quality products, the two types of defects in product development must be clearly understood.

Type I defects—This type of defect is the result of a substantial failure in a critical aspect of the new product development process, such as:

- *Technology failure*—a new product fails to deliver the advertised performance or product capability.

- *Market failure*—a new product does not have economic utility for its targeted customers, or the uniqueness of its application is not accepted in the market.

- *Procedural failure*—a new product possesses a fundamental flaw in its core or underlying technology (in the basic physics, mathematics, or software logic).

- *Opportunity failure*—a new product is delivered to the market with a timing that is not synchronized to its market window of opportunity in order to fully capitalize on the development.

- *Implementation failure*—the production technology is not sufficiently mature to deliver the new product in sufficient commercial quantities to satisfy the market demand.

For this type of defect, a quality goal of "zero defects" is achievable, but achievement of this goal will not necessarily result in sustained (beyond a single product life cycle) competitive advantage for the company! Note that product designers can be held accountable for these errors because they are all "special cause" in nature—errors due to failures in their controllable work processes. This means that the root cause(s) of these problems can be determined and lessons can be learned to prevent recurrence of the cause(s) in future development projects. Individual project managers can manage using these lessons learned to "mistake-proof" their development program.

Type II defects—This type of defect represents an opportunity cost of investing resources in pursuit of a low-payoff or no-payoff project, compared to alternative uses of the same resources for building competitive advantage. This type of defect is a direct result of research focused on the wrong subject and is precipitated by failure in the design management system—this represents a common-cause failure—and management should be held accountable. Such common-cause defects are not preventable by individual product development managers but are avoidable by the management team through more effective long-range planning and decision-making.

Achieving "zero defects" in this category is probably neither achievable nor desirable. Why? If an organization makes no mistakes, then it takes no risk and subsequently misses potential opportunities. The future is uncertain, customers are fickle, and there is no sure knowledge of which technologies will have the highest potential value. Decisions about where to invest in the face of uncertainty represent probabilities of success, and therefore a degree of uncertainty (potential for failure) must be expected in the results. If a product development organization does not fail sometimes, then it might not be pushing the leading edge of its targeted technology! A performance goal for this type of defect should be set as a control mechanism such that success of new product developments "achieves an 80% implementation rate" for all projects initiated in both categories of new product development (variant features added to current products and creation of "first-commercial-use-products" through the application of intellectual capital).

If these are the two dominant types of defects, how should management measure the goodness of contribution from its new product development projects?

Developing a performance measurement system. It is important to use a "balanced scorecard" type of approach for developing a set of new product development process-performance measures. This means that measures should reflect several perspectives that provide a comprehensive view of organization-wide performance and also indicate actionable areas for the focus of management's efforts to improve the quality of work output. This set of metrics should address the following focus areas:

▶ *Market contribution*—the proportion of new knowledge in the form of intellectual capital introduced to the market through the new product development process.

▶ *Financial contribution*—the contribution of new products and intellectual capital to the revenue stream.

▶ *Customer contribution*—the effect of new product development on the satisfaction and purchasing behavior of customers.

▶ *Productivity contribution*—the improvement effect in time to market for the design and development of new products.

▶ *Employee contribution*—the contribution of the human work environment to the feeling of creativity and the motivation of employees to work innovatively.

In order to address these five focus areas of the product development process, several measures could be considered: comparative growth in knowledge above primary competitors (percentage of total technology patent applications), sales revenue due to new products and licensing fees for intellectual property, customer satisfaction (with products and services), organizational productivity for new product introduction, and employee satisfaction with their work environment and "capacity to create." Each of these five focus areas is described below:

Market contribution—Knowledge share growth is a measure providing an indication of the extension of the technological body of knowledge capital and organizational core competence to those disciplines, which are strategic for the product development road map of the organization. What percentage of the global patent applications does the group submit relative to other companies? Are there any surprises among the companies doing related work? Are new competitors on the knowledge horizon?

Financial contribution—This measure of the "bottom line" contribution of new products is a critical factor in demonstrating the effectiveness of capital investment to the top management team. Although individual products are typically chosen based on surpassing a return on investment (ROI) hurdle rate or a return rate on capital employed (ROCE) criterion, it is essential to check "achieved" results against the predicted results using some financial metrics:

- Growth in royalty income from license fees
- Growth in passive income
- Growth in "knowledge capital"
- Growth in revenue-growth contribution for new product introductions
- Distribution of revenue by year of technology introduction (vintage chart)
- Enhancement in R&D investment efficiency (Salomon Index)
- Decrease in the R&D project payback period or break-even time (BET)
- Growth in return on research

Customer contribution—The satisfaction of customers is an important indicator of the contribution that designers make to their clients' businesses. Two customers must be evaluated to correctly perceive the results of a new product development effort:

- Product-line manager satisfaction with the quality of the development program's design contribution.
- Satisfaction of the national registrar for trademarks and patents with the originality of IPR (intellectual property rights) applications (conversion rate of applications to patents).

Perception indicators of client satisfaction must be compared against the expectation factors for "quality deliverables" of the new product development process in order to assess the level of satisfaction against the level of "defects" in the total performance. In addition, comparisons should be made between satisfaction level and the revenue contribution of the new product programs.

Productivity contribution—The classic productivity indicators, such as the ratio of units of output per units of input, make no sense in new product development. The just-in-time (JIT) manufacturing way to measure productivity uses the number of units produced during a standard cycle time period (the *takt* time or beat of the manufacturing machine). Using this style for measurement, R&D productivity is the measure of the cycle time to transition an idea from theory to reality. Some of the ways that cycle time measures can be used to represent R&D productivity include:

- Percentage share of technology breakthroughs relative to all classes of competition.
- Transition cycle time of new technology to "protected property" (e.g., patents).
- Convergence toward a 6σ performance level in improvement of product-reliability growth demonstration tests as compared to the customer-design standard.

▶ Growth rate in "knowledge share" (percentage of new patents) compared to the total new patents granted in a selected core technology.

Employee contribution—This indicator is a measure of the capacity to create that employees feel based on the motivational elements in the design environment that has been provided by the organization. Over the past fifteen years, many studies on the subject of "innovation" and/or "creativity" have highlighted factors that contribute to a motivating, inventive environment. While management can build what they believe to be a creative environment, it is important to understand the feelings and attitudes of the design employees' perception. In new product development, people are the most valuable asset. Development of the competence of the workforce and establishment of a challenging work environment are two factors that management must reinforce on a regular basis. Trends in measurement of the perceived "capacity to create" and degree of support from management can be developed through an annual survey that assesses the employees' environment. Employee perception measures must be correlated with investments and participation in development and professional performance (contributions that extend the total body of knowledge in a particular technological field—e.g., published papers, books, patents, etc.) to create a superior working environment for design and development.

The key performance indicators (KPIs) for new product development must be specified and their performance measured to establish a baseline level for comparison of future improvements, a benchmark to provide external objectivity, and a historical trend as a means to quantify improvement across business cycles. A sample measurement specification format is included at the end of this appendix.

Third: Conduct a self-assessment audit of best practices

The final element required in a DFSS readiness assessment is an analysis of the set of current practices used by the organization for new product development as compared to the leading practices found at best companies that have achieved good success in their development of performance indicators for Six Sigma achievement.

These practices fall into two categories: broad factors that enhance the ability of the organization to adapt DFSS into its culture, and specific best practices that prepare an organization for a full, organization-wide DFSS deployment.

Critical cultural stimulants for success in Six Sigma implementations

There are three additional, pragmatic factors that enhance the ability of organizations to succeed in implementing Six Sigma.

One critical success factor in Six Sigma implementation is your organization's ability to define project scope in a way that projects can be accomplished in a reasonable time frame so that results are accrued faster at the bottom line. In many organizations, there is a proclivity to define projects with such broad scope that it seems they take forever to achieve the desired results. Other organizations have a more successful rate of project completion because they choose the scope of projects in a way that makes them easier to complete. In the final analysis, the number of projects completed drives the return an organization achieves on its Six Sigma investment—the more projects completed, the higher the return.

Another critical success factor is constancy of purpose for organizational management in its vision for strategic direction. Does Six Sigma align to the organization's long-term strategic direction, and has this direction persisted long enough that employees believe that all efforts tied to this direction have the full attention of the top management team? Whenever possible, Six Sigma should be integrated with the organization's top concerns and interpreted as an implementation toolkit for its strategic projects.

A third critical success factor is the approach that the organization takes toward the development of its employees. Many organizations experience great difficulty in finding challenging jobs to keep all high-potential employees productively and energetically engaged in activities that enhance their careers by broadening and deepening the knowledge of the organization and its business. Six Sigma provides additional career-enhancing opportunities through newly created positions for Black Belts and Master Black Belts. The knowledge that these people gain will not only enhance their careers, but will better prepare them for cross-functional positions where they can make positive contributions and further develop a general manager's breadth of business knowledge. If these positions are used to develop the breadth and depth of thinking about the business for high-potential employees, then they become trained in the "general manager's mind-set"—one of the most challenging employee development requirements that an organization faces.

Best practices that support DFSS implementation

Many organizations have long histories of working to improve their product design and development processes. Over the course of the past quarter-century, a number of best practices have been demonstrated and documented at leading-edge technology firms, whose challenge has been to consistently reduce their time to market while at the same time increasing product quality and decreasing product cost. This challenge is multifaceted and requires enlightened management thinking in order to outpace the competition and remain at the leading edge of technological innovation in product-line planning. Of course, the bottom-line performance of new products is the most critical indicator of an organization's ability to consistently lead in its industry. In product development processes, a set of "business imperatives" has emerged that can serve as a checklist for organizations to determine if they have surpassed the "state of the art." This set of imperatives includes the following:

- Determine what matters to customers and how much performance differential is significant to them.

- Establish a set of performance expectations that serve the targeted customers of the product and ensure that their needs are met at both the fundamental and the differentiating feature levels.

- Deliver on the key performance expectations that have been set for customers and validated as significant expectations by sound market research.

- Create a product portfolio to manage the introduction of new technologies and user features in a way that minimizes technology risks while maximizing market development opportunities.

- Design all new products to minimize failure risks at the part, process, and product perspectives and to surpass the quality performance of the products they replace or compete with.

- Design products for robust performance in the operating environments of the ultimate user (that customer who places their hands on a product to use it).

- Create new product development design rules that are based on best practices of the design team in prior versions and use a quantitative assessment of design risk for making choices, rather than a heuristic "safety factor" approach.

- Involve suppliers early in the design process to ensure a systems approach for the use of their parts in the design and to ensure that supply-chain processes are robust and do not contribute potential problems from the ultimate customer perspective.

- Stabilize design requirements early in the design process to eliminate last-minute changes that are counter-productive.

- Predict product reliability for design alternatives to ensure that all new product designs are better than products previously delivered to the market and that the customer's next experience is superior to their last product experience.

- Test product to the point of failure to identify and then prevent these failure modes from being delivered to the market.

- Document product development with computer-aided design (CAD) products that link parts and tolerance analyses and manage configuration changes so they are reflected in design documents as well as the bill of materials that is used with suppliers for purchased parts.

- Integrate CAD with automated manufacturing (i.e., CAM) for critical suppliers of custom parts in order to ensure rapid prototyping of designs.

- Foolproof the production processes to prevent operator error and eliminate the escape of mistakes to customers as well as stabilize material flows in production.

- Ensure that all measurement systems are able to precisely detect the performance differences that are significant to customers and that the sample size for testing is statistically significant to demonstrate that the desired performance has been met.

- Minimize engineering changes to reduce all potential risk from introducing new product failures and test each change to ensure that it meets the original product-specification requirements that were tied to customer success factors.

If you are doing these things, then you have attacked many of the environmental issues that create success in implementing DFSS at the product-design level. If your organization has not implemented these practices, then you must also redesign the management system for new product development as well as the implementation of the statistical and management methods at the project level.

Procedure for conducting a self-assessment

How can an organization perform a self-assessment of its readiness to implement a DFSS business-improvement initiative? Try the following set of steps:

1. Customize the criteria for the readiness assessment and the scale to be used in making the self-assessment.

2. Develop a standard procedure for conducting a self-assessment.

3. Train local business-area leaders in the procedure for leading a self-assessment.

4. Conduct self-assessments using intact product development management teams.

5. Consolidate the results from all business areas in a way that identifies those areas that are most prepared for a DFSS implementation.

6. In those areas where your organization scores either neutral or below, identify the specific countermeasures to include in your deployment plan in order to ensure overall success of your change-implementation efforts.

What do you do if this readiness assessment indicates that your organization is not ready for implementing DFSS? The answer is that you create a pathway forward by developing and implementing a change management process to move you closer to the place where you are ready for successful change. This can be accomplished during the pilot phase of a DFSS program by following a change model to ensure that all the appropriate steps are taken for a successful change—emphasizing those areas where your management team feels there is a need for improvement.

Measure Name:	Performance indicator name.
Operational Definition:	Objective definition of the indicator, including boundary conditions and logical constraints.
Measurement Tree:	Business Y–level indicator: indicator name.
	Value to Executives: Description of how to interpret it. Process Y–level metric: metric name.
	Value to Managers: Description of how to interpret it. Work process X–level measure: measure name.
	Value to Operators: Description of how to interpret it.
Customer Focus:	Accountable internal process owner. External target customer. External investor/owner.
Desired Performance:	Performance expectations, stretch goal, or target.
Calculation:	The formula for calculating the indicator.
Counting Rules:	The rules for including or excluding sample data.
Defect Definitions:	Operational definition of the major defects.
Failure Modes:	Major failure modes identified in the process analysis.
Measurement Owners:	Responsible manager (business Y). Responsible supervisor (work-process Y). Responsible worker (work-process X).
Process Control Point:	Where data is collected and the process is controlled.
Type of Data:	Data definition (e.g., probability [scaled from 0 to 1.0]).
Recording Schedule:	The frequency of data recording.
Reporting Period:	Daily, reported in a monthly management scorecard.
Data Format:	Format of data at the point of collection.
Graphical Output:	Description of graphical output from the analysis (e.g., rolling trend chart with each month's raw data and summarized using a box-and-whiskers plot of history compared to targeted performance).
Baseline Performance:	To be determined (initial data from analysis).
Current Performance:	To be determined (initial data from analysis).
Target Performance:	To be determined during the strategic planning process.
Benchmark Performance:	To be determined (initial data from first study).
Action Limits:	To be determined (these limits are set relative to current and desired performance levels to ensure prompt action to mitigate out-of-control types of conditions).
Review Schedule:	Weekly review (process)/monthly review (staff).
Management Authority:	Senior business leader accountable for performance.
References:	To be determined.

Appendix B
Design for Six Sigma Body of Knowledge

"The statistical method is only good science that has been brought up to date by recognition that all laws are subject to variation. Your study of the statistical method will not displace any other knowledge that you have; rather, it will extend your knowledge and make it more useful."

~ W. Edwards Deming

Knowledge-based disciplines

Dominant business disciplines, such as accounting and finance, sales and marketing, and engineering, can be characterized by their special vocabulary and body of knowledge that define their unique contribution to a business organization. It can be said that no discipline really becomes important to management until it has both a shared vocabulary (so that people can communicate with meaning about it) and a documented body of knowledge that people can be trained to execute. All disciplines have a hierarchy of knowledge that defines their cognitive processes. This hierarchy is additive, starting with knowledge and ending in wisdom:

▶ **Knowledge**: facts and data that define a subject.

▶ **Understanding**: information that answers specific questions about the subject.

▶ **Wisdom**: the ability to create new knowledge based on understanding.

Mastery of a subject occurs when an individual is able to operate at the wisdom level for the differentiating factors in the discipline's body of knowledge and has all the prerequisite knowledge and understanding necessary to support their wisdom. Thus, a body of knowledge is a critical legitimizing factor for any discipline, as it permits a discipline to operate within the same business context as other recognized disciplines. While many disciplines have a natural affinity for support by certain groups (e.g., professional societies such as the Project Management Institute [PMI], American Society for Quality [ASQ], and American Production and Inventory Control Society [APICS]) and academic departments (e.g., engineering, accounting, business, etc.), design for Six Sigma is a multidisciplinary methodology that has been largely developed by practitioners and therefore does not have a natural support system for developing its body of knowledge. By developing and promulgating this design for Six Sigma body of knowledge, the methodology can be advanced toward a more general application and broader acceptance.

What is a body of knowledge?

A body of knowledge represents the professional knowledge base for a competence or professional designation (e.g., the project management body of knowledge of the Project Management Institute, or the quality-engineering body of knowledge from ASQ). There are two different aspects of a body of knowledge: The first is *logically structured content* that defines what must be known to achieve mastery of this field, while the second assigns *levels of cognition* that must be achieved in the content so that the performance for a specific depth of mastery can be adequately defined. To make a judgment about any individual's degree of mastery of a body of knowledge, it is necessary to define the performance criteria and assessment methods to be used in order to assess a person's competence for the purpose of a third-party certification (e.g., certified project manager or certified quality engineer).

There are six levels of cognition that indicate the intended *complexity level* of the content to be taught in curriculum and provide a structure for assessment. These levels are based on "Levels of Cognition" (adapted from Benjamin S. Bloom's *Taxonomy of Educational Objectives*, 1956) and are ranked in the following list according to their relative degree of complexity:

▶ **Knowledge level.** Being able to *remember* or recognize terminology, definitions, facts, ideas, materials, patterns, sequences, methodologies, principles, etc. This is also commonly referred to as recognition, recall, or rote knowledge (*information recognition*).

▶ **Comprehension level.** Being able to *read and interpret* descriptions, communications, reports, tables, diagrams, directions, regulations, etc. (*conceptual understanding*).

▶ **Application level.** Being able to *use and apply* ideas, procedures, methods, formulas, principles, theories, etc., in job-related situations (*contextual treatment*).

▶ **Analysis.** Being able to break down (*decompose*) information into its constituent parts and recognize the parts' relationship to one another and how they are organized; identify sub-level factors or salient data from a complex scenario (*construction*).

- **Synthesis**. Being able to put parts or elements together in such a way as to show a pattern or structure not clearly there before; identifying which data or information from a complex set is appropriate to examine further or from which supported conclusions can be drawn (*innovative integration*).

- **Evaluation**. Being able to make judgments regarding the value of proposed ideas, solutions, methodologies, etc., by using appropriate criteria or standards to estimate accuracy, effectiveness, economic benefit, etc. (*critical judgment*).

How is the DFSS body of knowledge structured?

The following table illustrates the linkages among the body of knowledge's training and development learning objectives, cognitive levels, performance criteria (which can be used to indicate achievement of the cognitive levels), and appraisal methods (which can be used to assess or evaluate the achievement of a skill, knowledge, or competence).

Learning Objectives	Cognitive Levels	Performance Criteria	Appraisal Methods
Understand Know Recognize Identify	Knowledge— information recognition	Describe item	Personal reflection; Test
Discuss Document Define Compare Contrast Choose Select Depict	Comprehension— conceptual understanding	Distinguish item	Team discussion; Table talk; Test
Collect Measure Construct Chart Plot Use Apply Translate Interpret	Application— contextual treatment	Interpret item	Case study; Project; Test
Calculate Determine	Analysis—decomposition and construction	Analyze item	Homework; Case Study; Exercise; Project; Test
Plan Negotiate	Synthesis— innovative integration	Facilitate item	On-the-Job Project; Case Study; Essay; Exercise
Create Develop	Evaluation— critical judgment	Create new item; Design/modify item; Critique item design	Teach; Coach; Mentor

What content defines the DFSS body of knowledge?

The design for Six Sigma body of knowledge (DFSS BOK) is organized using a logical structure as its knowledge architecture borrowed from the DMADV analysis process for the top-level definition in its outline. At the second level are the tools, methods, skills, aptitudes, and knowledge that support each specific phase of DFSS. At the third and subsequent levels of indenture of the DFSS BOK, the specific content that must be mastered is defined, while a final level of indenture defines the cognitive requirement to be achieved for mastery of that item.

A preliminary version of the DFSS BOK was developed by the author and reviewed by subject-matter experts in related fields. This outline represents a work in progress and is being published in order to expand this conversation about having a DFSS BOK and its specific content.

Any suggestions for improvement or changes to the DFSS BOK can be made to the author at gregbss@aol.com.

The design for Six Sigma body of knowledge (preliminary version)

This version of the DFSS BOK is structured into a work-breakdown structure for the DFSS process. The next phase in this process will be to create a version of the BOK that includes the next level of content and assignment of cognitive levels using a panel of recognized subject-matter experts. At that time, the BOK will be ready for third-party review and open comments.

Work-breakdown structure of design for Six Sigma (DFSS)

1	**Recognize**
1.1	Business Strategy
1.1.1	Values-Based Leadership
1.1.1.1	Shareholder Value
1.1.1.2	Brand Value
1.1.1.3	Moral Values and Ethics
1.1.1.4	Business Values
1.1.1.5	Business Governance
1.1.2	Value Proposition
1.1.2.1	Business Purpose
1.1.2.1.1	Vision and Strategic Intent
1.1.2.1.2	Core Competence
1.1.2.2	Customer Value
1.1.2.2.1	Market Research
1.1.2.2.1.1	Demographic Market Analysis
1.1.2.2.1.2	Customer Identification
1.1.2.2.1.2.1	Segmentation Analysis
1.1.2.2.1.2.2	Customer Persona

Appendix C
Data Analysis and Experimentation

"Scientific research is a process of guided learning. The object of statistical methods is to make that process as efficient as possible."

~ George E. P. Box

Experimental design synthesizes statistical methods

Designed experiments begin with hypotheses about the potential for relationships among functional parameters. Plans are made to collect samples of data in order to demonstrate relationships that are analyzed using regression analysis and reported using ANOVA tables. Although DOE is more than the sum of these parts, these statistical methods must be understood in order to design and conduct a designed experiment.

In order to understand what a designed experiment is, it is essential to first understand what research is in general. There are three major types of research designs, which can be classified according to the answers to two questions. The first question is: Does the design use random assignment to groups? If random assignment is used, then it is called a true experiment or a randomized experiment. If random assignment is not used, then a second question is asked: Does the design use either multiple groups or multiple waves of measurement? If the answer to this question is yes, then this would be called a quasi-experimental design. If the answer is no, then we would call it a non-experiment. The simplest form of a non-experiment is a single-shot survey design that consists of only a single observation (true Theory O). This is the type of research design that is used in many surveys for narrative questions. This three-fold classification is useful for understanding the internal validity of a design. Randomized experiments are the strongest of these three designs, and they are especially helpful when seeking to establish a cause/effect relationship among experimental factors.

The focus of this appendix is on experimental design, so the quasi-experiment and non-experiment will not be covered in this discussion. Our concern will be with establishing causation and determining the transfer function $Y = f(X)$. This means that we will be attempting to resolve two logical conditions (which appear much like the results of a test of hypotheses):

If X, then Y.

If not X, then not Y.

In some types of experiments, it is essential to establish this dual condition by creating two different conditions for the research: one in which the same people, context, time, and conditions are treated with the change desired (called the treatment group), and a second identical group that is not treated the same way (called the control group). In reality, "same" is not possible. But creating two situations that are comparable is possible, and then one group can receive the treatment, and the other group would not receive the treatment, but in all other respects the two groups would be treated the same. Then, the only significant difference between these two groups is that one was influenced by the treatment while the other was not. Statistical tests can demonstrate whether a difference in outcomes exists under these circumstances.

Thus, the real question is: How do you create groups that are "equivalent"? The key to achieve equivalence is through probability, where the truth is known within a probability range (confidence interval) based on randomization of the factors in the experiment. The simplest experiment is a hypothesis test that looks at two groups that have been randomly assigned and compares the observations (measures) by testing the differences between the means using a t-test or a one-way analysis of variance (ANOVA).

Types of experiments

There are many types of experiments and applications of experimental design. The list presented below is a partial taxonomy of experiments for further consideration:

▶ Comparing two treatments:

  ▶ Paired

  ▶ Unpaired

▶ Comparing more than two treatments:

  ▶ Completely randomized designs (not blocked)

- Randomized block design (one blocking variable)
- Designs with more than one blocking variable
- Measuring the effects of variables:
  - Factorial designs
  - Two-level factorial designs
  - Two-level fractional factorial designs
- Building models:
  - Empirical model-building
  - Mechanistic model-building
  - Least squares model
  - Response surface
  - Analysis of variation
  - Time-series analysis
  - Simulation analysis

Principles of good design

What does it take to have a good experimental design? Some characteristics of a good experimental design include the following:

- Doesn't require too many levels of the controlled variables.
- Provides for replication, or partial replication, in order to estimate variance.
- Fast to analyze.
- Provides orthogonal, minimum-variance estimates of desired effects.
- Easy to block, or equivalently easy to construct from a small block of runs.
- Uses center points to "calibrate" the model against current performance.

Experimental signal and noise

Measurements (or observations of data) can be divided into two components: signal and noise. Signal is related to the variable of interest—this is the primary factor that is being measured, the treatment whose effect is being studied in an experiment, the independent variable that is being changed to observe its influence on a dependent variable, or a change that is being implemented to improve the output of a process. Noise consists of all the random factors in the situation that make it harder to observe this signal—the way that an observer looks at a measurement gage, the error contained in a measurement system, the difference in attitude among employees, etc. A ratio of the signal to the noise describes the relative influence of the factor relative to its environmental background. In research, it is preferable to have a strong signal (a powerful relationship or influential factor) and very good measurement (this means low noise). In this situation, there is a much greater opportunity to observe the effect of a treatment than if there is a strong signal and a weak measurement system (high noise) or a weak signal and a strong measurement system. In order to cope with these situations, experimental design seeks to either enhance the signal or reduce the noise. Taking either of these actions improves the quality of the research outcome. Signal-enhancing experimental designs are called factorial designs because they focus almost entirely on a program of factors (variables in the treatments or X-factors), components of their variation, and dimensions of performance (levels). Typical factorial experiments employ several different level treatments to evaluate their relative effect on the dependent variable (Y).

One way to apply a signal-to-noise ratio in analysis is to consider how it is affected by the two statistics that are used to classify data distributions. If one wants to detect the difference between two groups of data, one can conduct a statistical test to compare their means. However, this test approach does not take into account the variability around the means. A small difference between means will be hard to detect if there is a lot of noise or variability around these means. In addition, a large difference between means is easily detectable if the noise and variability are low. Differences between groups are much more observable when the signal is high and the noise level is low. Signal and noise effects can be evaluated as follows:

$$Effect = \frac{Signal}{Noise} = \frac{\text{Difference between group means}}{\text{Variability of groups}} = \frac{\bar{x}_T - \bar{x}_C}{SE\,(\bar{x}_T - \bar{x}_C)} = t - value$$

where:

C = control group

T = treatment group

The difference between a level of a treatment group and that of a control group is called the size of the "effect." The numerator of the ratio is the actual difference between the means of the two groups. The denominator of the ratio is an estimate of the variability around the means that is calculated as the standard error between the two means. The standard error incorporates information about the standard deviation (a measure of the variability around the mean) for each of the two groups. This ratio is called a t-value.

Probability equivalence

The expectation of an experiment is to determine how closely two groups of interest are related to each other. There is no expectation that the groups will be exactly the same, only that we might infer relationship based on probability. This means that we know perfectly the odds that we will find a difference between the two populations. This is achieved through the mechanism of random assignment to groups. We can calculate the chance that the two groups differ based on their assignment alone. If the two groups will be different in 5 out of 100 opportunities, then the level of statistical significance (α) is 0.05. When we assign participants to groups randomly, then the only reason that a difference exists beyond this level of significance is due to the treatment that is imposed on the groups.

There are actually three methods to estimate the treatment effect for an after-the-fact test of a randomized experiment. All three yield mathematically equivalent results. Each of these methods was developed independently of the others, and it was only after they were created that their equivalence was observed. The first, and easiest, method is to compute an independent t-test. A second method is to compute a one-way analysis of variance (ANOVA) between the two independent groups. The third method is to use regression analysis to regress the observed values onto a dummy-coded treatment variable. Even though these three methods provide the same analytical result, regression analysis has the most general application and is used as a means for explaining many experimental results.

Testing statistical hypotheses

A statistical hypothesis test is a formal way of asking and answering the question: "How certain are we that a change has occurred in our process?" Hypothesis tests can be done to evaluate whether the process mean has shifted or whether the dispersion of the process has changed.[1] It is important to understand the following:

- What is a "statistical hypothesis," what types exist, and how do they relate to critical design parameters?

- What is the distribution of chance events, and how does it relate to the null hypothesis?

- What types of decision risks are associated with the null and alternate hypotheses?

- How does statistical significance balance against practical significance?

- What role does sample size play in relation to statistical hypotheses?

- What is the general process for establishing and testing a statistical hypothesis?

---

[1] Indeed, statistical control charts are a form of hypothesis testing—does the new data observation fall into the same distribution that was used to establish the grand mean and the control limits? A CUSUM control chart is actually a form of hypothesis testing that is used to shift performance of a controlled variable to a new level while continuously operating the process.

Hypotheses represent the translation of a practical question into a statistical question. In this manner, the "real-world" problem is represented in terms that are suitable for scientific examination and testing. In essence, hypotheses are statements related to the parameters of a given probability distribution—for example, the mean and/or the variance that are related to a specified probability distribution for the given values of the data. In other words, hypotheses are statements that allow us to represent all possible outcomes prior to conducting an investigation. Following the statistical investigation, we simply accept or reject each hypothesis, which in turn provides a foundation for making practical decisions.

There are two types of hypotheses: null hypotheses and alternative hypotheses. A null hypothesis assumes that the change we find in our process is simply due to random variation in our sampling (the distribution of chance events), with the change not being statistically significant. This particular hypothesis is most often referred to as the "null hypothesis" and designated as "H_o." The meaning of the null hypothesis is that the parameters under investigation are equal; in other words, there is an insignificant difference with respect to the parameter of interest (mean and/or variance).

In direct contrast to the null hypothesis is the alternative hypothesis (H_a). Alternative hypotheses are generally associated with distributions other than chance and, as such, are said to be "statistically significantly different" from the chance distribution. This means that any observed difference in the sample parameters under investigation is unlikely to have resulted by chance variations inherent to the sample. If the observed difference in the sample cannot be explained by chance variations, then we conclude that sample membership is, in one or more respects, different from the qualifications necessary for membership in the population of interest. Thus, we accept the alternative hypothesis of inequality and conclude the sample was drawn from a population other than the one under investigation.

Following the concept of "innocent until proven guilty," the null hypothesis assumes that the parameter in question is unaffected by any changes. In other words, any differences between the two distributions initially are presumed to be due to random variation from one sample to another. The alternative hypothesis bears the "burden of proof" that manipulating the parameter has led to a detectable change that is statistically significant. The computations must lead to a high probability (rarely less than 90%, and often much higher) that the change is real, before we reject the null hypothesis.

When designing a hypothesis test, we must take into account decision risks due to the possibility of random variation leading us to an erroneous conclusion. We consider risk appropriately when we establish a level of risk that we are willing to accept (in advance of the investigation). Once this has been done, we have all the information necessary to determine a "rational" sample size. Mathematical equations exist for this purpose; however, we must balance this computation against the practical limitations of cost, time, and available resources in order to arrive at a "rational" sampling plan. There are two types of risk, called alpha and beta. Alpha risk (α) represents the probability of accepting the alternative hypothesis—that is, concluding a change has occurred—when in fact the process is unchanged. Beta risk (β) is the likelihood of concluding, in error, that no change has occurred.

The sample size for the experiment is determined by the alpha and beta risk, along with the magnitude of change or significant difference (δ) that must be detected. Too small a sample increases alpha and beta risk; too large a sample might cause us to conclude that a change has occurred, even when the change is too small to be of practical significance.

Types of Statistical Change

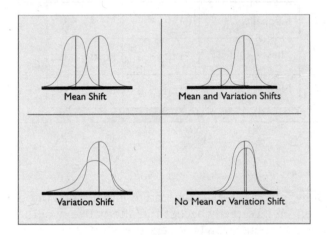

| Mean Shift | Mean and Variation Shifts |
| Variation Shift | No Mean or Variation Shift |

Hypothesis testing begins by writing equations for the null and alternative hypotheses, describing the kind of change for which we are testing. Unless and until we exceed some "threshold" level of certainty that the alternative hypothesis should prevail, we accept the truth of the null hypothesis.

We can construct the alternative hypothesis in several ways. Frequently we expect (or hope) that manipulating the parameter has a specific, directional effect on the process parameter. That is, we are looking specifically for either an increase or a decrease in the parameter, but not both. Such hypothesis tests are referred to as one-sided tests. On the other hand, two-sided tests apply when we only want to detect whether any kind of change has occurred, without regard to directionality.

The types of hypotheses tested include the following:

Tests of Hypothesis

Null hypothesis (H_0): Nothing has changed:

For tests of process mean: $H_o: \mu_0 = \mu_1$

For tests of process variance: $H_o: \sigma^2_0 = \sigma^2_1$

Alternative hypothesis (H_a): Change happened:

	Mean	Variance
Inequality	$H_a: \mu_0 \neq \mu_1$	$H_a: \sigma^2_0 \neq \sigma^2_1$
New < Old	$H_a: \mu_0 < \mu_1$	$H_a: \sigma^2_0 < \sigma^2_1$
New > Old	$H_a: \mu_0 > \mu_1$	$H_a: \sigma^2_0 > \sigma^2_1$

Alpha and beta risk

When we do a hypothesis test, it can lead to either alpha or beta risk. Alpha risk occurs when we incorrectly accept the alternative hypothesis. Beta risk occurs when we erroneously fail to accept the alternative hypothesis.

In order to perform hypotheses tests to detect whether a change has occurred in our process, we must choose a sample size based on the possibility that our sample might not reflect the true behavior of the process. Whenever we analyze the data distributions, two sources of variation are present:

▶ Identifiable effects, such as changes in a critical design characteristic due to manipulating one or more process parameters. Sometimes we refer to these as "black noise," "special cause" variation, which are observed best in samples taken that show long-term effects of change (to observe these changes, the sampling process should be designed so that these events are observed between the sampled rational sub-groups).

▶ Random effects, which are sometimes referred to as "white noise," "common cause" variation, which are best observed in samples taken that show the short-term effects of change (to observe these changes, a sampling process should be designed so that these events are observed within the sampled rational sub-groups).

The Type I alpha error occurs when we incorrectly accept the alternative hypothesis. In other words, this indicates that we believe in error that we have changed a process. The Type II beta error corresponds to concluding incorrectly that a process has NOT changed. Thus, we erroneously fail to accept the alternative hypothesis.

The relationships among these errors can be presented in "truth table" format, as shown below:

Tests of Hypothesis Errors

		Valid Hypothesis	
		(H_o)	(H_a)
Accepted Hypothesis	H_o	No Error	Type II Error Beta (β)
	H_a	Type I Error Alpha (α)	No Error

Type I and Type II errors cannot be committed simultaneously, since a null hypothesis cannot be true and false at the same time. To understand probabilities of the relationships and determine the magnitude of risk that is acceptable for the given hypothesis, consider the following table of risk acceptability:

Range of "Acceptable Risk"

Error Impact	Approximate Range of Risk	
Minor Rework	0.10	0.05
Major Rework	0.05	0.01
Injury/Litigation	0.01	0.001
Death	0.001	0.00001
Catastrophic Death	0.00001	???

How can these risks be managed to ensure that these errors do not occur? This is done by using the following approach:

▶ Identify the kinds of outcomes likely to result from a Type I error, and assess the impact of this error.

▶ Establish the appropriate level of statistical risk that corresponds to such outcomes and impact assessment.

▶ Identify the kinds of outcomes likely to result from a Type II error, and assess the impact of this error.

▶ Establish the appropriate level of statistical risk that corresponds to such outcomes and impact assessment.

▶ Determine how much change in the process parameter we need to detect. Take into account the degree of process improvement required to achieve the desired static and dynamic performance levels, along with the ability of the measurement system to detect a change in the parameter being evaluated.

▶ Determine sample sizes that correspond to the amount of change we need to detect, for the levels of alpha and beta risk that apply.

▶ The smaller the alpha and beta risks are, the larger the sample size becomes.

Test of means: Basic equations

If the t-value calculated from the data is larger than $t_{critical}$, we conclude that the result is statistically significant. However, just selecting an alpha risk of 0.05 and then calculating a $t_{critical}$ value based on the sample size (and its degrees of freedom) is not enough. We must also set a beta value and decide how much reduction in the mean is required. In considering these factors, the sample size needed to draw a conclusion might change, and it might be necessary to collect more data before computing the test statistic.

What does a test of difference look like? Consider the following circumstance, where the data indicates a mean of 4.2 and a standard deviation of 1.2 based on a sample size of 16 observations. Does another observation of 4.8 belong in this distribution? While the alpha risk is explicitly chosen (0.05), the beta risk is a function of sample size due to its relationship to the power of the test $(1 - \beta)$. Given this situation, the hypothesis can be tested using a one-sample t-test as illustrated below.

Since the calculated t value is greater than $t_{critical}$ (95% probability), then at our chosen alpha level it can be interpreted as an unusual event and not likely to be included in the population, so we would reject the null hypothesis. Based on the underlying probability distribution, a p-value (probability value) can be calculated for the observed t-value. A direct test can be performed using the logical decision: If the p-value for $t_{observed}$ is greater than $t_{critical}$ (or the $t_{critical}$ is less than the p-value for $t_{observed}$), then reject the null hypothesis. Graphically, this relationship between the confidence interval and the null hypothesis can be represented as follows:

95% Confidence Interval

$\bullet$ H$_o$

Thus, we would reject the null hypothesis, as the p-value for inclusion in the distribution is not included in the confidence interval.

Test of Differences

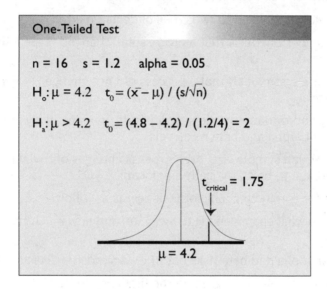

One-Tailed Test

n = 16   s = 1.2   alpha = 0.05

$H_o: \mu = 4.2$ $t_0 = (\bar{x} - \mu) / (s/\sqrt{n})$

$H_a: \mu > 4.2$ $t_0 = (4.8 - 4.2) / (1.2/4) = 2$

$t_{critical} = 1.75$

$\mu = 4.2$

Types of hypothesis tests

▶ Two means: t-test
▶ Two variances: f-test (homogeneity of variance tests in Minitab)
▶ Two proportions (attribute data):
  ▶ T-test approximation of binomial distribution
  ▶ Exact binomial test in Minitab
▶ More than two means: ANOVA
▶ Expected vs. actual distribution: chi-square test

▶Changing how a process is performed can have specific effects on the "critical-to" characteristic(s) of that process:

   ▶The mean can change.

   ▶The standard deviation (and variance) can change.

   ▶Both mean and standard deviation can change.

   ▶The response can remain unchanged.

▶Statistical hypothesis tests answer the question: "How certain are we that a process parameter has changed?" Specific hypothesis tests enable us to determine whether specific changes have happened to a CT characteristic.

▶Random variation can lead to two types of decision error:

   ▶Concluding erroneously that a process has changed (Type I alpha error).

   ▶Concluding erroneously that a process did not change (Type II beta error).

▶Establishing appropriate sample size depends on using likely outcomes to select the right alpha and beta risk levels.

▶With a big-enough sample size, even process changes of trivial magnitudes can appear to be statistically significant.

▶The process for conducting a hypothesis test is as follows:

   ▶Determine what characteristic to evaluate, and how much change is needed.

   ▶Establish alpha and beta risks based on acceptable decision risks.

   ▶Determine sample size based on the first two steps.

   ▶Establish null and alternate hypotheses.

   ▶Collect data.

   ▶Compute test statistic.

   ▶Compare test statistic with critical value.

   ▶If the p-value is > 0.5, reject the null hypothesis (this is the logical equivalent of accepting the alternative hypothesis).

   ▶Act on the decision.[1]

How data is collected is another aspect of experimental design. There are two aspects to experimental randomization: selection and assignment. Random selection refers to how a sample of data is drawn from its underlying population—it is related to sampling and can improve the external validity of

---

[1] For a description of standards relating to statistical methods, see: International Standards Organization, *Guidelines for Selection of Statistical Methods in Standardization and Specification*, Technical Report, TR 13425, second edition, 15 November 2003.

(ability to generalize) the results. A random sample is most important to ensure that the participants in an experiment truly represent the larger group from which they are drawn. Random assignment is how a sample that has been drawn is assigned to different groups or treatments in the experiment. Random assignment is most important in experimental design, as it ensures internal validity in the results. This means that all the experimental groups are handled equivalently prior to their treatment with the causal factor. In experimental designs, it is possible to have both random selection and assignment, either random selection or assignment, or neither random selection nor assignment (non-random).

Analysis of variance

An ANOVA model describes the expression $Y = f(X) + f(\varepsilon)$, where the X terms include the main effects (A, B, and C in the illustration below) and all the interaction effects (AB, BC, and AC are the two-way interactions in this example, while ABC is a three-way interaction). The term $f(\varepsilon)$ describes the effects of other analytical factors that are not included in the model (like a missing factor D as a Red X effect), lack of fit for the proposed model to the observed variation, and measurement errors that are accumulated from the data observations for the modeled factors.

Test of Differences

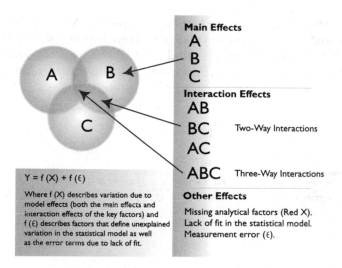

Main Effects

A
B
C

Interaction Effects

AB
BC — Two-Way Interactions
AC

ABC — Three-Way Interactions

$Y = f(X) + f(\varepsilon)$

Where $f(X)$ describes variation due to model effects (both the main effects and interaction effects of the key factors) and $f(\varepsilon)$ describes factors that define unexplained variation in the statistical model as well as the error terms due to lack of fit.

Other Effects

Missing analytical factors (Red X).
Lack of fit in the statistical model.
Measurement error (ε).

In a practical way, what does an ANOVA model look like? An easy way to observe a model's design is to look at it in a matrix format showing relationships among experimental factors. Here is an example:

Age	Method	Person	Pre-Test		Post-Test	
			Prompted	Unprompted	Prompted	Unprompted
Young	Structured	1				
		2				
		3				
		4				
	Unstructured	5				
		6				
		7				
		8				
Old	Structured	9				
		10				
		11				
		12				
	Unstructured	13				
		14				
		15				
		16				

In the above design, age is blocked to determine if there is a difference between young and old participants relative to their learning style (structured or unstructured) based on pre-test and post-test considerations for both prompted and unprompted tests. Each subject is observed by four different measurements, two taken at each of two different times.

Consider a second experimental design:

Test Intervention		No Instructions				Instructions Provided			
Treatment level		A	B	C	D	A	B	C	D
Experience	Person								
1	1								
1	2								
1	3								
2	4								
2	5								
2	6								

In this experiment, experience is a blocking factor. Each person is tested using four levels of treatments within two test interventions. Under this experiment, each person has one factor to classify the individual and eight combinations of factors. Note that if an additional factor is added (with three levels of performance), then 24 observations are required for each subject. This increase in the number of trials required is one reason for conducting screening experiments to determine which factors are the most important in the final experimental design.

After data is collected in some format, it can then be structured for analysis:

Sample	X_i	$(X_i - X_{i \, BAR})$	$(X_i - X_{i \, BAR})^2$
1	X_i Data		
2	X_i Data		
3	X_i Data		
4	X_i Data		
5	X_i Data		
6	X_i Data		
7	X_i Data		
8	X_i Data		
9	X_i Data		
10	X_i Data		
Σ	ΣX_i	–	Sum of Squares
Mean	$X_{i \, BAR}$	–	–
σ^2	σ^2	–	Mean Square Error
σ	σ	–	Mean Square Error

This method is called the "least squares method" because it looks at the differences of individual observations from the mean of the overall observations squared. The mean square term is calculated by:

mean square = sum of squares / degrees of freedom (Df)

Degrees of freedom

Degrees of freedom are calculated based on the number of observations for a term. For example, when you have three samples, then the last factor has been completely determined by all those that precede it. Generally stated, in any sample, the last coordinate of an n-dimensional variation vector is always equal to minus the sum of the first n − 1 coordinates. This means that an n-dimensional variation vector is completely determined by its first n − 1 coordinates. We express this by saying that an n-dimensional variation vector has n − 1 degrees of freedom (Df).

Two types of variation are considered in the above analysis: the *within* and *between* treatment sums of squares, where:

$$SS_{TOTAL} = SS_{TREATMENT} + SS_{ERROR}$$

This sum-of-squares decomposition is usually displayed in a tabular form. Because it contains estimates of variances, this table is called the analysis of variance (ANOVA) table. In an ANOVA table, the first column identifies the source of variation, the second and third columns are the sum of squares and degrees of freedom, the fourth column gives the mean squares, and the last column contains the F-ratio:

$$F = MS_{TREATMENT} / MS_{ERROR}$$

ANOVA Table

Effect	Estimate	SS	Df	MS	F
A					
B					
C					
AB					
AC					
BC					
ABC					
ε					
Total					

This table can also be constructed to demonstrate how the variation is broken down according to the modeled effects using the following structure:

ANOVA Table

Source	Sum of Squares	Degrees of Freedom	Mean Square (Variance)	$F_{Observed} = MS_{Factor}/MS_{Error}$	P Value Based on F and DF
Between	SS_{Factor}	$g - 1$	$SS_{Factor}/(g-1)$	MS_{Factor}/MS_{Error}	P(F)
Within	SS_{Error}	$g(n-1)$	$SS_{Error}/g(n-1)$		
Total	SS_{Total}	$(n * g) - 1$			

Where:
g = number of groups
n = number of data points in each group

$$R^2 = \frac{SS_{Factor}}{SS_{Total}}$$

Note that the statistic R^2 can be calculated using the ratio of the sum of the squares for the factors to the total sum of squares. The R^2 statistic describes how much of the total variation has been explained by the terms included in the ANOVA model.

ANOVA hypothesis test

The test performed uses the null hypothesis (no difference) that all of the treatments are the same:

$$H_0: \mu_1 = \mu_2 = \mu_3 = \mu_4 = ... = \mu_k$$

The alternative hypothesis that stands in contradiction to this null hypothesis is that at least one of the treatment means is different: H_1: not all μ_i are the same. Note that the within-treatment mean square error is an estimate of σ^2, which is true even if the treatment means are not the same. But the between-treatment mean square ($MS_{TREATMENT}$) is an estimate of the σ^2, only if the treatment means are the same. If the treatment means are different, then the $MS_{TREATMENT}$ tends to be much larger than σ^2. Most computer programs calculate a "p-value" that corresponds to the F-value that is calculated from the ratio of $MS_{TREATMENT} / MS_{ERROR}$. If the p-value is less than or equal to α, then we reject H_0 until further data is obtained. If $p > \alpha$, then we have no reason to say that the null hypothesis of equality of means is wrong based on this data set—in other words, there is no statistical difference between the treatment means.

Residuals analysis

A statistical analysis of the $f(\varepsilon)$ term is called a residuals analysis; it indicates the goodness of fit of the model to the data. Three different tests are typically used in the residuals analysis: normality of the residuals, residuals versus fits, and residuals versus the order of the data. When the statistical distribution of the residuals data is examined, it should come from a normal distribution if all variation that is included (the "unexplained" variation) comes from purely random factors. If there is coherence in the residuals (e.g., one indicator of coherence would be non-normality, which could indicate the presence of a signal amidst this noise), then there is a chance that there is another term that should be included in the model (this is especially true when the R^2 value does not explain all of the variation). The "residuals versus fits" analysis looks for patterns or unexpected values when residual values are compared with the fitted or expected values based on the analysis. A "residuals versus order of the data" analysis illustrates any time dependency in the "lack of explanation" of the variation, which could be due to seasonality or other time-series considerations.

The third statistical component of an experimental design is regression analysis. The statistical model used in regression analysis is that of a straight line, which is defined mathematically as:

$$Y = mX + b, \quad \text{which can be rewritten as} \quad Y = b + mX$$

where:

Y = a dependent Y-axis point in a Cartesian coordinate system

X = an independent X-axis point in a Cartesian coordinate system

m = the slope of the line

b = the intercept point on the Y axis when $X = 0$

This equation is modified slightly in its application for regression analysis:

$$Y_i = \beta_0 + \beta_1 X_i + \varepsilon_i$$

Notice that the regression equation is the same as the straight line, where β_0 equals b, which is the Y intercept; β_1 is the same as m, the slope of the line; and X_i is the same as X. In order to conduct a general analysis between two groups, we convert the X_i into a Z variable that has only two values: a 0 if the observation comes from the control group, or a 1 if the data comes from the treatment group. This type of variable is sometimes called a "dummy variable" because it is coded and replaces the parametric expression in the analysis (e.g., it represents a factor that has two levels—"off" and "on"—or "control group" where $Z = 0$ and "treatment group" where $Z = 1$). The relative magnitude of these beta coefficients indicates their relative contribution to the regression equation effects.

It is essential to interpret this model correctly. The slope of the line in this model (β_1) is the same as the difference between the means for the two groups. The two points on this plot indicate the average values for the two groups (control and treatment). The line that connects the two dots helps to indicate the magnitude of their difference. The slope of the line is the change in Y over the change in X. But the change in X is always equal to 1, so the slope of the line must be equal to the difference between the average Y-values for the two groups. Thus, β_1 is the value that would be obtained by subtracting the two means from each other (e.g., subtracting the control group from the treatment group). A positive value indicates that the treatment group is higher than the control group, while a negative value indicates that the treatment group is lower. (Note: The chart that illustrates this relationship among these points is called a main effects plot.) But just knowing the difference between means does not take into account the variability of the scores. A regression analysis reports on whether the β-values are statistically significant. They report a t-value that tests whether the β-value differs from zero. It turns out that the t-value for the β_1 coefficient is the exact number that would be obtained from a t-test for independent groups. This is also the same number as the square root of the F-value in the two-group one-way ANOVA (because $t^2 = F$). Other tests of goodness in the regression analysis include R^2 and residuals analysis, which are the same elements in ANOVA.[2]

Learning from experiments

The basic purpose of a designed experiment is to learn how a process operates and how to influence its performance. As observed earlier, there are many different approaches to formulating an experimental design. But each of these tools has a different degree of learning that occurs with its application. The following list indicates the relative degree of learning inherent with different types of experimental designs:

Most Learning:

    Statistical process control

    Evolutionary operation (EVOP)

    Response surface methods

    Full factorial design with replication

    Full factorial design with repetition

    Full factorial design without replication or repetition

    Fractional factorial or screening designs

Least Learning:

    One factor at a time (OFAT) analysis

$$H_0: \mu_1 = \mu_0$$
$$H_0: \mu_1 = \mu_2$$
$$H_0: \mu_1 = \mu_3$$

What is a factorial design?

Factors are independent variables that are managed under the experimental design. An experiment compares "K" levels (treatments) of performance for each factor that is considered in the design. Factors can be either controlled or noise factors in the experiment. Frequently, analyses might require investigation of more than two levels (K) (treatments) of a single factor (e.g., looking at financial results over several years, or productivity across several different production lines). This is the model for a completely randomized experiment. The assumption made in an analysis of data with K levels is $Y_{ij} = \mu_i + \varepsilon_{ij}$,

---

[2] Note that the squared Pearson coefficient of correlation (r^2) is equal to R^2.

where Y is the response variable for the jth trial for the ith treatment, μ_i is the ith treatment mean, and the ε_{ij} are independent $N(0, \sigma)$ random variables. This equation describes the statistical model that links the observations and the parameters of the underlying populations. The assumptions in this model are that the data is measured independently, the measurements are normally distributed (Anderson-Darling test), and the measurements have common variance (Levine's test).

The design of an experiment is much more important than the analysis of the experiment. A poorly designed experiment can never be retrieved; it is a problem that haunts an analyst forever. However, a poorly analyzed experiment can always be reanalyzed. The design is also important because the design of a study will determine how the data should be analyzed. Most experiments consider inputs or process or product interventions that are planned by the analyst to demonstrate a causal linkage between the factors in the experimental model (transfer function). The levels of an input factor are the values of the input factor (X) being examined in the experiment. The output factor (Y) is permitted to obtain an independent value that relates to the dependent values of the factor levels chosen.

▶ For a quantitative (variables data) factor such as temperature, when an experiment is conducted at two temperatures (high and low, for instance), then the factor is said to have two levels.

▶ For a qualitative (attributes data) factor that is binomial (either off or on), when an experiment is conducted for these two settings, then this factor is said to have two levels.

A two-level design with three possible factors has 2^3 (or eight) possible combinations of factors and levels. For a three-factor experiment, the factors (variables) would include the following eight combinations: total equation (A + B + C), each of the main effects taken independently (A, B, and C), the pairs of two-way interactions (AB, AC, and BC), and the three-way interactions (ABC). This total of eight different variable combinations leads to the naming of this form of experimental design as a 2^3 design. In order to simplify the application of the design factors, a coding scheme is used to identify the combinations of variables in each experimental "run" or trial. A coding scheme is equivalent to using a set of dummy variables to combine the factors in the design for further analysis. Two of the schemes for coding factors that indicate whether the "factor" is on or off (as used by popular statistical software packages to specify their experimental designs) are as follows:

+/- (On/Off) Coding Scheme				1/0 (On/Off) Coding Scheme			
Factor	A	B	C	Factor	A	B	C
Run 1	-	-	-	Run 1	0	0	0
2	+	-	-	2	1	0	0
3	-	+	-	3	0	1	0
4	+	+	-	4	1	1	0
5	-	-	+	5	0	0	1
6	+	-	+	6	1	0	1
7	-	+	+	7	0	1	1
8	+	+	+	8	1	1	1

A designed experiment occurs when planned changes are made to the key process input variables (KPIVs) (these are CTQ input factors, or process X factors) in order to observe the corresponding changes in the key process output variables (KPOVs) (these are the CTS outputs, or process Y factors). A transfer function ($Y = f(X)$) is used to record the information from the trials (runs), as in the following data-collection format:

Number of Runs (Experimental Trials)	Factor X_1	Factor X_2	Factor X_3	Factor Y	Resultant Y_{BAR}	Resultant $Y_{STD-DEV}$
1						
2						
3						
...						
N						

How might such a transfer function ($Y = f(X)$) be mathematically defined? There are two basic approaches used to specify the transfer function:

▶ Exact definition from theoretical knowledge or first principles.

▶ Approximating the function using similar function translation or statistical data collection (DOE or simulation).

However, when the process is an exact transfer function, then a designed experiment is not needed, as in the following example:

▶ **Output Y**: Minimize cost of transportation from your warehouse to six of your customers' sites.

▶ **Input X's**: Cost per unit of distance and distance of route.

Then:

$$Y = (cost/unit\ of\ distance) * (distance\ of\ route)$$

Orthogonal arrays

For a two-level, full factorial design with k factors, the general design structure is given by the following rule (called Yates Standard Order): The first column (X_1) starts with the coded factor −1 and then alternates the factor's signs for all 2^k runs. The second column (X_2) starts with −1 repeated twice and then alternates with two in a row of the opposite sign until all 2^k of its places have been filled. The third column (X_3) starts with −1 repeated four times, followed by four repetitions of +1's and so forth, for the remaining 2^k places. In general, the ith column (X_i) starts with 2^{i-1} repeats of −1 and then follows with 2^{i-1} repeats of +1's and continues this pattern to the end of the 2^k places. In a design matrix, the first column indicates the run number; in a 2^3 design, there are eight runs (not counting replications or center points). Graphically, this design might be shown as a cube, where the corners represent the high and low values for the three factors, and the arrows indicate increases in the magnitude of the factors from low to high values. The 2^3 design matrix for Yates Standard Order is illustrated below next to this DOE hyper-cube.

Yates Standard Order

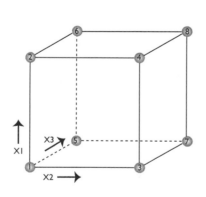

2³ Design Matrix				
Run	X_1	X_2	X_3	Y
1	−1	−1	−1	Y_1
2	1	−1	−1	Y_2
3	−1	1	−1	Y_3
4	1	1	−1	Y_4
5	−1	−1	1	Y_5
6	1	−1	1	Y_6
7	−1	1	1	Y_7
8	1	1	1	Y_8

Orthogonal designs are balanced designs. Each factor is statistically independent from the others. They enhance the ability to detect and quantify interactions. The design described by Yates Standard Order above is orthogonal because the columns are balanced (the sum of the coded variables is zero in each column) so that the effects of any one factor "balance" out across the entire experiment. Suppose v and w are two columns of a design matrix. These two columns are orthogonal if:

$$\sum_i (v_i \, w_i) = 0$$

If all pairs of columns v and w associated with different terms in the model are orthogonal, then the design is orthogonal. If the design is not orthogonal, then results calculated in a DOE will almost certainly be in error.

Design for Six Sigma

Appendix D
References

"Those who don't know history are doomed to repeat it."

~ George Santayana

1. Akao, Yoji, *Quality Function Deployment: Integrating Customer Requirements into Product Design* (Portland, OR: Productivity Press, 1990).

2. Akao, Yoji, and Shigeru Mizuno, *Quality Function Deployment: The Customer-Driven Approach to Quality Planning and Deployment* (Tokyo: Asian Productivity Organization, 1994).

3. Akiyama, Kaneo, *Function Analysis: Systematic Improvement of Quality and Performance* (Portland, OR: Productivity Press, 1991).

4. Allen, Thomas J., *Managing the Flow of Technology: Technology Transfer and Dissemination of Information within the R&D Organization* (Cambridge: MIT Press, 1977).

5. Altshuller, Genrich S., *Creativity as an Exact Science* (New York: Gordon & Breach, 1988).

6. Amran, Martha, and Nalin Kulatiklaka, *Real Options: Strategic Investments in an Uncertain World* (New York: Oxford University Press, 1998).

7. Barlow, Richard E., Carlo A. Clarotti, and Fabio Spizzichino, *Reliability and Decision Making* (London: Chapman & Hall, 1993).

8. Baumol, William, *The Free-Market Innovation Machine* (Princeton, NJ: Princeton University Press, 2002).

9. Birolini, Alessandro, *Quality and Reliability of Technical Systems: Theory, Practice, Management* (New York: Springer-Verlag, 1994).

10. Block, Heinz P., and Fred W. Geitner, *An Introduction to Machinery Reliability Assessment* (New York: Van Nostrand Reinhold, 1990).

11. Bralla, James G., *Design for Manufacturability Handbook*, second edition (New York: McGraw-Hill, 1998).

12. Breyfogle, Forrest W., *Implementing Six Sigma* (New York: John Wiley & Sons, 1999).

13. Breyfogle, Forrest W., James M. Cupello, and Becki Meadows, *Managing Six Sigma* (New York: John Wiley & Sons, 2000).

14. Brown, John Seely, ed., *Seeing Differently: Insights on Innovation* (Boston: Harvard Business School Press, 1997).

15. Brue, Greg, *Six Sigma for Managers* (New York: McGraw-Hill, 2002).

16. Burgelman, Robert A., and Leonard S. Sayles, *Inside Corporate Innovation* (New York: Free Press, 1986).

17. Buzzell, Robert D., and Bradley T. Gale, *The PIMS Principles* (New York: Free Press, 1987).

18. Chowdhury, Subir, *Design for Six Sigma* (New York: Kaplan Professional Company, 2002).

19. Chowdhury, Subir, *The Power of Six Sigma* (Dearborn, MI: Dearborn Financial Publishing, Inc., 2001).

20. Christensen, Clayton M., *The Innovator's Dilemma* (Boston: Harvard Business School, 1997).

21. Christensen, Clayton M., and Michael E. Raynor, *The Innovator's Solution* (Boston: Harvard Business School, 2003).

22. Christensen, Clayton M., Scott D. Anthony, and Erik A. Roth, *Seeing What's Next: Using the Theories of Innovation to Predict Industry Change* (Boston: Harvard Business School Press, 2004).

23. Conti, Tito, Kondo Yoshio, and Gregory H. Watson, eds., *Quality into the 21st Century: Perspectives on Quality and Competitiveness for Sustained Performance* (Milwaukee, WI: ASQ Quality Press, 2003).

24. Cooper, Robert G., *Winning at New Products: Accelerating the Process from Idea to Launch*, second edition (Cambridge, MA: Perseus Books, 1993).

25. Cooper, Robert G., *Product Leadership: Creating and Launching Superior New Products* (Cambridge, MA: Perseus Books, 1998).

26. Cooper, Robert G., Scott Edgett, and Elko Kleinschmidt, *Portfolio Management for New Products* (Cambridge, MA: Perseus Books, 1998).

27. Crawford, C. Merle, *New Products Management*, fifth edition (New York: McGraw-Hill, 1997).

28. Creveling, Clyde M., David Antis, Jr., and Jeffrey Lee Slutsky, *Design for Six Sigma in Technology and Product Development* (New York: Pearson Education, 2002).

29. Cusumano, Michael, and David Yoffie, *Competing on Internet Time: Lessons Learned from Netscape and Its Battle with Microsoft* (New York: Free Press, 1998).

30. Dimancescu, Dan, and Kemp Dwenger, *World-Class New Product Development: Benchmarking Best Practices of Agile Manufacturers* (New York: AMACOM, American Management Association Press, 1996).

31. Dodson, Bryan, *Weibull Analysis* (Milwaukee, WI: ASQ Quality Press, 1994).

32. Drucker, Peter F., *Innovation and Entrepreneurship* (New York: HarperCollins, 1985).

33. Eccles, Robert, and Nitin Nohira, *Beyond the Hype: Rediscovering the Essence of Management* (Boston: Harvard Business School Press, 1991).

34. Eckes, George, *Making Six Sigma Last* (New York: John Wiley & Sons, 2001).

35. Eckes, George, *Six Sigma Team Dynamics* (New York: John Wiley & Sons, 2003).

36. Eckes, George, *The Six Sigma Revolution* (New York: John Wiley & Sons, 2000).

37. Ellis, Lynn, *Evaluation of R&D Processes: Effectiveness through Measurements* (Boston: Artech House, 1997).

38. Elsayed, Elsayed A., *Reliability Engineering* (New York: Addison Wesley Longman, 1996).

39. Foster, Robert N., *Innovation: The Attacker's Advantage* (New York: Macmillan, 1986).

40. George, Michael L., *Lean Six Sigma* (New York: McGraw-Hill, 2002).

41. Goldratt, Eliyahu M., and Jeff Cox, *The Goal*, second edition (Boston: North River Press, 1992).

42. Goldratt, Eliyahu M., *Critical Chain* (Boston: North River Press, 1997).

43. Grief, Michel, *The Visual Factory: Building Participation through Shared Information* (Portland: Productivity Press, 1991).

44. Harrington, H. James, and Leslie C. Anderson, *Reliability Simplified: Going beyond Quality to Keep Customers for Life* (New York: McGraw-Hill, 1999).

45. Harris, Betsi, and Ehrlich Harris, *Transactional Six Sigma and Lean Servicing* (New York: SLP, 2002).

46. Harry, Mikel, and Richard Schroeder, *Six Sigma: The Breakthrough Management Strategy* (New York: Doubleday, 2000).

47. Hauser, John R., *Design and Marketing of New Products*, 2nd edition (Englewood Cliffs: Prentice Hall, 1980, 1992).

48. Hirano, Hiroyuki, *Putting 5S to Work: A Practical Step-by-Step Approach* (New York: PHP Institute, Inc., 1993).

49. Howard, William Jr., and Bruce Guile, eds., *Profiting from Innovation: The Report of the Three-Year Study from the National Academy of Engineering* (New York: Free Press, 1992).

50. Hoyland, Arnljot, and Marvin Rausand, *System Reliability Theory: Models and Statistical Methods* (New York: John Wiley & Sons, 1994).

51. Iansiti, Marco, *Technology Integration* (Boston: Harvard Business School Press, 1998).

52. Imai, Masaaki, *Kaizen: The Key to Japan's Competitive Success* (New York: McGraw-Hill, 1986).

53. Ireson, W. Grant, and Clyde F. Coombs, Jr., *Handbook of Reliability Engineering and Management* (New York: McGraw-Hill, 1988).

54. Jain, R. K., and H. C. Triandis, *Management of Research and Development Organizations*, second edition (New York: John Wiley & Sons, 1997).

55. The Juran Institute, *The Six Sigma Basic Training Kit* (New York: McGraw-Hill, 2001).

56. Kececioglu, Dimitri, *Reliability Engineering Handbook*, volumes 1 and 2 (Englewood Cliffs, NJ: Prentice-Hall, 1991).

57. Kececioglu, Dimitri, *Reliability & Life Testing Handbook*, volumes 1 and 2 (Englewood Cliffs, NJ: Prentice-Hall, 1993, 1994).

58. Kerzner, Harold, *Project Management: A Systems Approach to Planning, Scheduling, and Controlling*, 6th edition (New York: John Wiley & Sons, 1998).

59. King, Bob, *Better Designs in Half the Time: Implementing Quality Function Deployment (QFD) in America* (Salem, NH: GOAL/QPC, 1987).

60. Klinger, David J., Yoshinao Nakada, and Maria A. Menendez, AT&T *Reliability Manual* (New York: Van Nostrand Reinhold, 1990).

61. Lloyd, David K., and Myron Lipow, *Reliability: Management, Methods, and Mathematics*, second edition (Milwaukee, WI: ASQ Quality Press, 1984).

62. Lowenthal, Jeffrey N., *Six Sigma Project Management* (Milwaukee, WI: ASQ Quality Press, 2001).

63. Matheson, David, and Jim Matheson, *The Smart Organization: Creating Value through Strategic R&D* (Boston: Harvard Business School Press, 1998).

64. Matthews, Brian, and Watts Wacker, *The Deviant's Advantage: How Fringe Ideas Create Mass Markets* (New York: Crown Business Publications, 2002).

65. McGrath, Michael, Michael Anthony, and Amram Shapiro, *Product Development: Success through Product and Cycle-Time Excellence* (Boston: Butterworth-Heinemann, 1992).

66. McLean, Harry W., HALT, HASS, & HASA: *Accelerated Reliability Techniques* (Milwaukee, WI: ASQ Quality Press, 2000).

67. Meyer, Christopher, *Fast Cycle Time* (New York: The Free Press, 1993).

68. Miles, Lawrence D., *Techniques of Value Analysis and Engineering*, second edition (New York: McGraw-Hill, 1972).

69. Miller, William, and Langdon Morris, *Fourth Generation R&D: Managing Knowledge, Technology, and Innovation* (New York: John Wiley & Sons, 1999).

70. Moore, Geoffrey A., *Crossing the Chasm: Marketing and Selling Technology Products to Mainstream Customers* (New York: HarperCollins, 1991).

71. Nadler, David, and Michael Tushman, *Competing by Design: The Power of Organizational Architecture* (New York: Oxford University Press, 1997).

72. Nakajima, Seiichi, *Introduction to TPM: Total Productive Maintenance* (Portland, OR: Productivity Press, 1988).

73. Nakajima, Seiichi, TPM *Development Program* (Portland, OR: Productivity Press, 1989).

74. Naumann, Earl, and Steven Hoisington, *Customer-Centered Six Sigma* (Milwaukee, WI: ASQ Quality Press, 2001).

75. Nikkan Kogyo Shimbun Ltd., *Poka-Yoke: Improving Product Quality by Preventing Defects* (Portland, OR: Productivity Press, 1988).

76. Nonaka, Ikujiro, and Hirotaka Takeuchi, *The Knowledge-Creating Company: How Japanese Companies Create the Dynamics of Innovation* (Oxford, U.K.: Oxford University Press, 1995).

77. O'Connor, Patrick D. T., *Practical Reliability Engineering*, third edition (New York: John Wiley & Sons, 1991).

78. Pande, Peter S., Roland R. Cavanagh, and Robert P. Neuman, *The Six Sigma Way* (New York: McGraw-Hill, 2000).

79. Pande, Peter S., Roland R. Cavanagh, and Robert P. Neuman, *The Six Sigma Way Team Fieldbook* (New York: McGraw-Hill, 2001).

80. Pande, Peter S., and Lawrence Holpp, *What Is Six Sigma?* (New York: McGraw-Hill, 2001).

81. Prasad, Biren, *Concurrent Engineering Fundamentals, Volume 1: Integrated Product and Process Organization* (Englewood Cliffs, NJ: Prentice Hall, 1996).

82. Prasad, Biren, *Concurrent Engineering Fundamentals, Volume 2: Integrated Produce Development* (Englewood Cliffs, NJ: Prentice Hall, 1997).

83. Pugh, Stuart, *Total Design: Integrated Methods for Successful Product Engineering* (Reading, MA: Addison-Wesley, 1991).

84. Pugh, Stuart, *Creating Innovative Products Using Total Design* (Reading, MA: Addison-Wesley, 1996).

85. Pugh, Stuart, and Bill Hollins, *Successful Product Design: What to Do and When* (Boston: Butterworth, 1990).

86. Pyzdek, Thomas, *The Six Sigma Handbook* (New York: McGraw-Hill, 2000).

87. Reinertsen, Donald G., *Managing the Design Factory: A Product Developer's Toolkit* (New York: Free Press, 1997).

88. Rhodes, Richard, *Visions of Technology* (New York: Simon & Schuster, 1999).

89. Rogers, Everett M., *The Diffusion of Innovation*, 5th edition (New York: Free Press, 2003).

90. Rosenau, Milton D., *The PDMA Handbook of New Product Development* (New York: John Wiley & Sons, 1996).

91. Roussel, Philip, Kamal Saad, and Tamara Erickson, *Third-Generation R&D* (Boston: Harvard Business School Press, 1991).

92. Schwartz, Peter, *The Art of the Long View* (New York: Doubleday, 1991).

93. Shina, Sammy G., *Six Sigma for Electronics Design and Manufacturing* (New York: McGraw-Hill, 2002).

94. Shirose, Kunio, Yoshifumi Kimura, and Mitsugu Kaneda, P-M *Analysis: An Advanced Step in* TPM *Implementation* (Portland, OR: Productivity Press, 1995).

95. Smith, Anthony M., *Reliability-Centered Maintenance* (New York: McGraw-Hill, 1993).

96. Smith, Dick, Jerry Blakeslee, and Richard Koonce, *Strategic Six Sigma* (New York: John Wiley & Sons, 2002.

97. Smith, Preston G., and Donald G. Reinertsen, *Developing Products in Half the Time* (New York: Van Nostrand Reinhold, 1991).

98. Snee, Ronald D., and Roger W. Hoerl, *Leading Six Sigma* (New York: Pearson Education, 2002).

99. Star, Harold, and Stephen J. Snyder, *Understanding the Essentials of the* Six Sigma *Quality Initiative* (New York: 1st Books Library, 2000).

100. Taguchi, Genichi, *Introduction to Quality Engineering: Designing Quality into Products and Processes* (Tokyo: Asian Productivity Organization, 1983).

101. Taguchi, Genichi, *System of Experimental Design: Engineering Methods to Optimize Quality and Minimize Costs* (Dearborn, MI: American Supplier Institute, 1988).

102. Taguchi, Genichi, Subir Chowdhury, and Shin Taguchi, *Robust Engineering* (New York: McGraw-Hill, 2000).

103. Tayntor, Christine B., *Six Sigma Software Development* (New York: CRC Press, 2002).

104. Terninko, John, Alla Zusman, and Boris Zlotin, *Systematic Innovation: An Introduction to* TRIZ (*Theory of Inventive Problem Solving*) (New York: CRC St. Lucie Press, 1998).

105. Treacy, Michael, and Fred Wiersema, *The Discipline of Market Leaders* (New York: Perseus Publishing, 1997).

106. Trigeorgis, Leonos, *Real Options: Managerial Flexibility and Strategy in Resource Allocation* (Cambridge, MA: MIT Press, 1996).

107. Tushman, Michael, and Charles O'Reilly, *Winning through Innovation: A Practical Guide to Leading Organizational Change* (Boston: Harvard Business School Press, 1997).

108. Ulrich, Dave, Steve Kerr, and Ron Ashkenas, *The GE Workout* (New York: McGraw-Hill, 2002).

109. Ulrich, Karl T., and Steven D. Eppinger, *Product Design and Development*, 2nd edition (New York: McGraw-Hill, 2000).

110. Utterback, James, *Mastering the Dynamics of Innovation* (Boston: Harvard Business School Press, 1994).

111. Watson, Gregory H., *Six Sigma for Business Leaders* (Salem, NH: GOAL/QPC, 2004).

112. Watson, Gregory H., *Strategic Benchmarking* (New York: John Wiley & Sons, 1993).

113. Watson, Gregory H., *Business Systems Engineering* (New York: John Wiley & Sons, 1994).

114. Watson, Gregory H., ed., *Technical Foundations of Six Sigma* (Milwaukee, WI: ASQ Quality Press, manuscript in process).

115. Wheeler, Donald J., and R. W. Lyday, *Evaluating the Measurement Process*, 2nd edition (San Francisco: Addison-Wesley, 1990).

116. Wheelwright, Steven C., and Kim Clark, *Leading Product Development* (New York: The Free Press, 1995).

117. Wheelwright, Steven C., and Kim Clark, *Revolutionizing Product Development* (New York: The Free Press, 1992).

118. Womack, James, and Daniel T. Jones, *Lean Thinking* (New York: Simon & Schuster, 1996).

119. Yang, Kai, and Basem El-Haik, *Design for Six Sigma: A Roadmap for Product Development* (New York: McGraw-Hill, 2003).

120. Zacks, Shelemyahu, *Introduction to Reliability Analysis: Probability Models and Statistical Methods* (New York: Springer-Verlag, 1992).

About the Author

Gregory H. Watson is president and managing partner of Business Systems Solutions International, Inc., and an adjunct professor of industrial engineering at Oklahoma State University. Previously he was a business executive with Xerox, Compaq, and Hewlett-Packard and a lieutenant commander in the U.S. Navy.

Mr. Watson is a past president of the American Society for Quality and was appointed to the prestigious International Academy for Quality in 1997, where he is currently serving as secretary/treasurer. Mr. Watson has been appointed a companion of the British Institute for Quality Assurance and elected a fellow of the American Society for Quality, Australian Organization for Quality, Quality Society of AustralAsia, and World Productivity Council. He received the Lancaster Medal from the American Society for Quality in 2001 and, in the same year, received the President's Award from the Association for Quality and Participation.

Mr. Watson is the author of *Six Sigma for Business Leaders* (GOAL/QPC, 2004), *Business Systems Engineering* (John Wiley & Sons, 1994), *Strategic Benchmarking* (John Wiley & Sons, 1993), and six other books on related business subjects. He is a frequent contributor to and member of the editorial board for *Six Sigma Forum Magazine*. Mr. Watson was the founder and serves as co-chair of the International Standards Organization Six Sigma Advisory Committee to the technical committee on statistical matters. He holds master's degrees in the fields of systems management, legal studies, and industrial engineering.

Mr. Watson was certified as a quality engineer by the American Society for Quality in 1991, and he received his Master Black Belt from the Six Sigma Academy in 1997. He has worked with numerous organizations in designing and deploying their Six Sigma systems. A few of the organizations that he has assisted include American Express, DuPont, ExxonMobil, Ford Motor Company, Johnson Controls, Monsanto, Nokia Mobile Phones, Noranda, and Toshiba.

Mr. Watson lives in Espoo, Finland, with his wife Inessa and her very special daughter Crista. He can be contacted at gregbss@aol.com.

Kudos!

Glossary

activity-based costing (ABC)
Determining the actual cost of a product or service by tracing the cost back to the specific activities that produce or provide it.

Affinity Diagram
A method that enables a team to generate a large number of ideas and then organize natural groupings among them to understand the essence of a problem and identify solutions.

Analytic Hierarchy Process (AHP)
A decision-support tool that provides a logical approach for making a complex decision by enabling the decision-maker to determine trade-offs among options to find the most appropriate choice.

attribute
A characteristic that can have only one value (e.g., 0 or 1, green or red, go or no-go).

balanced scorecard
A measurement system based on gathering a comprehensive set of performance measures to enable an organization to determine its strengths and areas needing improvement.

baseline
A current or historical level of performance that is used as a standard of comparison for future performance improvements.

benchmarking
The practice of establishing performance targets and change projects based on how an organization's processes compare with the industry's best practices.

block diagram
A graphical linkage of blocks, which are labeled with noun-verb phrases, that indicates the logical sequence of a series of events. A block diagram is the elemental graphical form of a process model or flowchart.

brand value
The market's sustained confidence that a company can provide enduring customer satisfaction.

business process
An end-to-end sequence of activities that defines one or more business functions required to deliver goods or services to a customer. Processes serving external customers are considered core business processes; those serving internal customers are considered support services.

business-process improvement
The practice of flowcharting a process, accurately identifying customer needs, identifying non-productive work, and redesigning the process to better meet customer needs with less chance for errors and at a lower operating cost.

business Y
An output indicator of success in delivery of desired business results, such as shareholder value and brand value.

catchball

Give-and-take dialogue that occurs among organizational levels during negotiation and leads to shared objectives or consensus on direction in a policy-deployment-planning system.

Cause & Effect/Fishbone Diagram

A diagram that enables a team to identify, explore, and graphically display, in increasing detail, all possible causes of a problem in an effort to identify its root cause(s).

charter

A written commitment (or contract) by management that states the purpose and objectives of an improvement-project team. Resources, performance targets, participants, and review authority are specifically addressed.

confounding

A combined effect or statistical condition that occurs when two or more variables (or their interactions) are evaluated together so that the unique effects of each variable cannot be separated.

continuous improvement

A step-wise, incremental, continuous effort to improve performance of a process or sequential improvement in the performance of a product's features over time. The idea that management improvement is necessarily a continuous activity to ensure ongoing customer satisfaction and improved performance.

control chart

A graphical rendition of a characteristic's performance across time in relation to its natural limits and central tendency. It is used to evaluate whether a process is in a state of statistical control.

control point

A physical location or point in time in a work process at which critical measurement observations are taken and control can be exercised over the quality or quantity of the throughput.

core business process

A process that delivers a critical business outcome (i.e., a key driver to providing value to external customers).

cost of poor quality (COPQ)

The sum of costs incurred for efforts made to prevent and detect problems and to correct internal and external failures. COPQ is often offset by the *return on quality*, which is the benefit received from reductions in scrap, rework, and lost time, plus a productivity improvement from using the failure time to produce additional products.

Cp

An indicator of the potential performance capability of a centered or ideal process as indicated by a comparison of the voice of the customer (i.e., what the customer wants) to the voice of the process (i.e., what the process is able to provide). It is measured as the ratio of specification tolerance width to six standard deviations in process variation as indicated using short-term data.

Cpk

An indicator of the actual performance capability that a process achieves, taking into account the real-world result of the process performance. It is measured as the minimum of the difference between the process average and the distance to the upper and lower specification limits divided by three standard deviations in process variation using short-term data.

critical to quality (CTQ)
Describes product or service characteristics that significantly influence one or more CTSes in terms of quality.

critical to satisfaction (CTS)
Describes characteristics that are critical to the way customers use, apply, or consume an organization's products or services.

customer dashboard
A measurement system based on connectivity among performance indicators based on causality, reducing variation to improve processes, and process ownership that includes accountability for performance.

customer focus
The concept that top priority must be given to working on factors that satisfy short- and long-term customer needs. All decisions must be made in full understanding of their impact on external customers. Some organizations also extend this principle to their internal customers.

cycle time
The total time required to successfully complete all the tasks that are required for a work process.

defects per million opportunities (DPMO)
A measure of quality that indicates the number of defects observed in a million opportunities for producing the given defect. Each defect opportunity must be independent of the others. Defect sequences that are conditional on the occurrence of an initial defect are considered together as a single defect opportunity.

defects per unit (DPU)
An estimated number of defects observed at the end of the production process (or upon customer delivery) when the exact number of opportunities is unknown. The estimate is based on the number of defects found during inspection.

Design for Six Sigma (DFSS)
A methodology for designing new processes, products, or services or completely redesigning ones that already exist to achieve 3.4 defects per million opportunities or less.

design of experiments (DOE)
A methodology that involves the investigation of factors whose variation might impact the output of a work process. It is used to enhance the predictability of a process.

DMADV
An innovation process that ensures that an organization's products, processes, or services consistently meet current customer requirements. The term *DMADV* is an acronym for the process's five sequential steps: Define, Measure, Analyze, Design, and Verify.

DMAIC
Six Sigma's rigorous approach for statistical problem solving. The term *DMAIC* is an acronym for the process's five sequential steps: Define, Measure, Analyze, Improve, and Control.

entitlement
The best performance results obtainable without adding more resources.

Failure Mode and Effects Analysis (FMEA)
A method of identifying specific ways in which a product, process, or service might fail and developing countermeasures for those failures.

fault tree analysis (FTA)
A tool for evaluating a process's design, operation, and reliability. All factors affecting the process's success or failure are placed in a single diagram for evaluation.

5S workplace streamlining
A lean-enterprise method of creating a clean and orderly workplace that exposes waste and errors. The term *5S* stands for Sort, Shine, Set in Order, Standardize, and Sustain.

flowchart
A block diagram that illustrates the sequential actions and decisions that represent the steps of a process. It might follow a logical, geographical, physical, or functional means to break a process down into smaller steps or activity increments.

Function Analysis System Technique (FAST)
A mapping technique that graphically depicts work processes and products and identifies function dependencies.

Gantt chart
A program-planning method used to indicate the projected start and completion times for scheduled activities of a project. Its horizontal bars show which tasks can be done simultaneously over the life of the project.

hidden factory
A part of a process that adds no value for the customer and involves fixing things that weren't done right the first time.

just-in-time delivery (JIT)
To deliver a product exactly when it is needed at the quality level required. JIT reduces required inventory levels.

kanban system
A production-control system that uses cards or tickets as visual signals to trigger or control the flow of materials or parts during the manufacturing process.

Kano analysis
A tool for classifying and prioritizing customer needs. It enables a company to rank requirements for different customers to determine which are most important.

key process input variable (KPIV)
A performance indicator that describes in-process performance of work in progress or identifies the performance contribution of suppliers to internal work processes. (See *process X*.)

key process output variable (KPOV)
A performance indicator describing key business-results areas from an external viewpoint outside the organization. (See *business Y*.)

line of sight
A linked and aligned performance-relationship structure that enables executives to see how front-line workers deliver the company strategy and permits front-line workers to understand how their activities deliver the company strategy.

measurement systems analysis (MSA)

The study of an organization's measurement system to determine its reliability. An improperly functioning measurement system can introduce variability that negatively impacts process capability.

MECE analysis

A $y = f(x)$ analysis where the top-level metrics provide an operating definition for sustained success, and these metrics cascade to actionable measures with local accountability. The term *MECE* stands for mutually exclusive, completely exhaustive. The breadth is mutually exclusive, with no logical overlaps, and the depth is completely exhaustive, with no missing considerations.

multi-vari analysis

A method of identifying patterns of variation within a work process.

non-value-added

Activities or tasks performed during the production of a product or service that do not contribute to meeting customer requirements. Their elimination from the work process does not degrade its overall performance or results.

Pareto chart

A chart that ranks problems by their relative frequency or importance to help a team focus on causes that offer the greatest potential for improvement if solved.

Plan-Do-Check-Act (PDCA) Cycle

A structured, systematic approach for developing and implementing actions of any type. The first step is to plan for action by collecting and analyzing data and developing alternatives. The second step is to implement the selected alternative on a small scale to pilot the change. The third step is to evaluate the results and compare them with expected values. The fourth step is to adopt the change if the desired results were achieved.

poka-yoke

The discipline of applying simple, low-cost methods to either prevent mistakes or detect them immediately and request a corrective action before the mistakes can be repeated and the defects passed on to customers.

problem statement

A succinct statement that describes what the problem is, where and when it occurs, potential reasons why it occurs, how the process operates at the point of the problem, and who is involved in the problem or in a potential solution.

process average

The central tendency of a given process characteristic across a given amount of time or a specific point in time.

process capability

A ratio of the "voice of the process" to the "voice of the customer" that measures the process variability relative to the customer specification and the nominal or target value for performance. This ratio relates customer requirements to actual process performance (see *Cp* and *Cpk*).

process model

A block diagram that illustrates the flow of a work or business process and illustrates the boundaries of the process, its major inputs, and outcomes delivered. It might be broken down from the process level to the activity level and perhaps further broken down to the task level.

process X
An indicator of performance for a work process. It is an independent variable in the equation $y = f(x)$.

Pugh matrix
A tool that helps determine which potential solutions are more desirable than others. All solutions are evaluated in terms of their strengths and weaknesses and then assigned scores. This tool is usually associated with the QFD method.

quality function deployment (QFD)
A methodology for aligning the design of an organization's products and services with the expectations of its customers.

realization review
An assessment of the financial benefits realized after a protracted implementation phase of a Six Sigma project. It is done to ensure that the project's anticipated benefits were realized and whether they transferred to the bottom line.

Recognize step
The step in the Six Sigma analysis process during which an organization's top-level managers determine the strategic issues the organization faces and prioritize the selection of improvement projects.

road map
A time-sequenced program for introducing future product or process developments. It indicates what will be developed and when it is targeted for delivery.

rolled throughput yield (RTY)
A process to determine the probability that a product will make it through a multi-step process correctly the first time it is produced or that a process will work correctly each time it is used.

root-cause analysis
The process of identifying sources of variation to identify the key sources causing a problem. Eliminating these root causes will make the biggest impact toward solving the problem.

SIPOC
A diagram that enables a team to develop a high-level understanding of a process under study, including the upstream and downstream links. The term *SIPOC* stands for Suppliers, Inputs, Process, Outputs, and Customers.

SMED
A method of reducing the time required for setups and changeovers of production machinery so that these operations do not interfere with continuous workflow or productivity. This technique was developed by Shigeo Shingo as part of the Toyota Production System. The term *SMED* stands for Single Minute Exchange of Dies.

standard deviation
A statistical indicator of variability, dispersion, or spread of values in a statistical distribution.

statistical process control (SPC)
The application of statistical methods and procedures relative to a process and a given set of performance standards.

storyboard
A graphical summary of the progress of a project and the methodology used. It is used to track data, decisions, and actions and to create a pictorial record of an improvement project.

stratification
The separation of data into subsets that share similar characteristics.

SWOT analysis
A planning device for capturing all the factors that a leadership team needs to consider as they plot their organization's strategic direction. The term *SWOT* stands for strengths, weaknesses, opportunities, and threats.

systematic innovation process (SIP)
A process used to engage teams in a structured approach to innovation by applying appropriate tools in a facilitated process.

Theory O
A style of management where decisions are based on opinion and anecdotal information rather than validated by objective facts.

Theory X
A style of management where decisions are dictated by management without input, feedback, or challenge from other members of the organization.

Theory Y
A style of management where decisions are made with the participation of an entire group and each group member has an opportunity to make his/her personal opinion heard. Also called consensus management.

tollgate review
A method of reviewing progress and checking key deliverables at the completion of each step of the DMAIC and DMADV processes.

total cycle time (TCT)
The total elapsed time from customer-need identification to delivery of a product, from new-product design concept to cost-effective production, or from identification of a new business opportunity to stable operations.

total productive maintenance (TPM)
A process that ensures every piece of equipment used in a production process is always able to perform its required tasks so that production is never interrupted due to equipment failure.

trend analysis
The use of a run chart to study observed data for a process-performance measure over a period of time in an effort to see trends or patterns in its real-time behavior.

TRIZ
A systematic approach for creating innovative solutions to technical problems. It is especially useful for new product development, service delivery, and solving production problems.

value-added
Activities or tasks performed during the production of a product or service that increase its value to the customer.

variation

Any quantifiable difference between individual measurements. Such differences can be classified as being due to either common causes (i.e., random) or special causes (i.e., assignable).

voice of the customer (VOC) analysis

A method for identifying the key drivers of customer satisfaction. This enables an organization to effectively design, deliver, and improve its products and services.

Work-Out

A group decision process conducted in a constrained workshop. A cross-functional team meets and develops a defined position based on solid data analysis and recommends a course of action. A team of managers listens to the presentation; challenges the team on assumptions, data analysis, and logic; and then either makes a firm yes-or-no decision or sets a date for the decision to be made after requesting additional data to drive a conclusion.

$\overline{X}$ & R Chart

A type of control chart that displays variability in the process average and range across time and represents the process's capability over time.

y = f (x)

A formula that enables an organization to identify key process drivers and determine what factors in a process can be changed to improve the CTQs.

yield

The percentage of production output that is in conformance with the specification. Can be calculated as a first-pass yield (the percentage of product that goes through production without rework) or rolled throughput yield (the probability that a product will be produced right the first time).

zero defects

A long-range concept that implies the end state of a never-ending improvement process. It is viewed as the achievement of Six Sigma–quality performance.

dditional publications to help you
with your Six Sigma Initiative...

The Lean Enterprise Memory Jogger™

Richard L. MacInnes

Competitiveness in the New Economy demands streamlined operations and a total organizational effort to more quickly improve bottom-line performance, from shop floor to boardroom. *The Lean Enterprise Memory Jogger™* provides quick access to lean principles and practices with comprehensive, "how-to-do-it" guidance on:

~ Introduction to Lean Concepts
~ Goals of the Lean Enterprise
~ Visual Management
~ Mapping the Value Stream
~ Error Proofing
~ Quick Changeover
~ Standard Operations
~ One-Piece Flow
~ The Kanban System
~ Lean Metrics
~ Total Productive Maintenance
~ A Lean Glossary

At a Glance

~ Reduce waste across the board
~ Shorten cycle times
~ Eliminate non-value-added activities
~ Improve customer satisfaction
~ Align business performance projects more closely with core objectives for maximum shareholder value

2002. 166 pages. ISBN 1-57681-045-3. 3.5" x 5.5".
Code 1077E

The Black Belt Memory Jogger™

Six Sigma Academy

Why use it? What does it do? How does it work? How do I do it? These are the step-by-step questions that help guide your Black Belts through the more than twenty-one Six Sigma tools and concepts spelled out in this extraordinary Six Sigma teaching tool from GOAL/QPC.

Starting with a clear depiction of the DMAIC model and the roles and responsibilities that help ensure that Six Sigma methodologies become ingrained in the organization, *The Black Belt Memory Jogger™* clarifies concepts and tools, from Critical To Flowdown through Control Plans, illuminating these methods in twenty-four detailed chapters of Six Sigma know-how.

No Black Belt should undertake a Six Sigma project without a copy of *The Black Belt Memory Jogger™* in his or her pocket. As a quick reference under tight deadlines, it will help keep projects—and concepts—on track. As a teaching tool for team members, it has no equal; it is small and easy to carry, comprehensive yet concise, and most of all, written from a training perspective so every topic and every page goes quickly to the critical point of interest. As a mentoring aid, *The Black Belt Memory Jogger™* is the perfect way for mentors, team leaders, and team members to come together and begin to build new levels of Six Sigma success. 2002. 266 pages. ISBN 1-57681-043-7. 3.5" x 5.5". **Code 1075E**

Content at a Glance

- ~ Roles and Responsibilities
- ~ Project Management
- ~ Critical To Flowdown
- ~ Basic Statistics
- ~ Process Maps
- ~ Rolled Throughput Yield
- ~ Sigma Values
- ~ Cause & Effect/Fishbone Diagram
- ~ Measurement Systems Analysis
- ~ Capability Indices
- ~ Graphical Analysis
- ~ Multi-Vari Charts

- ~ Central Limit Theorem
- ~ Confidence Intervals
- ~ Hypothesis Testing
- ~ Transforming Data
- ~ Correlation & Regression
- ~ Binary Logistic Regression
- ~ Design of Experiments
- ~ Failure Mode and Effects Analysis
- ~ Control Charts
- ~ Control Plan
- ~ Total Productive Maintenance and Preventative Maintenance

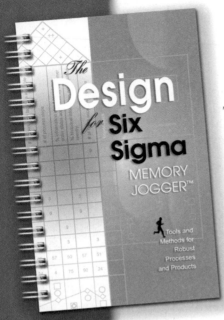

The Design for Six Sigma Memory Jogger™

If the question "How can I design a process that is capable of delivering products and services that meet Six Sigma performance levels?" keeps you awake at night, we have the answer that will let you rest easy.

Based on the Define-Measure-Analyze-Design-Verify (DMADV) methodology, The Design for Six Sigma Memory Jogger™ guides you, step-by-step, through the design process and clearly and concisely presents tools for:

~ Identifying the Voice of the Customer

~ Prioritizing Critical to Quality characteristics

~ Creating high-level & detailed design elements

~ Assessing risks

~ Testing designs

~ Validating process capability

Using The Design for Six Sigma Memory Jogger™ as both a teaching tool and performance support aid, team members will hit the ground running, mapping their next steps, using tollgate reviews to report progress, and documenting their project quickly and clearly.

Portable, concise, easy to read, and packed with wisdom, The Design for Six Sigma Memory Jogger™ allows team members to know how they "fit in" and enables them to make a maximum contribution to the project team. 2004. 266 pages. ISBN 1-57681-047-X. 3.5" x 5.5". **Code 1078E**

At a Glance

~ Why you need Design for Six Sigma

~ Overview of DMADV with an explanation of the differences between DMADV and DMAIC Six Sigma methods

~ Detailed tools and methods for performing each DMADV step

~ Resources for advanced and industry-specific applications

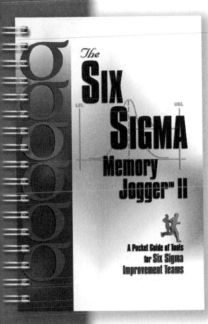

The Six Sigma Memory Jogger™ II

GOAL/QPC

The Six Sigma Memory Jogger™ II is the indispensable training and performance support resource for Six Sigma project team members.

Beginning with an overview and introduction to Six Sigma concepts, primary terminology, and the basics of the DMAIC method, this valuable pocket guide presents forty-eight Six Sigma tools, including the CTQ (Critical To Quality) Tree, FMEA (Failure Mode and Effects Analysis), Kano Model, MSA (Measurement Systems Analysis), process sigma, regression, SIPOC (Suppliers, Inputs, Process, Outputs, and Customers), VOC (Voice of the Customer) Data-Collection System, and the y = f (x) formula.

The Six Sigma Memory Jogger™ II helps team members to quickly learn the key tools of Six Sigma and to effectively work with their Black Belt leaders. Text is enriched with diagrams, charts, and tables. Information is presented with instructor-type questions and bulleted responses that cut quickly to the core of every issue. Thoughtful tips throughout head off misunderstandings before they can take root. Examples and case studies clarify complex concepts and make learning fun. 2002. 266 pages. ISBN 1-57681-044-5. 3.5" x 5.5". **Code 1076E**

At *a Glance*
~ Six Sigma Overview
~ DMAIC

This updated version of *The Memory Jogger™ II* contains these tools that support Six Sigma:
~ Charter
~ Commitment Scale
~ Communication Plan
~ CTQ Tree
~ Data Collection
~ DOE
~ FMEA
~ Focused Problem Statement
~ Hypothesis Testing
~ Involvement Matrix
~ Kano Model
~ MSA
~ Operational Definitions
~ Process Management Chart
~ Process Sigma
~ Regression
~ SIPOC
~ Six Sigma Storyboard
~ Taguchi Loss Function
~ Tollgate Review
~ VOC Data-Collection System
~ y = f (x) Formula

Project Management Memory Jogger™

Paula Martin and Karen Tate

The *Project Management Memory Jogger*™ can help jump-start project management and bring projects in on time and within budget. Using this tool is the most cost-effective way to ensure that your project teams achieve high-quality results. It provides every member of your organization with an easy-to-use road map for managing all types of projects. Learn how to deal with typical problems to ensure a successful project every time. Written for all employee levels within the organization, it teaches readers how to plan a project, create a project charter, work as a team, create a project plan, implement the project, and close out the project. 1997. 175 pages. ISBN 1-57681-001-1. 3.5" x 5.5". **Code 1035E**

At a Glance
~ Meet critical deadlines while staying within budget limits
~ Allocate scarce resources and exceed customer requirements

Facilitation Dynamics: Interactive Video Series™

Teaching "must-have" facilitation skills to your organization is now faster, easier, and more cost-effective than ever with our new interactive Facilitation Dynamics series. This video-based series is a complete learning package that shows the techniques of facilitation in action. Each video presents real-life examples of common pitfalls and demonstrates the facilitation strategies needed to avoid them. The videos help viewers hone their observation skills and learn how and when to use the facilitation techniques. **Code 5220**

Facilitation at a Glance!

An easy-to-use quick reference to facilitation, this book is packed with useful information, tips, and techniques. Anyone can learn and use facilitation skills to increase leadership effectiveness and help teams become more productive. *Facilitation at a Glance!* will assist both new and experienced facilitators in their efforts to maximize team effectiveness and achieve increased productivity. **Code 1062E**

Toll Free: 800.643.4316
Sales Direct: 603.893.1944
Fax: 603.870.9122
service@goalqpc.com • www.goalqpc.com

GOAL QPC

Six Sigma
for Business Leaders

Six Sigma integrates lean thinking to increase the efficiency of all business

D	M	A	I
STREAMLINE			STREAMLINE
Identifies all the process constraints and bottlenecks that cause chronic problems in work throughput.	Measures process time elements (setup, cycle, and waiting) to find all non-value-added components. Applies 5S methods to improve visual operations.	Evaluates process bottlenecks, flow, and buffer management. Captures early process-performance improvements.	Applies principles of both SMED and kanban. Simulates change to the process and verifies the most promising changes with a pilot experiment.

▶ A Guide to Implementation

▶ Gregory H. Watson

that cause chronic problems in work throughput.	and waiting) to find all non-value-added components. Applies 5S methods to improve visual operations.	flow, and buffer management. Captures early process-performance improvements.

Six Sigma for Business Leaders
A Guide to Implementation

Greg Watson

This 6" x 9" book summarizes the best practices associated with the Six Sigma approach and puts them into a context for senior management to use as a guideline for implementing Six Sigma in their companies.

It is intended to support leadership teams as they design their Six Sigma initiative and manage the execution of Six Sigma through aligning it with their business strategy. This book supports executive- and champion-level Six Sigma training for business leaders and process owners. This practical text answers fifty questions that an organization must address to initiate, develop, and sustain a successful Six Sigma deployment. Some sample chapter titles are:

~ What does an executive sponsor do?
~ How can Six Sigma improve financial value?
~ Why is a formal project charter important?
~ What is the DMAIC problem-solving process?
~ How does the Improve step of DMAIC work?

2004. 227 pages. ISBN 1-57681-049-6. 6" x 9". **Code 1207P**

Order online today at www.goalqpc.com

www.goalqpc.com